FOUNDRY ENGINEERING

[*A Textbook for Engineering Students*]

AF623378

T.R. BANGA
(Ex-Principal, Govt. Polytechnic College, Alwar)

TAHIL MANGHNANI
Ex-Head of Production Engg.
(Khaitan Polytechnic College, Jaipur)

KHANNA PUBLISHERS
Operational Office
4575/15, Onkar House, Ground Floor,
Darya Ganj, New Delhi 110 002
Phones : 011-23243042, 011-23243043 & Mob. 981154146(
E-mail : contactus@khannapublishers.in

Published by :

Romesh Chander Khanna & Vineet Khanna
for **KHANNA PUBLISHERS**
2-B, Nath Market, Nai Sarak
Delhi- 110 006 (India)

Website : www.khannapublishers.in

© 1979 and onward

This book or part thereof cannot be translated or reproduced in any form without the written permission of the Authors and the Publishers. The right to translation, however, reserved with the author alone.

Copyright: Author and Publishers Jointly

Hologram & Description

To all readers of our books, from yourself if being defrauded by pirates to prevent, please make sure that there is an Hologram on the cover of our books with the below specifications. If you find any book without Hologram and Description, please mail us at **contactus@khannapublishers.in**

Thanking you

ISBN No. 978-81-7409-285-4

First Edition : 1997
Fifth Edition : 2014

***Price :* ₹ 249.00**

PREFACE

This New Edition of the book is totally as per demand of readers.

The book contains text for Engineering Students of Mechanical, Metallurgical and Production branches explaining basic concepts and principals as applied to casting processes.

The subject matter is presented in a simple way and diagrams are simple and self-explanatory according to the needs of students and industry.

The authors are thankful to Mr Vineet Khanna, M/s Khanna Publishers, Delhi for the improvement of this book.

The authors will be glad to receive comments and suggestions for further improvement.

—T.R. BANGA
—TAHIL MANGHNANI

CONTENTS

Chapter *Pages*

1

Importance of Foundry

History and Development of Metal Casting

The casting of metals is one of the oldest industries in the world. This is evidenced by the fact that metal castings were made by the Egyptians about the year 4000 B.C. The huge columns that supported King Solomon's Temple are recorded as having been made of bronze, 9 metres high and 2.75 metres in diameter, the thickness of metal being about 100 millimetres. Throughout the history of the Greeks and Romans reference is made to the use of metal bells and ornaments for adornment of the ancient temples of worship.

A life size portrait made of cast bronze from Mesopotamia dates back to about 2250 B.C. By the end of the medieval period, decorated bronze castings were seen in the European church and domestic life. Earlier castings of cast iron were perhaps those of common shots and grave slabs.

The first use of metal, because of its beauty, was for ornamental purposes, and, as man became more familiar with it, he developed it for use as a weapon to protect his family against enemies.

Craftsmen have been making metal casting for either artistic or utilitarian purposes for more than five thousand years. Specimens, which cover this period, are housed in museums throughout the world, not for portraying the development of foundry industry but for illustrating the art of ancient China, the earliest types of machinery, medieval kitchenware, Roman civilization, etc.

The first foundry centre came into existence in the days of the Shang dynasty in China (1766-1822 B.C.). History of Greeks and Romans reveal the use of decorative ornaments and metallic

bells. In about 1540, Biringuccio wrote on metal founding. Prior to that, founding was an art and a craft with all its secrets confined to certain families.

Development of the art of founding progressed slowly by the '*rule of thumb*' method until about the seventeenth century. Scientists began to study the peculiarities of the metal known as cast iron. Experiments with types of furnaces and fuels have been carried on continuously since that time. Modern foundries and their products are the results of these experiments.

The first known cast iron casting made in America is reported to have been an iron cooking pot cast in the year 1642.

Reumur (1683-1757) worked on metal founding and produced malleable cast iron. He studied various factors which influenced the production of grey, white and mottled cast iron. In 1709, Abraham Darby succeeded in smelting in coke-fired blast furnace, which opened a route for large-scale use of cast iron in construction.

A number of cast iron foundries came into being after the Industrial Revolution in Britain. In 1879, the collapse of the Tay Bridge made the people go beyond the rudimentary judgement of the moulders and study the founding variables and their effects on the structural properties.

Middle of twentieth century saw marked developments in founding. Newer techniques were invented, casting phenomenon could be understood better, more and more young men took interest and training in this field. Many engineering institutes started teaching metal casting as an independent subject.

Castings are made in innumerable alloys. But for commercial purposes, they fall into the following groups :

(*i*) Iron which includes ordinary grey iron, white iron, black heart and white heart malleable.

(*ii*) Special-purpose grey iron which includes Mechanite, spheroidal-graphite and all types of alloyed iron.

(*iii*) Steel, both plain carbon and alloyed.

(*iv*) Copper-base non-ferrous metals *e.g.*, brass, bronze, gunmetal, etc.

(*v*) Light alloys *e.g.*, aluminium and magnesium.

(*vi*) Miscellaneous groups *e.g.*, zinc-base die casting alloys and white metals.

The smallest commercial castings regularly made will weigh 2 gm, while the heaviest in Great Britain are ingot moulds weighing 100 to 160 tonnes. After being poured, these large castings will require about three weeks to cool down. For melting the above range of alloys, furnaces ranging from a tiny crucible to a tilting type open-hearth having a capacity of more than 100 tonnes, are used.

Most of castings are made in moulds compounded of green sand (*i.e.*, moist sand), dry sand, or specially-bounded sands (*i.e.*, by resin, linseed oil, or sodium silicate). Moulds are consolidated either by mechanical or hand ramming around a removable pattern, or by loam moulding.

Hollows are formed by inserting cores carrying the shape of the desired hollow. A mixture of dried sand and linseed oil, starch, dextrin, synthetic resin or proprietory bond is formed to the desired shape in a core box, then baked in an oven to form a hard transportable compact mass.

All castings are not made in sand. Thousands of tonnes of pipe castings are made by centrifugal process in metal moulds. Many new methods of bonding sands to form moulds and cores have been developed. Die-casting utilizes metal moulds and an advance on this is '*mounting of metal moulds on turntables*'.

Modern Foundries

The modern foundry is a well-organised business, efficiently operated to maintain quality as well as quantity production of castings at a low cost.

In order to maintain these standards modern buildings have been constructed to house the several departments in a manner that will provide efficient production. Mechanised units have been installed whenever possible to relieve the worker of great physical strain. Laboratories have been established in which tests are constantly being made of all materials used in the production of castings.

Much thought has been given to the physical conditions under which the foundry worker is to be employed, such as heating, lighting and ventilation. In general, the working conditions in the modern foundry compare favourably with those in all other industries.

Great developments have been made in the foundry industry during the last fifty years : One of the most promising of these new

processes is the '*Shell-moulding system*' invented by Cronin in Germany during the World War II. It produces a casting of closer dimensional tolerances that is obtained in normal foundry practice, thus much reducing or even eliminating machining costs. The process finds its major use in the manufacture of small repetition castings.

Another development of recent years is the '*Carbon Dioxide (CO_2) Process*', which admits of the hardening or setting of a mould or core form by gassing it with CO_2. Sand is compounded by adding sodium silicate. CO_2 converts it into a viscous material which hardens the mould or core in seconds. Considerable degree of mechanization has been applied to its operation on a repetitive scale for large and small moulds and cores.

"*Lost Wax Process*" has been greatly expanded to cover such work as the making of thousand of small components accurate as cast to hundredths of a millimetre. In modern process, material placed around wax-pattern (the investment) is such that, after processing (which involves the use of very high temperature baking), the casting is produced repetitively to accuracy possible only by machining.

With development of all types of moulding machinery, including those which lead to automation, there have been outstanding developments in core-blowing and in making of hollow cores by shell and CO_2 processes much in demanded in die-casting.

Inspection facilities have been reinforced by more powerful X-ray sets, gamma-radiography, mass spectrography, application of ultrasonics, etc.

Foundry can shape parts weighing from a few grams to hundreds of tonnes. A cast steel mill housing manufactured by British Steel Corporation weighed 200 tonnes whereas an investment casting for dental implant in cobalt-chromium alloy weighed only 9 grams.

In United States, foundry industry produces more than 30 million tonnes of castings every year and employs more than half a million people. There are more than 7000 foundries (both ferrous and non-ferrous).

Today, in India, there are more than 8000 foundries (both ferrous and non-ferrous). Indian ferrous foundries produce about 12.5 lac tonnes of castings. Big foundries in India are at :

(*i*) Hindustan Machine Tools Ltd., Bangalore (now it is Bengaluru).

(*ii*) Bharat Heavy Electricals Ltd., Bhopal.

(*iii*) Chittaranjan Locomotive Works, Aasansol.

(*iv*) Steel Plants at Durgapur, Rourkela and Bhilai.

Uses of Foundry to Modern Industry

Foundry work is a branch of engineering that deals with the melting of metals and the pouring of molten metal into moulds from which castings are obtained. Casting is one of the basic tools of shaping metals and alloys.

It is basic industry. Let us consider its importance in the world of today, which depends extensively upon metal and metal products. These products would be non-existent if it were not for the foundry, as we cannot obtain metal in a usable form from the earth.

The basic simplicity of casting process proved to be a boon for growth of foundry industries. Today, a wide variety of components from domestic use to space vehicles are produced by founding.

The conveniences enjoyed in the modern home depend largely on foundry products :

(*i*) Grey iron castings appear in the form of bath tubs, sinks, wash basins, soil pipe, furnaces, cooking utensils etc.

(*ii*) Brass and bronze castings are found in the form of hardware, parts of washing machines, and other household mechanical equipment.

(*iii*) Aluminium and magnesium castings appear in the form of cooking utensils and parts of refrigerators, food mixers and vacuum cleaners.

(*iv*) Our modern land, sea and air transportation systems depend upon castings for their operation. An average automobile has 300 kg or more of cast metal parts in its construction.

Modern communication and lighting systems would be impossible without castings. Modern civilization would not be so far advanced as it is today if it were not for the foundry and its products.

The foundry industry is a progressive one, always, looking ahead, and, as it improves, so will civilization.

CHART
Classification of Casting Metals and Alloys

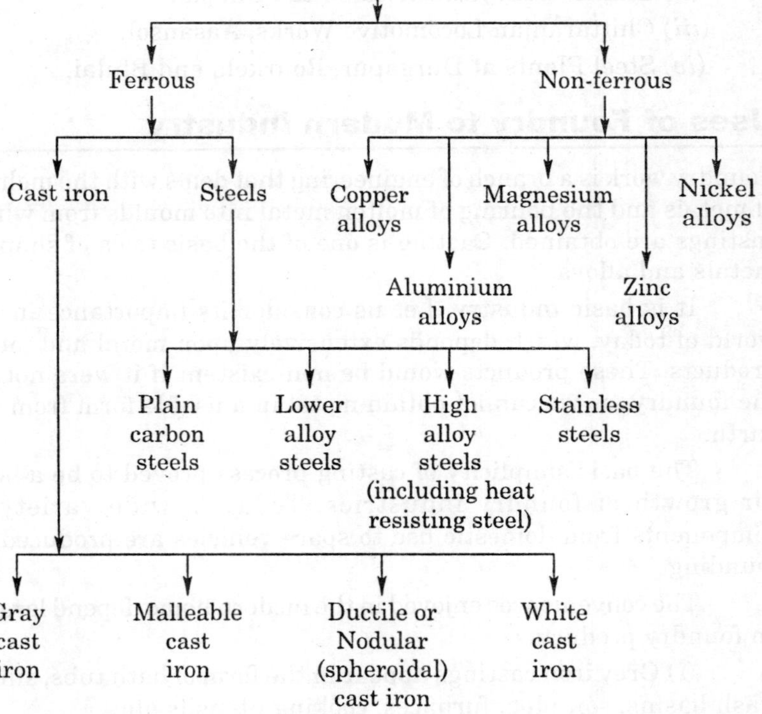

Advantages of Casting Process

1. Products with intricate shapes are produced at a cheaper rate.

2. The process of casting if done with accuracy reduces the machining time.

3. Certain metals and alloys, due to their metallurgical properties cannot be shapped by mechanical working but these can be cast easily. Cast iron is difficult to fabricate because of its brittle behaviour but can be easily cast into different shapes.

4. The casting technique is simple, as the number of operations in this technique are less.

5. The total per unit of production is less as it gives faster rate of production.

6. The wide range of alloys having different compositions and properties can be cast easily.

7. In some light metals, strength, lightness and good bearing qualities can only be produced by casting.

8. It is possible to make a cast-weld product. Complicated parts can be cast as 2 or 3 pieces and then joined by welding.

9. Castings weighing a few grams to several tonnes can be produced. Hence size is not a limitation.

10. As the metal can be placed exactly where it is required, large saving in weight is obtained.

11. This process is ideally suited to the production of models or prototypes required for developing a new design.

Disadvantages

1. This process is not economical, when parts casted are very small in *quality*.

2. Casted products are susceptible to defects like blow holes, hob tears, porosity and shrinkage etc.

The complete process of producing castings is divided into five stages, these are :

(*a*) Pattern making

(*b*) Moulding and core making

(*c*) Melting and casting

(*d*) Fettling

(*e*) Testing and inspection

Each process is explained in detail in the subsequent chapters of the book.

QUESTIONS

1. Give the main advantages and disadvantages of the casting process over other methods of fabrication.
2. Explain the main stages by which the metal flows in a foundry.
3. Describe in what circumstances casting will prove to be the most economical manufacturing process.
4. Give the applications of casting process.
5. Explain in short the history of foundry.

2

Basic Metallurgy of Cast Metals

Crystalline Nature of Metals

As a molten metal is cooled to its freezing temperature solidification begins in the regions of lowest temperature. Submicroscopic metal crystallites, called *'nuclei'* first form and then grow, generally in pine tree or dendritic fashion. The growing arms of the dendrites impinge one upon another, and further growth takes place by formation of small arms upon the original branches of individual dendrites until the mass is completely solid. The solid dendrites are called *'grains'* or *'crystals'*.

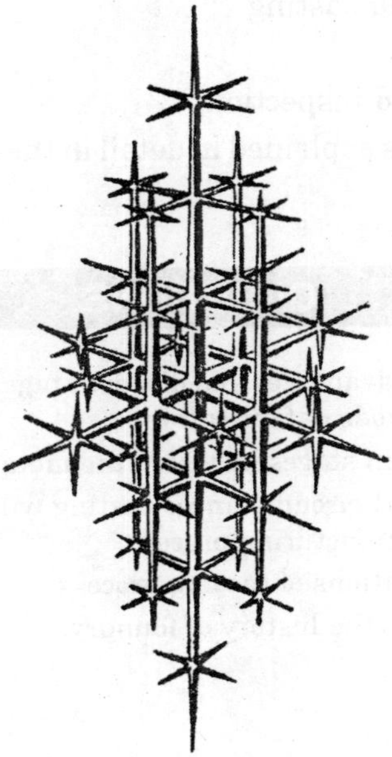

Fig. 2.1. Growth of a metal dendrite.

The atoms line themselves through the entire grain in evenly spaced columns and rows so that the final structure may be pictured as many '*unit cells*' (also called '*space lattices*') stacked one upon another.

(*i*) Austenitic iron, copper and aluminium process the '*face centred cubic structure*' unit cells. This structure has an atom located in the centre of each face, as well as one in each corner of a cubic lattice.

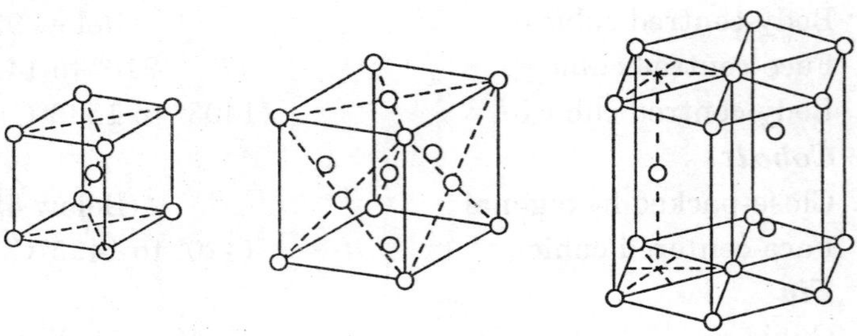

(A) (B) (C)

Fig. 2.2. Some common arrangements of metal *atoms* (Unit cells or Space-lattices)

A—Body centred cubic lattice, B—Face centred cubic lattice,

C—Hexagonal close-packed lattice.

(*ii*) Ferritic iron and chromium possess '*body-centred cubic structure*' unit cells. This structure has an atom on each corner of a cubic and one in the centre.

(*iii*) Magnesium and zinc have '*close-packed hexagonal space lattice*' which has one atom in each corner as well as one in each face.

These differences give unique properties to the metals of each class. The characteristics arising from the differences in basic structure are very important in metal working but are not particularly significant to foundry processing.

Some metals may exist in several lattice forms, depending upon the temperature. When a metal exists in more than one lattice form, it is said to be '*allotropic*' in character. Those metals that exist in only one form are :

Face-centred cubic :

Ca, Sr, Ni, Cu, Rh, Pd, Ag, Ir, Pt, Au, Pb, Al, Tl.

Body-centred cubic :

Li, Na, K, Rb, Cs, V, Mo, Ta, W, Ba, Cb.

Tetragonal (face-centred) in hexagonal (close-packed) :

Be, Mg, Zr, Os, Zn, Cd, Te.

Of the commercially important metals, iron, cobalt, tin, titanium, manganese and chromium may exist in more than, one lattice form, *i.e.*, they exhibit allotropy. Following elements have allotropic forms indicated :

Iron

Body-centred cubic α (Below 910°C)
Face-centred cubic γ (910° to 1403°C)
Body-centred cubic δ (1403° to 1535°C) (mp)

Cobalt

Close-packed hexagonal (Below 420°C)
Face-centered cubic (420° to 1495°C) (mp)

Tin

Cubic α (Grey below 13°C)
Tetragonal β (White 13° to 230°C) (mp)

Managense

Cubic, 58 atoms per unit cell α (Below 678°C)
Cubic, 20 atoms per unit cell β (678° to 1100°C)
Tetragonal γ (1100° to 1135°C)
Tetragonal δ (1135° to 1250°C) (mp)

Chromium

Close-packed hexagonal β (Below 20°C)
Body-centred cubic α (20° to 1800°C) (mp)

Titanium

Close-packed hexagonal α (Below 880°C)
Body-centred cubic β (880° to 1725°C) (mp)

A combination of lattices produces a crystal. A *crystalline substance* is defined as one in which the atoms are arranged in a definite and repeating order. Single crystals are very rarely used in practice. However, they are employed in investigation of fundamental behaviour of materials.

Characteristics of Pure Metals

Pure metals possess certain characteristic properties which make them desirable for specialised applications :

(*i*) They have very high electrical conductivity ; hence commercially pure copper or aluminium are used for electric wiring bus bars, or other carriers of electric current.

(*ii*) They have excellent thermal conductivity and so commercially pure copper is used for the tuyeres in water-cooled blast furnaces.

(*iii*) As compared with their alloys they have higher melting point, higher ductility, lower tensile and yield strengths and sometimes better corrosion resistance.

In foundry, generally higher melting point or pure metals sometimes leads to difficulty in (*a*) pouring castings, (*b*) more severe mould metal reaction, (*c*) greater tendency toward cracking, (*d*) making castings sound due to their mode of solidification, *i.e.*, '*risering*' properly.

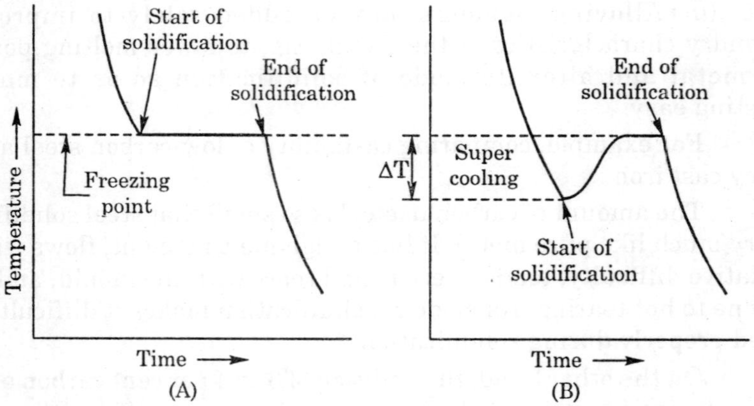

Fig. 2.3. Cooling curves of a solidifying pure metal.

A—Equilibrium cooling (slow solidification),

B—Supper-cooling (rapid cooling).

(*iv*) Pure metals melt and freeze at a single temperature, the melting point (or freezing point) ; above this temperature they are completely liquid, and below completely solid (under equilibrium conditions).

(*v*) When pure metals are cooled rapidly, solid crystals are sometimes formed at the freezing point. At a temperature (ΔT) below the freezing point, nucleation of solid suddenly occurs, and the heat of fusion liberated may increase the temperature tc that of the equilibrium freezing point. Such cooling of a liquid metal below the normal solidification temperature is called **'Under-cooling'** or **'Super-cooling'**.

Super-cooling also can occur in commercial alloys and has a direct bearing on the metallurgical structure of these alloys, *e.g.*, size, shape and distribution of graphite in grey cast iron can be directly related to '*super-cooling*' effects.

Characteristics of Alloys

White pure metals are desirable for certain specialised applications, alloying elements are usually added to cast metals to improve their properties :

(*i*) Alloyed metals, or alloys, are generally stronger than pure metals : the tensile strength of pure iron may be improved by proper alloying and heat treatment.

(*ii*) Alloying elements are also added to improve strength at high temperature, machinability, corrosion resistance, colour etc.

(*iii*) Alloying elements may be added solely to improve foundry characteristics of the metal, *e.g.*, to lower melting point of metal and alter its mode of solidification so as to make casting easy.

For example, comparing castability of low-carbon steel and grey cast iron :

The amount of carbon in steel is so small that steel solidifies very much like pure metal. It has a high melting point, flows with relative difficulty, tends to erode and react with the mould, and is prone to hot tearing. Its mode of solidification makes it difficult to feed properly during solidification.

On the other hand, the addition of 3 or 4 per cent carbon and silicon gives cast iron which freezes altogether differently and several hundred degrees lower. Mould-metal reactions, hot tearing, and risrering difficulties are all very much reduced.

Grey iron is considered an '*easy*' alloy to coast ; steel a '*difficult*' alloy.

(*iv*) Alloying elements increase the range over which melting occurs. Pure metals melt and freeze at a single temperature. Alloys, in most cases, do not.

For a given alloy, there is a particular temperature (the '*liquidus*' temperature), above which it is all liquid. There is another, lower temperature (the '*solidus*' temperature), below which it is all solid. Between these two temperatures is a region where liquid and solid co-exist.

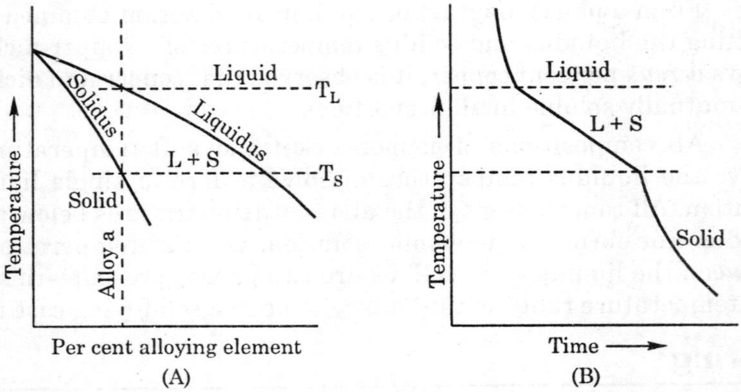

Fig. 2.4. Effect of alloying on solidification temperature of metal.

A—Solidification temperature *versus* per cent alloying element.

B—Ideal cooling curve (equlibrium cooling) of alloy.

Molten alloy '*a*' cooled slowly. Freezing begins at T_L and is complete at T_S. Rate of cooling is rapid until liquidus temperature T_L is reached. Rate of cooling is slow from T_L to solidius temperature T_S. Rate of cooling : again is rapid during solidification.

Such an alloy, in this temperature range has some consistency because of the solid material existing, but little or no strength because of the liquid interspersed with the solid. It has the consistency of '*mush*', and for this reason the portion of a solidifying casting whose temperature lies between the liquidus and solidus is often termed '*mushy zone*'.

Solid Solution Alloys

One of the ways in which two metals may combine to form an alloy is by solid solution, where the atoms of one element become a part of the space lattice of the other element. Several types of solid solutions are possible. In steel, the carbon atoms wedge themselves in the interstices between the iron atoms ; they dissolve interstitially in iron crystal structure.

A more common type of solid solution, however, is represented by the copper-nickel alloys. Both copper and nickel are face-centred cubic metals. If an alloy is composed of 50% copper atoms and 50% nickel atoms, the alloy will have a single crystal structure which is also face-centred cubic. One-half the atom sites in the crystal structure will be filled with copper atoms and one-half with nickel atoms. The metals, in effect '*dissolve*' in each other's crystal lattice to form a solid solution.

From a phase diagram or equilibrium diagram obtained by plotting the liquidus and solidus temperatures of a copper-nickel alloys *versus* per cent copper, it is observed that copper and nickel are mutually soluble in all proportions.

All compositions of copper-nickel alloys at temperatures above the liquidus temperature dissolve to form a single liquid solution. All compositions of the alloys at temperatures below the solidus line form a single solid solution. Only at temperatures between the liquidus and solidus are two phases present—this is the temperature range of the '*mushy*' zone in a solidifying casting.

Coring

Solidification in castings is seldom slow enough to attain the ideal diffusion (homogenization) in the solid. Such ideal solidification is called '*equilibrium solidification*'.

Most frequently, solidification of castings occurs under non-equilibrium conditions, in which lack of complete diffusion in the solid state results in '*coring*' which means the outer surface of the dendrites having considerably higher copper content (in coppernickel alloys) than the centre.

Coring in the solidification process is extremely common in cast alloys. It not only alters the final casting microstructure, it also can effect the temperature range over which alloys freeze.

In most cases, coring does not appear to be particularly deleterious to the mechanical properties or serviceability of cast parts.

If necessary, however, coring can be eliminated by reheating the alloy to allow diffusion (homogenization) to take place. Reheating during heat treatment serves the same purpose as casting slowly ; the atoms are able to move about (diffuse) more easily and with enough time at temperature, the structure becomes homogeneous and coring is eliminated.

Eutectic Alloys

Metals that are not mutually soluble in all proportions combine as mechanical mixtures to form alloys. Alloys of this type are made up of two chemically (and sometimes structurally) different types of crystals, mechanically mixed on a very fine scale.

Some metals are completely insoluble in each other in the solid states ; *e.g.,* tin and cadmium. Alloys of tin and cadmium are made up of very fine crystals of pure tin and pure cadmium.

More frequently, however, alloys possess limited solid solubility *e.g.,* aluminium-copper alloys. alloys that freeze as mechanical mixtures usually do so by a *'eutectic reaction'*.

Steel with 0.9% carbon is a saturated solid solution of iron and iron carbide and is known as *'Entectoid'*, under 0.9% as *'Hypoeutectoid'* and over 0.9% as *'Hypereutectoid'*. The temperature at which maximum solubility for a metal occurs is known as the *'Euctectic temperature'*.

Nearly all simple aluminium-base and magnesium-base alloys, and the most widely used cast metal of all, cast iron exhibit eutectic freezing.

In some of the high-strength light-metal-base alloys, the eutectic structure is brittle and damaging to mechanical properties. In these cases, the eutectic is dissolved by heat treatment.

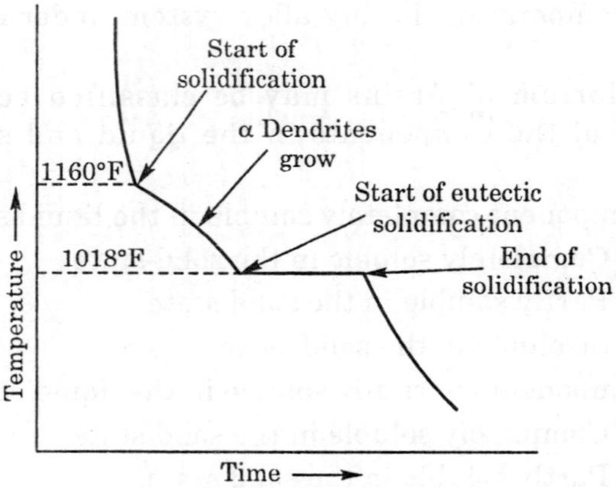

Fig. 2.5. Cooling curve for 10% copper-aluminium alloy illustrating eutectic mode of freezing. Freezing begins at 1160°F. Maximum solubility for copper reached at 1018°F (5.6% copper dissolved) known as *'Eutectic temperature'*. Eutectic freezed at a single temperature.

For some purposes *e.g.,* wear resistance certain eutectic structures are desirable, and no attempt is made to alter them. In grey cast iron, graphite occupies more volume as a solid than when it is dissolved in the liquid iron. Properly controlled the expansion of graphite during the late stages of eutectic solidfication can be employed to counterbalance metal shrinkage during freezing.

Intermetallic Compounds

Some metals in certain percentages tend to form compounds (intermetallic compounds) with one another. Alloys containing large amounts of such compounds are technically unimportant as they are hard, brittle and lacking in strength and ductility. However, such compounds appear in small amounts in many engineering alloys, *e.g.,* nickel-magnesium alloys.

Phase Diagrams

The liquidus and solidus temperatures of say two metal alloys are plotted on the ordinate *versus* percentage of one of the two metals on the abscissa. Such a plot constitutes a '*phase diagram*' or '*equilibrium diagram*' for the system. An equilibrium diagram may be defined as a plot of the composition of phases as a function of temperature in any alloy system under equilibrium conditions.

Equilibrium diagrams may be classified according to the relation of the components in the liquid and solid states as follows :

(*i*) Component completely soluble in the liquid state.

(*a*) Completely soluble in the solid state.

(*b*) Partly soluble in the solid state.

(*c*) Insoluble in the solid state.

(*ii*) Components partially soluble in the liquid state.

(*a*) Completely soluble in the solid state.

(*b*) Partly soluble in the solid state.

(*iii*) Components completely insoluble in the liquid state.

(*a*) Completely insoluble in the soild state.

The first type of equilibrium diagram in which the components are completely soluble in the liquid state is most common in engineering alloys.

These diagrams are used by the metallurgist and foundryman in many ways :

(*i*) They indicate the phases present (at equilibrium) in a given alloy at any temperature. From this information, the metallurgist can often deduce what physical and mechanical properties the alloy is likely to possess.

(*ii*) It can also be determined if heat treating is likely to improve properties of metals and what heat treatments may be useful in improving these properties.

(*iii*) Phase diagrams indicate the solidification temperatures of alloys. So they are useful in estimating the required pouring temperature for casting a given alloy.

(*iv*) They also indicate the range of temperatures over which a casting will solidify. This range of solidification has an important bearing on many foundry characteristics, particulary shrinkage hot tearing and fluidity.

Most commerical foundry alloys contain three or more metals. The construction of phase diagrams to represent these alloys is difficult at best, and interpretation of such diagrams is time consuming. In nearly all cases it is adequate to use a '*pseudo-binary*' diagram to obtain an understanding of the nature of these alloys, *e.g.*, phase diagram for an iron-2% silicon alloy containg varying amounts of carbon.

Solid State Transformations

So far we have dealt with transformations or changes that occur in alloys when they cool from the liquid to the solid state. Changes can also occur when the metal is completely solid. These changes form the basis for all metal heart-treating operations.

(*i*) The simplest solid state change is a '*composition change*' in an alloy phase, *e.g.*, elimination of cored structures by heat treating (*i.e.*, heating for prolonged times at elevated temperatures below the alloy melting point).

(*ii*) A second type of solid state reaction is a '*phase change*' which takes place by precipitation of new grains over range of temperature. This solid state change is the basis for age-hardening.

(*iii*) Other changes in the solid state may occur at a single temperature, *e.g.*, a eutectic-like reaction. Such a reaction is called a '**Eutectoid**' where one solid decomposes (on cooling) to form by diffusion two different types of crystals.

This reaction accounts for many of the valuable engineering properties of steel. Eutectoid point in steel occurs at 0.80% carbon and at 723°C.

(*iv*) A quite different kind of reaction occurs in certain crystal structures which transform not by diffusion but by mechanical moment, or shear, *e.g.*, martensite in steel.

QUESTIONS

1. Describe with neat sketch the crystalline nature of metals.
2. Explain with diagram the characteristic properties of pure metals.
3. Explain in short the following :

   (*a*) Solid solution alloys

   (*b*) Eutectic alloys

   (*c*) Solid state transformation.
4. Draw the phase diagram of the two metals and explain its characteristics.

3

Metallurgy of Commercial Non-Ferrous Cast Alloys

Introduction

Like cast iron and steel, most commercial cast non-ferrous alloys are not simple binary metals ; they often contain two or three other elements in small amounts which must be controlled to obtain desirable physical and mechanical properties.

Most of the popular non-ferrous metals can be readily cast to shape by the usual processes.

They can also be heat-treated to homogenize composition and structure or to develop special properties. For alloys susceptible to precipitation hardening, high temperature solutionizing anneals are used to bring some phase or constituent into solid solution. The part is then cooled rapidly and given a low-temperature hardening treatment.

Aluminium Alloys

These alloys are cast by any of the usual casting methods including sand, die, permanent mould and plaster casting processes.

The strength of pure aluminium (99.5%) is too low to be useful structurally. It can be strengthened by adding copper (to 10%), silicon (to 14%), magnesium (to 10%), or zinc (to 20%). Most aluminium casting alloys contain one or another of these elements as a major alloying constituent.

Smaller amounts of other elements, *e.g.,* chromium, titanium, nickel, sodium and tin may also be present for special purposes.

Properties. (*i*) Aluminium and magnesium and their alloys are useful where weight saving is important.

(*ii*) Aluminium alloys have a strength-to-weight ratio approximately equivalent to cast steels.

(*iii*) As compared to mild steel of the same load carrying capacity, aluminium alloy castings are one-third as heavy.

(*iv*) Aluminium and its alloys are chosen also for their relatively good strength, corrosion resistance, conductivity reflectivity (ability to take a fine surface finish), ease of casting and relative economy.

Common Aluminium Alloys Suitable for Sand Casting

(*i*) *Aluminium-copper Alloys.* Copper content may vary from 4 to 10%. It makes the alloy strong and hard.

These alloys are used for engine castings, crankcases, transmission housing etc.

(*ii*) *Aluminium-silicon Alloys.* Silicon content upto 5% improves casting characteristics and imparts greater resistance to corrosion.

These alloys are used for marine castings, pipe fittings, cooking utensils, parts of domestic machines like sewing machines, washing machines, etc.

(*iii*) *Aluminium-copper silicon Alloys.* About 4% copper and 3% silicon content aluminium alloys have good strength and high corrosion resistance.

These alloys are used for castings requiring pressure tightness and automobile engine parts.

(*iv*) *Aluminium-magnesium Alloys.* Magnesium content upto 4% improves machinability and corrosion resistance and reduces weight.

These alloys are used for kitchen-ware, food handling equipment, hardware, chemical fittings, etc.

(*v*) *Aluminum-copper-magnesium-nickel Alloy.* They contain about 3.5% copper, 1.5% magnesium, 2% nickel and rest aluminium.

These alloys are used for pistons, bearings, etc.

(*vi*) *Aluminium-manganese Alloys.* Manganese content about 1.5% to 2.5% produces leak-proof castings.

These alloys are used for tank and pipe fittings.

Precautions while casting

(*i*) Due to low melting temperatures of aluminium alloys, the sand moulds for aluminium castings require fine sand.

(*ii*) Due to a high rate of shrinkage, large sprues, gates and risers are necessary.

(*iii*) Soft cores metal chills are sometimes used to avoid cracking by shrinkage.

(*iv*) The molten metal should not be held for a long time so as to prevent excessive gas absorption, coarse and large grain size and should not be agitated too much after melting. Minimum agitation necessary to produce uniform composition should be given.

(*v*) The metal should not be heated to a temperature much higher (preferably below 790°C) than its melting point, as it tends to oxidise with increase in temperature.

Solidification of Aluminium Alloys. When the solidification of the metal in the mould starts, first the dendritic growth of the parent metal takes place and then the layers of solid solution progressively get deposited. By increasing the rate of solidification, considerable refinement in the dendritic structure can be obtained. The actual amount of dendrite formed depends on the percentage of alloying elements and the rate of cooling.

Alloys forming solid solutions upto higher percentage give a compact structure. The constituents which solidify near the liquidus tend to be coarse grained than those which solidify near the solidus. Grain size is established immediately below the liquidus.

Magnesium Alloys

Aluminium is the principal alloying element used with this metal. For engineering applications, the cast metal is usually alloyed with aluminium (4 to 10%), zinc (0 to 3%) and manganese (about 0.2%).

More recently developed alloys contain small amounts of zirconium, thorium, or rare earths.

Magnesium alloys can be cast in specially treated and moulds or in permanent moulds and can be pressure cast in cold dies. Pressure castings are not usually heat-treated, but sand and permanent mould casting are heat treated.

Moulding and core sands used in the production of magnesium alloy castings are usually treated with sulphur and ammonium fluoride. They are also moistened with some organic substance like glycol.

Properties. (*i*) Maguesium, about two-third the weight of aluminium and one-fourth that of steel, is the lightest of the commercial metals.

(*ii*) Magnesium alloys have excellent machining characteristics and high resistance to corrosion.

(*iii*) Most of magnesium alloys are susceptible to age-hardening. They are given a long solutionizing heat treatment at about 375°C, followed by aging at about 180°C. The first treatment, improves tensile strength and ductility, and the second increases hardness and yield strength with little increase of tensile strength and some loss of ductility.

Applications. (*i*) Magnesium alloys are extremely useful where light weight is essential.

(*ii*) These are extensively used for aeroplane parts, instrument housings, portable tools etc.

Copper-base Alloys

These alloys form the most important section of the non-ferrous foundry since a major proportion of the non-ferrous work consists of these alloys :

1. Copper-zinc alloys, *i.e.*, Brasses
2. Copper-tin alloys, *i.e.*, Tin Bronzes
3. Aluminium Bronzes
4. Silicon Bronzes.

They are usually cast in the alloy form. The alloys are first prepared from virgin metals by melting and casting in the ingot moulds. Metals having the highest melting points should be melted first and those having lower melting points should be introduced in the order of their melting temperatures. Additions, should be made gradually to avoid chilling action. Before pouring the mixture into the ingot moulds, it should be thoroughly stirred. Allowances should be made for volatilisation and oxidation.

For subsequent melting for casting purposes, the furnaces and may be coke, oil or gas fired crucible furnance, air furnance or electric furnance.

Following points should also be kept in mind while casting copper base alloys :

(*i*) Gating ratio best suited for the given alloy should be used.

(*ii*) Sands used must be finer and suitably bounded with oils, resins, molasses etc.

(*iii*) To avoid internal strains due to the difference in sectional thickness chilling practice is often employed in brass casting.

(*iv*) Pouring temperature should be carefully controlled to suit each individual alloy because melting temperature is different for different alloys.

(*v*) Molten metal should be held for shortest possible time.

(*vi*) Fluidity is found to be greatest only at a certain temperature. Pouring should be done at this temperature.

(*vii*) If pouring temperature is too high, metal gets oxidised and lost. This results in shrinkage and tendency to absorb gases causing gas-porosity.

(*viii*) Oxidised metal floats on the surface. It should be prevented from entering the mould.

(*ix*) There should be least amount of agitation and the metal should be poured at a steady rate.

1. **Copper-Zinc Alloys (Brasses).** Cast brasses are alloys of copper and zinc, usually with other agents added. Three principal groups of cast brass are :

(*i*) Red brass (2 to 8% zinc)

(*ii*) Semi-red brass (8 to 17% zinc)

(*iii*) Yellow brass (above 17% zinc).

In addition to zinc, brasses also contain 2 to 6% tin as hardener and 1 to 8% lead to improve machinability.

Yellow brass (also called '*Manganese Bronze*') with over 2% total of hardening additions such as aluminium, manganese, silicon, iron, and nickel has good corrosion resistance and high strength. It is used for marine propellers, gears, bearing races etc. It is more difficult to cast and machine than other brasses.

Leaded red brasses are the most popular of the cast copper-base alloys used for plumbing goods and steam-valves where moderate corrosion resistance, good machinability, moderate strength and ductility, and good castability are required.

Higher zinc contents of the semi-red and yellow brasses result in cheaper alloys of lower mechanical properties used mainly in the plumbing field.

2. **Copper-Tin Alloys (Tin Bronzes).** Cast copper-tin alloys (also called '*Tin Bronzes*') contain 5 to 10% tin with 0 to 4% zinc. Lead may be present in quantities of 1 to 10% or more for machinability and to improve casting characteristics. Compositions

over about 9 to 10% tin are avoided so as to prevent embrittleness of the cast metal.

Tin bronzes have excellent corrosion resistance and good properties at elevated temperatures. With lead, they make excellent bearings for use at moderate speeds.

3. **Aluminium Bronzes.** Commercial cast aluminium bronzes usually contain between 4 and 13.5% aluminium, 1 to 4% iron and some nickel and manganese.

They are heat-treated by quenching from 870 to 925°C to give an acicular structure resembling martensite followed by tempering at 480 to 700°C. This heat treatment increases strength and hardness at some expense of ductility.

Although aluminium bronzes are more difficult to cast than brasses and tin bronzes, they exhibit higher strength, hardness, and resistance to fatigue and shock. They also possess, higher hardness at elevated temperatures than brasses and tin broznes. Their colour resembles that of 10-carat gold.

Aluminium bronzes are useful for gears, propellers, pump parts, high strength bearings and fans.

4. **Silicon Bronzes.** They contain about 1 to 5% silicon and smaller amounts of zinc, tin, iron and up to 0.5% lead ; lead is added to improve machinability.

Silicon bronzes have very good resistance to sea water, alkalies and acids, with good mechanical properties.

Zinc Alloys

Zinc is most extensively used in castings for alloying with copper to form brass. In recent years, about 20% of zinc produced has been used for die-casting alloys.

Die-casting alloys are made of special high-purity zinc and contain about 4% aluminium, upto 2.5% copper and 0.1% magnesium, with minor impurities. They are commercially known as '*Zamak Alloys*'.

Low melting point of these alloys (about 400°C) facilitates die-casting. Such castings can be plated or otherwise finished to improve appearance and corrosion resistance. Tensile strength of zinc base-die casting may reach 4000 kg per sq. cm. and their elongation sometimes is as high as 15%.

These castings find extensive application in the automotive, camera, business-machine and household-appliance fields.

Nickel Alloys

Over 60% of the nickel produced is alloyed with cast iron and steel, and about 15 to 20% with copper.

Some important nickel alloys are :

(*i*) *Monel* is an alloy of 70% nickel and 30% copper. Additions of silicon and other elements to monel make the alloy age hardenable and more wear resistant.

Monel is used in wrought and cast form for its corrosion resistance and high strength.

(*ii*) *Nichrome* is an alloy of 80% nickel and 20% chromium. It is used for electrical resistance heaters.

(*iii*) *Inconel* is an alloy of 80% nickel, 14% chromium and 6% iron. It combines oxidation resistance with high strength at elevated temperatures. It is used extensively in cast and wrought form.

(*iv*) *Invar* contains 36% nickel and balance iron. It is an alloy with low coefficient of expansion.

(*v*) *Elinvar* has 36% nickel, 4 to 5% chromium and 1 to 3% wolfram. It has constant modulus of elasticity over a useful range of temperatures.

Effect of Impurities in Bronze

1. **Lead.** (*i*) Its small amounts are beneficial, and upto 1.5%, it increase tensile strength ductility and resistance to impact.

(*ii*) It is purposely added to bearing bronze castings to improve the bearing properties, and to castings subject to pressure to increase pressure tightness.

(*iii*) It is also assists the free cutting and easy machining properties.

(*iv*) It can be added up to 6% without undue segregation but above this 1 to 2% nickel, according to lead content will have to be added.

2. **Iron.** (*i*) It is present in all non-ferrous alloys and it is normally impossible for the foundry to eliminate it.

(*ii*) Under 0.3% it has little effect on the mechanical properties. The greatest danger of iron pick-up arises during remelting of turnings and borings. Efficient magneting machines are used for removing iron before melting.

(*iii*) High iron content (*i.e.*, over 0.5) causes trouble in casting, *e.g.,* metal may lack in fluidity and tend to give dirty castings. It

increases hardness or result in hard spots and causes unprotected machined surfaces to rust.

3. **Zinc.** (*i*) It is a hardening constituent, being approximately equal to half its amount of tin when present in bronze.

(*ii*) It acts as deoxidant.

(*iii*) It improves fluidity and castability of bronze. The alloy 85 copper, 5 tin, 5 lead, 5 zinc is most widely used.

(*iv*) Vapour pressure due to presence of high amounts of zinc tend to retard absorption.

(*v*) It is one of the main constituents of brass. Below approximately 39% zinc, brass is comparatively ductile. Above this amount, it has tensile strength but low elongation.

(*vi*) High-zinc content alloys should be rapidly melted and removed from the furnance as soon as the correct casting temperature is reached, otherwise high melting losses accompanied by a compositional and structural changes occur.

4. **Phosphorus.** (*i*) It is usually added in the form of 15% phosphorus copper, the main use of which is as a deoxidant.

(*ii*) It is also used for alloying purposes to make phosphorus bronze.

(*iii*) A very small amount goes into solution, and above this, copper phosphide is formed which itself is comparatively hard and brittle and increases Brinell hardness and lowers solubility of tin in copper.

5. **Nickel.** (*i*) It is not determinental in any quantity, but rather the reverse, tensile strength and elongation are slightly improved.

(*ii*) Its 1 to 2% is desirable in leaded bronze to prevent lead segregation by speeding up initial solidification.

(*iii*) Purposely added in larger amounts, it gives a series of high-strength alloys having very useful physical properties for special services, *e.g.*, Nimonic series with remarkable high-temperature properties has made possible the development of the jet engine.

6. **Aluminium.** (*i*) It is a constant hazard in the non-ferrous foundry producing gun metal castings.

(*ii*) A very small amount of aluminium, even as little as 0.01% causes loss of strength due to oxide films and inclusions resulting in porosity and lack of pressure tightness.

(*iii*) Bronze contaminated by aluminium can be successfully treated with aluminium removing fluxes which are commercially available for the purpose.

7. **Sulphur.** (*i*) It is responsible for a number of troubles and difficulties ranging from low strength and poor fluidity to porosity.

(*ii*) Gun mental readily absorb and react with sulphur dioxide which is always present in the furnace atmosphere from the combustion of fuel, particularly oil fuel.

(*iii*) Upto 0.3% sulphur, there is no effect on fluidity castability of porosity.

8. **Silicon.** (*i*) It is not a harmful impurity so long as the lead content is low.

(*ii*) In leaded bronze, it has a very bad effect, as it reacts with lead oxide forming lead silicate, and this affects mechanical properties and pressure tightness.

9. **Arsenic.** (*i*) Not much is known of its effect. Upto 0.3%, it appears to have not noticeable effect.

10. **Bismuth.** (*i*) It is a dangerous impurity.

(*ii*) Its presence results in poor physical properties, unsound castings, lack of pressure tightness.

Effect of Added Metals in Aluminium Bronze

1. **Iron.** (*i*) It is a cheap and very valuable addition.

(*ii*) It gives grain refinement resulting improvement in mechanical properties.

(*iii*) It helps to prevent self-annealing.

2. **Nickel.** (*i*) It has a grain refining action.

(*ii*) It increases tensile strength but decreases elongation.

(*iii*) Iron and nickel in combination give very superior properties in the as-cast state, *e.g.*, 10% aluminium alloy with 5% iron, 5% nickel has tensile strength of 7-7.5 tonnes/cm^2 and elongation of over 15%.

(*iv*) It increases still further the resistance to corrosion.

3. **Manganese.** (*i*) It is somewhat similar to iron, *i.e.*, it refines the grain and improves mechanical properties.

(*ii*) It acts as deoxidant. Upto 0.3% manganese with 0.02% magnesium is aimed at for deoxidation purposes.

Analogy between Aluminium-Bronze and Steel

(*i*) Aluminium bronze when quenched from a high temperature, gives greater strength with lower ductility. These properties can be further improved by a subsequent tempering treatment.

(*ii*) As with steel, the necessary heat treatment varies with the size and section of the castings, and small castings generally give better results.

Additions and Impurities in High-tensile Brass

1. **Tin.** It improves resistance to corrosion.

Normally, it is added upto 1% and some compositions do not include it.

2. **Lead.** It is not purposely added. Its presence in small amounts may come from scarp.

3. **Iron.** It plays an important part, but it is not soluble to any great extent, and forms a complex iron-rich constituent with copper and probably some tin, manganese or aluminium. This constituent provides nuclei for crystallisation, imparting a fine grain size.

4. **Manganese.** It acts as deoxidant and improves the tensile strength.

5. **Nickel.** It is not a zinc-replacing element, but behaves as copper. It is often added to manganese brass for use in marine propellers to increase corrosion and erosion resistance.

6. **Aluminium.** It has a high coefficient of equivalence, so that its small amounts have an important effect on both the structure and the mechanical properties.

7. **Phosphorus Silicon Magnesium.** They are kept out of manganese brass. Silicon and magnesium in particular are deleterious as both reduce ductility.

Effect of Added Metals on Aluminium Alloys

The elements commonly added to aluminium are copper, silicon, magnesium, nickel, manganese and zinc. Small amounts of titanium, cobalt, cerium and columbium are added to certain alloys to impart special properties.

Addition of hardeners, *e.g.*, copper, silicon and magnesium improves the tensile strength and casting properties.

More than double the strength of pure aluminium can be obtained by alloying with other metals but at the expense of ductility. With the correct heat treatment of suitable compositions, mechanical properties can be further improved.

1. **Copper.** Copper, silicon and magnesium are the most important of the elements added to aluminium. The relationship of copper to aluminium has, in fact, been likened to that of carbon in steel.

Under equilibrium conditions, 5.7% of copper enters into solid solution in aluminium at 548°C. But under 0.2%, it remains in solution at atmospheric temperature, copper aluminide ($CuAl_2$) precipitating in sub-microscopic form. This improves mechanical properties of heat-treatable copper-aluminium alloys.

2. **Magnesium.** It profoundly affects the properties of aluminium alloys. Silicon is invariably present in aluminium and its alloys. Magnesium and silicon form magnesium silicide (Mg_2Si) which, like copper aluminide ($CuAl_2$) is also an important precipitation-hardening constituent.

Solubility of Mg_2Si increases to about 1.6% at 580°C, but falls to under 0.4% at atmospheric temperature.

3. **Iron.** It does not enter into solid solution in aluminium and the structures are eutectiferous, consisting of aluminium and the compound $FeAl_3$.

All aluminium alloys contain iron (0.6-0.7%) as permitted impurity.

4. **Silicon.** It is a valuable addition to aluminium, either as a straight alloy upto 11-14% or as an addition in small amount with other metals.

Above 8% silicon, eutectic structure becomes exceedingly coarse when sand cast, resulting in poor mechanical properties. and particularly in low ductility.

Treatment of alloy at a minimum temperature of 750°C with either sodium salt or metallic sodium results in a fine dispersion of silicon with considerable gain in mechanical properties.

Difference between Ferrous and Non-ferrous Founding

(*i*) In a non-ferrous foundry, generally, there is a large proportion of small-size work and bench moulding is most common.

(*ii*) The metallurgical side of the non-ferrous foundry practice is very complex as large number of alloys with different compositions are available requiring knowledge about their metallurgical characteristics and properties.

(*iii*) The area of entry is to be increased because non-ferrous alloys chill and solidify comparatively at a faster rate.

(*iv*) Non-ferrous metals get oxidised quickly and tend to develop air aspiraion and turbulence. Hence careful precautions have to be taken during pouring.

(*v*) Non-ferrous metals possess high fluidity and seeping tendency at pouring temperatures. Hence, sands used for non-ferrous work have comparatively smaller grains.

(*vi*) When cooled from molten state, most of the non-ferrous metals contract to a large extent, to avoid shrinkage cavities and cracks, special care has to be taken.

Cores for non-ferrous casting moulds are prepared from materials which allow free contraction of the metal during its solidification and cooling around the cores.

QUESTIONS

1. Give the properties of aluminium alloys used in casting. Explain the important precautions while casting.
2. Give the list of common aluminium alloys suitable for casting. Explain in short their properties.
3. Give the composition and uses of magnesium alloys in short.
4. What points should be considered while casting copper base alloys ?
5. What do you mean by cast brasses ? Give the composition of :
   (*a*) Red brass
   (*b*) Semi-red brass
   (*c*) Yellow brass
6. Explain in short :
   (*i*) Copper tin alloys
   (*ii*) Zinc alloys
   (*iii*) Nickel alloys
7. Explain the difference between ferrous and non-ferrous founding.

4

Metallurgy of Cast Iron and Cast Steel

Introduction

Cast iron may be defined as a cast alloy of iron and carbon with other elements, and any carbon content in excess of some 2%, the maximum solubility of carbon in iron at any temperature. In practice, cast iron usually contains from 2.5 to 4.5% of carbon, while other constituents, as silicon, sulphur, phosphorus and manganese are always present.

The iron ore consisting essentially of iron oxide. Fe_2O_3 or Fe_3O_4, with silica and other impurities is reduced by means of coke and being removed by means of a flux of limestone. The resultant pig iron constitutes the chief raw material of the iron founder.

Grading of Pig Irons

The varying quality of the blast furnace product, from white to grey iron, is caused by the condition of the carbon. Carbon occurs either in the free state, as graphite, or combined, as carbide of iron, Fe_3C, known as cementite. In most irons, it occurs partly in each state.

When the carbon is chiefly free, the pig iron shows a fracture which is dark grey or nearly black in colour, being known as *"grey iron"*. Here graphite occurs in thin plates with their long axes at right angles to the cooling surface, constituting cleavage planes.

When the carbon is all combined, the fracture is silvery white. Iron which is partly grey and partly white is known as **"mottled"**. The quantity of carbon separating in the free state depends chiefly upon the content of silicon. Increase in silicon content leads to production of iron progressively more grey, soft and weak.

In practice, this grading is expressed by a series of numbers, as from 1 to 4, and then mottled and white, denoting pig irons which at first are soft and open in fracture, but contain progressively less silicon, manganese and graphite, and more sulphur and combined carbon, throughout the series, thus becoming gradually

harder and more close in grain, until in white iron, an extremely hard and brittle product is obtained.

Table 4.1: Grading of Pig Iron according to its Carbon Content and Physical Characteristics

Sl No.	*Type or Grade*	*Characteristics*	*Applications*
1.	Pig iron No. 1	(*i*) Contains most of carbon in free graphite. (*ii*) Contains maximum silicon. (*iii*) Very soft, dark grey in colour. (*iv*) Extremely weak and brittle due to its graphite in the form of long flakes.	Chiefly used for thin castings where high fluidity is essential
2.	Pig iron No. 2	(*i*) Contains relatively less carbon in free state. (*ii*) Some carbon present in combined form as cementite. (*iii*) Less soft and lighter in colour.	—
3.	Pig iron No. 3	(*i*) Has still less free graphite and more carbon in chemically combined state. (*ii*) Harder having closer grains. (*iii*) Stronger and less fluid when molten	Very widely used for general castings work in combination with steel and C.I. scarp.
4.	Pig iron No. 4	(*i*) Carbon as graphite and silicon are much less. (*ii*) Percentage of chemically combined carbon increases with increase in sulphur content.	—
5.	Mottled Pig iron	(*i*) Contains both free carbon and chemically combined carbon in almost equal proportions about 2% each). (*ii*) Light grey in colour. (*iii*) Much less brittle and stronger than previous grades.	—
6.	White Pig iron	(*i*) Contains whole of carbon (3.2-3.5%) in chemically combined state. (*ii*) Has very close and smooth fracture whitish in appearance.	For open hearth steel making process.

Grading based on fracture must invariably be confirmed by analysis because the system of numbering based on fracture differs from place to place.

Pig iron cannot be put directly into any practical use due to its being in a highly impure state. It is first cast into some regular

forms like the *'pigs'* or ingots and these forms are remelted in foundries for casting the required objects. By remelting in a suitable furnace with additional elements added up if desired, a large proportion of the impurities are either eliminated or reduced and the pig iron is refined.

Iron-Carbon Constitutional Equilibrium Diagram (Fig. 4.2)

Some knowledge of rather complicated reactions which occur during cooling of iron-carbon alloys from molten state down to normal temperatures is necessary for successful practice.

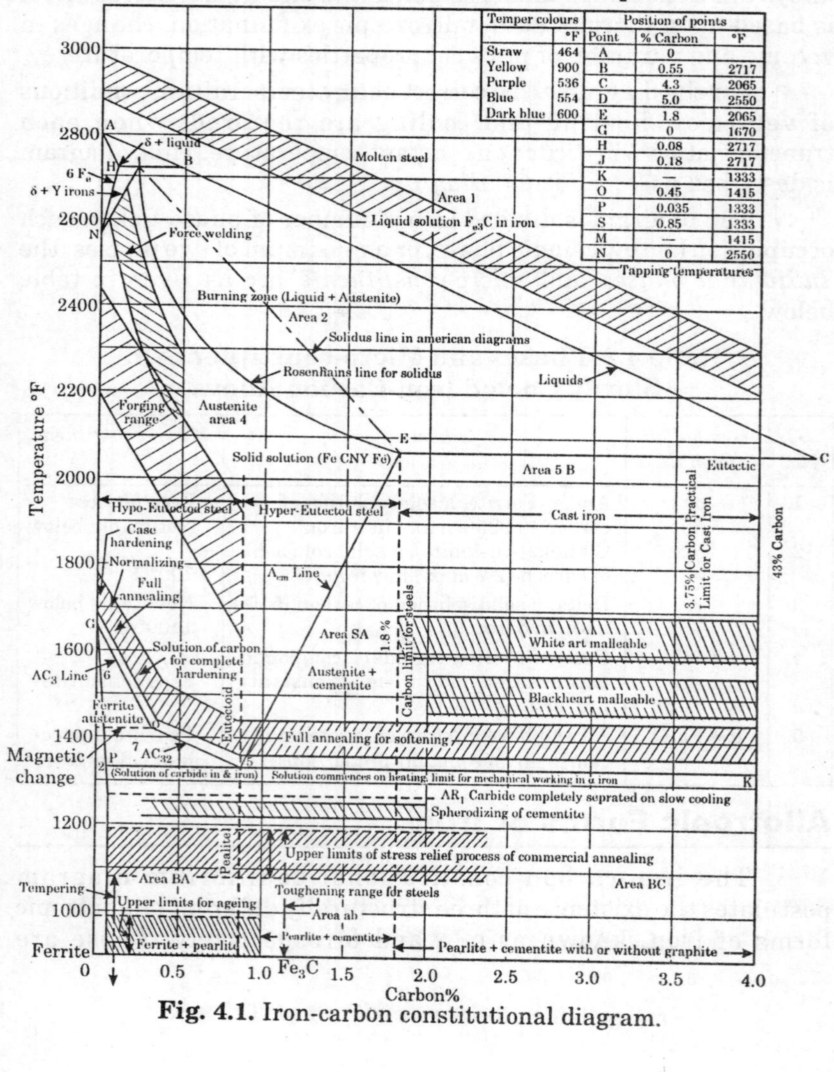

Fig. 4.1. Iron-carbon constitutional diagram.

For all practical purposes, cast iron may be regarded as rather impure steel containing flakes of graphite. Part of iron-carbon diagram relating to steel is shown in Fig. 4.4, which represents changes occuring in a steel of any given carbon content, both on solidification and in cooling slowly to a temperature of 600°C.

Composition of any steel can be represented by a point along the abscissa, and that of any temperature by another point along the vertical ordinate. Hence it is possible to show the constitution of any steel, at any temperature, graphically as in the figure.

At certain *'critical'* temperatures, constitutional changes occur. Thus, heating and cooling curves for all possible iron-carbon alloys are determined and assembled into one figure. Moreover, it is based upon thermal data, microscopic examination, changes in volume and variation of physical properties with temperature.

For the diagram to be correct at any temperature, conditions of very slow heating and cooling are required, when each transformation will occur at a constant temperature. Thus, diagram is described as *'equilibrium diagram'*.

The diagram is divided into a number of phase-fields, each occupied either by a single phase, or a maximum of two phases, the *'individual phases'* and *'micro-constituents'* are as given in table below :

Table 4.2: Phases and Micro-constituents in Slowly Cooled Iron-Carbon Alloys

S. No.	*Symbol or formula*	*Phase*	*Micro-constituent*
1.	α	Alpha (Ferrite, a solid solution of carbon (0.025% max.) in α-iron	Free ferrite
2.	γ	Gamma (Austenite), a solid solution of carbon (2% max.) in γ-iron	Not stable below 700°C
3.	δ	Delta, a solid solution of carbon (51%) max. in δ iron.	Not stable below 1400° C
4.	Fe_3C	Cementite (Iron carbide) a compound between iron and carbon of constant proportions.	Free cementite
5.	$\alpha + Fe_3C$	A two-phase mixture of ferrite and cementite of constant proportions.	Pearlite (a mechanical mixture

Allotropic Forms of Iron

The iron-carbon constitutional equilibrium diagram postulates the existence of three structurally different or allotropic forms of iron, known as α, γ and δ respectively. These are

discriminated from each other chiefly by their lattice structures and the temperatures at which they occur.

α-iron (*Ferrite*) has body-centred cubic lattice, in which the unit cell has an atom at each cube corner and one at the centre of the cube. It is found at temperatures between 910°C to 700°C. It has a maximum solid solubility for carbon of 0.025% at about 700°C, falling to about 0.008% at room temperature. It is strongly magnetic.

γ-iron (*Austenite*) has a face-centred cubic lattice, in which unit cell has eight atoms at the cube corners ; and six atoms, one at the centre of each cube face. It is found at temperatures between 1403°C and 910°C, having at these temperatures a solid solubility of 2% and 0.8% respectively. It is non-magnetic, or only feebly so.

δ-iron, like α-iron, has a body-centred cubic lattice. It differs from α-iron only in temperature at which it occurs between freezing (point of 1535°C and 1403°C), and in its greater solubility for carbon (0.51% max. at 1492°C).

β-iron was formerly thought to occur in low carbon steels above 768°C when α-iron, instead of remaining strongly magnetic, becomes only feebly so.

Physical properties like specific heat, rate of thermal expansion and resistivity also show changes on passing this temperature. The reverse change is exhibited on cooling.

Magnetic change point is known as *'Curie Point'*. It is not associated with any known structural transformation. β-iron is now a-days not usually recognised as a distinct variety.

The effect of carbon on the structure and properties of iron seems much out of proportion to the amount involved. Less than 0.03% carbon in the iron lattice is sufficient, when properly manipulated, to raise the tensile strength of otherwise pure iron from 3200 to 10400 kg per cm^2.

Alloys of iron and carbon, with other elements added for special purposes, make up the important classes of ferrous metals known as steels and cast irons. These alloys, particularly steels can be heat treated and a wide range of properties can be imparted to them by varying the cycles of heating and cooling.

A phase diagram for iron-carbon alloys is shown in Fig. 4.2 Below 1670°F (910°C), pure iron exists in the body-centred cubic form; it is known as ferritic iron or ferrite. Ferrite has relatively little solubility for carbon (about 0.025%). Between 1670°F (910°C) and 2540°F (393°C), pure iron assumes a face centred cubic lattice, and in this form can dissolve upto about 2% carbon. Face-centred cubic form of iron or iron alloys is termed *'Austenite'*.

When the solubility of iron for carbon is exceeded, the carbon precipitates in one of two forms, either as metastable Fe_3C compound (cementite), or as elemental graphite. In low-carbon or high carbon alloys cooled at a rapid rate, carbon always precipitates as cementite (Fe_3C). Phase diagram shows the products of Fe-Fe_3C reactions.

At higher carbon contents, cooling rate may be sufficiently slow that the true equilibrium 'graphite' will precipitate. Phase diagram for iron-graphite reaction is nearly identical with that for iron cementite reactions, differing only slightly at the dotted lines.

Normally cementite rather than graphite precipitates at less than about 2% carbon; which is the composition range of ordinary commercial steels. Above about 2% carbon either graphite or cementite may precipitate. depending on cooling rate and other factors. Composition range of most cast iron varies from about 2 to 5% carbon.

Cast Plain Carbon Steels

Cast plain carbon steels of upto about 0.5% carbon solidify by a peritectic reaction to form the single phase solid solution austenite.

The high diffusion rate of carbon results in very little coring during solidification.

Steels of over 0.5% carbon solidify directly to the austenite, over a temperature range. The microstructure of steels in the austenite region is sketched in Fig. 4.2 A.

Steel containing between 0.025% carbon and 0.80 carbon cool through a two-phase region where austenite and ferrite co-exist. In this range, ferrite precipitates at the austenite grain boundaries and partially consumes the original austenite grains (Fig. 4.2 B)

At 1333°F (723°C) a eutectoid transformation takes place whereby the austenite remaining in the steel transforms directly to a fine, platelike aggregate of ferrite plus cementite, known as pearlite (Fig. 4.2 D). The eutectoid reaction is similar to eutectic reactions, except that all reaction products are solid in the case of the eutectoid.

Steels of 0.80 carbon transform to an entirely eutectoid (pearlite) microstructure. They are known as *'Eutectoid'* steels (Fig. 4.2 E).

Steel containing less than 0.8% carbon are termed *'Hypoeutectoid'* and steels containing more than 0.8% carbon are *'Hypereutectoid'* steels.

Hypereutectoid steels begain to transform (on cooling from the austenite region) at the A_{cm} line (Fig. 4.2) with cementite forming, at the grain boundaries (Fig. 4.2 C). At the eutectoid temperature the remaining austenite transforms to pearlite, as shown in Fig. 4.2 F.

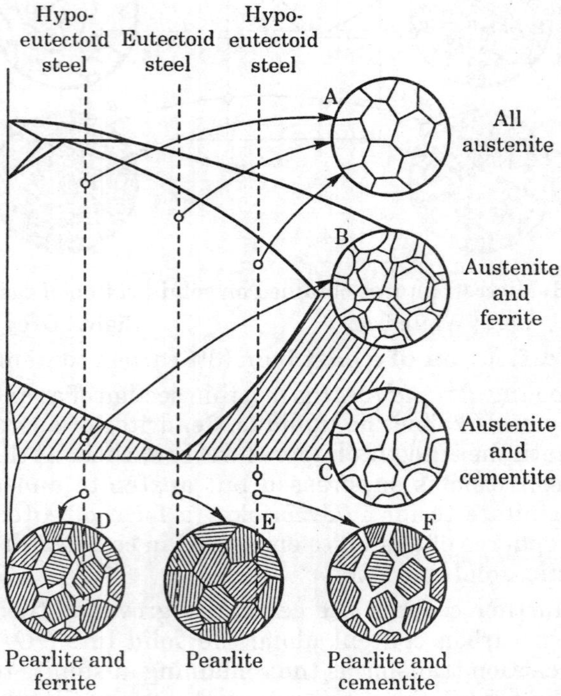

Fig. 4.2. Portion of iron-iron carbide phase diagram showing microstructures obtained by slow solidification and cooling.

Cast Iron

The metallurgy of cast iron is one of the most complex metallurgical systems. We have seen that the iron-iron carbide ($Fe-Fe_3C$) system is metastable in iron-carbon alloys and that the true system is iron-graphite (Fe-C). This distinction is mostly of academic interest in steels, since graphite seldom forms, but it is of great importance in cast irons.

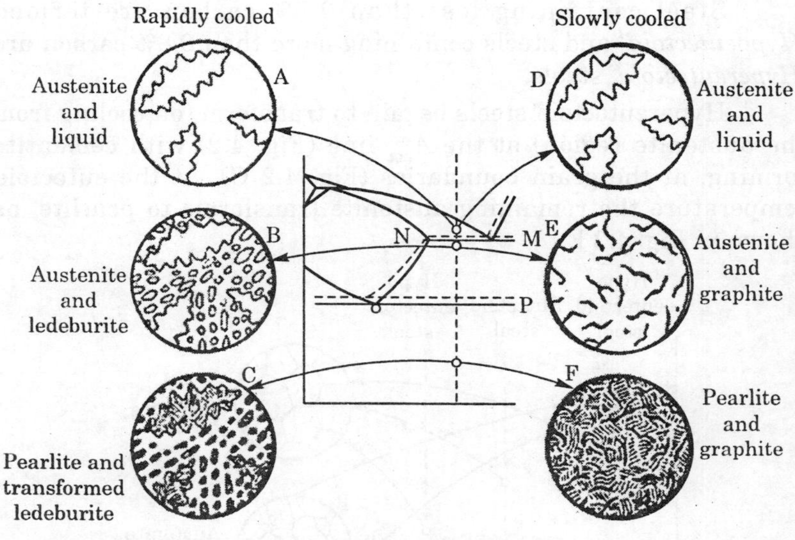

Fig. 4.3. Microstructures obtained on solidification of cast iron.
Left : White iron Right : Grey iron

Solidification of a cast iron (3% carbon content) Fig. 4.3:

(*i*) *Cooling at rapid rate* (as in a thin section of a sand casting). As the alloy cools below the liquidus, dendrites of austenite form and grow until the eutectic temperature is reached. At the eutectic, graphite formation is suppressed but austenite and cementite (Fe_3C) precipitate to form *'ledeburite'* (a form of eutectic which consists of spheres of austenite embedded in cementite) at the Fe-Fe_3C eutectic, solid line *'NM'*.

On further cooling, the cementite grows as the austenite decreases in carbon content along the solid line *NO*. At *O* the eutectoid reaction transforms the remaining austenite to pearlite. Figure 4.3 *A, B, C* show the microstructures illustrating the solidification and cooling of this alloy.

At room temperature, it is hard and brittle, and is called *'White Iron'* because the surface of a fractured piece of the iron is white and somewhat lustrous.

A high rate of cooling tends to prevent the formation of graphite, hence maintains the iron in a hard, unmachinable condition.

(*ii*) *Cooling at a slow rate.* In this case, austenite first forms from the melt, but eutectic freezing is now slow enough so that the products of the eutectic reaction are austenite and graphite. The reaction takes place at the dotted line *NM*.

The eutectic graphite tends to form as flakes surrounded by eutectic austenite. As cooling continues the austenite decreases in carbon content along the dotted line *NO*, and the graphite flakes grow. At the eutectoid temperature *OP,* remaining austenite transforms as before to pearlite.

Typical microstructures of an alloy cooled in this manner are shown in Fig. 4.5 *D, E, F*. The fracture surface appears dull grey, and the material is known as *'Grey Cast Iron'* or *'Pearlite Grey Iron'*.

(*iii*) *Cooling at a very slow rate.* Phase changes in such an alloy will be exactly like those of case (*ii*) above, except that, at the eutectoid, cooling will be sufficiently slow to permit graphite to precipitate rather than pearlite.

Actually, no new graphite flakes will form, but the ones present will increase in size. In this case the final microstructure will be only graphite flakes embedded in a matrix of ferrite ; this is termed *'Ferritic Grey Iron'*.

In ordinary castings, cooling is seldom slow enough to obtain the above structure, and most ordinary grey iron castings possess the structure of (*ii*) above, *i.e.,* graphite embedded in a pearlite matrix.

Sometimes the cooling rate of a portion of a casting may be intermediate between (*i*) and (*ii*). Then a structure containing patches of both white iron and grey iron is obtained known as *'Mottled Iron'*.

Effect of Graphite Shape

Graphite may be formed in cast iron as flakes, nodules, or spheroids (Fig. 4.4). Regardless of shape, graphite has very little

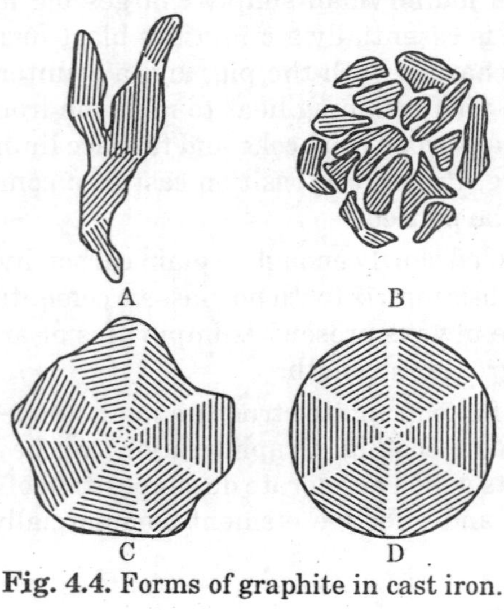

Fig. 4.4. Forms of graphite in cast iron.

A—Graphite basal planes aligned along major axes of flakes in grey iron.

B—Graphite basal planes oriented at random in malleable iron Contrary free MnS but no free FeS.

C—Graphite basal planes oriented perpendicular to radii of nodule in malleable iron containing free FeS.

D—Graphite basal planes oriented perpendicular to radii of spherulite in *'ductile iron'* treated with magnesium, cerium or other desulfurizing agent.

cohesive strength and reduces the effective metallic cross-section of the casting.

Graphite reduces tensile strength and ductility most in flake form ; the flakes are often interconnected, and their relatively sharp edges are potential areas of low ductility and weakness.

Graphite nodule is a more favorable form. From strength and ductility point of view, the ideal graphite shape is spheroidal.

Iron Silicon Carbon System or Commercial Grey Cast Iron

Pig iron from blast furnace is the starting material for both cast iron and steel. Typical pig iron contains about 3% carbon, 1.5% silicon, and smaller amounts of manganese, sulphur and phosphorus. Steel maker treats this in open-hearth furnace by diluting pig iron with twice as much or more steel scrap and removing most of the above elements by reacting them at 1650°C under a slag of carefully controlled composition.

Cast iron foundryman simply charges pig iron into cupola furnace, which is essentially a miniature blast furnace. Coke and limestone are charged with the pig, and a counter current of air burns the coke for furnishing heat to melt the iron. Some carbon and silicon are absorbed from coke and furnace lining, and the slag is self-adjusting. Proper composition cast iron comes from cupola spout ready to be poured.

If it is cooled slowly enough, a plain carbon hypoeutectic iron can have a pearlitic matrix (with no massive cementite). Practically, other alloys are always present as impurities or are intentionally added to give greater strength.

To get a flake graphite structure in an alloyed iron requires impractically slow cooling. Graphitization can be speeded up by adding elements which accelerate decomposition of cementite. The most practical and effective element commercially used for this

purpose is silicon. Such elements are called **'Graphitizers'**. Certain other elements *e.g.*, chromium, which prevent decomposition of cementite are called **'Carbide Stabilizers'**.

Comparison of *'Pseudo-binary'* diagram of iron-silicon carbon (2% silicon) with that of plain iron-carbon phase diagram illustrates the effect of silicon addition on solidification of a cast iron. In general, silicon.

(*i*) moves the cast iron eutectic point upward and to the left on the phase diagram, and

(*ii*) also results in a eutectic that does not solidify at a single temperature, but does so over a narrow range of temperatures.

Characteristics and Uses of Grey Cast Iron

(*i*) It contains 2.5-3.8% C, 1.1-2.8% Si, 0.4-1.0% Mn, 0.15 P and 0.1% S and rest Fe.

(*ii*) It is basically an alloy of carbon and silicon with iron.

(*iii*) It can readily be cast into complex and their sections desired shapes in sand moulds due to its high fluidity.

(*iv*) It is marked by the presence of graphite flakes in a matrix of ferrite, pearlite or austenite.

(*v*) Length of flakes varies from 0.05-0.1 mm.

(*vi*) Flakes of graphite occupy about 10% of the metal volume.

(*vii*) Fracture gives grey appearance.

(*viii*) Its melting point is lowest of all the ferrous alloys.

(*ix*) Its machinability is better then that of steel.

(*x*) It has high wear-resistance.

(*xi*) It has high vibration damping capacity.

(*xii*) As compared to steel it has low ductility and low impact strength.

(*xiii*) It possesses high compressive strength.

(*xiv*) It has excellent casting qualities.

(*xv*) It is a good combination of low cost with rigidity and hardness.

(*xvi*) It has shrinkage of 1 mm in 100 mm.

(*xvii*) It has a solidification range of 1300-1100°C.

Uses. It is used for :

(*i*) Ingot moulds, (*ii*) Machine tool structures, (*iii*) Manhole covers, (*iv*) Frames of electric motors, (*v*) Underground water and gas pipes, (*vi*) Piston rings, (*vii*) I.C. engine and steam engine cylinder blocks and heads, (*viii*) Sanitary wares, (*ix*) Tunnel segments, (*x*) Household appliances, (*xi*) Rolling mill and general machinery components.

Foundry Mixtures

In calculating the composition of the metal it is necessary to allow for the various changes that are found in melting in the cupola. The effect on the proportion of each consistuent charged varies with the proportion of steel in the charge, and the cupola conditions :

Table 4.3: Alteration in Composition brought about in Cupola Melting

S. No.	*Charges in composition*	*For low silicon mixture with 20-30% steel*	*For higher silicon mixtures containing only pig iron and scarp*
1.	Silicon content reduced	25%	16%
2.	Sulphur content increased	50%	25%
3.	Phosphorus content increased	5–10%	5–10%
4.	Manganese content reduced	30%	10–20%

Note. The approximate variation caused by melting in one's own cupola should be determined.

Charge of an iron suitable for cylinders and liners for steam engines, diesel engines, and gas engines, piston rings, etc. may contain : Silicon 1.2-1.4%, Phosphorus 0.3-0.5%, Manganese 0.8-1.2%. If necessary, low manganese content may be brought up by using spiegeleisen, ferro manganese or manganese briquettes.

An iron suitable for pipes, bed plates, condenser bodies, pump castings, and general castings from 12 to 40 mm thickness can be obtained by calculating on charge figures : Silicon 2-2.75% Phosporus 0.5-1%, Manganese 0.5-0.7%.

Table 4.4: Typical Composition of some Important Mixtures

Mixture for	*Total carbon per cent*	*Silicon per cent*	*Sulphur per cent*	*Phosphorus per cent*	*Manganese per cent*
C.I. Liner	3.42	0.76	0.10	0.30	1.06
C.I. Cylinder	3.51	1.05	0.112	0.33	0.89
C.I. Flywheel	3.17	1.41	0.126	0.27	0.85
C.I. Pump	3.58	1.89	0.116	0.48	0.61
C.I. Light and small castings	3.48	2.26	0.114	0.63	0.63
High-duty cast iron	2.98	0.84	0.116	0.34	0.57

Effects of Inoculation—Inoculated Cast Irons

Inoculated cast irons are obtained by adding to the molten iron in the ladle, a suitable proportion of graphitiser or inoculant like ferro-silicon, just prior to casting. The iron to which inoculant or graphitiser is added, should have a controlled and comparatively low carbon content, *i.e.*, between 2.4 and 3%.

The silicon in the basic mixture must be lower than that required to produce normal grey iron castings, the deficiency being made up by adding controlled amount of ferro-silicon, or other graphitiser, in proportion to the carbon content.

The graphitising of such an addition is much greater than when it forms part of the charge in the usual manner. The graphite is caused to separate as flake; which, however, is not of the coarse form assumed in the normal method of separation ; but is, instead comparatively fine and also distributed in a random manner.

Irons with finely dispersed graphite set in a pearlite matrix, while grey and machinable, are considerably stronger than ordinary cast irons, and can be made of tensile strength from 3 tonnes/cm^2 upwards. Their strength can be still further increased by using additional alloying elements, such as copper, molybdenum, nickel, etc.

Among inoculants are calcium silicide (Mechanite Process) and nickel shot and ferro-silicon (Ni Tensyl Process) :

Approximate composition of Mechanite iron for high strength purposes is total carbon 2.4–2.7%, silicon 1.1–1.5%, sulphur 0.05–0.14%, phosporus 0.10–0.20%, manganese 0.65–1% giving tensile strengths of 3 to 4 tonnes/cm^2 with B.H. No. 260–30 material however, being readily machinable. Thus, a specially made white C.I. composition is graphitised in the ladle with calcium silicide.

In Ni-Tensyl Process, the graphitising additions are finely divided ferro-silicon and nickel shot. These are added to a basic mixture of approximate composition : Total carbon 2.5%–3%, silicon 0.5–0.8%, sulphur 0.12% (max.), phosphorus 0.2% (max), manganese 0.7–1%. Such iron, frequently cupola melted, contains 50–90% steel scrap, the remainder being selected ordinary scarp or elected pig iron.

By inoculation in the ladle, the silicon is increased to 1.25–1.75 and nickel to 1–2%. A composition with about 1.5% of each gives satisfactory results over a wide range of casting thickness.

Thus, inoculants, like calcium-silicon, ferro-manganese-silicon, zirconium-silicon, ferro-silicon etc. when added to molten cast, change its structure and hence improve its mechanical properties without changing its composition and reduce its tendency towards chilled edges.

Acicular Cast Irons

During slow cooling of unalloyed cast irons, in the temperature range of some 700–600°C, the matrix changes from original solid solution austenite to lamellar pearlite. With increase in the rate of cooling, this transformation occurs less readily, and the pearlite becomes progressively finer.

If cooling is sufficiently rapid, transformation of the high temperature range is completely suppressed, and the structural change occurs at a much lower temperature (250°–150°C), with the production of martensite.

By quenching in an intermediate range in temperature, and holding for a sufficient time at that temperature, intermediate structure consisting neither of pearlite nor martensite, is obtained.

Acicular structures can be produced in unalloyed irons by precise control of cooling rates. But, in foundry practice, alloying with nickel and molybdenum is necessary to control transformation rates. Nickel-molybdenum acicular cast irons show high strength, good machinability at high hardness.

Recommended composition range for acicular cast iron :

Carbon 2.9–3.1%, silicon 2.6–2%, (sections upto 75 mm), 20–1.6% (sections 75 mm and over), sulphur 0.15 (max.), phosphours 0.15% (max.), manganese 0.9–1.2%, molybdenum 0.8-1%, nickel 1–1.4% (12–40 mm sections), 1.8–2.2% (40 to 60 mm thickness), 2.4–2.8% (60–100 mm thickness), 3–3.5% (100–175 mm thickness), 3.6–4.5% (175–250 mm thickness), chromium nil (upto 75 mm thickness), 0.25% (max.) upto 150 mm thickness), 0.5% (max.) (150 mm thickness and over).

Increase in strength occurs on tempering acicular nickel-molybdenum cast irons in 260–370°C temperature range due to relief of stresses and transformation within the residual austenite-martensite of the matrix.

Spheroidal Graphite Cast Irons

In ordinary cast irons, the graphite assumes the form of elongated flakes, which act as stress raisers, and reduce the strength and ductility of the material.

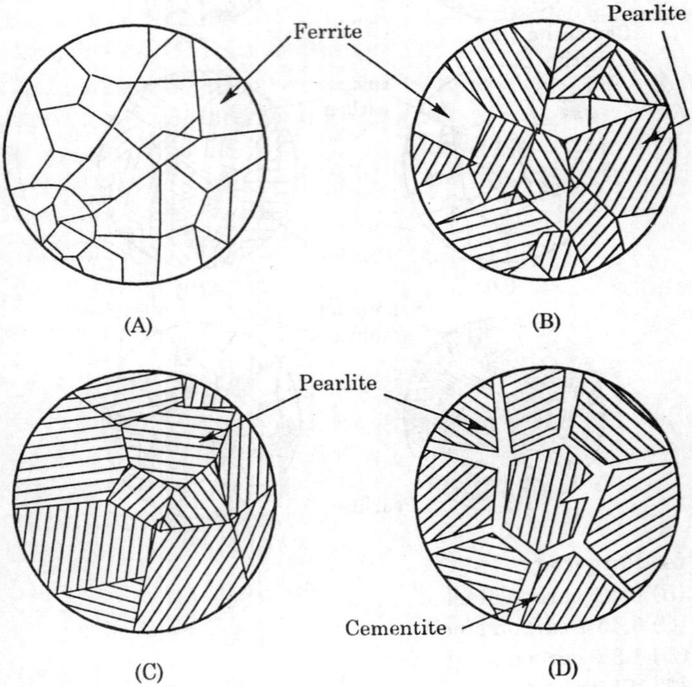

Fig. 4.5. Micro-constituents in Iron and Steel.

The latest development in cast iron foundry practice in recent years is the production of spheroidal graphite cast iron. Castings can be made directly in the foundry with graphite in spheroidal form. The British Cast Iron Research Association developed the process depending on the addition of small amounts of cerium to controlled compositions of molten iron, while the process developed in the U.S.A. uses magnesium. Magnesium process has been found to be both more adaptable and cheaper, but sometimes it is advantageous to use a combined addition.

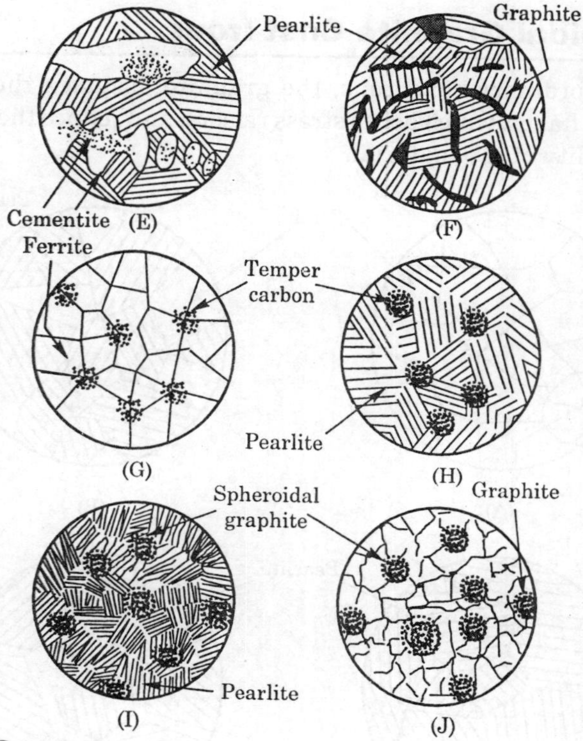

(*A*) Pure iron
(*B*) 0.4% carbon steel
(*C*) 0.45% carbon steel
(*D*) 1.3% carbon steel
(*E*) White cast iron
(*F*) Grey cast iron
(*G*) Blackheart malleable cast iron
(*H*) Whiteheart malleable cast iron
(*I*) Spheroidal graphite iron as cast
(*J*) Spheroidal graphite iron annealed

Fig. 4.6. Diagrammatic representation of Micro-structure of steel and cast iron.

In spheroidal graphite cast iron (known also as *'nodular graphite cast iron'*, *'nodular cast iron'* and *'ductile iron'*), by suitable treatment of the molten metal, the graphite in the metal as cast, instead of separating in the form of flakes, occurs as spherical nodulus. These nodules break up the continuity of the metal to a much smaller extent ; while the stress raisers (graphite flakes) are no longer present, and ductility is much greater.

Such transformation in graphite type can be effected by adding small quantity of cerium (0.02–0.2%) to irons which solidify grey. Cerium adding should be followed by the addition of one of the usual inoculants. A comparatively short annealing improves the properties still further.

The base metal should be of high carbon content, of hypereutectic type, with a silicon content of over 2.3%, and low in sulphur (0.05% max.), and phosphorus (0.1 max).

The process may be applied to all types of alloyed or unalloyed grey cast iron with generally a doubling of strength and a marked increase in ductility and shock resistance.

Mechanical properties of typical cerium-treated nodular iron (total carbon 3.8%, silicon 2.17%, sulphur 0.015%, phosphorus, 0.052%, maganese 0.92%, copper 2.17%, cerium 0.054%) :

Tensile strength 7.5 tonnes/cm^2

Transverse rupture stress 15 tonnes/cm^2

Deflection 6.75 mm

Compressive strength 15 tonnes/cm^2

Brinell Hardness 300

Use. These irons may be used as cast, but preferably after normalizing or annealing, according to the properties desired.

Advantages. High carbon content of these irons ensures :

(*i*) ready castability and

(*ii*) their properties, approaching those of steel. There properties can be developed in castings of all sizes and section thicknesses.

Grey Cast Iron finds use due to :

(*i*) Its cheapness and ease of machining ;

(*ii*) Low melting temperature (1140–1200°C) ;

(*iii*) Ability to take good casting impressions ;

(*iv*) Wear resistance ;

(*v*) High damping capacity ;

(*vi*) A reasonable tensile strength of 1000–3000 kg/cm^2 associated with a very high compressive strength, making it very suitable for applications requiring rigidity and resistance to wear.

Classification of Cast Iron

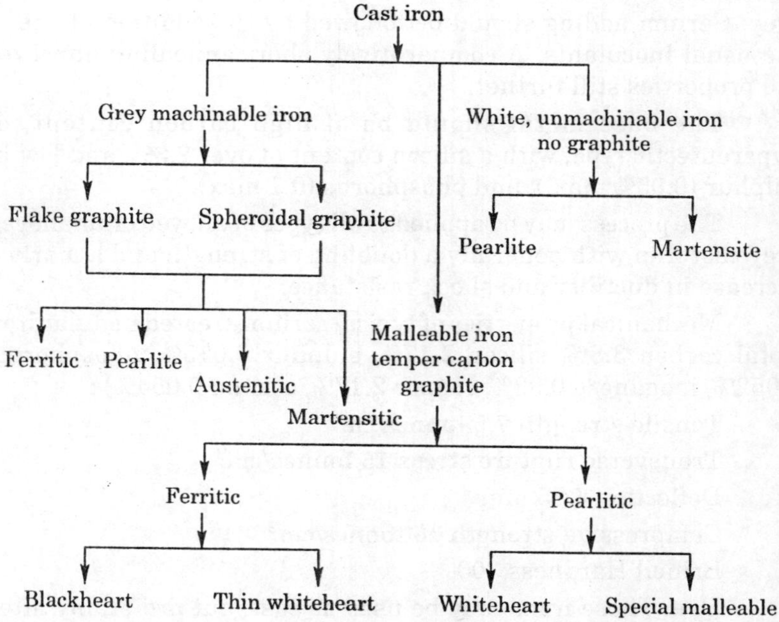

Alloying Elements and Their Effect on the Properties of Cast Iron

Alloying elements are classified in two groups :

1. Elements present inherently in the metal, as impurities or otherwise, *e.g.*, carbon, silicon, phosphorus, sulphur, manganese.

2. Elements added to improve properties of cast iron, *e.g.*, chromium, nickel, copper, manganese, magnesium, vanadium, titanium.

1. **Elements present Inherently**

(*i*) *Carbon.* It is the most important element present in cast iron. It lowers the melting-point of the metal and produces more graphite. Hence, it favours a soft, weak iron. Its content varies between 2 to 4.5%. It determines to a great extent, the mechanical properties of the casting. It is either present in the combined form (in the form of iron-carbide) or as free graphite. Iron carbide imparts strength and hardness whereas graphite causes softness and porosity in thicker sections. For general purpose casting, graphite is useful for making a soft and easily machinable iron.

Graphite in the form of long flakes is harmful as it makes the metal brittle. Size of flakes is controlled and reduced.

(*a*) by using inoculation treatment.

(*b*) by superheating the metal prior to casting to 1510—1710°C.

(*c*) by addition of suitable alloying elements.

Iron with lower carbon content (2.8 to 3.1%) has relatively higher freezing point (*i.e.*, lower fluidity), better heat and oxidation resistance, higher solidification shrinkage. Higher shrinkage requires elaborate risering. It has lower machinability, damping capacity but higher tensile strength and elasticity.

(*ii*) *Silicon.* Silicon is introduced into cast iron not only *via* the pig iron and scrap, but is also used as an addition in various forms to the molten metal to effect a final control over the structure of the ultimate product.

Silicon is the second most important alloying element in iron. It is a graphitizing element as it tends to decompose iron carbide (Fe_2C) into ferrite and graphite.

Change in silicon content will give a wide range properties in iron having a constant carbon percentage ; even if the cooling rate is kept the same during solidification.

Some elements like manganese, chromium, vanadium, molybdenum etc. deaccelerate the graphitizing effect of silicon and are called *'chill inducing elements'*.

Some elements like copper, aluminium, nickel, titanium zirconium etc. help silicon in graphitizing and are called *'chill restraining elements'*.

Silicon mainly occurs in solid solution and improves tensile strength and hardness. Iron gets thoroughly graphitized if silicon is above 3%. Iron with about 6% silicon is resistant to scales at high temperatures but is very brittle. Iron with 12 to 15% silicon and about 1% carbon is very brittle, but has high resistance to corrosion and action of acids.

(*iii*) *Manganese.* Manganese is always present in cast iron being derived mainly from pig iron. Special additions of ferro-manganese are often made in the furnace to increase the proportion of this element when desired.

The main reason for adding manganese to cast iron is to neutralize the harmful effect of sulphur. Its first effect is to combine with any sulphur present forming manganese sulphide which gets distributed uniformly.

Sulphur is a carbide-forming element of hardener. So, with a given sulphur content, increase in amount of manganese results in softening of the metal due to neutralization of sulphur content.

Manganese is not harmful to the properties of iron. In heavy casting cooling is slow and manganese sulphide collects at the surface forming slag layer due to its lower density and protects the metal from chilling effect.

Manganese is rarely present in ordinary cast iron in excess of about 1.2%. In special cases, however, large additions are made in the production of highly alloyed cast irons.

(*iv*) *Sulphur.* Sulphur is almost invariably present in cast iron as an impurity picked up from the fuel used in the preparation of the original pig and in remelting in the foundry.

The effect of sulphur is closely tied up with that of manganese as explained above. Sulphur present in iron tends to form iron sulphide. Freezing point of this sulphide is lower than that of iron. So, sulphide destroys the cohesion between the grains by forming a thick grain boundary of itself.

Sulphur has a powerful chilling tendency on the iron ; special precautions have, therefore, to be taken for its control and removal. In grey-iron casting it should never exceed 0.15%. On the other hand, sulphur is a powerful carbon-stabilizer and helps to retain iron-carbide in white cast iron.

(*v*) *Phosphorus.* The amount of phosphorus present in iron varies very widely from 0.92 to 1.6%. It is present partly in solid solution with ferrite and partly as iron-iron phosphide eutectic. Its presence is often undesirable, since it introduces into the structure of the metal, areas of hard, brittle iron phosphide constituent. This phosphide makes the casting mechanically weak, destroys its resistance to shock and decreases its toughness.

But phosphorus gives added fluidity to molten iron, and is, therefore, particularly useful for casting thin sections and intricate shapes. it also imparts wear resistance. When it exceeds 0.3%, it affects the tensile and bending strengths adversely.

There is no commercial method of removing phosphorus from pig or cast iron in foundry practice.

Table 4.5: Typical Analyses of Commercial Cast Irons

S. No.	*Application*	*Per cent*				
		C (Total)	S_i	M_n	*P*	*S*
1.	Auto cylinders	3.25	2.25	0.65	0.15	0.10
2.	Auto piston	3.35	2.25	0.65	0.15	0.10
3.	Auto castings	3.40	2.60	0.65	0.30	0.10
4.	Auto piston rings	3.50	2.90	0.65	0.50	0.06
5.	Machinery iron :					
	Light section	3.25	2.25	0.50	0.35	0.10
	Medium sections	3.25	1.75	0.50	0.35	0.10
	Heavy sections	3.25	1.25	0.50	0.35	0.10
6.	Water pipe :					
	Light and medium	3.60	1.75	0.50	0.35	0.08
	Heavy	3.40	1.40	0.50	0.80	0.08
7.	High strength iron	2.75	2.25	0.80	0.10	0.09
8.	Heat resistant iron	3.50	1.15	0.80	0.10	0.07
9.	Caustic pots	3.60	1.00	0.75	0.20	0.07
10.	Ingot moulds	3.50	1.00	0.90	0.20	0.07
11.	Car wheel iron	3.35	0.65	0.60	0.35	0.12
12.	Pressure cylinder	3.25	0.25	0.65	0.20	0.10
13.	Valves head fittings	3.30	2.00	0.50	0.35	0.10

2. **Alloying Elements added to improve properties.** The elements normally used as additions to cast iron are chromium, molybdenum, copper, nickel and aluminium for production of ordinary low-alloy cast iron.

For production of certain special types of alloys iron higher proportions of silicon and manganese are used.

Smaller proportions of vanadium, titanium and zirconium may be added as de-oxidizers. After doing their work, they are removed in the slag and are not generally found in the finished casting.

Chromium is a carbide former while copper and nickel are graphitizing elements. Beneficial effects of these elements on the structure and properties of the metal may be combined in a balanced addition so that the chilling power or chromium in just neutralized by the graphitizing effects of copper and nickel. Molybdenum does not influence amount of combined carbon very strongly. All these alloy additions have some influence in refining structure and improving the mechanical properties of the casting.

(*i*) *Chromium.* Additions of chromium are beneficial in a cast iron provided that its effect in forming chill does not result in casting which are hard giving trouble in machine shop. Chromium is, therefore, more often used in combination with graphitising elements such as higher silicon, nickel or copper. Iron in which the chilled or white structure is desired, chromium may be helpful. However, it tends to induce brittleness in the metal. It stabilizes the carbides and is often useful, therefore, in castings requiring heat resistance.

Chromium is added in appreciable amounts when high resistance to heat and corrosion are required. When silicon is present upto 0.5%, chromium is used to neutralize the silicon effect. Chromium is usually accompanied with nickel *viz.*, Ni-Hard alloy cast iron contains 4% nickel and 1% chromium, which has hardness of chilled or white cast iron without losing toughness.

30% nickel, 10% chromium alloy cast iron is even harder and is almost equal to stainless steel in corrosion resistance and taking high polish.

2% carbon, 5% silicon, 1% manganese, 2.5% chromium, 18% nickel alloy cast iron is very much used as heat resisting metal. It is easily machinable and can be temper-hardened.

(*ii*) *Nickel.* It is chill-restraining or graphitizing element instead of chill-inducing one like chromium. Its presence below 1% refines distribution of graphite. At high temperatures, it reduces stability of carbides.

1 to 2% nickel in cast iron eliminates hardspots, gives increased density and soundness, makes the metal more fluid and easier to cast and easily machinable. It resists heat very well without being brittle and gives good surface finish. Nickel does not decompose the carbide of pearlite like silicon but it refines and hardens it.

Usually nickel and chromium are used in combination to have advantages of both *viz.*,

(*a*) 1.7% nickel, 0.4% chromium, 3.4% carbon, 1.25 silicon, 0.5% phosphorus alloys cast iron is best combination for heavy duty castings such as C.I. dies for forging work.

(*b*) 4% nickel, 1% chromium cast iron is used for I.C. engine cylinder liners.

(*iii*) *Copper.* The limit of solubility of copper in iron is low (upto 3%). It is a mild chilled-resisting element about one-tenth effective than silicon. Its presence helps in giving corrosion resistance.

Table 4.6: Structural Effects of Alloying Elements on Cast Iron

S. No	Name of Alloying element with its category	Percentage of alloying element in pearlitic iron.	Chilling Effect	Effect on carbides at high temperatures	Effect on graphite structure	Effect on combined carbon in pearlite	Effect on matrix
1.	Chill-inducing elements :						
	(*i*) Chromium	0.15–1.0	Increases	Strongly stabilizes	Mildly refines	Increases	Refines pearlite and hardens
	(*ii*) Vanadium	0.15–0.5	Increases	Strongly stabilizes	Refines	Increases	Refines pearlite and hardens
2.	Mildly chill-in ducing elements :						
	(*i*) Manganese	0.3–1.25	Mildly increases	Stabilizes	Mildly refines	Increases	Refines pearlite and hardness
	(*ii*) Molybdenum	0.3—1.0	Mildly increases	About neutral	Strongly refines	Mildly increase	Refines pearlite and strengthens
3.	Mildly chill restraining : Copper	0.5—2.0	Mildly restrains	About neutral	About neutral	Mildly decreases	Hardens
4.	Chill-restraining elements :						
	(*i*) Carbon	...	Strongly restrains	Decreases stability	Coarsens	Strongly decreases	Produces ferrite and softens
	(*ii*) Silicon	...	Strongly restrains	Decreases stability	Coarsens	Strongly decreases	Produces ferrite and softens
	(*iii*) Aluminium	...	Strongly restrains	Decreases stability	Coarsens	Strongly decreases	Produces ferrite and softens
	(*iv*) Nickel	0.1—3.0	Restrains	Mildly decreases stability	Mildly refines	Mildly decreases and stabilizes at eutectoid	Refines pearlite and hardens
	(*v*) Titanium	0.05—0.10	Restrains	Decreases stability	Strongly refines	Decreases	Produces ferrite and softens
	(*vi*) Zirconium	0.1—0.3	Restrains	... ...	About neutral	... ...	Produces ferrite and softens

In thicker-sections, amount of copper added is more restricted because cooling is slow and copper tends to separate out in the casting with disastrous results. In case of thin sections, which solidify rapidly copper upto 3% can be allowed.

Copper is alloyed in combination with nickel and chromium, *viz.*, 3% copper, 12% nickel, 7 to 8% chromium C.I. used for pump parts.

(*iv*) *Molybdenum.* Molybdenum added to cast iron is generally less than 1%. It has no particularly market effect on the amount of combined carbon but it is very useful for strengthening the metal. it is more often used in combination with nickel, chromium or copper.

Acicular cast iron is produced by a combined additon generally of nickel and molybdenum. The microstructure corresponds to Bainite in steel and is the result of controlled transformation. Proportions of these alloying elements are adjusted for the size and thicknesses of the casting. Acicular structure results in high strength and improved shock resistance. For 25 mm thickness, 1% nickel and 1% molybednum is a typical composition.

(*v*) *Manganese.* For non-magnetic properties in iron, manganese is used as an alloying element.

5 to 10% manganese, 10 to 15% nickel alloy C.I. called **'NOMAG'** is adopted for electrical casting *e.g.*, switch covers, insulator supports, motor exteriors, etc. It is practically non-magnetic having a low permeability and high electrical resistance. Both magnetic and eddy current losses are cut down resulting saving in power. It can be easily machined.

(*vi*) *Magnesium*. It helps in converting the graphite flakes to nodular form resulting in increased strength, hardness and elongation. This iron is called *'Ductile Iron'* due to greater toughness and ductility.

For parts which are too intricate to be cast in steel or which can not be made strong enough by adopting grey C.I., magnesium is used as an alloying element.

(*vii*) *Vanadium*. It is also a chill-inducing or carbide forming element like chromium. At high temperatures, it strongly stabilizes the carbide. It helps uniform distribution of graphite flakes and reduces the size of the grain. It improves hardness, wear resistance, tensile and bending strengths but decreases machinability.

(*viii*) *Titanium.* It is added in amounts as small as 0.01%. It readily combines with nitrogen forming inactive inclusions of titanium nitride.

It strongly refines the grain structure and improves the mechanical properties like strength and toughness.

High Strength Irons

Modification of Micro-structure and properties of cast iron can be brought about by :

1. Use of special melting and casting technique.
2. Addition of alloying elements.
3. Heat treatment, particularly of white iron.

1. **High duty irons due to casting technique.** High duty irons are made by additing to the cupola, steel scrap which slightly reduces the carbon content and in particular the amount of free graphite together with the production of a pearlitic matrix.

Other methods consist of super-heating the molten metals in a separate furnace, whereby the graphite is greatly refined. Alternatively, an iron which would normally cast white can be graphitised by certain compounds (*e.g.*, calcium silicide in mechanite) in the ladle to give strength of 3000 to 4500 kg/cm^2.

2. **Addition of alloying elements.** The most common of the special element added to cast iron are nickel, chromium, copper and molybdenum, *Nickel* tends to produce grey iron, in which respect it is less powerful than silicon. Consequently in castings of widely varying section, silicon can be reduced slightly and nickel added to prevent chilling in thin section, but still retaining a close structure in thick ones.

Chromium, by forming carbides, acts in the opposite way to nickel, but at same time it exerts a grain refining action. These elements, singly or together, are commonly found in motor cylinder irons.

Molybdenum nodulises the graphite and promotes a fine pearlite but it is used preferably with other elements such as nickel or chromium.

Classification of High Strength Alloy Iron

(*i*) Pearlitic irons
(*ii*) Acicular irons
(*iii*) Martensitic irons
(*iv*) Austenitic irons
(*v*) Spheroidal graphite cast iron.

(*i*) *Pearlitic Irons.* 0.5–2% Ni (Cr upto 0.8% and Mo upto 0.6%). Used for many general castings.

High carbon Ni–Cr-Mo cast iron is useful for resisting thermal shock in applications *e.g.*, die casting moulds and brake drums.

Cr (0.6)–Mo 0.6 irons are useful for engine liners, press sleeves, dies, etc., where wear resistance in relatively heavy sections is important.

Cast iron with 1% each of Cr and Mo is used for piston rings.

(*ii*) *Acicular Irons.* C 2.9–3.2, Ni 1.5–2, Mo 0.3–0.6. Copper can replace Ni upto 1.5%. This rigid, high strength, shock resisting material is used for diesel crank shafts, gears and machine columns.

With correct amounts of Ni and Mo correlated with cooling rate of a particular casting, the pearlitic change point can be suppressed and an acicular intermediate constituent (ferritic needles in austenitic matrix) can be produced with high mechanical properties.

Acicular C.I. is very much tougher than any of the pearlitic C.I of lower strength. Tensile strength of acicular C.I. with about 3% C will vary from 4000 to 5500 kg/cm^2 in large sections.

Phosphorus should not exceed about 0.15% in presence of molybdenum, otherwise a compound is formed which improvises the matrix of molybdenum. Large variations in silicon content can be tolerated, but chromium in excess of 0.4% is harmful.

The structure changes rapidly at 600–750°C and these irons should not be used above 300°C.

(*iii*) *Martensitic Irons.* 5 to 7% Ni with other elements. Very hard irons used for resisting abrasion, *e.g.*, metal working rolls.

(*iv*) *Austenitic Irons.* Non-magnetic, with 14–25% Ni, Cu, Cr are frequently added. These have good resistance to corrosion and heat *e.g.*, Ni-Resist.

Outstanding characteristics of Austenitic Cast Irons as compared with ordinary C.I. :

(*a*) Resistance to corrosion

(*b*) Market resistance to heat.

(*c*) Non-magnetic, with suitable compositions.

(*d*) A high electrical resistance with a low temperature coefficient of resistance.

(*e*) A high coefficient of thermal expansion.

(*f*) No change points.

(*v*) **Spheroidal Graphite C.I.** Production of spheroidal graphite in the as-cast state is an outstanding development of a new iron, due to the use of cerium and magnesium. Combined use

of cerium and magnesium followed by ferro-silicon as an inoculant is used to produce spheroidal graphite. Remelting causes a reversion to flake graphite due to loss of Mg. Mg-treatment desulphurises the iron to below 0.02% before alloying with the iron, and for economic reasons, the sulphur content should be as low as possible.

S.G. iron can be used with a pearlitic matrix or ferrite after a short annealing or with an anicular or austenitic matrix when suitably alloyed.

High Alloy Cast Irons

(*i*) *High Silicon Cast Irons.* Cast iron containing 5 to 7% silicon known as *'Silal'* possess special heat resisting properties. In addition to their oxidation resistance, they are strong at high temperatures but are brittle under ordinary conditions. These are used for certain types of furnace castings.

Cast iron alloyed with 12 to 14% silicon known as *'Tantiron'*, *'Duriron'* and *'Ironac'* is used for acid-resisting castings. It is white in fracture and unusually hard and brittle. Castings cannot be machined. They are so weak that they fracture like glass when dropped on the floor. However, they are important since they provide a remarkable degree of resistance to strong mineral acids.

(*ii*) *High Manganese Cast Irons.* Cast irons alloyed with manganese upto 3% are used for special structures, *e.g.*, crushing rolls. Castings tend to become white as manganese is a carbide-forming element. This tendency decreases in heavy sections resulting castings with a hard matrix showing high degree of wear resistance.

With greater additions of manganese, the castings tend to become white and unworkable. So, they are used in combination with elements like nickel.

(*iii*) *High Chromium Cast Irons.* They are white due to the carbide-forming tendency of chromium. They are important for their heat resistance.

Cast irons containing upto about 30% chromium have, in addition to high resistance, strength at high temperatures, good wear-resistance and corrosion-resistance. They generally contain low total carbon even below 1%. Hence they show all round good mechanical properties with machinability.

(*iv*) *High Nickel Cast Iron.* (*a*) Castings containing over 2% nickel tend to be hard. They can be air-hardened and heat-treated.

(*b*) 4.5% nickel cast iron is martensitic. This structure is associated with excellent wear resistance. If casting are white or chilled, the iron is called *'Ni-Hard'*, which is used for grinding and crushing parts, chilled rolls, sand handling equipment.

(*c*) Castings containing above 18% nickel are austenitic in structure, relatively soft, show high resistance to heat and corrosion and are non-magnetic.

(*d*) 14% nickel, 6% copper, 2% chromium is well-known special austenitic iron *'Ni-Resist'*, corrosion and heat resisting, non-magnetic.

(*e*) 11% nickel, 7% manganese is well known non-magnetic cast iron *'Nomag'*. It is also austenitic in structure.

(*f*) 18% nickel, 2% chromium, 4.5% silicon is well known *'Nicrosilal'* austenitic cast iron, heat corrosion resisting.

(*g*) Cast iron containing 34 to 36% nickel, 2% chromium shows abnormally low thermal expansion about five or six millionths per degree centigrade. It is used in measuring gauges subjected to fluctuating temperatures.

Steel Foundry Metallurgy

Steel is essentially an alloy of iron and carbon. For foundry purposes, carbon content in straight carbon steel is generally less than 0.6%, but for certain special castings its percentage may even exceed 1%. Steel can be regarded as a purified form of cast iron, and its manufacture in refining process applied to charges consisting of pig iron and cast iron scrap. Elements which are normally present in cast iron, *e.g.*, carbon, silicon, manganese, sulphur and phosphorus have a proportionately far greater influence in steel than in cast iron. They must, therefore, be controlled, and in some cases eliminated to the maximum possible extent.

Element in Steel. (*i*) *Carbon* is the controlling element on which the properties ultimately obtained in steel depend. Lower the carbon content, higher the melting point and more difficult to handle and cast in foundry but steel is softer and more ductile.

Carbon content is rarely below 0.1% for foundry purposes. Lowest carbon is used for electrical castings which are required to have good magnetic properties.

Increasing carbon upto 0.6%, the liquid metal becomes more fluid and, therefore, more suitable for general castings. Higher carbon increases strength, improves other desired properties and makes it more responsive to heat treatment.

Table 4.7: Some High Alloy Cast Irons

S. No.	*Name of high Alloy Cast Iron*	*Total Carbon*	*Silicon*	*Manganese*	*Sulphur*	*Phosphorus*	*Nickel*	*Copper*	*Chromium*	*Properties*
1.	Silal	2.2	5.5	0.5	0.1	0.1				Heat resistance
2.	High silicon C.I.	1	13–16	0.2–51	0.05	0.8				Acid resistance
3.	High chromium C.I.	2.5–3.2	1.0	0.5	0.05	0.1			10–14	Heat resistance
		1.5–2.5	1.0	0.5	0.05	0.1			21	—do—
		1.0–2.5	1.2–2.0	0.5	0.05	0.1			30–34	—do—
4.	Ni-Hard	2.8–3.5	0.5–1.0	0.6–1.2	0.12	0.4	4.5		1.5	Wear resistance
5.	Ni-Resist	30	1.5	1.2	0.12	02	14	6	2-4	Corrosion and heat resistance. Non-magnetic.
6.	Nicrosilal	1.7	4.5	0.8	0.10	02	18		2	Corrosion and heat resistance
7.	Nomag	3.0	1.5	7.0			11			Non-magnetic
8.	Low expansion C.I.	2.2	1.5	0.8			34-36		2	Minimum thermal expansion

(*ii*) *Silicon* is usually present only in small quantities in steel (generally less than 0.5%). Silicon within this limit has not a very profound influence on foundry and mechanical properties of steel.

In tool steels, the amount is usually less than 0.2% owing to the tendency for graphite to form.

(*iii*) *Manganese,* as in cast iron, is generally considered a desirable element. It may be present upto 1% in plain carbon steel castings. There are special steels of high manganese content.

Manganese confers depth of harderning, but also a particular liability to crack in quenching, for which reason high carbon steels, intended to be quenched in water, should contain less than 0.5%.

Manganese raises the yield point and Izod values.

(*iv*) *Sulphur and phosphorus* are both considered most undesirable in steel for general purposes.

(*a*) Sulphur exists as either manganese sulphide (MnS) or ferrous sulphide (FeS). The ferrous sulphide forms brittle, low melting point yellowish-brown films around the solid steel crystals and causes the metal to split when forged.

High melting point manganese sulphide is only slightly soluble in iron and collects into large globules irregularly distributed through the steel. It is plastic at high temperatures, being elongated into threads by rolling without seriously impairing the properties of the material.

The manganese should be about five times that theoretically required to combine with sulphur present. Modern free-cutting steels use 0.2% sulphur and 1.5% manganese with low phosphorus. But in tool steels, the sulphur should not exceed 0.035%.

Sulphur induces hot-shortness, and tends to make steel brittle.

(*b*) Phosphorus also has a strong embrittling influence. As far as possible it must be eliminated.

Both ferrous sulphide and phosphorus have a powerful tendency to segregate. Every effort is made to keep phosphorus to 0.02–0.05%.

Phosphorus forms a compound Fe_3P which dissolves in iron upto 1.7%, but in the presence of 3.5% carbon its solubility is reduced to 0.3% and the excess forms the brittle eutectic found in cast iron.

Advantages accure from the presence of phosphorus in certain cases :

1. With 0.08%, the tendency of tin plates to stick together is prevented.

2. With 0.07% in presence of 0.3% copper, increased resistance to atmospheric corrosion is obtained.

All processes of steel making consist of (*a*) Reduction of undesirable impurities, *e.g.*, sulphur and phosphorus and excess quantities of silicon and carbon normally present in C.I., (*b*) adjustment of composition of silicon and carbon for producing the desired combination of properties.

Casting of Steels

Difference between moulding and casting of steel and iron

(*i*) In case of steel casting, usually high silica sands bounded with refractory clays are used because melting points of steel are higher involving higher pouring temperatures which necessitate sands of greater refractoriness.

(*ii*) All steel castings must be fed in the heaviest sections so as to make the metal free from solidification shrinkage. In case of iron, solidification shrinkage is relatively low, hence this factor is not so important.

(*iii*) No carbonaceous material or washers are used on mould faces for steel casting because molten steel has a tendency to dissolve carbon.

(*iv*) In steel casting, new facing sand having high refractoriness is generally used on the contact faces. In other part of mould, backing up sand of inferior grade is used so as to reduce cost.

(*v*) Before pouring steel into the moulds, it must be thoroughly dioxidised to obtain sound castings. If it is not chilled, it spits and boils in the ladle due to dissolved oxygen and defect like gas holes, gas porosity and sponginess are produced.

Low carbon steels may be chilled or not but alloy steels are invariably chilled in one of the following ways :

(*a*) By adding small amount of deoxidising elements like aluminium, manganese, silicon, etc. to molten metal in the ladle for controlling grain size.

(*b*) By allowing the metal to remain in the crucible for a longer time so that the silicon of the crucible may combine with the oxygen forming slag of the surface.

(*c*) By normalizing.

(*vi*) To get sound castings, directional solidification should be aimed, at, *i.e.*, solidification should start from the point which is farthest from the riser and should proceed progressively towards the riser.

Ways to achieve directional solidification

(*a*) By designing the casting properly.

(*b*) Due to a high rate of solidification shrinkage in steel casting, heavy risering is essential so that riser remains molten for a longer time than the section to be fed by it. Hence, risers of proper size and shape should be used and they should be most appropriately placed.

(*c*) By using external or internal type chills.

(*d*) By using gating methods capable of setting up favourable temperature gradients in the metal during pouring.

(*e*) By using exothermic compounds in the moulds for differential cooling.

(*f*) By using mould materials of varying thermal properties in different portions of the mould so as to have desired change in the rate of heat loss.

(*vii*) By designing the sprue properly because it is important for getting sound casting.

The sprue should be large enough so that (*a*) mould cavity gets filled up completely without misruns, seams or laps, (*b*) a metal head is formed quickly so that mould gases may be prevented from being aspirated into the mould.

The sprue should be small enough so that (*a*) it can be kept full during the entire pouring operation and (*b*) metal may not enter the mould with high velocity causing splashing and turbulence.

Solidification of steel. In sand castings, freezing starts with skin formation. Actual rate of freezing varies with size and shape of the casting.

For given metal with the given type of mould, freezing time decreases if :

(*i*) Heat of fusion is low.

(*ii*) Specific heat is low.

(*iii*) Freezing range is short.

(*iv*) Freezing temperature is high.

(*v*) Conductivity is high.

Actual ratios of freezing times of various metals in chill and sand castings vary from 4 : 1 to 20 : 1.

As observed from Iron-carbon diagram :

(*i*) At room temperature, an iron containing no carbon will be 100% ferrite and will consist of microscopic polygonal grains.

(*ii*) A steel containing 0.8% carbon will be 100% pearlite and will consist of microscopic pearlitic grains made up of alternate laminations or bands of ferrite and cementite.

(*iii*) Steel containing varying amounts of carbon between 0 and 0.8% will consist of varying amounts of ferrite and pearlite depending upon actual composition.

(*iv*) Steel containing carbon between 0.8 to 1.4% will contain pearlite and cementite in varying amounts.

Steel castings are likely to become unsound due to absorption of gases by molten metal while pouring. For producing casting free from defects and promoting proper solidification, manganese and silicon compounds are frequently used. Silicon, in liquid state, combines with oxygen forming iron manganese-silicate, a part of which gets precipitated as slag and floats on the surface. The reminder goes into the casting as inclusion.

Silicon upto 0.6% is usually used. Above this amount, it may cause embrittlement of steel castings.

Properties of Fine and Coarse-grained Steels

Fine grained steel (3 to 16 grains per sq. cm.) has the following characteristics compared with a coarse grain (¼ to 2 grains per sq. cm.) :

(*i*) Enhanced toughness in plain steels, but increase is less in alloy steels.

(*ii*) Shall over-harden less tendency to warp and crack.

(*iii*) Carburises less deeply, absence of grain growth in core permits single quench from the carburising temperature.

(*iv*) Less tendency for cracks to originate in flash trimming of forgings.

(*v*) Mass production machining is more difficult.

(*vi*) Deterioration by quench and strain ageing is reduced.

Greater standardisation can, therefore, be obtained by using a steel with an inherent grain size suitable for a particular purpose.

Production of Malleable Cast Iron

Ordinary cast iron being hard and brittle is not suitable for articles (*i*) which are to be thin and light, or (*ii*) which are subjected to shocks and vibrations, or (*iii*) for small castings used in textile and agricultural machinery. Graphite present in the iron in the form of flakes is a source of weakness and causes brittleness.

If white cast iron is annealed continuously at a temperature of 950 to 1000°C, it has been found that the carbon precipitates out in the form of a very fine nodular form. Graphite flakes, when converted in such a finely divided form, are not so harmful and make the iron malleable.

Malleable iron is obtained by the heat treatment of white iron so that the reaction $Fe_3C \longrightarrow 3Fe + C$ (graphite) is completed. Heat treatment breaks down hard carbide structure of ledeburite and converts it to a matrix of nearly all ferrite in which iron, '*ferritic malleable iron*' has typical mechanical properties of 5000 kg/cm^2 tensile strength, 3000 kg/cm^2 yield strength, and 20% elongation.

By other heat treatment cycles, the matrix can be made pearlitic, resulting in a material of higher strength, and somewhat lower ductility.

The important metallurgical *distinction between malleable and grey iron* is what in malleable iron the graphite is not present in flakes which embrittle the cast metal but in nodules which are not as harmful to strength properties.

Furnaces employed for production of malleable cast iron are cupola, air furnace and electric furnace.

Two kinds of malleable cast iron are

(*i*) Whiteheart malleable cast iron.

(*ii*) Blackheart malleable cast iron.

(*i*) *Production of Whiteheart Malleable Cast Iron.* It was developed in Europe. It is made from cast iron low in silicon and manganese and high in sulphur. It chills even in a sand mould giving white cast iron without flaky graphite. White iron so given is then packed in red haematite ore and heated slowly for 5 to 6 days of 950 to 1000°C in an annealing furnace. It is then slowly cooled in the same furnace.

Carbon present in iron slowly diffuses out, gets oxidised by haematite and is thus removed. The resulting product has a very little carbon and is soft, though and malleable. Whiteheart malleable cast iron has its fracture brightly crystalline with a rim

of dull grey matrix. Maximum thickness of castings suitable for this process is 20 mm.

(*ii*) *Production of Blackheart Malleable Cast Iron.* It is made similarly by heating in an annealing furnace at 950 to 1000°C for about 3 to 6 days. In this process carbon is not removed as in Whiteheart process. It is packed in sand on crushed slag instead of packing it in haematite ore.

During cooling of castings, the combined carbon separates out, but all the carbon does not change into graphite state. It changes into another form of free carbon termed *'temper carbon'*.

This separation of carbon from combined state renders the casting less brittle, *i.e.* malleable. Blackheart malleable cast iron has its fracture dark grey or black in appearance. It is most commonly produced and used in automobile industry in India. Maximum thickness of castings suitable for this process is 25 to 35 mm.

Table 4.8: Typical Chemical Compositions of Malleable Cast Iron

S. No.	*Types of Malleable Cast Iron*	*Total carbon*	*Silicon*	*Manganese*	*Sulphur*	*Phosphorus*
1.	Whiteheart	3.2–3.9	0.4–1.1	0.1–0.4	0.1–0.3	0.1
2.	Blackheart	2.2–2.8	0.7–1.1	0.3–0.4	0.03–0.1	0.1

Both Whiteheart and Blackheart Malleable cast irons are less brittle than ordinary cast iron. They are more stronger more ductile and more fluid.

Malleable cast iron is produced and adopted mainly for thin walled and small articles *viz.*, hinges, door keys, spanners, all kinds of mountings, gear wheels, cranks, levers, small cast parts for agricultural and textile machinery, etc.

Characteristics and Uses of Malleable Cast Iron

Characteristics: (*i*) It can be hammered and rolled for obtaining new shapes.

(*ii*) It is obtained from hard and brittle white iron through a regulated heat conversion process.

(*iii*) It posses high yield strength.

(*iv*) It has good vibration damping capacity and wear resistance.

(*v*) It has a solidification range of 1400–1330°C.

(*vi*) It has shrinkage of 1.5 mm in 100 mm.

(*vii*) It can be used from – 15 to 650°C.

(*viii*) It has low to moderate cost.

(*ix*) It has a low coefficient of thermal expansion and a high Young's modulus.

(*x*) Ferrite malleable C.I. has ferrite matrix, pearlite malleable C.I. has pearlite matrix and alloy malleable C.I. (containing Cr and Ni) possesses corrosion resistance and high strength.

Uses : It is used for :

(*i*) Gear cases, (*ii*) Automotive crankshaft, (*iii*) Crankshaft sprocket, (*iv*) Conveyor chain links, (*v*) Automotive industry, (*vi*) Electrical line hardware, (*vii*) Agricultural implements, (*viii*) Universal joint yoke, (*ix*) Truck tendem axle assembly components, (*x*) Rear axle banjo housing.

Ductile Cast Iron

Ductile iron can be obtained without an extensive malleabilizing cycle. The original as-cast graphite is caused to grow as spherulites rather than flankes. For doing this, specific agents like magnesium or cerium are added to the melt mechanism of action of these agents is not yet fully understood.

For obtaining spherulites, it is necessary :

(*i*) to desulphurize the iron almost completely, then

(*ii*) add magnesium or cerium and, finally,

(*iii*) add a post-inoculant like ferrosilicon.

Typical properties of as-cast ferritic ductile iron : Tensile strength 5000 kg/cm^2, yield strength 3500 kg/cm^2, elongation 20%. For pearlitic ductile iron : Tensile strength 8000 kg/cm^2, yield strength 5500 kg/cm^2, elongation 60%.

Characteristics and Uses of Ductile or Nodular Cast Iron

Characteristics : (*i*) It contains 3.2–4.2% C, 1.1–3.5% Si, 0.3–0.8% Mn, 0.08% P and 0.02% S.

(*ii*) Unlike long flakes as in grey C.I., graphite appears as rounded particles, or nodules or spheroids.

(*iii*) Sphroidizing elements, when added to the melt, eliminate sulphur and oxygen and cause nodulization.

(*iv*) Properties depend on composition and cooling rate.

(*v*) It possess very good machinability. Soft annealed grades can be turned at very high feeds and speeds.

(*vi*) Its damping capacity is intermediate between C.I. and steel.

(*vii*) It possess good wear resistance and excellent cast ability.

Uses : It is used for :

(*i*) Farm implements, (*ii*) Tractor implements, (*iii*) Earth moving machinery, (*iv*) Construction machinery, (*v*) Paper industry machinery, (*vi*) Compressor and pump components, (*vii*) Steel mill rolls and mill equipment. (*viii*) I.C. engines, (*ix*) Pipes, (*x*) Valves and filttings.

Characteristics and Uses of White Cast Iron (Mottled Iron)

Characteristics : (*i*) It is named so because its freshly broken surface shows a bright white fracture.

(*ii*) It has almost all its carbon chemically combined with iron as iron carbide (Fe_3C), which is a very hard and brittle constituent.

(*iii*) White C.I. contains 1.8–3.6% C, 0.5–2.0% Si, 0.2–0.8%, Mn, 0.18% P and 0.10% S.

(*iv*) Cast iron is made to solidify as white C.I. by using a fairly low silicon content.

(*v*) Under normal circumstances, it is brittle and unmachinable.

(*vi*) White iron castings can be made in sand moulds.

(*vii*) White iron can also be made on the surface of grey iron castings of special composition.

(*viii*) First step in producing malleable iron castings are white iron of a particular chemical composition.

(*ix*) Iron of proper composition, if cooled rapidly, free carbon changes to combined form giving rise to white iron.

(*x*) Its shrinkage is 1 mm in 100 mm.

(*xi*) Its solidification range is from 1400 to 1330°C.

(*xii*) It possesses excellent abrasive resistance.

Uses : It is used for :

(*i*) Production of malleable iron castings.

(*ii*) Manufacture of components requiring hard and abrasion resistant surface.

Non-ferrous Cast Alloys

(*i*) Copper alloys, (*ii*) Aluminium and its alloys, (*iii*) Magnesium alloys, (*iv*) Zinc alloys, (*v*) Nickel alloys.

Copper and its Alloys

Raw copper used for *Cast copper base alloys is classified as* :

(*i*) *Electrolytic Copper or High Conductivity copper.* It contains 99.9% Cu, 0.04% O_2, 0.005% each Pb and Fe, 0.002% Ag, 0.001% Bi. It is used for electrical purposes.

(*ii*) *Deoxidized Copper.* It contains 99.85% Cu, 0.05% As, 0.03% Fe, 0.003% Bi, 0.05% P, 0.01, Pb, 0.10% Ni, 0.003% Ag, 0.005% Sb.

(*iii*) *Arsenical Deoxidized Copper.* It contains 0.04% As, 0.04% P. It is used for welded tanks and vessels.

(*iv*) *Arsenical tough pitch Copper.* It contains 0.4% As, 0.065% O_2, 0.02% Pb, 0.15% Ni, 0.006% Ag, 0.01% Sb, upto 0.005% Bi, upto 0.02% Fe.

(*v*) *Oxygen-free Copper.* It contains 0.005% Pb, 0.001% Ni, 0.001% Ag, upto 0.0005% each Fe and Bi. Melting and casting is carried out in non-oxidized atmosphere.

Characteristics of Copper

(*i*) High electrical and thermal conductivity.

(*ii*) Ductile and malleable.

(*iii*) Moderate in strength and hardness.

(*iv*) Non-magnetic.

(*v*) Very good corrosion resistance.

(*vi*) Very good machinability.

(*vii*) Can be soldered brazed and welded.

(*viii*) Can be easily polished, plated with good appearance.

(*ix*) Easily form as Alloys with Zn, Sn, Al, Pb, Ni, Si, etc.

(*x*) Cast copper alloys cannot be easily worked but can be brazed and machined. They can be cast into intricate shapes with sand casting, die casting shell moulding and centrifugal casting.

Table 4.9: Some Important Cast Copper-base Alloys and Their Uses

S. No.	*Name of alloys*	*Composition (%)*	*Application*
1.	Tin bronze	8–10 Sn, 2–4 Zn, Rest Cu	Structural bronze, pressure casting, bearings, bushings.
2.	Leaded tin bronze	6–8.5 Sn, 0.5–1.5 Pb, About 4 Zn, Rest Cu	Steam pressure castings, electrical castings, pumps, gears, bushings.
3.	High lead tin bronze	5–10 Sn, 7–15 Pb, 1–3 Zn, Rest Cu	High pressure and high speed bearings corrosion resisting pumps.

4.	Aluminium bronze	1–4 Fe, 9–11 Al, Rest Cu 4–Ni (sometimes)	Heavy duty parts, marine components, guides, bushing, steams, valve seats, acid resistant pumps, oxidation and corrosion resisting parts requiring strength at high temperatures.
5.	Leaded nickeld bronze	4–5 Sin, 1.5–4 Pb, 2–8 Zn, 20.25 Ni, Rest Cu	Marine castings, dairy compoments, valves hardware.
6.	Leaded red brass	4–5 Sn, 5–6, Pb, 5–7 Zn, Rest Cu	Pipe and tube fittings, pumps impellers, small gears, hardware, plumbing items.
7.	Leaded yellow brass	1 Sn, 1–3 Pb, 24–36.7 Zn, 03 Al, Rest Cu	Ornamental castings, hardware, valves and fittings.
8.	Silicon brass	14 Zn, 3.5–4 Si, 0.5 Pb, Rest Cu	Die cast parts, small gears, structural parts
9.	Gun metal	5–10 Sn, 2–5 Zn, Rest Cu	Good tensile strength and corrosion resistances. Hydraulic valves and gears, castings, steam pipe fittings, bearings.

Aluminium and its Alloys

Characteristics : (*i*) Light weight (one-third weight of steel), (*ii*) Good electrical conductivity, (*iii*) Good corrosion resistance, (*iv*) Ductile and malleable, (*v*) Non-magnetic, (*iv*) High thermal conductivity, (*vii*) Tensile strength about equal to that of structure steel (*viii*) Coefficient of expansion more than that of steel, (*ix*) Forms alloys with Cu, Cr, Ni, Fe, Zn, Si, Mg and Mn, (*x*) Can be cast in sand moulds, shell, moulds and permanent metal moulds, (*xi*) Do not work well above 300°C, (*xii*) Exhibit toughness and more strength below atmospheric range.

Table 4.10: Classification of Aluminium Alloys, Properties and Uses

S.No.	*Name*	*Composition*	*Properties and uses*
1.	Al-Si-Mg-Mn alloy	8–13 Si, 0.17–0.3 Mg, 0.25–00.5 Mn, Rest Al	Large castings to work under heavy duty loading, easily machinable, high corrosion resistance.
2.	Al-Mg alloy	9.5–11.5 Mg. Rest Al	Simple castings to work under dynamic loading and corrosive conditions.
3.	Al-Si-Cu alloy	4.5–6 Si, 1–3 Cu, 0.35–0.6 Mg, Rest Al	Good castability castings to work under severe loading and high temperatures.

4.	Al-Mg Mn alloy	4.5 Mg, 0.5 Mn, Rest Al	
5.	Al-Cu alloy	4.5 Cu, Rest Al	
6.	Al-Cu-Ni alloy	4 Cu, 2 Ni, Rest Al	
7.	Al-Mg alloy	1.5 mg, Rest Al	

Applications

(*i*) In heavy duty structures *viz*., bridges, conveyor supports, cranes, hoists, etc.

(*ii*) In transportation industry *viz*., engine parts, structural framing, hardware, doors, windows, tanks, furnishings, fittings, trim and decorative fittings, etc. in trains, cars, buses, trucks, aeroplanes.

(*iii*) In architectural industry *viz*., window frames, doors, hardware, roofings, coping, railing, sills, fasteners, lighting fixtures, grills, solar shadings, gratings, etc.

(*iv*) In process industry *viz*., tanks, drums, pipes, heat exchangers, precipitators, Centrifuges, valves, fittings to handle organic chemicals and petrochemicals, gratings, smoke stacks.

(*v*) In electrical industry *viz*., overhead cables, electrical conductors.

(*vi*) In food industry *viz*., food preparing equipments, refrigeration, storage, bakery equipments, packing containers.

(*vii*) Cryogenic uses.

(*viii*) Mangles and Wafflemolds.

Magnesium Alloys

Characteristics. (*i*) Not employed in pure state as weak in strength, (*ii*) Mg can be alloyed with Al, Mn, Zn, Zr, Th, etc. for engineering uses, (*iii*) Mg-alloys prove to be superior to Al-alloys regarding strength-weight ratio, (*iv*) M-alloys can be readily cast in sand and permanent moulds.

Table 4.11: Important Magnesium Casting Alloys, their Composition and Uses

S. No.	*Composition*	*Properties*	*Uses*
1.	0.5 Zn, 0.3 Mn 8 Al, Rest Mg	Ductile, strong, shock resistant, good castability, work upto 150°C, crack resistant.	General purpose, pressure tight parts
2.	4.5 Zn, 4.7 Zn Rest Mg	Can be satisfactorily cast and welded. Creep resistant upto 350°C.	Pressure tight parts.

3.	4 Zn, 0.7 Zr, 1.2 RE, Rest Mg		
4.	5.5 Zn, 0.7 Zr. 18 Th, Rest Mg		
5.	07 Zr, 1.7 Re, 2.5 Ag, Rest Mg	Very high strength, can be used upto 250°C, can be welded.	Pressure tight castings

Note: —RE means Rare Earth metals.

General Applications

(*i*) In Aeroplanes, helicopters, missiles and satellites, *viz.,* framings, engines, flooring, sealing, gear boxes.

(*ii*) In ground transportation vechicles *viz.*, engines, transmission pumps, differentials, body panels, etc.

(*iii*) In material handling equipments *viz.*, gravity conveyors foundry equipment, hand trucks, grain shovels, barrel skids, ladders, scaffols, hoppers.

(*iv*) In storage reservoirs, electric and pneumatic portable drills and hammers, chain saws, etc.

(*v*) Components of printing equipment, textile machinery, type writers, calculators, dictating machinery, binocular and camera bodies.

(*vi*) In producing litanium, Zirconicum, beryllium, Uranium, etc.

Zinc Cast Alloys

For these, die casting process is most commonly used for zinc die castings, weighing from a few grams to 20 kg.

Some Implement Zinc-base Die-castings. (*i*) 0.10% Cu, 3.5-4.3% Al, Rest Zn has shrinkage of about 1.3 mm/100 mm and solidifies at about 380°C.

		Ni	Cu	Al	Mg	Pb	Cd	Sn	Fe	Zn
(*ii*)	(*a*)	0.005–0.02	0.25	3.5–4.3	0.005–0.02	0.003	0.002	0.001	0.075	Rest
	(*b*)	–	0.25	3.5–4.3	0.02–0.05	0.005	0.004	0.003	0.1	Rest

Uses : Zinc-base die castings find use in hardware items, radiator grills, carburettor body, door handles, etc.

Nickel Cast Alloys

(*i*) *Ni-Cu Alloys*. 70% Ni, 30% Cu, solidification range 1372–1335°C, Shrinkage 2 mm/100 mm.

(*ii*) *Ni-Cu-Si Alloy*. 30% Cu, 3.5% Si, Rest Ni, solidification range 1335–1260°C, Shrinkage 2 mm/100 mm.

Characteristics : (*i*) High corrosion resistance, (*ii*) Strong resistance to high temperatures, oxidation, creep.

Uses : For gas turbine blades, pump and valve parts for chemical plant.

QUESTIONS

1. Give the composition of cast iron. Explain the difference between grey iron and mottled iron.
2. Write short note on :
   (*a*) Iron-carbon equilibrium diagram.
   (*b*) Allotropic forms of iron.
3. Give the characteristics and uses of grey cast iron. What is inoculated cast irons?
4. Explain spheroidal graphite cast iron. Give its uses and advantages.
5. Describe the classification of cast iron into a chart.
6. Explain high strength iron and give their applications.
7. How malleable cast iron is produced? Explain in brief.
8. Give the characteristics and uses of :
   (*a*) Malleable cast iron
   (*b*) Ductile cast iron
   (*c*) White cast iron
9. Give some examples of non-ferrous cast alloys with uses.

5

Pattern Making

Introduction

A pattern may be defined as a model of anything, constructed in such a way that it can be used for forming an impression called *"mould"* in damp sand or other suitable material. When this mould is filled with molten metal or substances that solidify, a reproduction of the pattern known as *"casting"* will be formed. The process of making a pattern is known as *"pattern making"*. The person who makes the pattern is known as *"pattern-maker"*.

Difference between Pattern and Casting

Main difference between the two is that of their dimensions. Pattern is slightly larger in size than the casting because :

(*i*) Pattern is given contraction allowance of about 1 to 2 mm per 100 mm.

(*ii*) Pattern carries machining or finishing allowance for cleaning and finishing the desired surfaces.

(*iii*) Pattern is given draft allowance of 1° for external and 3° for internal surfaces.

(*iv*) Pattern is provided with core prints.

Moreover,

(*i*) Pattern may be in two or three pieces whereas casting is a single piece.

(*ii*) Pattern differs in material of which it is made.

(*iii*) Pattern may not have all slots and holes like those in casting because they are machined afterwards.

Materials Used for Making Patterns

The following materials are generally used for making patterns :

1. Wood.

2. Metals, *e.g.*, brass, cast iron, aluminium alloys, white metal etc.

3. Plaster.

4. Plastic compound.

5. Wax.

Wooden Patterns

Wood is the most common material for pattern, the main *reasons* being (*a*) its cheapness, (*b*) ease of availability, (*c*) ease of shaping, (*d*) lightness (*e*) ease with which it can be joined, (*f*) wood can be cut and fabricated into numerous forms by gluing, bending, and carving, (*g*) its surface can be easily made smooth by sanding (*h*) its surface can be preserved by applying a coating of shellac, which is the most commonly used finishing material for wooden pattern.

The common *drawbacks* in wood owing to which sometimes other materials have to be employed are :

(*a*) It is readily affected by moisture.

(*b*) It changes its shape when the moisture dries out of it, and when it picks up moisture from the damp moulding sand.

(*c*) It wears out quickly as a result of sand abrasion.

(*d*) If not stored properly, it may warp badly.

(*e*) Its strength is low and it tends to break on rough usage.

Owing to these reasons wooden patterns do not last long, and they are generally used when a small number of castings are to be produced.

Wood used for pattern making should be properly dried before it is used. It should be straight-grained, free from knots and free from excessive sapwood.

The chief Indian varieties of timber used for making patterns are :

(*i*) *Burma and C.P. Teak.* This wood is straight-grained, light, easy to work, has little tendency to break and warp, and has reasonable cost.

(*ii*) *White Pine.* It is commonly used for pattern making owing to its extreme lightness, softness, ease of working and cheapness. it is particularly suitable for patterns and core boxes for producing a relatively few castings of small size, approximately below 30 in number and under 50 cm in size.

(*iii*) *Mehogany.* This wood being harder and stronger than pine wood is used for all types of patterns, including those for production work during machine moulding. However, this wood cannot be used where the quantity of moulds to be made is too high, the design of casting is too intricate or where a high degree of accuracy is needed.

Other woods which may also be used in making patterns depending on the relative cost and ease of availability are sal, deodar, shisham, walnut, maple, cherry, birch, kail, etc.

Wooden patterns are used when the number of casting to be produced is small and for large size patterns.

Metallic patterns

These are advantageously used when a large number of castings are desired from a pattern or when conditions for wooden pattern are too severe. Advantages of metallic patterns are :

(*i*) They do not change their shape when subjected to moist conditions.

(*ii*) They are free from warping in storage.

(*iii*) They are very much suited to machine moulding because of their accuracy, durability and strength.

(*iv*) They can withstand abrasion and rough handling.

(*v*) Sometimes, they may not require to be cast from wooden patterns but can be machined to desired shape.

(*vi*) Easy to obtain smooth surface finish.

(*vii*) They possess excellent resistance to swelling.

Commonly a metal pattern is itself cast from a wooden pattern called *"master pattern"*. When metal patterns are to be cast form master patterns, double shrinkage must be allowed. For example, if the metal pattern is to be made of aluminium and the castings are to be of cast iron, the shrinkage allowed on the wooden master pattern will have to be 18 mm per meter for aluminium, plus 10 mm per metre for cast iron, making a total of 28 mm per metre.

The main *drawbacks* with metallic patterns are :

(*i*) Expensive than wood and hence not generally suited for small production.

(*ii*) Less easy to shape and work.

(*iii*) Tendency to get rusted *viz.*, cast iron.

(*iv*) Excessive weight.

(*v*) Cannot be repaired easily.

The metals mainly used for making patterns are :

(*i*) *Cast iron*. Besides its low cost, it is strong, gives a good smooth mould surface with sharp edges, is resistant to the abrasive action of the sand and can be easily cast to obtain any desired shape. It can be easily machined and filed.

The main drawbacks with cast iron are its excessive weight, is easily broken being brittle, gets rusted too much and hence requires dry storage.

It is used for some highly specialised types of patterns.

(*ii*) *Brass*. It is strong, does not rust, takes a better surface finish than cast iron, is able to withstand the wear of the moulding sand, is easy to join by soldering and breaking, can be easily worked and machined, can have very thin sections, possesses high strength and toughness.

But brass patterns are heavier and costlier than cast iron.

Brass is used in patterns, particularly when metal patterns are small *viz.*, match plate patterns.

(*iii*) *Aluminium*. It is probably the best all round metal because it melts at a relatively low temperature, is soft and easy to work, light in weight, and resistant to corrosion, rust and abrasive action of sand. Besides, it also gives sufficient strength and good surface finish.

Aluminium, being rather soft, is liable to be damaged by rough usage. It is difficult to repair.

It is preferably used for making big size patterns when the operator's fatigue is the main consideration and the pattern is required to be exceptionally light.

(*iv*) *White Metal*. The main characteristics of white metal which is an alloy of antimony, copper and lead are the low melting temperature (200°C), ease of pouring, little appreciable shrinkage immunity from the effects of chill, and good castability.

White metal is not used to any great extent for patterns but is the best material that can be used for making intricate and fine shapes. It is very much used for the lining of stripping plates required for moulding the patterns in machine moulding work. It is used in most die-casting production and, therefore, is often called **die-casting alloy**.

(*v*) *Steel*. Steel patterns have excellent resistance to swelling and wear. They have fair machinability, high strength and good repairability. However, they possess poor resistance to rust and corrosion excessive.

Can be easily worked and machined, can have very thin sections, possess high strength and toughness.

Plaster Patterns

Plaster patterns and core boxes are made of gypsum cement. Gypsum cement has a high compressive strength (upto 300 kg/cm^2), and controlled expansion. By means of careful design and use of reinforcements, plaster patterns may be made to have strength upto 1150 kg/cm^2. It can be readily worked with wood working tools. When the plaster is mixed with water, it forms a plastic mass capable of being cast into a mould made earlier by a master pattern or may be swept into desired shape or form by sweep and strickle method. Unlike the metals, gypsum cement expands on solidification and so, by choosing cement of proper expansion coefficient, the shrinkage of casting can be completely offset and no shrinkage allowance may be given on the pattern.

Owing to these qualities plaster patterns are very much coming into use for the construction of patterns, and core boxes of small dimensions requiring high precision.

Plastic Patterns

Plastics (Phenolic thermo-setting resings) are now finding their place as a modern pattern material because they do not absorb moisture, are strong and dimensionally stable, resistant to wear, possess good compressive and flexural strength, better impact strength, good resistance to chemical attack, have a very smooth and glossy surface, and are light in weight. Due to its glossy surface it can be withdrawn from the mould very easily without damaging the mould. Moreover, the plastic material has a very low solid shrinkage. Phenolic resin plastic best serves the purpose. It is manufactured from a combination of carbolic acid and formaldehyde. Best plastic for patterns is epoxy resin.

For preparing plastic patterns, dies or moulds are first prepared in two halves in metal or plaster of Paris. The thermo-setting resin is then poured in the required amount into the moulds. When these moulds which carry resin are heated to a specific temperature, the resin solidified and the patterns are produced.

Plastic patterns are made by one of the following techniques :

(*i*) *Solid casting.* In this technique, resin mixture is poured into a plaster mould, where it will harden and get cured at 50–65°C for 2 to 3 hours. For making the mould, wooden master pattern may be used.

(*ii*) *Casting with a core.* This technique is used for making small and medium size patterns of simple shapes.

(*iii*) *Wet lay-up technique.* This technique is suitable for making comparatively large patterns.

For large scale production numerous plastic patterns of similar shape and size can be mounted on match plates so as to reduce the unit cost of casting.

However, plastic patterns are fragile and thus light section require metallic reinforcing. They do not work well when subjected to severe shocks as in machine moulding *viz*. jolting.

Wax Patterns

These are used in investment casting process. Their use helps in imparting a high degree of surface finish and dimensional accuracy to castings.

Wax pattern is prepared by pouring heated wax into the split moulds or a pair of dies while the latter are kept water-cooled. The dies after having been cooled down are parted off. Now the wax pattern is taken out and used for moulding.

Wax pattern need not be drawn out solid from the mould. After the mould is ready, the wax is poured out by heating the mould and keeping it upside down.

Old Casting used as Patterns

Sometimes in case of emergency when the time is the main factor, old castings are used as patterns.

To increase the thickness and other dimensions so as to provide for finish machining and shrinkage etc. surfaces of old castings are lagged with thin strips of wood or leather. The castings. to be used as patterns should be well cleaned and made smooth so that they can be drawn out of the mould easily. To provide draw screws, holes can be drilled and tapped in the castings. If necessary, core-prints may be made and attached to the casting.

Wooden Patterns with Metallic Coatings

Where metallic patterns cannot be economically employed and wooden patterns are also not found satisfactory due to low strength and lack of high finish, metallic coated patterns are many a times used for short production.

The wooden patterns are sprayed with a thin metallic coating of bismuth, size of aluminium of about 0.25 mm thickness. the metal

is fed in the form of wire into metal spray gun and is heated therein by an oxyacetylene flame. Metal spray is blown in an atomised form through a nozzle under pneumatic pressure over the surface of the wooden pattern.

Factor Affecting the Selection of Pattern Material

While selecting a pattern material for a given casting, the following factors should be considered :

(*i*) Design of casting *viz*., the minimum thickness desired, intricacy of parts, the degree of accuracy and finish desired in the casting.

(*ii*) The number of castings required. For large quantity metal patterns are preferred.

(*iii*) Method of moulding employed *viz*., hand moulding or machine moulding. In case of machine moulding, the type of moulding machine used.

(*iv*) Moulding material to be used.

(*v*) Chances of repeat orders.

Table 5.1: Summary of Advantages and Disadvantages of Material for Patterns and Core Boxes

S.No.	*Material Advantages*	*Disadvantages*
1.	*Wood*	
	(*i*) Cheap.	(*i*) Susceptible to moisture.
	(*ii*) Easily worked.	(*ii*) Tends to warp.
	(*iii*) Light in weight.	(*iii*) Wears out quickly due to sand abrasion.
	(*iv*) Harder wood more durable for heavy duty repetition moulding.	(*iv*) Weaker than metalic patterns.
	(*v*) Use of resin-acid glue eliminates nails and screws.	
	(*vi*) Strong resinous joints are not weakened by contact with moist sand.	
	(*v*) Easily available in large quantity.	

Table 5.1: Continued

	(*vi*) Easy to join. (*vii*) Easy to obtain good surface finish. (*viii*) Can be easily repaired. (*ix*) Wooden laminated patterns are strong and lighter in weight.	
2.	*Cast iron*	
	(*i*) Cheap.	(*i*) Heavy.
	(*ii*) Easy to file and fit.	(*ii*) Easily broken.
	(*iii*) Strong.	(*iii*) Edges of their sections which cool very quickly, may be too hard to machine.
	(*iv*) Gives a good smooth mould surface with sharp edges. (*v*) Resistant to abrasive action of sand.	
3.	*Brass*	
	(*i*) Strong, tough	(*i*) Heavier than C.I.
	(*ii*) Does not rust	(*ii*) Costly
	(*iii*) Takes better surface finish than C.I. (*iv*) Able to withstand wear of moulding sand. (*v*) Small patterns are easily rectified, built up of fitted by soldering. (*vi*) Very thin sections can be cast without danger of encountering un-machinable edges.	
4.	*80% Aluminium Alloy (with 14% Zn, 3% Cu 1.5% Fe and 1.5% Si)*	
	(*i*) Easy to cast	(*i*) Softer than brass or C.I.
	(*ii*) Very light	(*ii*) Liable to be damaged by moulder's ramming.
	(*iii*) Does not rust	

Table 5.1: Continued

	(*iv*) Easily machined. (*v*) Shell moulding patterns and plates are heated to about 250°C and must be of metal.	
5.	*White metal*	
	(*i*) Best material for lining stripping plates	(*i*) Soft
	(*ii*) Can be cast into narrow cavities	(*ii*) Easily worn away by moulding sand.
	(*iii*) Low melting point 260°	
6.	*Quick-setting Compounds*	
	(*i*) Excellent medium for patterns used for hand ramming and for squeeze machines.	(*i*) Fragile and very light sections must be reinforced metal.
	(*ii*) Twin match plates may be cast into iron or steel frames to prevent damage in handling.	(*ii*) Hard wood or metal is preferred for jolt machines where patterns are subjected to severe shocks.
	(*iii*) Resin patterns made in plaster of Paris moulds show a smooth hard surface resistant moist sand. (*iv*) Are made more quickly thad metal patterns.	

Jointing Meterials for Pattern Construction

During fabrication of patterns. Nails, bolts and screws are commonly used for jointing purposes.

Where the pattern is to be roughly handled and where the joints have a tendency of getting loose, screws are particularly used.

When the pattern is split type or has loose pieces attached to it, wooden or metallic dowel pine are often used.

Where a permanent joint is required, glue is commonly used as an adhesive material, Cold glue does not require any heating and is applied in cold state. It is available in liquid form and is of

plastic resin type made from milk curds. Hot glue is animal or vegetable glue. It is to be heated and made liquid before applying. It needs a few hours for setting.

Patterns Finishing

The patterns should first be sanded with abrasive paper for smoothness because the degree of finish that can be obtained on the casting depends largely on the smoothness of the pattern. Thus, the tool marks are removed and surface becomes uniform all over. A coarse abrasive is used first and then a fine one. Sanding is done either by rubbing the sand paper over the surface of the pattern by hand or a sanding machine is employed.

Sanding machine makes use of rotating disc or a moving belt on whose surface abrasive material is glued or bounded. It is either of portable type or a sationary model.

After sanding, the pattern is coated with a thin layer of shellac, which imparts a hard and smooth surface. The wood grains absorb shellac thus rendering the surface smooth. Generally, three coats of shellac are required and after each coat, the surface should be sanded lightly with a fine sand paper and dried. Pattern shellac consists of flake shellac and alcohol in the ratio of 1 : 2 respectively. Sometimes, oxalic acid is also added to the mixture for lustre.

After coating with shellac, the patterns are painted according to the colour coding for different parts of the patterns and core-boxes.

Colour Coding or Distinguishing Colours for Patterns and Core-boxes

To keep out moisture, all surfaces of a wooden pattern and core-box are coated with shellac. For identification of their different parts, they are coloured with standard shades.

Table 5.2: Colouring and Marking System for Wooden Pattern Equipment in Foundries (IS : 1513–1959)

S. No.	*Part of pattern*	*Colour / Mark*
1.	As cast surfaces to be left unmachined	Red or Orange
2.	Surfaces to be machined	Yellow
3.	Core prints for unmachined openings and end prints :	
	Periphery	Black
	Ends	Black
4.	Core prints for machined opening :	
	'A' Periphery	Yellow strips on Black
	'B' Ends	Black
5.	Pattern joint (split pattern)	
	'A' Cored section	Black
	'B' Metal section	Clear section
6.	Touch core :	
	Cored shape	Black
	Legend	Touch
7.	Seats of and for loose pieces and loose core prints	Green
8.	Stop offs	Diagonal black strips with clear varnish
9.	Chilled surfaces :	
	Outlined in	Black
	Leg end	Chill

With the present widespread use of unpainted metal and plastic patterns, the colour code is less widely used.

Patterns Fillets

Fillets are provided in order to avoid sharp inside corners in the patterns. The fillets help the molten metal to flow easily into the mould cavity over the edges and strengthen the casting at its inside corners.

Fillets may be made of leather, wax, wood, plastic, fibre or metal. Leather fillets are used on costly patterns as they are more durable. Wooden fillets are used for very large radii. Wax fillets

are easy to form in the desired sizes with the help of fillet irons (Fig. 5.1) which are available in sizes varying from 3 to 12 mm. Wax fillets are specially used for small radii upto 10 mm. Plastic or fibre fillets are not very durable and are used as cheaper substitutes.

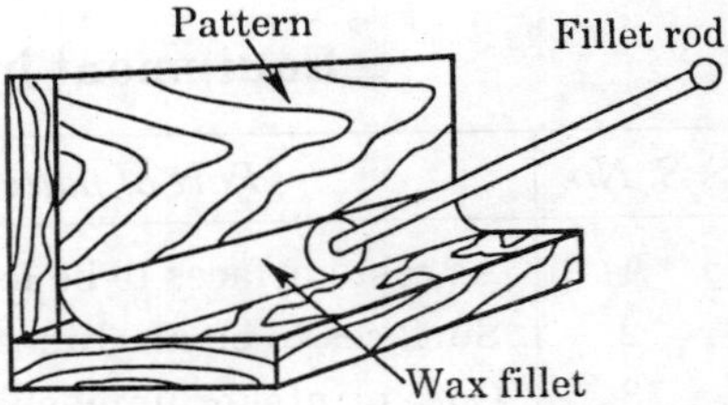

Fig. 5.1 Application of a wax fillet.

Pattern Allowances

The patterns are not made the exact size as the desired casting because such a pattern would produce undersize casting. When the pattern is prepared, certain allowances are given on the sizes specified in the finished component drawing so that the casting produced from that pattern after it has been finished and machined will conform to the specified sizes.

While designing patterns, the allowance commonly considered are given below :

Shrinkage Allowance. All the metals used for casting contract and shrink in size after solidification and cooling in the mould. To compensate for this, the pattern must be made larger than the finished casting by an amount known as *"pattern maker's contraction"*. The pattern maker is provided with a special rule or scale called *"Pattern maker's contraction rule"*. In laying measurements of the pattern, the pattern, maker allows for this contraction by using this rule which is slightly longer than the ordinary rule of the same length. There may be different contraction rules for different casting metals but generally a rule is used on each side of which, there are two scales, total number of scales being four for four commonly cast metals, *e.g.*, steel, cast iron, brass and aluminium. The graduations on each scale are oversized by a proportionate amount, *viz.* when constructing a pattern for cast iron, the pattern maker uses a contraction rule measuring about 10 mm longer per metre than the conventional rule because cast iron shrinks 10 mm per metre. A master pattern from which metal patterns are cast may have double shrinkage allowance.

Table 5.3: Typical Shrinkage Allowances for Important Casting Metals

S. No.	*Metal*	*Contraction (per cent)*	*Contraction (mm per metre)*
1.	Grey cast iron	0.7 to 1.05	7 to 10.5
2.	White cast iron	2.1	21
3.	Malleable iron	1.5	15
4.	Steel	2.0	20
5.	Brass	1.4	14
6.	Aluminium	1.8	18
7.	Aluminium alloys	1.3 to 1.6	13 to 16
8.	Bronze	1.05 to 2.1	10.5 to 21
9.	Magnesium	1.8	18
10.	Zinc	2.5	24
11.	Maganese steel	2.6	26.5

The contraction values given above and those considered on contraction rules are only average figures. The actual contraction in a casting depends on a variety of factors given below :

(*i*) Thickness and other dimensions of casting.

(*ii*) Design and intricacy of casting.

(*iii*) Resistance of mould to shrinkage.

(*iv*) Moulding material used and its hardness.

(*v*) Method of moulding used.

(*vi*) Pouring temperature of the molten metal.

Problem 5.1. *Grey cast iron castings are to be provided from an aluminium pattern, which is to be made from a wooden pattern. A dimension on the drawing of C.I. casting is 80 mm. Determine the correct dimension on the wooden pattern considering the contraction only.*

Solution.

$$\text{Allowance for aluminium} = \frac{80}{1000} \times 17.0 = 1.36 \text{ mm}$$

$$\text{Allowance for grey cast iron} = \frac{80}{1000} \times 8.5 = 0.68 \text{ mm}$$

Therefore, total shrinkage allowance

$$= 1.36 + 0.68 = 2.04 \text{ mm}$$

Thus, the dimension of the wooden pattern

$$= 80 + 2.04 = 82 \text{ mm} \textbf{ Ans.}$$

Finishing Allowance or Machining Allowance. The rough surfaces of castings that have to be finished or machined are made to dimensions somewhat over those shown on the finished working drawings. The extra amount of metal which is provided on the surface to be machined or finished is called **machine finish allowance**. The edges of such surfaces are indicated by a finish symbol or mark *V*, or *f*.

Machining allowance is given due to the following :

(*i*) Castings get oxdized in the mould and during heat treatment. Scales thus formed require to be removed.

(*ii*) For removing surface roughness and other imperfections from the castings.

(*iii*) For obtaining exact dimensions on the casting.

(*iv*) To achieve desired surface finish on the castings.

The amount that is to be added to the pattern, *e.g.*, the finish or machining allowances depends upon the following factors :

(*i*) Method of machining used, *e.g.*, turning, grinding, boring etc. Grinding removes lesser metal than turning.

(*ii*) Characteristics of metal, *e.g.*, ferrous or non-ferrous, or soft and easily machinable etc. Ferrous metals get scaled whereas non-ferrous do not.

(*iii*) Method of casting used. *e.g.*, centrifugal casting requires more allowance on the inner side. Die-castings need little machining whereas sand-castings require more machining.

(*iv*) Size and shape the casting *e.g.*, for the surface which is to remain at the top, the allowance should be greater since the impurities tend to collect at the top. If the casting is too long, there is tendency to warp and greater allowance is required.

(*v*) Degree of finish required in the casting.

(*vi*) Casting conditions, *e.g.*, whether casting surface is rough or semi-finished. These include nature of moulding material etc.

(*vii*) Number of cuts to be taken machining allowance is directly proportional to the number of cuts required finishing.

The standard of finish allowance for ferrous metals, *e.g.*, iron and steel, is 3 mm. The normal and sufficient allowance for non-ferrous *e.g.*, brass, bronze and aluminum is 1.5 mm.

Table 5.4: Approximate Machining Allowances for Different Metals and Alloys

S. No.	*Name of metal or alloys*	*Machining allowance (mm)*
1.	Cast iron	
	(*i*) Large size casting	10
	(*ii*) Machine size castings	3
2.	Cast steel	
	(*i*) Large size castings	12
	(*ii*) Machine size castings	4.3
3.	Non-ferrous *viz.*, Aluminium, Brass, Bronze, etc.	
	(*i*) Large size castings	5
	(*ii*) Medium size castings	1.5

Draft Allowance or Tapper Allowance

When a pattern is drawn from a mould, there is always some possibility of damaging the edges of the mould. This possibility is greatly decreased if the vertical surfaces of a pattern are tapered slightly inward. This slight tapper inward on the vertical surfaces of a pattern is known as the *'draft'*. Draft is expressed in millimetres per metre on a side, or in degrees. Amount of draft needed depends upon (*i*) the shape of the casting, (*ii*) depth of casting, (*iii*) moulding method, (*iv*) mould material. Generally, a draft of 3 to 6 mm per metre should be provided for precision castings.

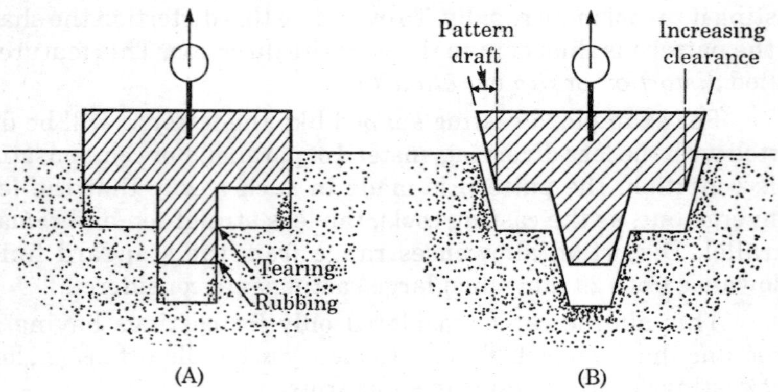

Fig. 5.2. Example of pattern taper.
(Tapper exaggerated for illustration)

Draft is thus given to provide light clearance for the pattern as it is lifted up. Pattern can be removed from the sand without treating away the sides of the mould and without excessive rapping or shaking by the moulder. The moment, the pattern lifting is started, all its surfaces are free or the sand and so, pattern can be removed without injuring the mould.

The amount of draft also depends on :

(*i*) Method of moulding.

(*ii*) Length of the vertical side of the pattern.

(*iii*) Intricacy of the pattern.

For general castings, the draft on exterior surfaces is about 10 to 20 mm per metre and that on interior surfaces, *e.g.*, holes, it is 40 to 60 mm per metre.

Rapping or Shaking Allowance

When the pattern is shaken for easy withdrawal, the cavity in the mould is slightly increased in size. This causes the size of the casting also to increase. In order to compensate for this increase, the pattern should be initially made slightly smaller.

In small and medium sized castings, this allowance can be ignored but for large sized castings or in ones that must fit together without machining or where high precision is desired, rapping or shake allowance is provided by making the pattern slightly smaller to the extent based on experience.

Distortion or Camber Allowance. Sometimes the castings because of their size, shape and type of metal, tend to warp or distort during the cooling period. This is due to uneven shrinkage, uneven metal thickness or to one surface being more exposed than another, casting it to cool more rapidly. To overcome this distortion the shape of the pattern is thus bent in the opposite direction. This feature is called *distortion* or *camber allowance*.

For example, a casting shaped like the letter U will be distorted with the legs diverging, instead of parallel. For compensating this condition, the pattern is made in such a way that the legs converge but, as the casting cools, the legs straighten and remain parallel. Distortion allowances range from the standard finish allowance upto 20 mm when large castings are considered.

This allowance is considered only for castings having an irregular shape and which have tendency to get distorted *e.g.*, long flat castings castings with unequal arms.

Considerations during Pattern Design and Construction

While designing and constructing the patterns, following points should be given due consideration :

(*i*) Suitable allowances for contraction, machining, draft, distortion and rapping should be provided wherever necessary, keeping in view the size, shape and design of the casting.

(*ii*) Keeping in view the number of castings to be prepared, the method of moulding and possibility of repeat orders, the wood should be chosen.

(*iii*) A fillet should be provided on the pattern, wherever there is a sharp corner. A concave connecting surface or the rounding of a corner caused by two intersecting surfaces or planes is called a **fillet**. These fillets or rounded corners help in easy withdrawal of the pattern, easy flow of metal in the mould and improve the appearance and finish of the casting. Internal strains become less and the casting becomes more sound.

(*iv*) Abrupt change in sectional thickness causes undue internal strains, which may sometimes cause the casting to crack. The section and wall thicknesses should be as uniform as possible. Whenever there is a change from light section to a heavy section or *vice versa,* the change should be very gradual.

(*v*) The pattern should be finished carefully because the finish on the casting much depends on how the pattern is finished. After preparing the pattern, the tool marks and other slight irregularities should be removed by sanding. No tool work should be done after sanding otherwise the cutting edge of the tool will be spoiled by small abrasive particles that get embedded in the pattern surface.

(*vi*) After sanding, the pattern should be finished by applying two to three coats of shellac, which fills up the pores and imparts a smooth finish.

(*vii*) If the pattern is to be preserved for a long time, it can be painted with some good quality paint according to standard colour scheme.

Types of Pattern

The type of pattern selected for a particular casting will depend upon several conditions *viz.* :

(*i*) The shape and size of casting.

(*ii*) Number of castings required.

(*iii*) Method of moulding employed.
(*iv*) Anticipated cost or difficulty of the moulding operation.
(*v*) Other factors which may enter the situation because of characteristics peculiar to the casting.

If the pattern is required for producing only a few castings, it should be constructed in the cheapest possible way. Similarly when the casting is of simple and regular shape the corresponding pattern may also be identical and in single-piece. If the casting, on the other hand, is of intricate nature involving changes in section, the pattern may be made in number of pieces involving the use of additional loose pieces, if necessary.

Several of the more common types of pattern are listed and described below :

(*i*) Single-piece pattern
(*ii*) Split pattern
(*iii*) Match plate pattern
(*iv*) Cope and drag pattern
(*v*) Gated pattern
(*vi*) Loose-piece pattern
(*vii*) Sweep pattern
(*viii*) Segmental pattern
(*ix*) Skeleton pattern
(*x*) Shell pattern
(*xi*) Built-up pattern
(*xii*) Boxed-up pattern
(*xiii*) Lagged-up pattern
(*xiv*) Left-hand right-hand pattern.

Single-piece or Solid Pattern. Pattern made with out joints, partings, or any loose pieces in its construction is called a *'single-piece'* or *'solid'* pattern. Such a pattern is not attached to a frame or plate. It is, therefore, also called as a *loose pattern*. They are cheaper. The moulder has to cut his own runners, feeding gates and risers when using such patterns. This moulding operation takes more time, therefore, these patterns are not recommended except for limited production.

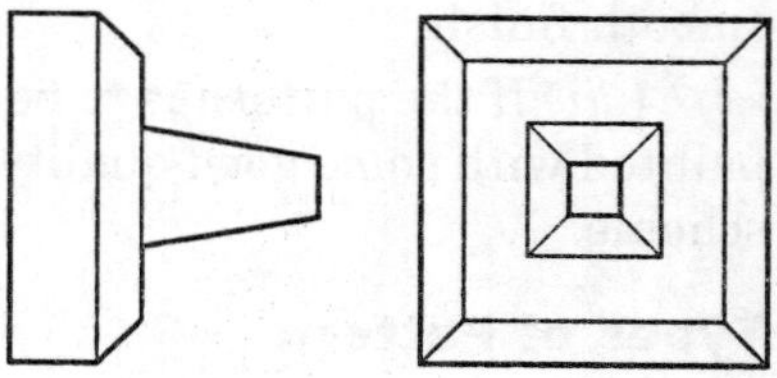

Fig. 5.3. Solid pattern.

Single-piece pattern is generally used for large casting of simple shape.

Under this heading, the simplest type of pattern is the *'flat-back pattern'* (Fig. 5.3) which may have a few or no irregularities and no core print. The mould cavity of this pattern will be either entirely in the drag or entirely in the cope. This mattern has the largest horizontal cross-sectional area which serves as the parting surface in the mould.

A few examples of castings which are made by making solid patterns are soil tamper, stuffing-box and gland of steam engine.

Split Pattern. A split type of pattern is used when the pattern if made is single-piece will give rise to withdrawal difficulties from the mould. For castings of intricate design or unusual shape, split patterns are employed to form the mould. These patterns are made in two parts so that one part may produce the lower half of the mould, and the other, the upper half. The two part may or may not be of the same size and shape. These are held in their proper relative position by means of dowel-pins. Dowel-pins are fast in one piece and fitting holes bored in the other piece. The surface which is formed at the line of separation of the two parts, usually at the entre-line of the pattern, is called as the *'parting surface'* or *'parting line'*. This surface is also the parting surface of the mould.

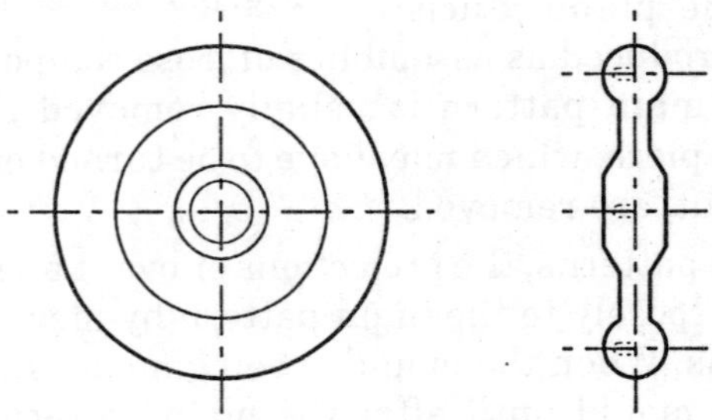

Fig. 5.4. (*a*) Two-piece split pattern.

Sometimes it is necessary to construct a pattern for a complicated casting which required three or more parts instead of two for making the complete pattern. Such pattern is called as *'Multi-piece pattern'*. For a three-part pattern, a flask having three parts may be used. Some types of three part patterns can be moulded in a two part flask.

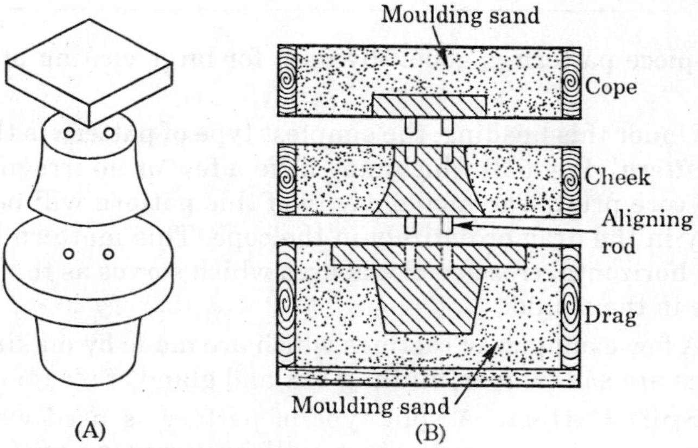

Fig. 5.4. (*b*) Three-piece split pattern.

A few examples of castings which require the use of split patterns are spindles, cylinders, steam valve bodies, water stop cocks and taps, bearings, small pulleys and wheels.

Loose-piece Pattern. The loose-piece patterns are needed when the casting is such that the pattern cannot be removed as one-piece, even though the pattern is split and the parting line is made on more than one plane. Such patterns are produced as assemblies of loose component pieces. In this case the main pattern is usually removed first. Then the separate loose piece, which may have to be turned or moved before taking them out, are removed.

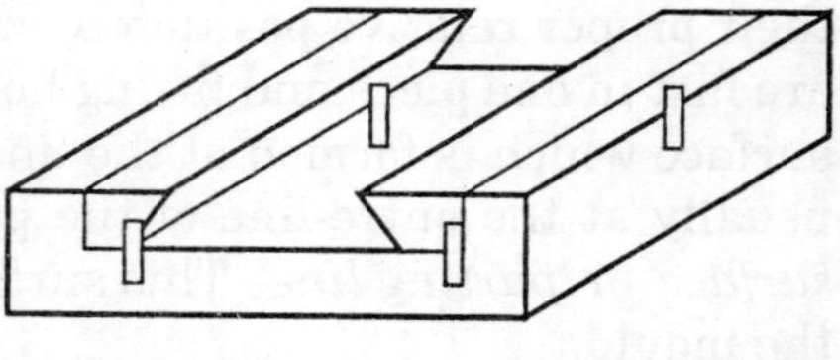

Fig. 5.5. Loose-piece pattern.

In these patterns, the projections or over hanging parts have to be fastened loosely to the main pattern by means of wooden or wire dowel pins. When the mould is being made, such loose pieces remain in the mould until after the main pattern is withdrawn and are then drawn out separately through the cavity formed by the main pattern.

Complicated patterns of this type usually need more maintenance are slower to mould.

Cope and Drag Pattern. In producing large castings, the complete moulds are too heavy to be handled by a single operator. Cope and drag patterns are, therefore, used for efficient moulding.

The patterns are made in halves, split on a convenient joint line. Separate cope patterns and drag patterns are built and mounted on individual plates or boards. Thus, one moulder or group of moulders may prepare the cope half of the mould while another moulder or group works on the drag half.

This planning of labour distribution increases production rate.

Match-plate Pattern. When split patterns are mounted with one half on one side of a plate and the other half directly opposite on the other side of the plate, the pattern is known as a *'match-plate pattern'*. One pattern or a number of patterns may be mounted on a match plate. The pattern is made of metal, and the plate making the parting line may be either metal or wood. For metal match plates, aluminium is commonly used.

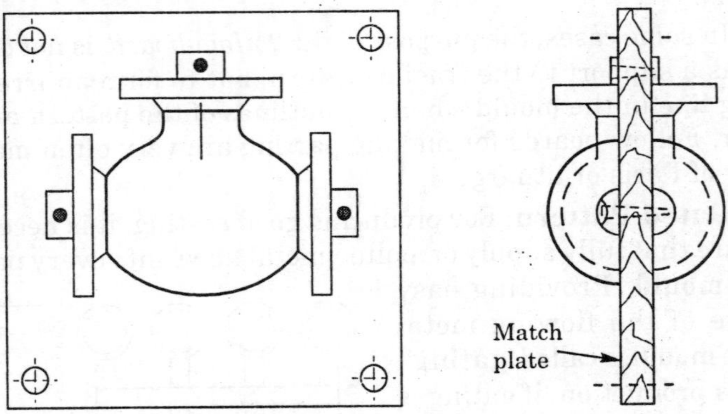

Fig. 5.6. Match-plate pattern.

To the drag side of the plate, patterns for gates and runners are fastened in their correct positions. When the match plate is lifted off the mould, all patterns are drawn, and the cope of upper half of the mould matches prefectly with the drag or lower half of the mould. The gates and runners are also completed in the same operation.

Match plate patterns are used for producing small castings in large quantities in moulding machines which give accurate and rapid production.

Match plate patterns are expensive to construct, but the initial cost is justified in mass production.

Follow Board Patterns. The patterns which have thin, sections, such as the one shown in the figure, tend to become distorted or to collapse, under the stress of ramming. Sagging of

thin pattern due to ramming can be easily overcome by constructing a block which may fit inside the pattern to serve as a support during ramming. This supporting block is known as *'follow board'*.

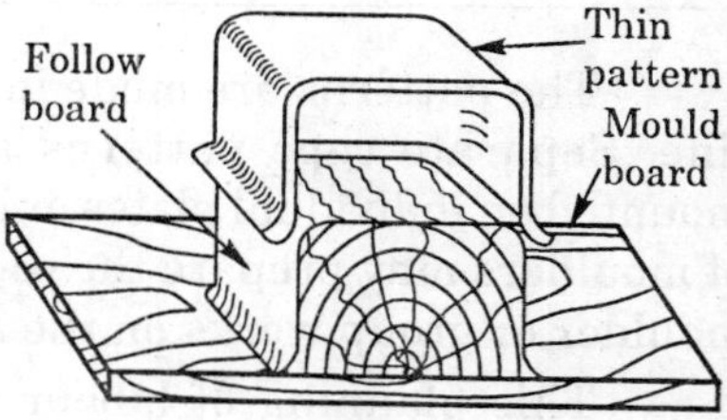

Fig. 5.7. Follow-board pattern.

In some cases, the purpose of the follow-board is not only to serve as a support to the fragile (thin) pattern, but it also forms an irregular parting line in the mould when the outlines of the pattern are irregular. For making partings, follow-boards are very often made of litharge or plaster-of-Pairs.

A great many stove and furnace patterns are made on follow-boards, and these are often *'master pattern'* for casting metallic patterns.

In some cases, the purpose of the *'follow-board'* is not only to serve as a support to the fragile pattern, but to form an irregular parting line in the mould when the outlines of the pattern are not regular. Follow boards for making parting are very often made of plaster of Paris or litharge.

Gated Pattern. For producing good casting, it is necessary to ensure that fully supply of molten metal flows into every portion of the mould. Providing easy passage of the flowing metal into the mould is called **'gating'**. In mass production, if gating is made by hand operations, it will require sometime. To save time, a number of castings are produced in a single multi-cavity mould by joining a group of patterns. The gates of runners for the molten metal are formed by the connecting parts between the individual patterns. By this arrangement, the time ordinary spent by the moulder in cutting gates and drawing patterns is eliminated. These groups of patterns with gate formers attached to them are called *'gated patterns'* as shown in the figure.

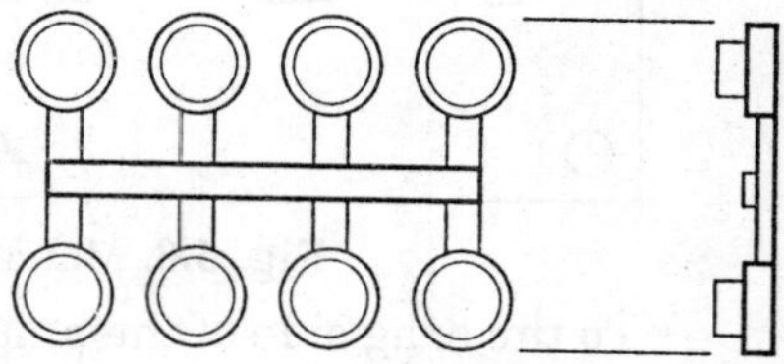

Fig. 5.8. Gated patterns.

Gated patterns are used for mass production of small castings. They are made of wood or metal.

Sweep Pattern. Moulds and cores of symmetrical and regular shape, particularly in large sizes, are sometimes shaped

by means of sweep patterns. The sweep pattern consists of a wooden board having a shape corresponding to the shape of the desired casting. It is arranged to rotate about a central axis as explained in Fig. 5.9.

The sand is rammed in place and the sweep board is moved around its axis of rotation so as to give the moulding sand the desired shape of the casting.

This method is very economical since no actual pattern is needed and the pattern costs are kept a minimum by eliminating expensive pattern construction. Sweep patterns are employed for moulding parts having circular sections. The curved sweep may be used to form part of the mould for a large cast iron kettle and the straight sweep, for any shape of groove or ridges.

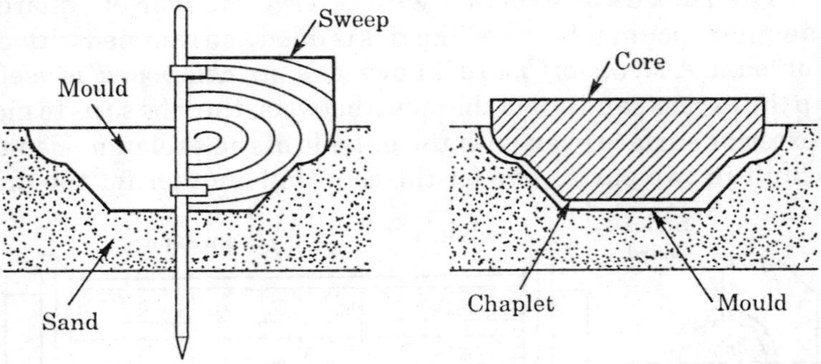

Fig. 5.9. Sweep pattern.

Segmental Pattern. They are also known as *'part patterns'*. These are generally applied to circular work, *e.g.*, rings, wheel rims, gears, etc.

Segmental patterns are sections of a pattern arranged in such a manner as to form a complete mould by moving to form each section of the mould.

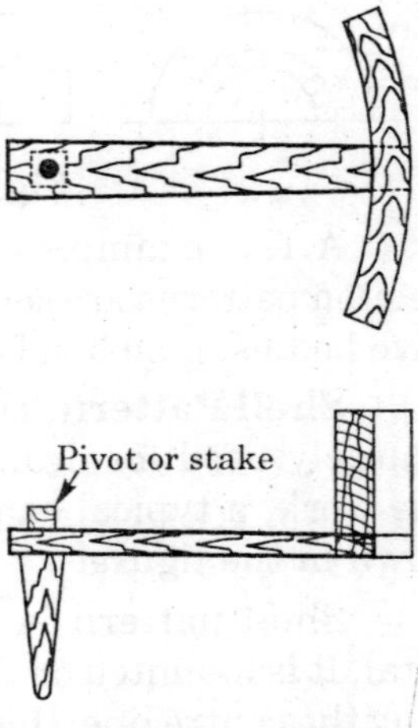

Fig. 5.10. Segment pattern.

When a mould is to be made using this pattern a vertical spindle is firmly fixed in the centre of drag flask. The mould bottom is rammed and swept level. Now the segmental pattern is fastened to the spindle. Moulding sand is rammed between

the outside of the pattern and the flask, and on the inside, except at the ends of the pattern. After ramming one segment, next segment is rammed ; and so on, until the entire perimeter of the mould is completed.

Skeleton Pattern. For very large castings patterns would require a tremendous amount of timber for fully solid pattern. Specially if the number of castings required is small, it may not be economical to prepare solid pattern. In such cases the pattern is made of wooden frame and rib construction so that it will form a partially exterior or interior outline of the casting. This frame-work is called a *'skeleton'*. It is employed to give the general contour and size of the desired casting.

The ribbed construction with a large number of square or rectangular openings between the ribs is filled and rammed with clay and or loam. A *'strike-off board'* known as a *'strickle board'* is used to scrap the excess sand out of the space between the ribs so as to make the exterior surface even with the outside of the skeleton. Usually, it is built in two parts ; one for the cope and another for the drag.

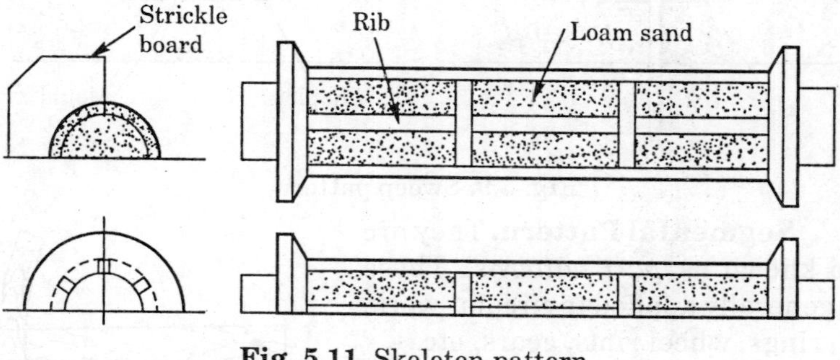

Fig. 5.11. Skeleton pattern.

A few examples of castings which are made by making skeleton patterns are soil and water pipes, valve bodies, pipe bends and boxes.

Shell Pattern. This type of pattern is largely used for drainage fittings and pipe work, a typical example of which is shown in the figure.

Shell pattern is usually made of metal. It is mounted on a plate and parted along the centre line, the two halves being accurately doweled together. Usually, these short bends are moulded and cast in pairs.

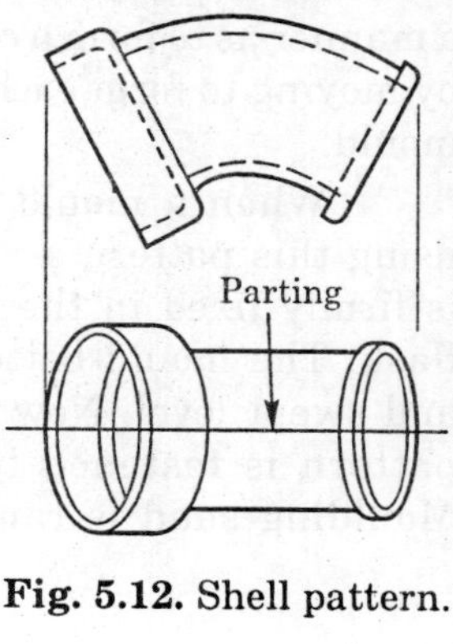

Fig. 5.12. Shell pattern.

The shell pattern is a hollow construction like a shell. The outside shape is used as a pattern to make the mould while the inside is used as a core-box for making core.

Built-up Pattern. As is obvious from the name, built-up patterns are composed of two or more pieces. For special pulleys, patterns are built-up of segment of wooden strips. The segments are made by cutting strips of wood to the curvature required. The thickness desired is built-up by gluing them in layers.

Flanges are also made similarly. This building-up is necessary sometimes because it is difficult to make an intricate shape in a block of wood for constructing a pattern. But it is easier to build-up the shape by gluing or joining number of segmental pieces together.

Boxed-up Pattern. In this type of pattern, the planks or strips of wood are joined together either by glue, nails, or screws so that a pattern is made like a box.

This method economises wood for large pattern and makes them lighter in weight.

The box construction is employed in making many patterns specially for castings having regular outline and rectangular form.

Lagged-up Pattern. Cylindrical patterns *e.g.*, barrels, pires of columns are built up with lag or stave construction to ensure proper shape. Longitudinal strips of wood, called *'lags'* or *'staves'*, are bevelled on each side for making the joint tight outside. These lags are glued and nailed or screwed to the wooden end pieces called *'heads'* as shown in the figure.

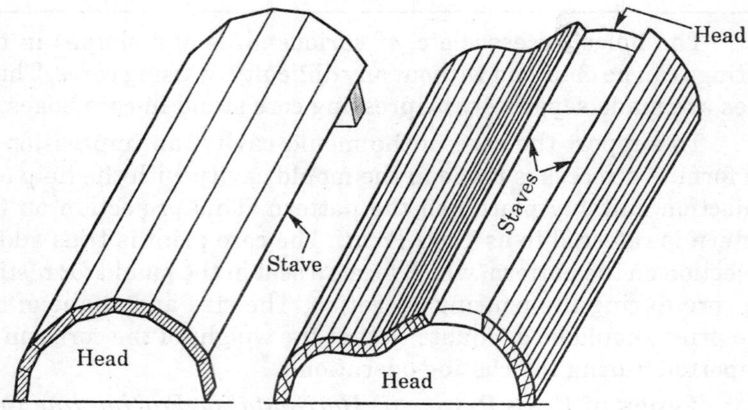

Fig. 5.13. Lagged-up pattern.

Such a construction gives the maximum strength and permits building close to the finished outline of the pattern. Thus there is comparatively little excess stock to be removed to obtain the required contour or shape.

Left and right-hand pattern. Some patterns are required to be made in pairs, and when their form is such that they can not be reversed and they have the centres of hubs, bosses, etc., opposite and in line, they must be made left and right-hand separately.

A few examples where a pair of right and left-hand patterns is required, are legs for wood-turning lathe, J-hangers for overhead shafting, legs for garden bench, legs for paddle type sewing machine, brackets for luggage racks in the railway carriages, etc.

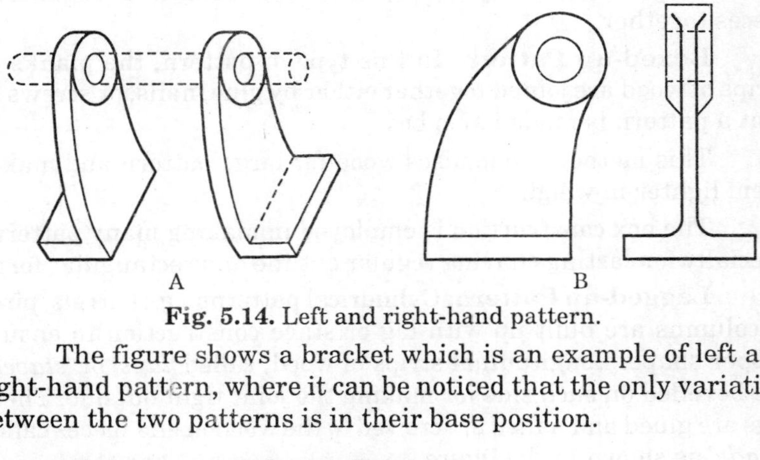
A B

Fig. 5.14. Left and right-hand pattern.

The figure shows a bracket which is an example of left and right-hand pattern, where it can be noticed that the only variation between the two patterns is in their base position.

Core Prints and Core Boxes

The holes, recesses etc. of various sizes and shapes in the castings can be obtained without any difficulty by using cores. These cores are made separately by pressing core stand in core boxes.

To support the core in the mould cavity, an impression in the form of a recess is made in the mould cavity with the help of a projection suitably placed on the pattern. This projection on the pattern is referred to as *'Core Print'*. The core print is thus added projection on the pattern, which forms a seat in the mould for resting the core during the pouring operation. The size and shape of the core print should be adequate so that the weight of the core can be supported during the casting operation.

Types of Core Print. (*i*) *Horizontal or Parting line Core Print* (Fig. 5.12). Such a print forms a seat into which core is laid

horizontally in the mould. It is most commonly used on two piece or split patterns. For locating a certain core at a desired angular relationship with respect to the central axis, a flat portion at one end is made to coincide with a flat portion of the core print.

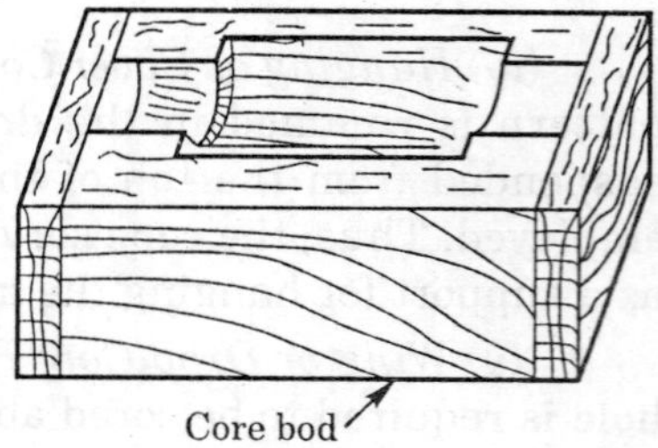

Fig. 5.15. Half core box.

(ii) Vertical or Cope and Drag Core Pring (Fig. 5.13). It is another type of commonly used core print. It is located on the cope and drag sides of a pattern and will form a seat for a core that stands vertically in the mould. Considerable taper (10–15°) is provided on this core print particulary on the cope side so that pattern withdrawal and replacement of cope on the drag are facilitated.

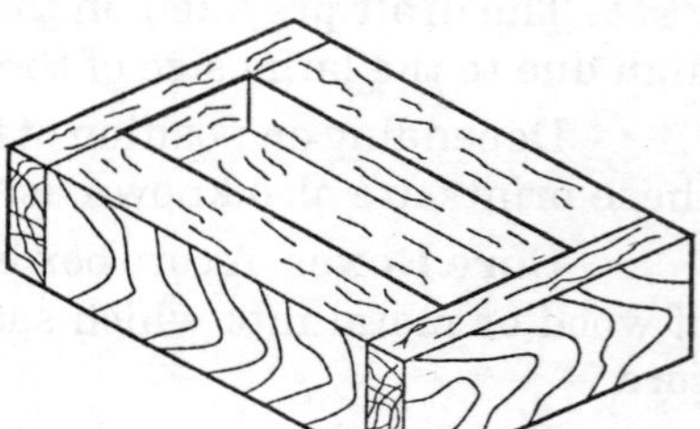
Fig. 5.16. Dump or slab core box.

(iii) Balancing Core Print (Fig. 5.14). When a horizontal core does not entirely through the casting and its shape is such that it is not possible to support the core from both sides, a balanced print is used.

In such cases, the core and core print are so designed that the part of the core in the mould cavity balances the part which rests in the core seat *i.e.*, the core is supported at one end only. Also, the shape of the print may not be necessarily the same as that of the core in the mould cavity.

To aid in supporting of the core in the cavity, chaplets can be used. The chaplets are small pieces of metal. Their height is equal to the space between the core and the mould wall. They should be of the same metal as that of the casting.

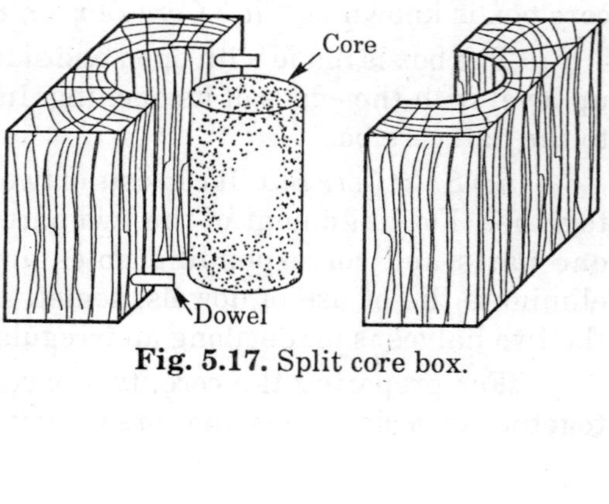

Fig. 5.17. Split core box.

(*iv*) *Hanging or Cover Core Print* (Fig. 5.16). When the entire pattern is rammed in the drag and the core is required to be suspended from the top of the mould, this type of core print is employed. Thus, the cope serves as a cover for the mould and also as a support for hanging the main body of the core.

(*v*) *Wing or Drop Core Print* (Fig. 5.17). When a recess or a hole is required to be cored above or below the parting line in the mould, this type of print is employed.

The draft provided on the vertical walls of the core is fairly high due to the large size of the core print required in this case.

Depending on position of the core in the mould and its shape, these prints are also known as *'Chair'* or *'Tail'* core prints.

Core Boxes. A core box is essentially a type of pattern made of wood or metal into which sand is rammed or packed to form a core.

The core box is made exactly to the shape and size of the core required. It must conform to the type of the core print used on the pattern. While preparing core boxes, the same accuracy should be maintained as is kept in the construction of the pattern.

Type of Core Boxes. Several types of core boxes are used according to the shape of the core as described below :

(*i*) *Half Core Box.* This type of core box is used when the shape of the core required is such that it can be prepared in two identical halves. After shaping to form with the help of this core box one after the other, the two halves are baked and pasted together to complete the core.

(*ii*) *Dump or Slab Core box.* This type of core box is designed to form a complete core requiring no pasting.

If the shape of the core thus made is a slab or rectangle, the core box is known as *'Slab Core Box'* or *'Rectangle Core Box'*.

The box is made with open one side and the sand is rammed up level with the edges of its opening. In appearance, it is similar to the half core box.

(*iii*) *Split Core Box.* It consists of two halves which are clamped together. For alignment of the two parts, dowel pins are fixed in one parts and corresponding holes are made in the other. To eliminate the of use of dowels, sometimes the parting surface of the two halves is made along an irregular line.

For preparing the core, two parts of the core box are held together by a clamp and the cores and it is rammed from one side.

After striking off the excess sand, the core box is unclamped and rapped. Thus, a complete core is produced in a single ramming.

A *"book type of box"* is similar to a split core box, consisting of two halves, hinged together, opening and closing like a book to form a complete core.

(*iv*) *Strickle Core Box*. When the core is required to have an irregular surface which can be easily rammed by other methods, a strickle type core box is used.

The shape of the core is produced by striking off the core sand from the top of the core box with a piece of wood called a strickle board. The strickle is cut to correspond exactly to the contour of the required core.

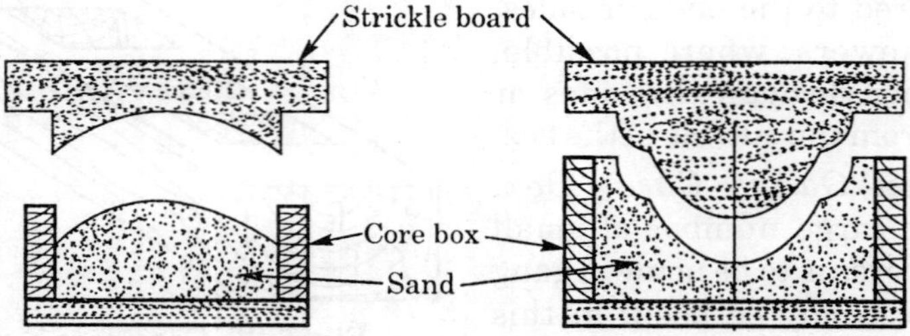

Fig. 5.18. Strickle core box.

Also for large sized work for which a regular core box if prepared will be too expensive, the strickle board is often used.

(*v*) *Right and left hand core Box*. When two half cores made in the same box can not be pasted together to form an entire core, right and left-hand core boxes become necessary.

The core halves are made in these two boxes and pasted together to form the completed core.

(*vi*) *Core Box with Loose Pieces*. The joints and devices used for fastening loose pieces to patterns may also be used for the similar purpose in the core box work.

In some cases, both the havels of the core which are not identical may be prepared from a single core box with the help of loose pieces.

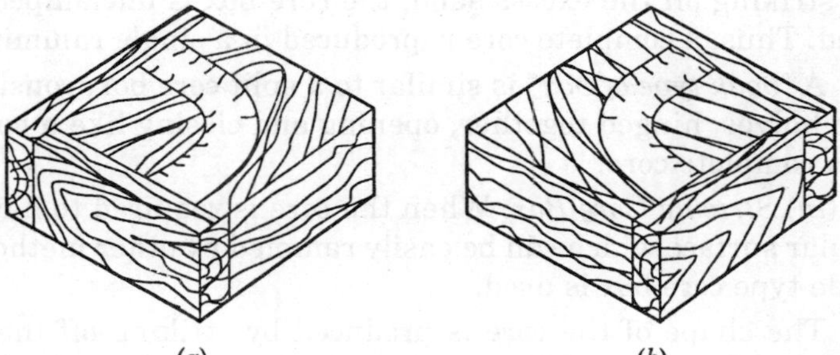

(a) (b)

Fig. 5.19. Right and left-hand core Box.

Bosses, hubs, etc. are skewered to the ends or sides, the skewers, where possible, drawing through the sides or ends from the outside of the box.

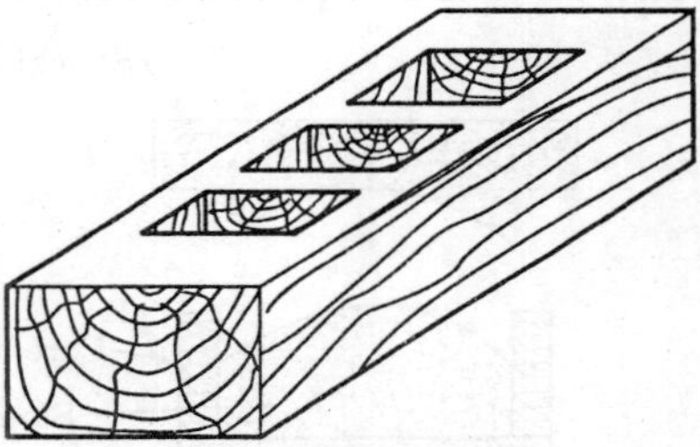

Fig. 5.20. Gang core box.

(*vii*) *Gang Core Box.* Where large number of small sized cores is to be made, a gang core box may be used. In this type of core box, several core cavities are rammed in a single operation.

(*viii*) *Sweep and Skelton Core Box.* This type of core box looks like a sweep and a skeleton pattern and is used for large sized cores required in small quantities.

Methods of Constructing Patterns

After deciding the moulding procedure and the form of the pattern, a layout of the pattern is made. In general, such layouts are reproductions of the blue prints laid out to full-size scale on a flat smooth wooden board. Sometimes, the boards for laying out large work are blackened on the face, and drawings are set down in chalk lines.

If more than one view is required, the additional views are shown down on the top of the first view ; the lines being coloured differently for distinction. The moulder often makes use of the pattern maker's drawings for reference until the castings are made. In such cases, they are wholly or partly varnished with shellac varnish for preserving them.

After completing the pattern layout, making allowances—shrinkage, finishing, draft, etc, the pieces to be used in the

construction of the pattern are shaped. The particular method to be used in any given case depends upon the shape and size of the pattern and the number of castings required.

In making patterns, it is particularly desirable that the grain of the wood runs in the direction of the greatest length of the piece being shaped. This provides strength and the chances of inaccuracy due to change in size of the pattern are eliminated.

In pattern finishing, all its angled corners are filled in with fillets. Sharp corners on a pattern cause the mould to be very weak as stresses concentrate at these parts. These corners, if not filled by the moulder, are often washed away by the metal flow spoiling the casting. Filling in the corners of the pattern gives a stronger and cleaner mould which improves strength and appearance of the casting.

Fillets may be made of wood, leather, metal or wax. If required fillet may be removed afterwards by machining.

1. **Constructing Flat Pattern.** It may be made by cutting a solid piece of wood to the desired shape. Or, it may be built up with a number of very thin pieces by gluing them together in such a manner that their grains run at right angles to the adjacent pieces.

The letter method is advantageous as one thick piece is more liable to shrink and alter in shape than several thin pieces well jointed and glued.

2. **Constructing Rectangular Pattern.** Such a pattern is built up in the form of a box. Firstly, *'grounds'* or *'bridges'* forming the foundation of this job are constructed. These are framed up with the joints half lapped together. These are then recessed out to receive longitudinal stays. The stays fix the grounds in position. Grounds and stays are now properly screwed, squared and levelled together forming a frame, strong and rigid, to receive the covering boards.

Top and bottom pieces of the covering are placed on, screwed to the grounds and stays with the outer edges flushing with the frame. In the end, sides are placed on. Boxed-up pattern is now trimmed off and the faces finished by planing.

3. **Constructing Cylindrical Pattern.** A cylindrical pattern to be finished by hand or by turning is built up with lag or stave construction. In such a construction, two or more end pieces called heads in the form of two half regular polygons are used ; lags being fastened to the heads.

In laying out the heads for a cylinder, a circle is scribed on a layout board corresponding to the outside diameter of the cylinder plus allowance for pattern turning. A centre line is drawn dividing the head into two half sections. The semi-circle is divided into a number of equal parts depending on the number of staves to be used. The staves are fastened to the heads by glue and nails or screws.

4. **Constructing a Ring-shaped Pattern.** Disc and Ring shaped patterns are built up by gluing a number of sectors or segments together. The sectors or segments are built up of successive layers of wood known as *'courses'*.

In each segment, the long wood grains are kept parallel to the chord of the circle. Thus, wood grains will follow the circle as nearly as possible and shrinkage of each segment will be uniform.

5. **Constructing Wheel and Pulley Pattern.** Two general classes of wheels are :

(*i*) Having plate or solid centre, called a *'webbed'* wheel.

(*ii*) Having spokes or arms.

In constructing webbed wheels with segment rims, the segments should run in continuous courses to form the face. A recess is turned in the centre course to receive the web which is circular form. Web is to fit the recess which is turned to receive the web. It is then glued and nailed in place.

In building patterns for armed wheels having spokes radiating from the centre, the spokes are worked to form before assembling them. The spokes are fastened to the rim by being built in during the turning process or after the rim is finished. Assembled arms are called a *'spider'*, and they can be fastened together at the hub or centre by a number of ways.

The most commonly used way of forming the rim is by means of a segment or part pattern that is moved in a circle as section of the mould is rammed as described under the heading *'segmental pattern'*.

6. **Constructing Gear Pattern.** Large gear rims are usually built up of segments as in case of pulleys or flywheels. The blocks of the teeth are fitted and fastened to the rim by gluing and nailing them into place.

7. **Constructing Filmsy Patterns.** A *'stop-off'* is a piece of stock placed on the drag of a thin pattern to add support. Very frequently, it becomes necessary to construct at thin pattern which

will naturally have a tendency to warp out of its true shape. This tendency to warp out can be overcome by adding narrow strips of materials known as *'stop-offs'*.

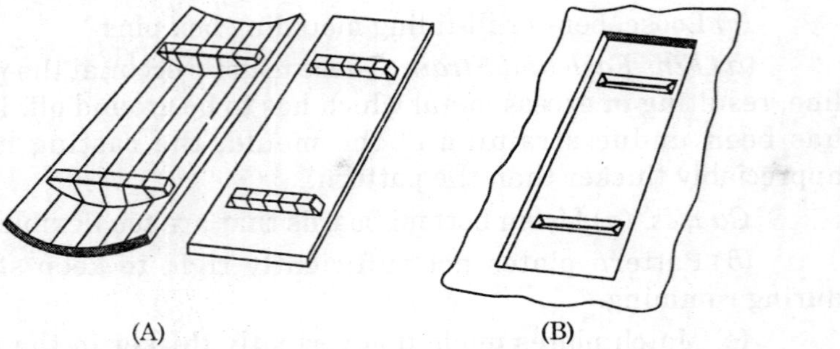

Fig. 5.20. Stop-off pieces to strengthen Filmsy Pattern.
A—Filmsy patterns strengthened by stopping-off pieces.
B—Depressions are filled up with sand.

When pattern is drawn from the mould the impression it makes is latter filled in with sand, rammed, and smoothed, off, and the resulting casting will not show the position of the stop-off.

Stop-off is a term which is also used to describe the process of reducing the size of a mould for the purpose of making a shorter casting. For doing so, the pattern maker provides a stop-off piece to enable the moulder to adjust the length of the mould to the correct length required.

The extra length in the cavity produced by a longer pattern is filled up and rammed with moulding sand. A stop-off piece may, thus, be used as a pattern enabling the pattern maker to avoid making of another pattern for a shorter casting.

8. **Constructing Strickle Board or Strike-off Board.** It is a thin piece of wood or metal to scrap off excess sand from a skeleton pattern. It is also used for cutting sand cores in halves, and sand moulds for large concentric castings *e.g.*, flywheels, gear wheels, cone pulleys, etc.

The strickle may be a straight edge for flat surfaces or shaped to the required contour or outline. All strickles should be levelled on their working edge.

Defects caused by Pattern and Moulding-Box Equip-ment

(*i*) *Mismatch.* It is a mismatching of the top and bottom parts of a casting at the mould joint.

Causes. (*a*) Worn or loose dowels in patterns made in halves.

(*b*) Faulty registering of top and bottom halves of patterns mounted on plates.

(*c*) Loose, bent or ill-filling moulding box pins.

(*ii*) *Fins Fash and Strain*. These usually occur at the parting line, resulting in excess metal which has to be ground off. If there has been undue straining of the mould, the casting may be appreciably thicker than the pattern.

Causes. (*a*) Using bottom boards that are too flexible.

(*b*) Pattern plates not sufficiently rigid to keep straight during ramming.

(*c*) Match plates made inadvertently thicker in the middle than near the edges.

(*d*) Use of patterns having insufficient taper, and needing excessive rapping to withdraw them from the sand result in fins.

(*e*) Top-part boxes inadequately weighed or cramped, permitting the top box to lift slightly, cause a fash along the mould joint.

(*f*) Change in shape of cores caused by rapping of core box to make it deliver the core.

(*iii*) *Variations in Wall Thickness*. Castings may have wall thicknesses either too thin or too thick.

Causes. (*a*) Worm core boxes giving oversize core dimensions.

(*b*) Worm core prints permitting a core to float or move.

(*e*) Lifting of cores caused by inadequate area of core print to resist the lift during casting.

(*iv*) *Crush*. This is a displacement of sand when closing a mould, and it shows itself as an irregular sandy depression in the casting.

Causes. (*a*) Core print too small for the core.

(*b*) Core too large for the core print.

(*c*) Excessive weight of the top part of a green-sand mould.

(*v*) *Swell*. It is swelling of the casting on the top side.

Causes. (*a*) Cause by the pressure of molten metal.

(*b*) Soft ramming.

(*c*) Insufficient weight of the mould during casting.

(*vi*) *Sand Wash*. Reveals itself as rough lumps of metal at some point of the casting and a corresponding area of rough holes or depression at other points.

Causes. (*a*) Inadequate draft on the pattern.

(*b*) Badly varnished patterns.

(*c*) Rough patterns.

(*vii*) *Core Blow.* This is an excessively smooth depression area on the inner surface of a cored casting, or a gas pocket in the casting above a cored cavity.

Causes. Using a core print too small to permit the rapid escape of the core gases during casting.

(*viii*) *Blind Cored Holes in Vertical Faces of Castings.*

Causes. (*a*) Making tail print with parallel sides.

(*b*) Inadeqate taper allowed at the back of the print.

(*ix*) *Blind Cored Holes in Horizonal Faces of Castings.* When a green-sand core or dry-sand core in a bottom part is made without a top core print *i.e.,* the upper end of the core is flat and pattern maker hopes it will make good contact with the flat face of the core, there is always danger that owing to core box wear resulting in a shorter core, or top part lift, there will be a thin flash of metal formed over the top of the core resulting in a blind hole.

The difficulty is ever present when making plate castings with a large number of perforations formed by cores. Satisfactory solution is to use boxes with top core prints, and to ensure that the boxes are cramped and weighted efficiently.

Pattern Making Tools

The pattern maker is basically a wood worker ; therefore, his tool kit will consist of most of the tools used by the cabinet maker, with the addition of some special tools that are used only in pattern making :

1. Measuring and Layout Tools :

(*i*) Rule (*ii*) Caliper Rule
(*iii*) Shrink Scale (*iv*) Flexible Rule
(*v*) Making Gauge (*vi*) Steel Square
(*vii*) Try Square (*viii*) Combination Square
(*ix*) T-Bevel (*x*) Dividers
(*xi*) Trammels (*xii*) Caliper

2. Sawing Tools :

(*i*) Coping Saw (*ii*) Compass Saw
(*iii*) Panel Saw (*iv*) Back Saw

(*v*) Dovetail Saw (*vi*) Pattern maker's Saw
(*vii*) Miter Saw.

3. Planing Tools :
(*i*) Block Plane (*ii*) Bench Plane
(*iii*) Rabbet Plane (*iv*) Router Plane
(*v*) Circular Plane (*vi*) Core box Plane
(*vii*) Spokeshave.

4. Boring Tools :
(*i*) Brace (*ii*) Hand Drill
(*iii*) Auger Bit (*iv*) Twist Drill
(*v*) Countersink (*vi*) Multi-spur Machine Bit
(*vii*) Bit Gauge (*viii*) Doweling Jig

5. Clamping Tools :
(*i*) Hand Screw (*ii*) Pattern Maker's Vice
(*iii*) C-Clamp (*iv*) Bar Clamp
(*v*) Pinch Dog

6. Miscellaneous Tools :
(*i*) Claw Hammer (*ii*) Mallet
(*iii*) Chisel (*iv*) Gouge
(*v*) Cabinet File (*vi*) Rasp
(*vii*) Nail Set (*viii*) Screw Driver
(*ix*) Brad Awl (*x*) Brad Pusher
(*xi*) Fillet Iron (*xii*) Cornering Tool.

Machine used in Pattern Making

Modern pattern-shop practice requires the use of basic wood-working machinery. Most of this machinery is similar to that of the cabinet or furniture shop. The size of machine equipment in a pattern shop will be determined by the size of the general run of work to be done.

Machines used for pattern making must be well built, their accuracy should be dependable. They should be well guarded to protect the worker from the harzards of operation.

The machines described below represent the minimum requirements for a well-planned pattern shop. These machines have been selected to illustrate the versatility of operations which may be performed with well-built equipment obtainable within a medium price range :

1. **Circular Saw.** It is used for ripping, cross cutting, mitering, beveling, rabbeting, and grooving lumber. The accuracy and versatility of this machine makes it indispensable in the modern shop. Although there are many types of circular saws, the basic working parts are common to all. Each has a flat surface or table upon which the work rests while being cut : a circular cutting blade ; a cut-off guide ; and a ripping fence.

The size of a circular saw is determined by the diameter of the cutting blade. Large blades enable deeper cuts to be made and therefore require larger components in every respect for handling larger work.

Tilting mechanisms on circular saws provide for angular cuts. These mechanisms are of no basic designs. In one case, the table tilts and the saw remains in a vertical plane. The other type has a tilting saw arbor and the table remains in a horizontal plane ; and this type is more convenient to operate, since it is easier to hold work flat on the table when the table remains horizontal. Both types of tilting arrangements are capable of tilting to a 45° angle.

2. **Band Saw.** It is designed to cut wood by means of an endless metal saw band that travels over the rims of two or more rotating wheels. The band saw is more limited than the circular saw in the number of operations which may be performed. However, the machine is almost indispensable for making curved or irregular cuts in wood.

The size of a band saw is determined by measurement taken from the saw blade to the flame. This measurement is about equal to the diameter of the upper and lower wheels. A 450 mm saw is capable of swing to the centre of a panel which is 900 mm in width.

The maximum width of the saw band is dependent upon the size of the machine. A 25 mm wide blade is used for general work on 500 mm or larger saw. Blades of 12 mm width are the largest practical blades for smaller band saws.

For curves of small radii, it is necessary to employ narrow saw blades which will not bend when the work is being turned. Saw blades are available in the following widths :

5 mm, 6 mm, 10 mm, 12 mm, 19 mm, 25 mm.

As in the circular saw, angular cuts are obtained by tilting the saw table. Some machines have stationary horizontal tables with a mechanism for pivoting the band-saw frame. This arrangement permits the sawing of heavy work at an angle while the work rests flat on the horizontal table.

3. **Jig or Scroll Saw.** It is indispensable for making intricate irregular cuts on small work. It may be used to do the same work as the band saw but on a smaller scale.

The size of a jig or scroll saw is dependent upon the blade-to-arm distance. A 600 mm machine is generally considered large enough for all practical purposes.

The table of jig saw may be tilted to accommodate angular work. Blades are available from less than 1.5 mm in width to 10 mm. One of the most useful characteristics of the jig saw is that it may be used conveniently for internal cuts by threading the blade through a hole bored into the work. This internal sawing procedure in not practical on any other common wood-working machine.

4. **Jointer.** After sawing lumber to size, the labour of planing straight edges on boards is largely eliminated by the use of the jointer. The jointer planes the wood by the action of revolving cutter head, which is generally fitted with three cutter knives. The board is hand fed against the revolving cutter head, which planes fine chips from the wood.

The size of the jointer is the same as the length of the cutting blade. 150 mm jointer will, therefore, plane the surface of a board which is 150 mm width.

A jointer is equipped with an adjustable fence for guiding the board at a pre-determined angle to the surface of the table. This fence may be adjusted to a right angle with the table or may be inclined for level and angular cuts.

The depth of cut is determined by the adjustment of the so-called *'infeed'* table, which, when lowered, produces a deeper cut.

As in the case of a hand plane, the long table surface of a well-built jointer insures accuracy in planing long work.

5. **Wood-turning Lathe.** It is especially useful to the pattern maker. Many castings are cylindrical in shape, and still additional castings are made up of parts which include sections of cylinders or other surfaces of revolution. Patterns for these cylindrical castings are usually made by the pattern maker on the wood-turning lathe.

Wood-turning lathe is a machine which rotates the wood stock while it is being shaped by the cutting action of one of the various-shaped turning tools as it is held against the rotating work.

The size of a lathe is determined by the so-called *'swing'* of the lathe and the maximum distance between centres. Swing is the distance from lathe centre to the bed multiplied by two. Thus

300 mm × 900 mm lathe can be used to turn work up to 300 mm in diameter, and also work of 900 mm maximum length.

Work that is long and slender is classified as spindle turning and is generally held in the lathe between centres.

Face-plate work is limited to disc-shaped pieces, which may be fastened to a face plate with screws and turned to shape without the use of the tailstock.

6. **Abrasive-Disc Machine.** This simple but still very useful machine for shaping or finishing flat surfaces on small pieces of wood is also called the *'disc sander'*.

An abrasive-disc machine consists basically of an electric motor with a metal disc mounted on its shaft, on which an abrasive disc is cemented.

An adjustable worktable is located below the centre of the face of the disc for supporting the work.

This machine is especially useful for sanding the draft on small patterns.

7. **Abrasive-Belt Machine.** It makes use of an endless abrasive belt which travels over two drums. This machine is especially useful in shaping patterns or parts of patterns that would normally require the use of hand tools.

The work is supported by an adjustable worktable that may be tilted at a predetermined angle. The size of the machine is governed by the size of the working surface of the belt.

Cloth-back abrasive belts are available in several grits for sanding or polishing wood or metal.

8. **Drills Press.** It has many uses in the pattern shop. In addition to drilling and boring holes, it may be used for mortising, shaping, and routing with the special attachments available.

It is available in many different sizes.

9. **Grinder.** It is used for sharpening and shaping tools. This bench grinder has two grinding wheels fastened to an arbor. Generally a coarse wheel is on one side of the motor and a fine wheel on the other.

A well constructed grinder has a lighted shield to protect the worker's eyes.

A container of water for cooling the work is conveniently located near the machine.

10. **Wood Trimmer.** It is most generally used for mitering mouldings accurately. It is not a motor-operated equipment.

It generally has two sharp knives which are fastened to a movable plate at an angle. This plate is moved from side to side by a hand lever.

An adjustable work fence is set either on the right or left of the table to the required angle ; and the plane operated by the handle, takes a shearing cut on the end of the wood.

11. **Wood Planer.** Its purpose is similar to that of jointer but it is specially designed for planing large size pieces at a comparatively faster rate reducing manual labour.

Wooden boards to be planed are fed by feed rolls along the table against a revolving cutter head. Cutter head is mounted on an overhead shaft which may be adjusted for regulating depth of cut.

Planer table is generally much wider and longer than that of a jointer to accommodate large planks. Hand feeding is eliminated as the planks are fed against the cutter by rolls.

12. **Wood Shaper or Wood Moulder.** It consists of a cutter head carrying a cutter rotating about a vertical axis. Its horizontal table is similar to that of a jointer.

Wooden piece is fed by hand along the table against the cutter and guided by an adjustable fence. The shape imparted to the surface of the wood is according to the profile of teeth on the cutter. A variety of shapes can be produced by suitably designing the cutter teeth.

13. **Mortiser.** It is used to facilitate the cutting of mortise and tenon which otherwise is a very laborious and time consuming operation.

Two types of mortising machines are generally used : (*i*) chisel type, (*ii*) chain type.

Chisel mortising machine consists of a revolving spindle carrying an auger bit at the bottom end. Auger bit rotates at a higher speed inside a square hollow chisel. Hollow chisel has four sides of equal width.

As hollow chisel is pierced into the wood, the auger bit bores the hole which is cut square by the sharp end of the chisel. Thus auger bit and chisel work together performing boring of a square hole. By shifting the work on the table, the mortise of the desired length with square ends and square bottom is produced.

Rotation of spindle is obtained from an electric motor and feed of tool into the work is obtained by pressing the foot lever. When foot lever is released, a return spring brings the tool to its initial position. Depth of mortise is regulated by an adjustable depth stop. Chain type mortiser uses chain cutter.

14. **Tenonner.** This machine is of several types *viz.*, (*i*) reciprocating type, (*ii*) circular saw type, (*iii*) rotary cutter type, (*iv*) hollow auger type.

In a rotary cutter type tenonner, the cutters, usually two in number, are mounted on two rotating cutter heads. Cutter heads are keyed on a driving spindle. They can be moved axially along the spindle for adjusting thickness of the tenon. Also they can be raised or lowered as a complete unit by raising or lowering the bracket carrying the spindle.

Work is fixed on a table which can slide along the bed of the machine. For limiting the travel of the table, stop both at the rear and the front are provided.

Pattern Storage

Patterns should be stored in weather proof store room where temperature and humidity are controlled. Suitable shelves and racks should be provided for storing patterns.

All patterns should be numbered to facilitate identification and tracing at the time repeat orders are received. A card should be filed in the office for each pattern. Name of the product, pattern number, manufacturing date, department, drawing number, location in store should be marked in this card.

QUESTIONS

1. What are the basic requirements of a pattern material?
2. Give the different types of materials commonly used for pattern making.
3. Explain the various types of allowances which should be provided in a pattern.
4. What is the influence of pattern allowances in the production of accurate castings?
5. Give the list of various tools and machines used in making a pattern. Explain each in short.
6. Describe the various types of core boxes. What are the usual allowances given on them ?
7. Explain in short the colour code for identifying the different parts of the pattern and core box.

6

Moulding Sand

Moulding Materials

The material used for making moulds is called *"Moulding Material"*. It should be such that mould cavity retains its shape till the molten metal solidifies castings are made in (*i*) Permanent moulds, which are made of ferrous metals and alloys *viz*., Grey C.I., steel, etc., (*ii*) Temperary moulds which are made of refractory sands, resins, wax, plaster of Paris, carbon, ceramics, etc.

Permanent moulds are generally used for casting low-melting point materials. They are very costly. Most of the castings are produced using refractory moulding materials mainly refractory sands.

Moulding Sands

The principal material used in moulding is the mould sand. All sands are formed by the breaking up of rocks due to the action of natural forces, such as frost, wind, rain, heat and water currents. Rocks are very complex in their composition. Sands contain most of the elements of the rocks of which they are fragments. Moulding sands in different parts of the world, therefore, vary considerably.

Sources of Moulding Sands in India

(*i*) Andhra Pradesh—Secunderabad
(*ii*) Uttar Pradesh—Haridwar
(*iii*) Maharashtra—Satara, Bhavnagar
(*iv*) Punjab—Batala
(*v*) Tamil Nadu—Avadi
(*vi*) Orissa—Rourkela
(*vii*) Bengal—Hoogli

Sources of moulding sands are :

(*i*) River beds, (*ii*) Sea,
(*iii*) Lakes, (*iv*) Deserts.

Important refractory materials are :

(*i*) Silica, (*ii*) Magnesite,
(*iii*) Zircon, (*iv*) Dolomite,
(*v*) Olivine, (*vi*) Sillimanite,
(*vii*) Graphite.

Moulding sands are classified according to the nature of their origin into two categories :

(*i*) Natural sand

(*ii*) Synthetic sand.

(*i*) **Natural moulding sand.** It is also called green sand. It is taken from river beds or is dug from pits. It contains only the binder and is used as received with water added. It can be used for making moulds as soon as it is received from its sources. It contains binder material from 5 to 20%. It needs additional water 5 to 8%. It may contain considerable organic matter.

This sand has the advantage of maintaining moisture content for a long time. It permits easy patching and finishing of moulds. It is employed for moulds for casting cast iron and non-ferrous metals. As compared synthetic sand, it is cheaper, needs lesser control. When mixed with bentonite, its properties are improved and it is known as *"Semi-synthetic sand"*.

(*ii*) **Synthetic moulding sand.** It is made in the foundry by mixing a relatively clay-free sand with a selected clay binder *e.g.*, bentonite, water and other materials as required. These are comparatively much better sands for moulding as the properties can be more easily controlled. As compared to natural sand, synthetic sand possesses greater refractoriness (above 1650°C), high permeability, more uniform grain size. It contains no organic matter. It acquires more modulability. It is easy to control its composition, requires less space for storing. It is more suitable for mass production in mechanised foundries. Advantages and disadvantages of synthetic sand against natural sand are given in the form of a table.

Reasons for using sand as mould material. Sand is the most important and principal mouling material used in foundry shop for all types of castings *e.g.*, ferrous, non-ferrous. The reasons for this are the characteristic properties, the sand possesses which are so valuable for the foundry purposes in the mould :

(*i*) The most important characteristic of sand is its refractory nature, *e.g.,* it can easily withstand the high temperature involved during the pouring of the molten metal and does not get fused.

(*ii*) Its chemical resistivity *e.g.*, it generally does not chemically react or combine with the molten metal and can be used over and over again.

(*iii*) A high degree of permeability, *e.g.* capacity to allow the gases and air to escape and at the same time the moulds maintain sufficient hardness and strength. This characteristic is extremely difficult to achieve in any other moulding material.

(*iv*) Sand can easily take any shape according to the shape of the pattern.

(*v*) Sand is extremely cheap and easily available everywhere.

All the above factors contribute in making the sand principal material for moulding.

Properties of a Good Moulding Sand

(*i*) **Property or Permeability.** Molten metal always contains a certain amount of dissolved gases, which are evolved when the metal solidifies. Also the molten metal, when comes in contact with the moist sand, generates steam and water vapour. If these gases and water vapour do not find passage to escape completely through the mould, they will forms gas holes and poures in the casting.

Therefore, the sand must be sufficiently porous to allow the gases or moisture present or generated to be removed freely while pouring. This property is known as *'Permeability'* of *'Porosity'*.

Sands which are coarse or have round grains exhibit more permeability. Soft ramming and clay addition in lesser quantities improve permeability. Inadequate permeability causes defects like surface blows, gasholes, mould blasting, etc.

(*ii*) **Plasticity or Flowability.** This property refers to the ability of the moulding sand to acquire a predetermined shape under pressure and retain the same when the pressure is removed. To obtain a good impression of the pattern in the mould, high plasticity is required of a moulding sand.

Moulding sand should respond to different moulding processes. Flowability of mould sand is its ability to get compacted to a uniform density. It assists moulding sand to flow and pack all around the pattern and take up the required shape.

When energy for compaction during ramming is transmitted through the sand mass (*viz*., sand slingers), good flowability is very essential. Flowability increases with the increase in clay and moisture content.

(*iii*) **Adhesiveness.** Moulding sand particles must be capable of adhering to another body. In other words, they should cling to the sides of the moulding boxes. It is due to this property that the sand mass does not fall out of the moulding box and the same can be successfully held in it.

(*iv*) **Cohesiveness.** The ability of sand particles to stick together is known as *'cohesiveness'* or *'strength'*. If this ability is not sufficient, it may lead to a collapse in the mould or during conveyance, turning over, closing or pouring, it may be partially destroyed or damaged.

This property of moulding sand in its moist or green state is known as *'green strength'* and in its dried or baked state as *'dry strength'*. Sand must have sufficient strength so that it may not be washed away during pouring.

(*a*) **Green Strength.** A mould having adequate *green strength* will not distort or collapse even after removing the pattern from the mould box. Green strength assist in making and handling the moulds. In the absence of green strength, dimensional stability and high accuracy cannot be achieved.

(*b*) **Dry Strength.** If green sand mould is likely to loose its moisture and get dried while waiting for getting poured or when it comes in contact with molten metal, the mould is *dried* or *skin dried* to withstand pressure and erossive forces of molten metal. Dry sand strength is related to grain size, binder and moisture content. There should b an optimum balance between dry strength and collapsibility of mould sand.

(*c*) **Hot Strength.** It is the strength of sand of mould cavity above 100°C. If hot strength is inadequate, mould is likely to enlarge break, erode, or get cracked.

(*v*) **Refractoriness.** The capability of the moulding sand to withstand the high temperature of the molten metal without fusing is known as *'Refractoriness'*. Moulding sands having poor refractoriness burn on to the casting. However, silica sands have high thermal expansion at 575°C.

As compared to casting of low melting point alloys, refractoriness is much more essential in casting of high melting point alloys like steel.

(*vi*) **Chemical Resistivity.** Moulding sand should not chemically react with the metal as otherwise the shape of the casting will be distorted and its surface spoiled.

Also the sand must not stick to the casting and should strip off easily leaving a clean surface.

(*vii*) **Collapsibility.** It is that property of the moulding sand, which determines the readiness with which it automatically gets collapsed after solidification of the casting and breaks down in knocking out and cleaning. If the mould or core does not collapse, it may restrict free shrinking of solidifying metal and cause the same to crack or tear.

(*viii*) **Fineness.** Finer mould sand resist metal penetration and produces smooth casting surface. Fineness and permeability are opposite to each other. Hence, these should be balanced for optimum results. Both these properties can be maintained by using mould coating on highly permeable mould surfaces.

(*ix*) **Low coefficient of expansion.** Mould sand should possess low coefficient of expansion.

(*x*) **Bench Life.** It is the ability of mould sand to retain its properties during storing, handling, or standing *e.g.*, in case of delay.

Table 6.1: Chemical Composition of Typical Moulding Sand

Silica (SiO_2)	...	81.4	to	92.4%
Alumina (Al_2O_3)	...	3.94	to	8.84%
Oxides of Iron (FeO, Fe_2O_3)	...	0.5	to	2.91%
Titanium Oxide (TiO_2)	...	0.12	to	0.43%
Calcium Oxide (CaO)	...	0.12	to	2.82%
Magnesium Oxide (MgO)	...	0.16	to	1.56%
Alkalis (Na_2O, K_2O)	...	1.7	to	4.37%
Loss on ignition	...	0.9	to	5%

Types of Moulding Sands

Moulding sands may also be classified, according to their use as under :

(*i*) **Green sand.** By green sand we denote sand in its natural more or less moist state. It is a mixture of silica sand with 18 to 30% clay and water 6 to 8%. The clay and water give bonding strength to green sand.

It is fine, soft, light and porous. Being damp, when squeezed in the hand it retains the shape given to it under pressure.

Moulds prepared in this sand are known as *'Green sand moulds'*. Cores can also be made out of green sand.

The rammed sand is dense, hence the structure is made porous by venting freely. As the hot metal is poured in it, sharp edges being weak, break and hence sharp edges are avoided in green sand moulding.

Green sand is generally used for casting simple, small or medium sized moulds. Larger output can be obtained from a given floor space as the cost and delay involved in drying the moulds is saved. Coal dust is mixed in green sand to prevent defects in castings.

(*ii*) **Dry sand.** The moulds prepared in green sand are dried or baked to remove almost all moisture of the moist sand. The structure in the moulding boxes becomes stronger and compact. Venting is necessary but not so much as required in green sand. For larger heavy moulds cowdung, house manure, horse hair are mixed with the sand of coarser grains.

Depending upon dried mould wall thickness, it may be called a *"skin dry mould"* or *"dry mould"*. Castings from dry sand moulds possess smoother surface. Dry sand mould possess greater strength, rigidity and thermal stability.

Dry sand moulds eliminate defects like pinholes etc. Moulds are dried by heating them at 175°C and skin-dried by torch. Skin drying is a localised drying process.

Dry sand moulding is employed for large and heavy castings.

(*iii*) **Loam sand.** Loam is mixture of clay and sand milled with water to a thin plastic paste from which moulds are build up on a backing of soft bricks. Patterns are not generally used for loam moulding and shape is given to the mould by sweeps.

Loam sand is high in clay, as much as 50% and dries hard. It also contains fire clay, graphite and fibrous reinforcements. It must be sufficiently adhesive to hold on vertical surfaces as it is applied as plaster to the rough structure of the mould. Chopped stray and manure are commonly used to assist in binding. The moisture content is from 18 to 20% to a consistency resembling mortar.

Table 6.2: Synthetic Sand Mixtures for Cast Iron—Green sand moulding

Class of work	*Old sand*	*New sand*	*Bond clay*	*Bentonite*	*Coal dust*	*Saw dust*	*Moisture per cent*
C.I. bath (for enamelling)	99.4 (System sand)	0.56	0.06	—	—	—	3
Pot castings (high duty iron)	54	36	4	—	6	—	3-3.5
Light castings (facing sand)	91	—	—	3	6	—	3.5
Light casting (high duty iron and steel)	99.7 (System sand)	0.25	—	0.05	—	—	3.8
Automobile cylinder castings (facing sand)	70	20	3.5	—	6.5	—	4
Hydraulic engineering castings (Hand and machine moulding)	97 (System sand)	1-3	—	—	0.7	0.1	6

Table 6.3: Natural Bonded Sand Mixtures for Cast Iron—Green sand moulding

S. No.	*Class of Work*	*Proportion of New sand per cent*	*Moisture (per cent)*	*Green compressive strength (gm/cm^2)*	*Dry compressive strength (gm/cm^2)*	*Green Permability A F.S. No.*
1.	General engineering ; light	25	5.5	510	1650	73
2.	Small electrical fittings	14	6	366	2200-2900	80-85
3.	Medium weight valves	10	5.5	350	2800-2900	60
4.	Small castings (high duty)	17	5.5	190	3000	40
5.	General engineering (upto 500 kg.)	35	6.8	375	1125-1270	121
6.	Machine tools ; small and medium weight	33	6.7	350	1830-2200	94
7.	Furnace plates	33	2-4.5	300	1550	100

Table 6.4: Moulding Sands for Steel (Synthetic)

Green sand		*Dry sand*	
New silica sand	25	New silica sand	15
Old sand	75	Old sand	85
Bentonite	1.5	Bentonite	0.5
Dextrine	0.25	Moisture	5
Moisture	3-3.5		

Table 6.5: Typical Mixtures of Loam Sand

Type 1		*Type 2*	
Silica sand	22 vols	Floor sand	10 vols
Clay	5 vols	New loam sand	10 vols
Manure	1 vol	Silica sand	3 vols
Moisture	18-22%	Ganister	3 vols
Dry strength (compression) (gm/cm^2)	1050-1760	Manure	2 vols
Permeability No. less than	5	Mineral blacking	2 vols

Loam is dried very slowly and completely before it is ready for casting. It is used for casting larger regular shaped castings, *e.g.*, chemical pans and drums etc.

(*iv*) **Facing sand.** It forms the face of the mould. It is used directly next to the surface of the pattern and it comes into contact with the molten metal when the mould is poured. It is, therefore, subject to the most severe conditions and hence must possess high strength and refractoriness. It is made of silica sand and clay, without the addition of used sand.

Facing sand may have a thickness of 20-30 mm. Its use reduces the mould material cost.

Table 6.6: Facing Sand for Green Castings

Type of sand	*Heavy C.I.*	*Medium C.I.*	*Light C.I.*	*Steel green sand*	*Steel dry sand*
Composition	28 new, 66 old, 6 coal dust	20 new, 76 old, 3-4 coal dust	25 new, 70 old, 5 coal dust	20 new, 75 old, 1.5 bentonite, 0.23 core gum	85 new, 15 old
Moisture	6-7	5.5-6.5	6-7	3-35	7-7.5
Permeability	30-40	35	30	170-180	110-120
Green strength (gm/cm^2)	635	370	320	625	530
Dry strength (gm/cm^2)	6700	5300	4600	4600	10000

Table 6.7: Non-ferrous Facing Mixtures

Class of work	*Facing mixture for dressing*
Phosphor-bronze and high melting point non-ferrous alloys.	Best fine plumbago 1 kg. China clay 1/2 kg. Molasses 375 gm. Mix with 2.25 litres hot water and dilute further if required for spray.
General brass and bronze castings.	Fine silvery plumbago 1/2 kg. Best white talc $1\frac{1}{2}$ kg, Molasses $\frac{1}{2}$ kg. Add 4.5 litres of water for use.
Light alloy casting.	Best white talc 1 kg, Whitening $\frac{1}{2}$ kg, Molasses $\frac{1}{2}$ kg, Make into thin cream with water for spray.

Different forms of carbon known as facing material (*e.g.*, plumbago powder, ceylon lead or grahite) are used to prevent the metal from burning into the sand. Sometimes they are mixed with 6 to 15 times fine moulding sand to make mould facings.

Facing and layer in a mould usually ranges from 20 to 30 mm. Facing sand is from 10 to 15% of the whole amount of mould sand.

(*v*) **Backing sand.** The accumulated moulding sand from cast up moulds which is used over and over again is known as *'Backing sand'* or *'Floor sand'*. It is used to fill in the mould at the back of facing layer so that it does not come in contact with the pattern. Old, repeatedly used moulding sand is mainly employed for this purpose. After it is used a number of times, the sharp edges of sand grain become rounded due to high temperature of molten metal and burning of clay content and the sand becomes weak in bonding strength.

The backing sand is sometimes known as *'black sand'* because old, repeatedly used moulding sand is black in colour due to the addition of coal dust and burning or coming in contact with molten metal. However before use, backing sand, should be cleaned off the foreign matter like fins, nails etc.

(*vi*) **System sand.** Mechanical foundries employ machine moulding. There, they use a so called *'system sand'*, to fill the whole flask. As the whole mould is made of this system sand, the strength, permeability, and refractoriness of the sand must be higher than those of backing sand.

System sand is prepared in a mechanical sand preparation and hardening system. No facing sand is used. Used sand is cleaned and reactivated by adding binders and special binders.

Table 6.8: Summary of Advantages and Disadvantages of Synthetic Sand against Natural Bounded Sand

Advantages	*Disadvantages*
1. Lower sand maintenance cost and no sand dumping.	High initial cost.
2. Improved permeability, lower Moisture, lesser chances of porous castings, chilling, etc.	Needs more careful control than natural bounded sand.
3. Easier to work mass production moulding.	Drying out gives friability and pashes.
4. Semi-skilled operatives can work on machine moulding.	Patching is difficult.
5. Old core sand and reclaimed sand can be used.	Balling up may give poor finish.

(*vii*) **Parting sand.** A mould is generally prepared into two or three boxes. These boxes are separated from adhering to each other by spreading a fine sharp dry sand called *'parting sand'*. Parting sand is also used to keep the green sand from sticking to the pattern.

It is clean clay-free silica sand. Some moulders use burnt core sand, *i.e.*, core sand cleaned from castings. These are also manufactured parting materials known as *'parting compounds'*. They are in powdered form and used by dusting them on parting surfaces.

When the oil has been mixed in moulding sand :

(*a*) lycopodium powder a parting compound is used.

(*b*) brick powder is used as parting sand to prevent mould sand to stick to the pattern, the only objection to its use is the high cost.

Parting compounds may be dry or wet. Dry parting substances are fine dried sand, charcoal, ground bone, lime stone, lycopodium powder (a yellow vegetable matter), tripolite a silicate rock), ground nutshells (walnut), talc (magnesium silicate), and calcium phosphate. These are used for wooden pattern.

Liquid parting substances are petrol-cum-jelly mixed with oil, paraffin, and stearic acid. These are used for metal pattern in machine moulding.

(*viii*) **Core sand.** Sand which is used for making cores is called '*core sand*' or '*oil sand*'. It is silica sand mixed with core oil which is composed of linseed oil, rasin, light mineral oil and other binders.

For the sake of economy, pitch or flour and water may be used in large cores. Core sand has been further discussed under core making.

(*ix*) **Molasses Sand and Oil Sand.** Sand using molasses or oil binders (linseed oil) are called '*Molasses sands*' and "*oil sands*".

Molasses sand is used small, thin, for producing intricate and accurate castings. It is also suitable for small non-ferrous gears.

Mould surface Coatings, Facings Dressings, Washer, or Blackings

Mould surface are coated after withdrawing the pattern from the mould box. Function of mould surface coating :

(*i*) To impart smooth surface to the casting.

(*ii*) To provide a better refractory surface.

(*iii*) To prevent metal penetration into intergranular voids in the mould faces.

(*iv*) To reduce surface defects on the casting.

(*v*) To impart greater care of cleaning the casting.

However, mould surface coatings reduce permeability at the mould surface. Hence, they should not contain gas-forming materials. They consist of :

(*i*) finely divided refractory oxides and silicates *e.g.*, silica, sillimanite, alumina, magnesia, talc, zircon, chromite, chamotte, molochite, etc.

(*ii*) Carbonaceous materials like graphite, plumbago, blacking etc.

Sillimanite and talc are applied to moulds for low melting point non-ferrous alloys. Graphite plumbago etc., is used in moulds for ferrous castings. They produce a reducing atmosphere at the interface of the mould and molten metal thereby decreasing metal penetration.

Mould surface coatings are either applied in the form of (*i*) dry powder, which is dusted over the mould face of (*ii*) liquid wash, which is applied by brush, swab, or spray mould wash needs check and control on its viscosity and specific gravity according to method of application *viz.* swab, brush etc.

Liquid wash should be evaporated or dried by gas torch or hot air. Volatile liquid wash like isopropyl alcohol is also used. Suitable binder like clay, molasses, or cereals is added to mould coating so that it does not crack or peel off.

It is advisable to use proprietory brand of mould coating rather than to use ones own. A few Indian brands are : (*i*) IVP products *viz.*, water soluble compounds and alcohol soluble compounds.

(*ii*) FOSECO products *viz.*, Terracote 2 for non-ferrous alloys, Terracote 41 for cast iron, Terrapaint 50Z for steel.

Principal Ingredients of Moulding Sands

(*i*) Silica sand grains

(*ii*) Moulding sand binder

(*iii*) Moisture

(*iv*) Additives

Silica sand grains. They impart refractoriness, chemical resistivity and permeability to the sand. They are of paramount importance in the moulding sand. They are specified according to their average *size* and *shape.*

Grain size and distribution influence sand properties like refractoriness, permeability, plasticity (flowability), surface fineness, strength etc.

Finer grains will be laying more closely to each other and so permeability will be less. But fine grains will impart more strength to the mould and so tendency of the mould towards deformation will be less. Fine grains give good surface finish.

Coarse and uniformly graded sands impart high permeability high flowability and maximum refractoriness. Normally, moulding sands posses grain size between 0.1 to 1 mm.

There are three distinct sizes of sand grains : fine, medium and coarse :

(*a*) For small and intricate castings the use of a fine sand is desirable, so that all the details of mould are brought out sharply.

(*b*) Medium sand is used in bench work and light floor work, *viz.*, making machinery castings having sections up to 50 mm.

(*c*) As the size of the casting increases, the sand particles like-wise should be coarser so as to permit the gases generated in the mould escape readily.

Grain size is determined by passing the sand through screens of sieves.

According to the shape, the grains are classified :

(*a*) **Rounded grains.** Grains which get rubbed against each other by the action of wind, waves or flowing water, acquire round shape. These have least contact with one another in a rammed structure. It makes the sand highly permeable to gases. Rounded grain sand lacks in strength possesses greater flowability. Grains too smooth and round should result in mould cracks, sand wash and scabs.

Table 6.9: Grading of Sand Grains

Classification		*Test sieves*	
Grade	*Particle size (mm)*	*Mesh No.*	*Aparture (mm)*
Gravel	Above 2.0	8	2.057
Very coarse sand	2.00–1.00	10	1.676
		16	1.003
Coarse sand	1.00–0.50	22	0.699
		30	0.500
Medium sand	0.50–0.15	44	0.353
		60	0.251
Fine sand	0.25–0.10	72	0.211
		100	0.152
		150	0.104
Coarse sand	0.10–0.05	200	00.76
		300	00.53
Fine silt	0.05–0.01	—	—
Clay	Less than 0.01	—	—

(*b*) **Sub-angular grains.** They are formed due to movement and moderate rubbing of angular grain with each other. This breaks sharp edges of grains and they acquire a sub-angular shape. They give comparatively less permeability than rounded grains. But they have higher strength.

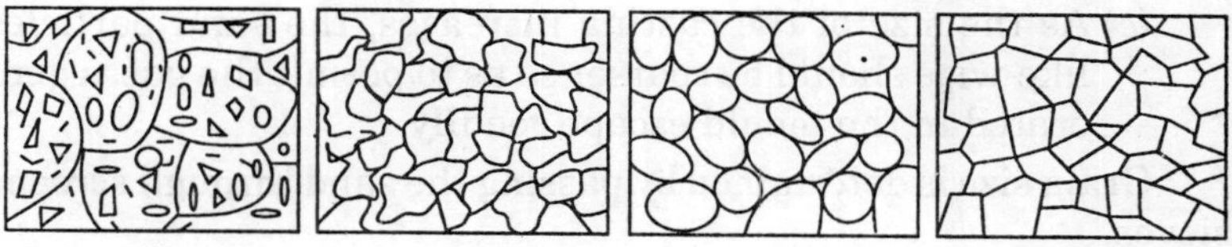

A-Compounded sand grains.
B-Sub-angular sand grains.
C-Rounded sand grains.
D-Angular sand grains.

Fig. 6.1 Types of sand grains.

(*c*) **Angular grains.** They result when the sand is formed due to decomposition of rocks without movement. It is also closely associated with frost and glacial action. These have defined edges. Their surfaces are nearly flat. They give still more strength and less permeability to the mould.

(*d*) **Compounded grains.** The grains, in some cases, are cemented together such that they do not separate when screened. They may consist of anyone of the above shapes or a combination of the above three shapes. They are not desirable because they tend to break down at high temperature.

Binder or Clay. Its purpose is to impart necessary bonding strength to the mould sand so that the mould does not lose its shape after ramming. As the quantity of clay increases, the permeability of the mould sand decreases.

Clay may be defined as those sand particles under 20 microns in diameter which fail to settle a distance of 25 mm per minute, when suspended in water. Average clay particles are of colloidal size, clays are essentially aggregates of extremely minute crystalline, usually flake-shaped particles, which can be classified on the basis of their structure and composition into a few groups called '*clay minerals*'.

Some of the clays are composed of particles of a single clay mineral, whereas others are mixtures of clay minerals. Some of the clays are composed, entirely of clay minerals whereas others contain mixtures of quartz, organic matter etc.

Table 6.10: Chemical Composition of Common Bonding Clays (*Per cent*)

Type of clay→	*Ordinary clay*	*Bentonite*	*Fire clay*
Silica (SiO_2)	53.7	61.5	45.1
Alumina (Al_2O_3)	25.4	22.1	33.4
Iron oxide (Fe_2O_3)	6.94	4.2	2.50
Calcium oxide (CaO)	0.34	1.74	1.20
Magnesium oxide (MgO)	2.04	2.27	0.94
Titanium oxide (TiO_2)	0.62	0.22	1.55
Alkalis ($K_2O + Na_2O$)	3.12	1.56	0.83
Loss on ignition	7.8	5.8	14.6
Fusion temperature °C	1390	1330	Above 1500

Clay consists of two ingredients ; fine silt and true clay. Fine silt is a sort of foreign matter or mineral deposit which has no bonding property. True clay imparts the necessary bonding power. When seen under high magnification, true clay is found to consist of extremely minute aggregates of crystalline particles, called '*clay minerals*'. Clay minerals are further composed of flake shaped particles about 2 microns in diameter which are seen to lie one on another.

As compared to sand grains sand binders are less refractory. Binders produce cohesion between the mould sand grains in green or dry state. They give strength to the moulding sand so that it can retain its shape as mould cavity.

Binders to the moulding sands should be added in minimum required quantity as it reduces permeability. Increasing binder content to a limit increases green compression strength ; after which this strength remains practically unchanged with increase in binder content. For bonding mould sands, clay binders are most commonly used.

Clay binders are classified as under:

(*i*) Fire clay

(*ii*) Bentonite

- (*a*) Sodium montmorillonite
- (*b*) Calcium montmorillonite

(*iii*) Illinite

(*iv*) Limonite

(*v*) Kaolinite

Clays are inorganic binders. Best clay is one which imparts the optimum combination of bonding properties, moisture mould strength, and low cost of producing the casting and produces a thin and adhesive film around the moulding sand grains.

When heated to high temperatures during pouring, clay gets baked and hardened. Clay is added to moulding sand from time to time so as to maintain adequate bonding strength of mould sand.

In natural moulding sand, clay and sand occur mixed in a proportion so that it can directly be used for moulding. But, in synthetic moulding sand, selected clays are added to obtain desired strength and plasticity.

Fire clay. It is a refractory clay usually found in coal mines. Hard black lumps are weathered and then pulverized for use in moulding sand. Particles are about four hundred times as large as bentonite particles. Thus, the same percentage of fire clay imparts lower strength to the mould.

Bentonite. It is the most commonly used clay binder as it produces the strongest bond in mould sand. In India, bentonite deposits are available in Bihar and Rajasthan. Bentonites are weathered product of volcanic ash. They are soft, creamy white powder. They are usually used for synthetic mould sand.

Table 6.11: Comparison of Sodium and Calcium type Bentonites

S.N.	*Characteristics*	*Montmorillonite*	
		Sodium	*Calcium*
(*i*)	Particle or flake size	Less than 0.00025 mm	Less than 0.00025 mm.
(*ii*)	Shrinking due to loss of water	Very high	Very high
(*iii*)	Swelling due to water	Very high gel-forming	Slight, little tendency to gel formation
(*iv*)	Softening point	1150-1350°C	980°C and above
(*v*)	Composition	Montmorill 90%, quartz 10%, mica, feldspar, etc.	Montmorill 85% quartz, 15%, limonite, etc.

Illite. It is a decomposition product of micaceous material due to weather. It is found in natural moulding sand. Illite

particles have thickness and width of 20 and 200 milli microns respectively.

Illite possess moderate shrinkage due to loss of water. It does not swell like bentonite but gives reasonable strength. It has a softening point of 1370°C. In temperature range of 500-550°C, irreversible dehydration takes place.

Kaolinite. It is the residue of weathered granite and basalt. It contains kaolinite 60%, illite 30%, and quartz 10%. Its particles possess thickness and width of 20 and 100-250 milli microns respectively. It is characterized by (*a*) low shrinkage due to loss of water, (*b*) very low swelling due to water, and (*c*) non-gel forming. Its softening point is 1650 to 1700°C.

Bond Formation or Bonding Action of Clays or Bonding Theories : clay (or binder) in presence of water tends to bind sand grains, together and makes it possible to construct the mould. Theories put forward to explain the phenomenon of bond formation are :

(*i*) Block and Wedge Theory
(*ii*) Surface Tension Theory
(*iii*) Electrostatic Bonding Theory

(*i*) **Block and Wedge Theory.** This theory is based on the inter-particle friction developed in non-plastic materials (in the form of particles) under pressure. Sand or clay sand particles act as blocks and wedges ; these, when rammed, get stuck or jammed against each other. Inter-particle friction so created results in bonding and resists further deformation.

(*ii*) **Surface Tension Theory.** According to this theory, bonding action of clays takes place due to surface tension of water, which surrounds the clay and clay-sand particles and fills the capillary interstices and the interstices of clay particles.

This theory was proposed because electrostatic bond was felt not to be so strong to explain the strength properties of green sand mixtures.

(*iii*) **Electrostatic Bonding Theory.** Electrostatic bond between clay and sand particles is established as under :

Sand grains and clay particles are mixed in presence of water. Water molecules break into H^+ (hydrogen) and OH^- (hydroxyl) ions. Due to unsatisfied valence bonds at clay-crystal surface, clay particle absorbs OH^- ions. These OH^- ions attract H^+ counter ions which then surround OH^- ions. When sand and clay particles are moistened in presence of each other, OH^- (hydroxyl) ions

surrounding clay particles attract H^+ (hydrogen) counter-ions of sand particles. An electrostatic bond is thus established between clay and sand particles.

Moisture. The purpose of clay will not be served until the requisite amount of moisture is added to it. Clay imparts bonding action and strength in the presence of moisture.

Water, when added to a clay moisture, it penetrates and forms a micro-film coating the surface of each individual flake. The molecules of water which form the micro-film on the flake are not in the original fluid state but they are in a fixed and definite position. On adding more water, thickness of the micro-film increases upto a certain limit after which, the excess water remains in the fluid state. The thickness of this water film varies with the clay mineral. Bonding property of clay depends on the maximum thickness of water micro film it can maintain.

When a mould is rammed, the sand grains are forced together. On each grain, the clay coating acts in such a way that it locks the grains in position and makes them retain the position. The bounding action is the best if the quantity of water added is just that is required to form the micro-film. Strength is reduced, and mould becomes weak, if the water added is in excess.

Amount of water added varies from 1.5 to 8%. Water is responsible for the bonding action of clays. It activates the clay in the sand and the clay-sand mixture and develops plasticity and strength. Water added, partly gets absorbed by clay and partly remains free (which is called **"Free Water"**).

Absorbed water develops proper bond and green strength. Free water acts as a lubricant, increases improves mouldability but reduces mould strength. Amount of water required to develop optimum properties is determined experimentally.

Additives

Materials other basic ingredient (*viz.,* sand binder and moisture) are also added to mould sand in small quantities for improving existing properties, developing certain other properties *viz.*, resistance to sand expansion defects, etc.

Additives include

1. Facing materials and
2. Cushion materials.

1. Facing Materials. These are used for obtaining smoother and cleaner surface on the casting and help easy peeling

off sand from surface of casting while shaking out. Some of the important facing materials are :

(*i*) **Sea coal or coal dust.** It is finely powdered bituminous coal. Amount of addition varies from 1% for small casting to above 10% for large castings. it is added to mould sand for cast iron to improve surface appearance and easy stripping.

(*ii*) **Pitch and Asphalt.** Pitch is distilled from soft coal at about 315°C. It is added upto 2%. Asphalt is a by product of petroleum distillation.

These are added to obtain fine surface finish on ferrous castings and improve hot strength.

(*iii*) **Graphite.** It may be natural or synthetic. It is added from 0.2 to 2%. It is added to improve surface finish of the castings and mouldability of foundry sand.

(*iv*) **Silica Flour.** It is pulverized silica which can pass through 200 mesh sieve. It is added upto 35%. It is added to improve surface finish and hot strength, resist metal penetration and minimize sand expansion defects.

(*v*) **Coke.** It may be added upto 5% and facilitates easy stripping.

2. **Cushion Materials.** These are added to burn at the time of pouring molten metal, giving rise to space to accommodate the expansion of silica sand of the surface of mould cavity. Thus, they prevent buckling of large felt surfaces of castings due to thermal expansion of silica sand grains.

Following are some of the important cushion materials.

(*i*) **Wood flour, Cereal hulls, Cellulose, etc.** These are added from 0.5 to 2%. They minimize sand expansion defects, improve flowability and collapsibility of sand.

(*ii*) **Perlite.** It is added for the same purpose as wood flour. As it possesses insulating properties, it is used as a riser insulator.

(*iii*) **Cereal or Finely ground corn flour.** These are added from 0.25 to 2%. They are added to increase green and dry strength, minimize sand expansion defects, and improve collapsibility. They reduce permeability and flowability.

(*iv*) **Fuel oil.** It is added from 0.01 to 0.1%. It improves mouldability of sand.

(*v*) **Iron oxide.** It is added to improve hot strength.

(*vi*) **Molasses and Dextrin.** Molasses resists the tendency of the mould to dry out. These are added to increase dry strength and edge hardness of the moulds.

(*vii*) **Dielthylene glycol.** It is added to improve surface finish of the castings. When added to bentonite bonded sand, it improves the tendency of the mould to surface drying.

(*viii*) **Ammonium bifluoride, Boric acid and Sulphur.** They are added to moulding sand for magnesium castings so as to prevent metal-mould reactions.

Specifications of Moulding Sands

The moulding sands are specified in terms of :

(*i*) the size and shape of the silica grains.

(*ii*) the clay content.

(*iii*) the moisture content.

Grain fineness number. The grain size is expressed by number known as Grain Fineness Number, which correponds to a standard sieve of 200 mm diameter having that number of meshes in it.

For determination of Grain Fineness Number of a given sand sample, a standard sieve set is used. This sieve set has a number

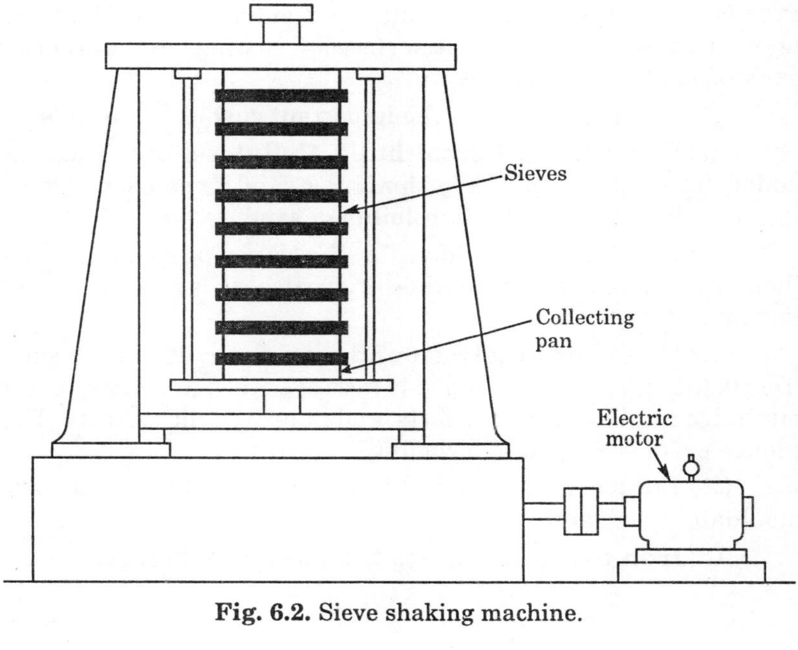

Fig. 6.2. Sieve shaking machine.

of sieves in it having varying number of meshes, placed one over another. Number of meshes in each sieve is known. The finest sieve is placed at the bottom and the coarsest at the top. After separating the clay and moisture, the sample under test is placed in the top sieve and the whole set is shaken in a sieve shaking machine for a definite time duration. The amount of sand which remains on each sieve is collected and weighed and is expressed in percentage of the original sample weight.

For each sieve, a multiplying number (constant) is given and so, the percentage collected on each sieve is multiplied by its multiplying number and all the products are added which gives the total product.

Grain Fineness Number

$$= \frac{\text{Total product}}{\text{Total sum of percentages collected on each sieve}}$$

Grain shape. It may be round, subangular, angular or compounded, which can be observed by visual examination using microscope or magnifying glass.

Clay content. For determining clay content in sands, an apparatus called, *'clay content tester'* is used. The sand sample under test is first dried and cooled. Then it is taken in a jar in a weighed amount (50 gm). To this, 475 c.c. of water and 25 c.c. of standard solution of NaOH are added and the jar is securely covered and sealed.

The appartus mainly consists of an arrangement for tightly holding one, two or more such jars in a frame and rotating the whole frame at about 60 r.p.m. by means of an electric motor. Thus, the solution gets shaken vigorously.

After about one hour's shaking, the jars are removed, unsealed. The sand adhering to the cover and sides is washed into the jar. Then, the jar filled up with water a pre-determined mark, usually 150 mm above the bottom, the contents allowed to settle for 10 minutes and water is siphoned off to a depth of 125 mm. Now more water is added upto the original mark and is again siphoned off after allowing the sand to settle for 10 minutes. A few more times, the process is repeated allowing only 5 minutes duration for settling through 125 mm.

In this way, the material which fails to settle 125 mm in 5 minutes, *i.e.,* 25 mm per minute is separated and removed from

the jar. This separated materials is clay. Remaining sand in the jar is carefully filtered, dried for half an hour and weighed.

The weight of the clay is given by the difference between the original weight and this weight of remaining sand.

Moisture content. (*i*) Using Direct reading moisture teller. For determining misture content weighed sand sample is taken, heated in an oven so that all the moisture is evaporated and reweighed. The difference in the weights will give the weight of the water evaporated. The percentage moisture can be calculated from this difference.

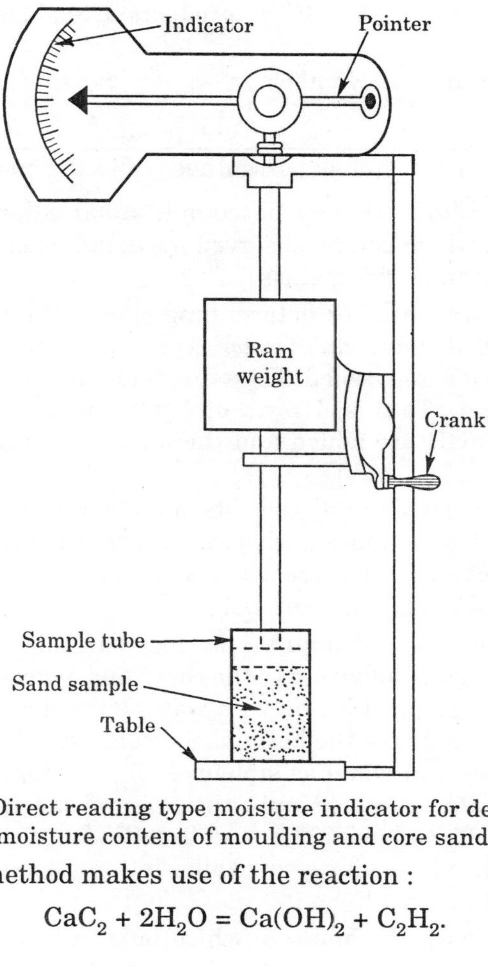

Fig. 6.3. Direct reading type moisture indicator for determining moisture content of moulding and core sand.

This method makes use of the reaction :

$$CaC_2 + 2H_2O = Ca(OH)_2 + C_2H_2.$$

Direct reading instruments called '*moisture tellers*' are used to determine moisture content without losing time. Their working depends on the pressure of acetylene gas generated by the chemical reaction of carbide with the moisture present in the sand.

Weighed amounts of sand sample and calcium carbide are placed in two compartments and then allowed to mix by shaking. The resultant pressure of the acetylene gas generated is indicated on a scale calibrated directly in percentage of moisture.

(*ii*) Using electrode probe devices.

(*iii*) Using measurements of microwave absorption in compacted sand sample.

(*iv*) Using Infrared heating : Prepared sand (20-50 gm) placed in the pan is heated by an infrared bulb for 2-3 minutes. Hence, moisture in the sand gets evaporated. Sand is taken out and reweighed. Difference in weights gives percentage moisture.

Chart 6.1: Sand Control Tests

On mould sands	*On core sands*
(*i*) Mould hardness test	(*i*) Core hardness test
(*ii*) Permeability test	(*ii*) Permeability
(*iii*) Strength tests	(*iii*) Strength tests
(*a*) Green and dry compression	(*a*) Green strength test
(*b*) Green tensile	(*b*) Baked strength test
(*c*) Green and dry shear	(*c*) Hot strength test
(*d*) Transverse or bending	(*d*) Retained strength test
(*e*) Hot strength test	
(*iv*) Moisture content test	(*iv*) Moisture content test
(*v*) Clay content test	
(*vi*) Grain fineness test	
(*vii*) Refractoriness test	

Testing of Moulding Sand

Besides determination of grain size and shape, clay content and moisture content, tests are generally carried out in foundries to evaluate the following properties of moulding sand :

(*i*) Sand mould hardness

(*ii*) Permeability

(*iii*) Strength

Sand mould hardness. It depends on the degree of ramming done on the mould. It is usually measured by a hardness tester.

The apparatus is like dial gauge having a small plunger protruding out of the flat base. When hardness tester is placed on the mould surface with its base on the latter, the plunger gets pressed and is forced into the sand. The distance through which it is forced in, will depend on the hardness of the sand mould. Plunger movement actuates spring and is indicated on a dial graduated from zero to hundred.

The density to which a green sand mould is rammed affects :

(*a*) the ability of the surface to withstand the wash and pressure of the molten metal, and

(*b*) the degree of relative permeability of the sand mould.

The dial depth indicator may also be fitted with a spring loaded ball, 5 mm diameter which may be pressed into the surface of the moist rammed sand. The depth to which the ball can be forced into the sand face under the constant load of 237 gm is indicated on a dial.

The average mould should indicate a hardness of about 50.

Table 6.12: Hardness Tests on Green Sand Moulds

S. No.	*Nature of Ramming*	*Hardness*
1.	Soft rammed mould	40
2.	Medium rammed	50
3.	Hard rammed	70
4.	Very hard ramming	85

Permeability. For absolute determination, permeability is tested with an apparatus known as '*Permeability Meter*'.

This apparatus has an arrangement which allows controlled amount of air to pass through a sand sample and the time taken for all the air to pass through the same is measred.

Permeability Number may be defined as the volume of air in c.c. that will pass through a sand sample of 1 sq. cm. cross-section and 1 cm high in size in 1 minute at a pressure of 1 gm. per cm^2.

Thus, Permeability Number $(p) = \frac{v.h.}{p.a.t}$

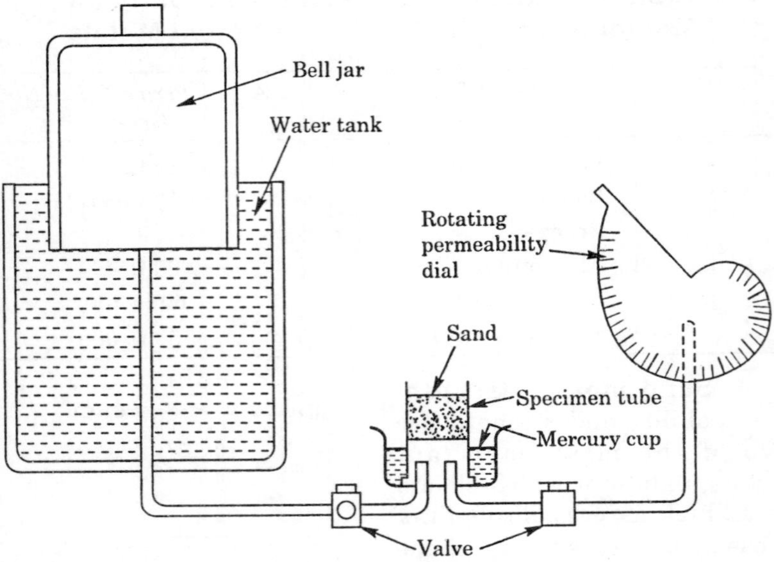

Fig. 6.4. Working principle permeability meter.

where v = volume of air in c.c.

h = height of sample in cm

p = pressure of air in gm/cm^2

a = cross-sectional area of sample in cm^2

t = time in minutes.

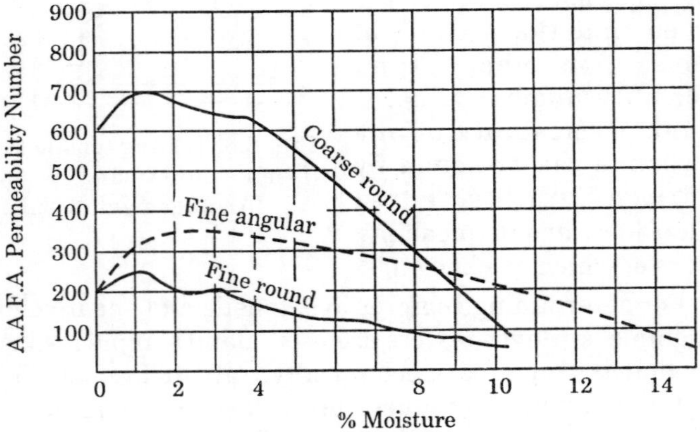

Fig. 6.5. Effect of moisture content on permeability of three different sands.

Table 6.13: Ranges for Green Permeability for Moulding Mixtures Used for Different Metals

S. No.	*Type of Sand*	*A.F.A. Permeability No. Green*
1.	Loam (15% moisture)	less than 5
2.	Cast iron	10 to 80
3.	Bronze	35
4.	Aluminium	20 to 40
5.	Steel-dry sand	60 to 100
6.	Steel-green sand	150 to 300

Sand mould strength. Permeability and strength are two of the most important factors, values of which should be as high as possible. Both of these depend on size and shape of sand grain provided the quantity of water used in mixing the sand should be just exactly correct. They also depend on the degree of hardness to which the sand is rammed.

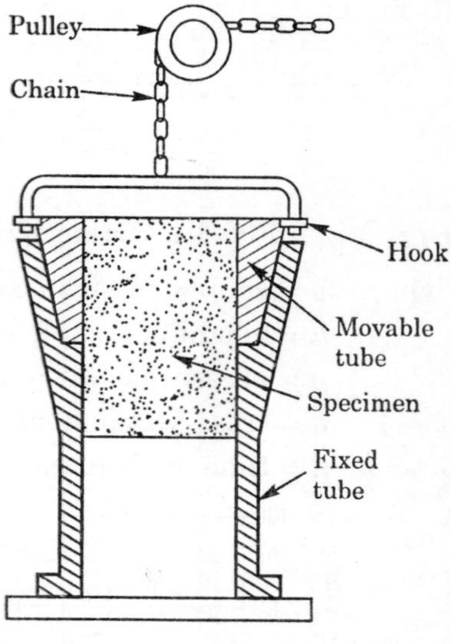

Fig. 6.6. Testing tensile strength of moulding sand specimen (Arrangement of Tubes)

If the sand hardness number does not exceed 85, it is observed that the product of hardness number and permeability number remains constant permeability of any sand sample can be found by comparison with a standard sand, hardness and permeability numbers of which are known.

For determining compressive, tensile and shear strength of sand sample, strength testers are used. Sand sample is placed in a holder and is squeezed mechanically until it breaks. The force applied in breaking it by squeezing is shown on an indicator. This force is compressive strength of sand. The same tester is used for testing shear and tensile strength by changing the holder.

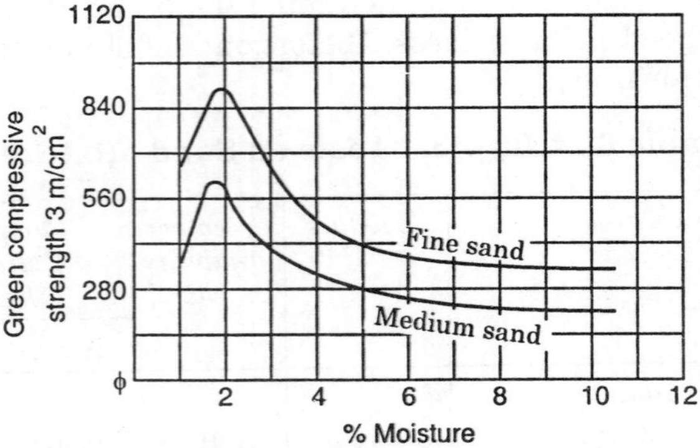

Fig. 6.7. Effect of moisture on green strength.

Green strength depends on :

(*a*) Grain size

(*b*) Shape and distribution of sand grains

(*c*) Type and amount of clay or other binder.

(*d*) Moisture content.

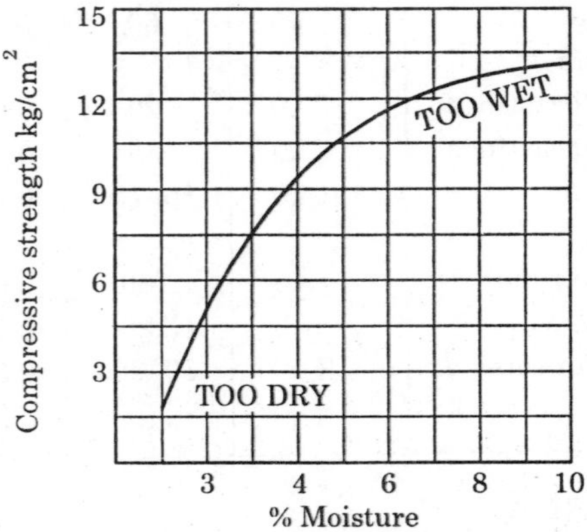

Fig. 6.8. Effect of moisture on dry strength.

Dry compressive strength of a moulding-sand mixture increases as moisture is added untill the sand is too wet to be workable (Fig. 6.8).

Hot strength test for testing hot strength, a double ended rammed cylindrical specimen about 28 mm in dia and 50 mm. in length is prepared. This specimen is tested by dilatometer, where specimen is heated from 250°C to 1400°C and tested in compression.

Refractoriness test. Cylindrical sand specimen is prepared. It is fired at 1550°C for 2 hours. Appearance and dimensional

changes, if any, are observed. Retaining shape and expansion upto 7% shows good refractoriness. Distortion and shinking indicates poor refractoriness.

Table 6.14: Typical Tests on Sand Mixtures

S. No.	*Casting*	*Moisture (%)*	*Green permeability No.*	*Compressive strength kg / cm²*	
				Green	*Dry*
1.	Cast iron				
	(*i*) Stove plate	9.0	10	0.500	0.170
	(*ii*) Radiators	7.0	35	0.400	4.000
2.	Cylinder blocks				
	(*i*) Average castings	7.0	35	0.500	5.000
	(*ii*) Synthetic-thin	3.5	70	0.675	5.000
3.	Non-ferrous copper base				
	(*i*) Small	6.0	25	0.600	3.400
	(*ii*) Large	5.5	60	0.850	5.100
4.	Aluminium				
	(*i*) Small castings	7.0	20	0.400	1.700
	(*ii*) Large castings	7.0	35	0.400	2.550
5.	Magnesium	4.0	80–150	0.675	8.500
6.	Steel				
	(*i*) Green sand	3.5	180	0.675	5.950
	(*ii*) Dry sand	7.5	120	0.750	12.75
7.	Oil sand for cores	2 to 5	50–200	0.040 –0.250	25.5 to 85

Mixing of Sand

A great deal of moulding and core sand is used by foundries. For making one tonne of sound castings 4 to 5 cubic metres of moulding sand are required. These are very few natural sands which possess all the qualities of moulding sand. It is, therefore, usual to make up the deficiency of sand by mixing it with other sands or other substances. Generally, it is mixed with small quantities of clay, lime, magnesia, potash, soda, horse manure, saw dust, cowdung, coal dust, etc.

Table 6.15: Moulding Sands for Cast Iron showing Variations in Composition

Type of Casting	*Ratio New sand to old*	*Ratio Coal dust to sand*	*Moisture (Per cent)*
Light :			
Minimum	1–100	1–500	3.5
Average	1–3	1–35$\frac{1}{2}$	6.0
Maximum	1–1	1–5	8.0
Medium :			
Minimum	1–40	0	3.5
Average	1–3$\frac{1}{2}$	1–18$\frac{1}{2}$	6.75
Maximum	1–1	1–50	7
Heavy :			
Minimum	1–12	0	3.5
Average	1–2	1–15	6.75
Maximum	2$\frac{1}{2}$–1	1–19	8.0

Silica is a high fusing material and makes the moulding sand capable of withstanding high temperature but it has no bond. Clay is, therefore, necessary bond to the moulding sand. Too much clay in sand causes cracking of the mould after drying. Addition of lime, magnesia, iron oxide, soda, etc. reduces melting point of silica. Small amounts of these elements are, therefore, added for making the casting soft.

Moulding sands are black in colour due to addition of coal dust, which makes the sand more open and helps to cool the mould after having been poured. As soon as the molten metal comes in contact with the sand containing coal dust, it dries the mould face and begins to heat the sand. Coal dust gives off carbon dioxide gas immediately. Water (moisture content) in the sand gets converted into steam. Coal dust thus absorbs fairly high amount of heat and cools the sand, preventing the grains from overheating and fusing. A protective film of carbon dioxide gases helps to keep the metal and sand separated from each other to guard against burning of sand on the casting surface.

Mixing moulding materials properly ensures uniform distribution of clay, moisture and other constituents between the sand grains. The more uniform this distribution, the better the qualities of the sand.

Preparation of Sand

Preparation of sand consists of :

(*i*) Sand Tempering

(*ii*) Sand Conditioning.

(*i*) *Sand Tempering.* For preparing foundry sand for making a mould, it should be tempered and cut through. The process by which sufficient moisture is added to the sand is known as '*sand tempering*'. For tempering the sand, water is thrown over the heap in a sheet by giving a backward swing to the pail. The pail of sand is then cut through, a shovelful at a time allowing the air through the clay in the sand breaking up the lumps. This moistens the clay in the sand and makes it adhesive. The heap is thus put in the best condition for working.

(*ii*) *Sand Conditioning.* It consists of preparing the moulding sand to make it suitable for ramming in flasks. New sand and used sand should be properly conditioned before use to obtain good castings.

Proper sand conditioning and preparation helps in the following ways :

(*a*) The binding material is distributed uniformly around the grains.

(*b*) The moisture is uniformly dispersed in the sand mixture. Also moisture content is properly controlled.

(*c*) The sand gets aerated which causes the sand grains to separate and increase the flowability of sand.

(*d*) The sand is supplied at the proper temperature.

(*e*) The foreign particles are separated from the sand.

The handling and conditioning of the moulding sand is done by hand for limited production *e.g.,* job shop production of castings.

In a mechanised foundry, proper equipments are provided for preparation of sand *e.g.,* tempering and conditioning :

(*a*) For sand mixing, a popular machine called '*Muller*' is used which kneads, shears, slices through, and stirs the sand in a heavy pot by means of several revolving rollers and knives.

(*b*) For screening the sand before mixing moulding materials, shaker, rotary and vibratory screens are used so as to remove large lumps of clay, pebbles, metal particles and other foreign matter as these may spoil the casting.

(*c*) For removing metal particles, magnetic separators are used.

(*d*) For aerating to separate sand grains after mixing by muller, aerators of various design are used. This operation of aeration is also called '*fluffing*'.

QUESTIONS

1. What are the basic requirements of a proper moulding sand?
2. Name the various additives used in moulding sand and describe how they affect the properties.
3. (*a*) Give why sand testing is important?

   (*b*) Explain the various tests required to determine the suitability, for steel castings, of sand obtained from :

   (*i*) a river bed (*ii*) a quarry
4. What do you know by water absorption capacity of sand? Give its main applications.
5. Explain the importance of mulling and explain how it affects the properties of a moulding sand.
6. Describe a systematic procedure which is followed in a sand conditioning installation.
7. Explain how green strength and permeability of sands are affected by

   (*i*) Grain shape (*ii*) Grain size.

   (*iii*) Grain distribution
8. What are the basic requirements of a core sand? How it differs from the moulding sand?

7

Core Making

Core Sands

Core is defined as that portion of the mould which forms the hollow interior of the casting or hole through the casting. The core means the mass of dry sand which is prepared separately, baked in an oven and then placed in the mould.

Characteristics of Cores and Core Sands. (*i*) The core should have sufficient strength and hardness in both green and dry states so that it may be able to support its own weight and with stand force of molten metal.

(*ii*) The core should be permeable to allow the escape of core gases.

(*iii*) The core should be able to withstand the high temperatures of the molten metal.

(*iv*) The core sand should produce minimum amount of gas when in contact with molten metal. Thus, very high permeability will not be needed. Consequently, greater will be imparted to the core.

(*v*) After the metal solidifies, the core should distintegrate and collapse, otherwise difficulty may be experienced in removing from the casting.

(*vi*) Core sand should be able to give smoothness and finish to the core surface.

Core Material or Ingredients of Core Sands

(*i*) Granular refractories

(*ii*) Binders (self-made and Patented)

(*iii*) Special additives

(*iv*) Moisture

Granular Refractories. They are silica sand (clean, pure and dry)

Zircon
Olivin
Carbon

Table 7.1: Important Properties of Granular Refractories used for Core Sands

Property	*Silica*	*Zircon*	*Olivin*	*Carbon*	*Chamote*
Density (kg/m^3)	1650	2700	1950	1050	1500
Specific heat	2.65	4.6–4.7	3.25–3.4	–	2.5–2.7
Melting point (°C)	1700	1900–2550	1750–1900	3550	1700–1750
Thermal expansion to 95°C mm/mm	0.020	0.005	0.015	0.008	0.007

Silica is the most widely used core base sand. For higher heat resistance and bulk density, zircon and olivin is sometimes prefered to silica sand for core making. In steel foundry, coarse white silica sand is used. In cast iron and non-ferrous foundries, finer river bank and lake sand is prepared.

Table 7.2: Chart Showing Types of Core Binders, Their Properties and Uses

- Organic binders
  - (1) Core oil (0.5–3% by weight) gives backed strength.
    - Vegetable (Lin seed oil)
    - Marine animal (Whale oil)
  - (2) Cereal binders (0.5–2% by weight gives green compression 0.07–0.16 kg/cm^2)
- Inorganic binders
- Others

Gelatinized starch (contains starch and glutin. Made by wet milling)

Gelatinized corn flour (Made by dry milling)

— (3) Water soluble binders

- Dextrin made from starch
- Molasses — Air hardens rapidly. Resists core sagging during handling. Increase in moisture gives higher tensile strength and edge hardness.

(4) Wood product binders

- Natural resins (Resin, thermoplastic
- Sulphite binders (contain resins water soluble. By-product of paper industry. Used upto 1.5% in green and dry sand cores. Mixed in pitch for large dry sand cores.
- Water soluble gums, resins and organic chemicals produced by steam explosion process.

— (5) Pitch (A coal tar produced. Added upto 3% or more as ground powder. Develops hot strength. May be used along with clay and sulphite binder.

— (6) Wood flour (It is ground hardwood cellulose. Added 1% or less for increasing flowability of sand collapsibility of cores and decreasing veining.

— (7) Protein binders (Hardens by baking)

- Casein
- Glue

— (8) Synthetic resins

- Urea formaldehyde
- Phenol formaldehyde

(Thermosetting. Available as dry powder of liquid. Harden quickly by baking 0.2% kerosene added to prevent sticking.)

Inorganic Binders

- Fire clay
- Bentonite
- Silica flour
- Iron oxide

These have been discussed under "*Mould Sand Binders*". They develop green strength, baked strength, and hot strength and give smooth surface finish. With these, more oil is required to be mixed.

Other Binders

- Portland cement (Hardens at room temperature.)
- Rubber cement (Hardens at room temperature.)
- Sodium silicate (Hardens as CO_2 gas is passed through it)
- Water (Varies between 2.5–7%. Binders and additives work only in its presence. Optimum quantity develops good green strength, edge hardness, scratch hardness and goods tensile strength after baking.

Patended Binders

- Foseco Products
  - Carsil (CO_2 binder)
  - Pertela (core oil)
  - Vitel (Air setting core binder)
- IVP products
  - IVO COL (Increases collapsibility)
  - IVATIN oils (Baking core oil)
  - IVCOSIL (CO_2 binder)
  - IVA-REZ (Synthetic resin)

Core Binders. For preparing cores, pure sand is used. Core sand has no natural bond. Hence some other materials are added to the sand to act as binders which cement the sand grains into desired shape and impart sufficient strength to cores to prevent breakage, distorition or erosion during core making, moulding and casting.

Various commercial binders available in the market mainly consist of oils, resins, sulphite, liquor, molasses and proteins. Generally, core oils are used as they are very economical and produce better cores. Core oils mainly contain vegetable oil like linseed oil or corn oil. Specially processed mineral oils are sometimes mixed for specific properties.

Rasin and pitch are thermoplastic binders. Their action depends on the heat to liquify and disperse them in sand. The powdered binder is mixed with core sand. On heating, the binder liquifies and coats the sand grains. On cooling, the dispersed liquid binds the sand grains together forming a united mass. Rosin which is a form of resin; is obtained by distillation and extracton from pine wood. By-products in petroleum and coal tar industries *viz.*, petroleum and coal tar resins are also used as binders. Use of synthetic resins is limited as they are costly. Addition of resin to core oil speeds up drying of core and reduces the volume of core gas. Pitch compounded with dextrine and steam coal is used for large cores.

Phenol and urea-formaldehyde thermosetting plastic core binders are becoming common due to their high strength, low gas formation, collapsibility and resistance to moisture absorption.

Molasses adds hardness to the core but lacks in strength. On the core molasses water may also be sprayed.

Table 7.3: Some Common Core Sand Mixtures

Purpose	*For C.I. cylinders*	*For brass and bronze castings*	*For aluminium castings*	*For small and medium size steel castings*
Sand	500 kg	500 kg	50 kg	500 kg
Core oil	45 litres	4.5 litres	1 litres	–
Cereal	2 litres	–	–	–
Casein	3–4 litres	–	–	–
Dextrine	–	–	–	4 + 5 kg
Bentonite	–	–	–	3 + 4 kg
Rosin	–	–	–	25 kg
Silica flour	–	–	–	35 kg

Table 7.4: Core Sand Mixtures

Purpose	*General purpose*	*Light grey C.I.*	*Large grey C.I.*	*Malleable ion castings*
Silica	100 kg (medium)	113 parts (AFS-56)	100 kg	
Starch	1.5 kg	–		
Core oil	1.5 kg	2 parts		1 part
Water	2.5 kg	–	4.5–5.5%	4.2%
Burnt core	–	–	360 kg (AFS–45)	
Bentonite	–	–	1.5 kg	
Pitch	–	–	2.5 kg	
Lake Sand	–	–	–	20 parts
Bank sand	–	–	–	75 parts (AFS–99)
Cereal	–	–	–	2.5 parts
Properties				
Permeability	200 cc/min	–	–	44 cc/min
Green compression	17 kg/cm^2	–	–	0.08 kg/cm^2
Dry compression	70 kg/cm^2	–	–	–
Dry tensile strength	17 kg/cm^2	–	–	–
Baked strength	–	–	–	5.5 kg/cm^2

Where easily collapsible cores are required, protein binders *viz.*, gelatin, glue, casein etc., are used.

Where high strength, hardness, quick drying and high temperature resistance is required, sulphite liquor obtained from paper and pulp industries in the form of concentrated liquid is used.

A typical oil sand mixture contains :

Silica sand 75 parts, core oil 1 part.

Core oil is composed of linseed oil 50 to 60%, resin 25% and remaining mineral oil.

Oil sands have become most common due to the following reasons :

(*i*) They are more collapsible than a clay-bounded loam core.

(*ii*) The baked cores are very hard and not easily damaged in handling or closing of mould.

(*iii*) The green and dry strengths of oil sand can be controlled by varying proportions of dextrine and oil.

(*iv*) They are easy to use for core making.

Except for very small cores, every core is internally reinforced with core wires or core rods for medium cores, and with cast-iron or fabricated steel devices known as core grids or arborbs for large cores. Reinforcement is required for the following reasons :

(*i*) To help the core retain its shape while it is damp (green compressive strength of core sand is very low–350 to 1000 gm/cm^2).

(*ii*) To provide internal hooks or staples by which the core can be lifted safely to a drying plate, and after drying lowered accurately into the mould.

(*iii*) To strengthen the core so that it withstands the tendency of the fluid metal to break and lift it during casting.

Core Coatings, Core Dressings, Core Washes, or Blackings. These are used like mould coatings. These may be applied by dusting (if in the form of solid powder), by dipping, spraying or brushing (if in the form of liquid).

Types of Cores

The cores used in foundries are classified according to their shape and position in the mould as under :

(*i*) *Horizontal core.* It is the most common type.

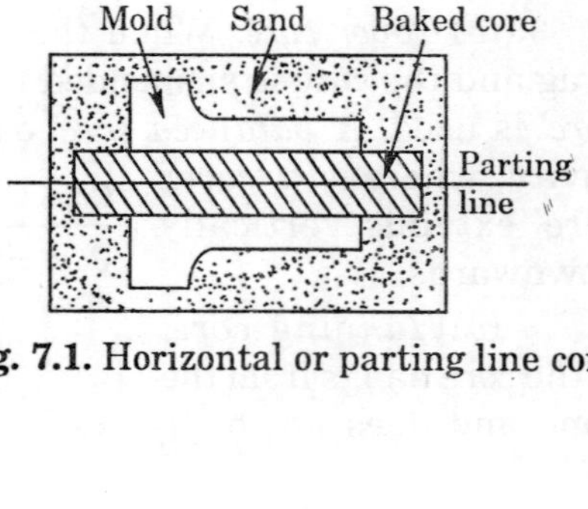

Fig. 7.1. Horizontal or parting line core.

It is usually in a cylindrical form laid in the mould horizontally. The ends of the core rest in the seats provided by the core prints on the pattern.

(*ii*) *Vertical core.* The core, when required to be placed along a vertical axis in the mould is known as '*vertical core*'. The upper end of the core is forced in the cope and the lower end in drag.

Horizontal and vertical cores are used in foundry work more frequently than cores of any other shape. These cores are, therefore, generally maintained in stock in various diameters and lengths and referred to as '*stock cores*'.

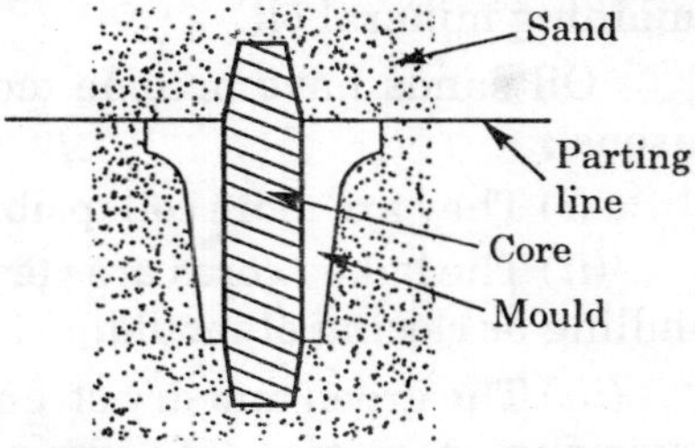

Fig. 7.2. Vertical or cope and drag core.

(*iii*) *Balanced core.* When the casting has opening only on one side and only one core print is available on the pattern, a '*balanced core*' is used. In such cases, the core print should be sufficiently large to support the weight of the core which extends into the mould cavity and it should be able to withstand the force of buoyancy of the molten metal which surrounds it. For supporting the core in the mould cavity, chaplets are often used.

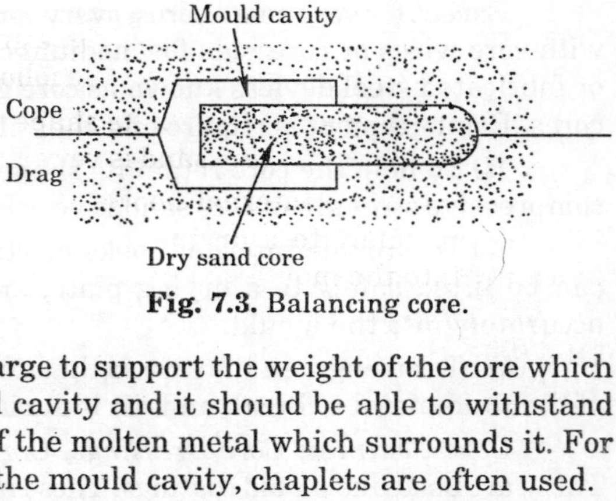

Fig. 7.3. Balancing core.

The chaplets are small pieces of metal, specially shaped to suit the cavity. Chaplets should be of the same metal as the casting because they finally go into it.

(*iv*) *Cover core.* When the entire pattern is rammed in the drag and the core is suspended from the top of the mould, a '*cover core*' is used. A '*balanced core*' extends horizontally in the mould cavity, whereas a '*cover core*' extends vertically downwards.

(*v*) *Hanging core.* If the core hangs from the cope and does not have

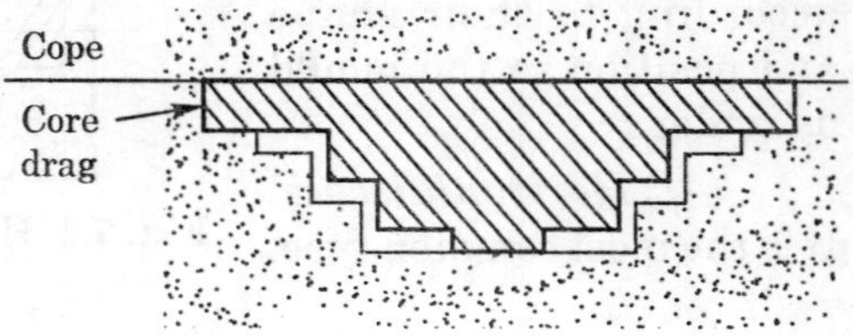

Fig. 7.4. Cover core.

any support at the bottom in the drag, it is referred to as *'Hanging core'*. In such cases, it may be necessary to fasten the core with a wire or rod extending through the cope.

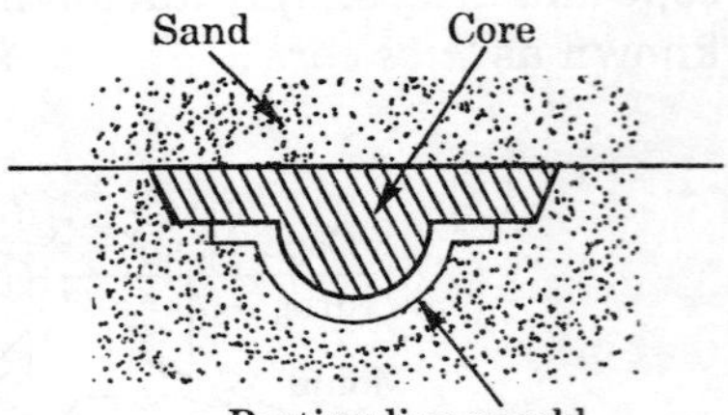

Fig. 7.4. (*a*) Hanging core.

(*vi*) *Wing core or stop off core.* It is used (*a*) When a hole or recess is to be obtained in the casting either above or below the parting line.

(*b*) When it is not possible to place the pattern in the mould such that the recess can be cored directly or with the above mentioned cores.

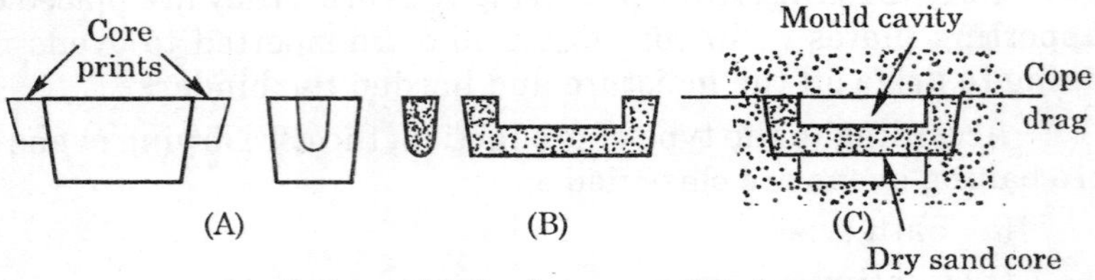

A —Pattern with the drop core prints for a hole above or below the parting surface.
B —Dry sand core.
C —Completed mould with dry sand core.
D —Stop off core.

Fig. 7.5. Wing or Drop Core.

The same core at times is also called *'tail core'*, *'chair core'*, *'sandle core'* etc. According to its shape and position in the mould.

(*vii*) *Ram up core.* Sometimes the core is set in the mould with the pattern before ramming it. Such a core is known as *'Ram up core'*. It is used (*a*) When cored detail is located in an inaccessible position. (*b*) For both interior and exterior portion of a casting.

(*viii*) *Kiss core.* When the pattern is not provided with core prints and no seat is available for the core to rest, the core is held in position between the

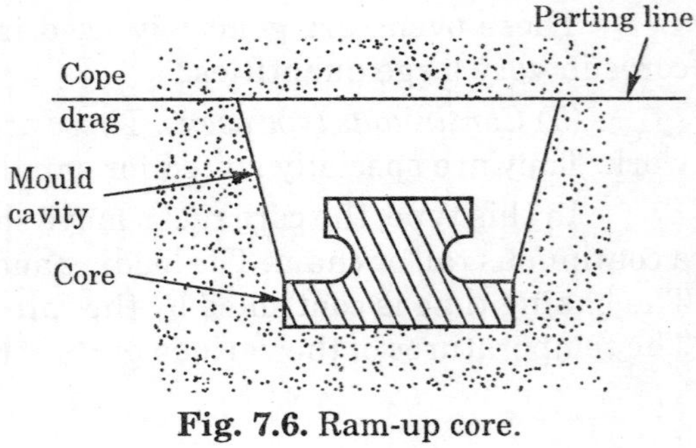

Fig. 7.6. Ram-up core.

cope and drag simply due to the pressure of the cope. Such a core is known as '*kiss core*'.

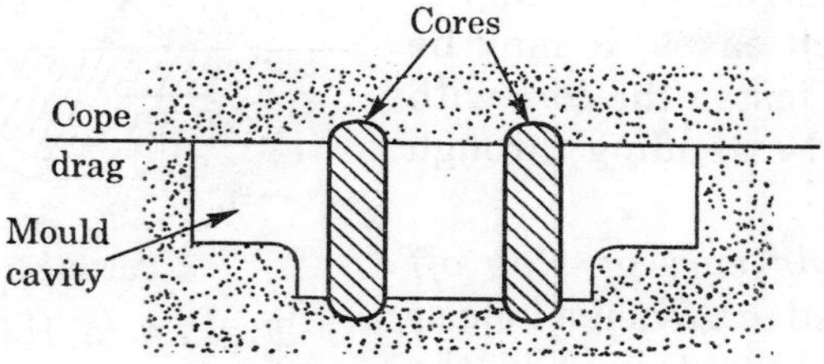

Fig. 7.7. Kiss core.

These cores are used when a number of holes are required in the casting and where dimensional accuracy with regard to the relative location of the holes is not important.

Core Drying. After preparing the cores, they are placed on supporting plates or in core driers and transported to ovens for baking to drive off the moisture and harden the binder.

According to the type of production, the core drying ovens or core baking ovens are classified as

(*a*) Bath type.

(*b*) Continuous type.

(*c*) Dielectrically heated type.

(*a*) *Batch type ovens.* These make use of portable racks. The racks loaded with cores are transported by lift trucks or monorail conveyors to the oven. Large cores are moved directly into the oven by rail. The racks are admitted into the oven either through two doors which swing open on hinges or through a single sliding door of counter-balanced type.

These ovens may also be '*drawer type*', in which the cores are placed in a number of sliding drawers. These drawers are operated by an overheated puller so that any one drawer or all at a time can be opened are closed.

These ovens are generally used in foundries not requiring cores in very large quantities.

(*b*) *Continuous type ovens.* These are used for high production work. They are specially suited for small cores.

In this type, the core racks move slowly through the oven on a continuous rail or chain. The loading and unloading is continuous. The baking time is controlled by the rate or travel of the conveyor. The temperatures of the various parts of the oven and the conveyor

speed are co-ordinated in such a way that the core comes out from the oven not only backed but also cooled. In some of the designs, for saving the floor space, the cores move vertically upwards through the oven and get baked. They get cooled on their return trip downwards.

Core drying ovens are heated by coal, coke, oil, gas or electricity depending on their availability, cost and the quality of core required. The temperature for baking depends on the type of binder, core size and backing time. The ovens are generally air circulated so as to distribute the heat uniformly all over and carry away the air saturated with moisture from the cores.

(c) *Dielectrically heated ovens.* These are modern core ovens employed for high quality cores using plastic binders.

The cores to be heated dielectrically are placed between the parallel plates or electrodes and a very high frequency current is passed. This high frequency current tends to deform the sand molecules. The sand molecules resist the deformation and required heating effect is produced.

In core ovens, adequate temperature control is necessary for maintaining the most effective temperature.

Testing of Core Sand

Core sand mixtures posses low green strength as compared to mould sand mixtures and use vertically acting compression testing machine. Green compressive strength of core sand varies between 0.035 to 0.105 kg/cm^2.

Green strength test. For testing green strength in tension, compression, shear and bending and permeability of core sands, same methods and equipments are used as in mould sand testing.

Hot strength test. Before testing, cores are baked. Hot strength of core sand is tested in the same manner as that of mould sand by using dilatometer.

Retained strength test. Core sand which exhibits lower retained compression strength is comparatively easier to disintegrate during shaking out.

Baked cylindrical specimen of standard core sand is heated to above 540°C and held at that temperature for 10–12 minutes approximately and allowed to cool down to room temperature. Then, cooled specimen is put to test for its copressive strength. If compression is more than 0.7 kg/cm^2, shaking out will be difficult.

Core hardness test. For testing green core hardness, the mould hardness tester with a larger indenter loaded having a light spring is used ; because green strength of core sand is lower than that of the mould sand.

For testing baked core hardness, the tester uses a knife-edge indenter, which is spring loaded and scratches the surface of the core. By drawing the tester slowly over a flat laked core surface hardness can be read directly from the tester dial.

Moisture content test. Some ingredients of core oils being volatile, evaporate at the evaporation temperature of the moisture. Hence, estimating moisture content by normal heating is difficult. Moisture content of core sand can however be determined by reacting the moisture of core sand with calcium carbide as already discussed under mould sand.

Gating Systems

All the passage ways through which the metal enters the mould cavity is known as *'Gating System'*. A pouring basin, sprue, runner, strainer core, gates etc., are included in *'Gating System'*.

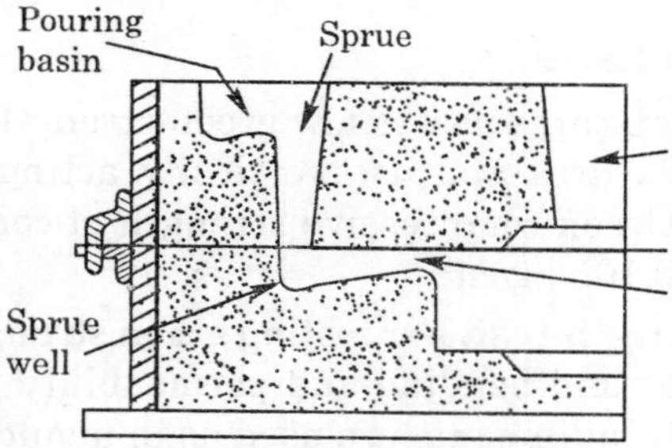

Fig. 7.8. Parts of gating system.

The main requisites of a gating system :

(*i*) The metal should flow through the gating system with minimum turbulence and aspiration of mould gases. Excessive turbulence causes aspiration of air and formation of dross.

(*ii*) The metal should be introduced in the cavity of the mould is such a way that a temperature gradient established on the mould surfaces and within the metal help the directional solidification towards the riser.

(*iii*) The cavity of the mould should be completely filled with molten metal in the shortest possible time.

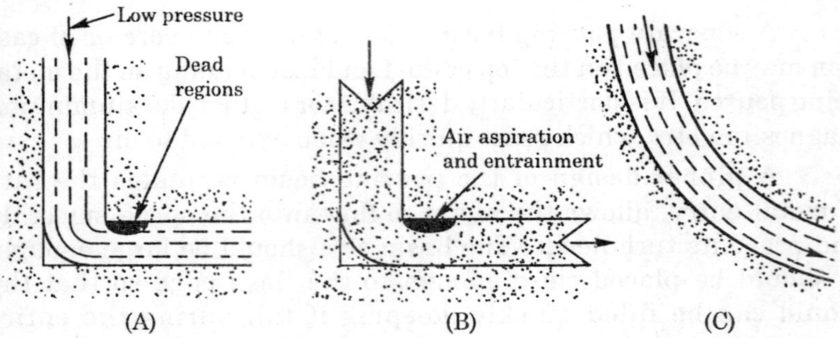

A, B—Turbulence and metal damage due to sharp corners.
C—Smooth metal flow due to streamlining of the corner.

Fig. 7.9. Metal flow in gating system.

(*iv*) The casting should be possible with minimum of metal in gates and risers.

(*v*) As the metal flows through the gating system, loose sand, oxides and slag should be prevented from entering the cavity of the mould by providing a proper skimming action.

(*vi*) The design of the gating system should be such that the entering of metal into the cavity of the mould is regulated properly.

(*vii*) The corrosion of the mould walls should be prevented.

Nowadays, the foundries usually design and test their gating system on one or more pilot castings. Then they mount the gates and turners directly on the pattern. The producing castings conforming to the desired specifications, the gating system should be designed carefully for better output and low rejects.

Pouring Basin. It is a tunnel-shaped opening made at the top of the sprue in the cope. The molten metal is brought from the furnace in the ladle and poured into pouring basin.

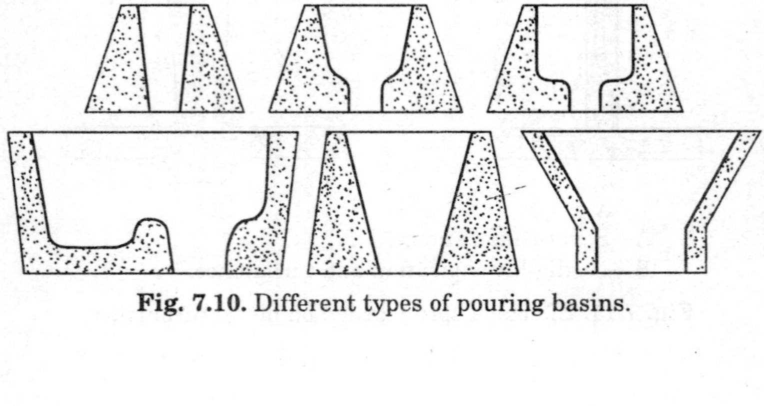

Fig. 7.10. Different types of pouring basins.

A separate pouring basin made of dry sand core or of cast iron may be placed on the top of the mould, depending on the metal being poured. It is particularly desirable for metals like aluminium, magnesium etc., which react quickly when exposed to air.

A proper design of the pouring basin regulates the rate of metal entry, allows the metal to flow into the sprue smoothly and prevents turbulence. The basin size should be large enough. It should be placed close enough to the flask edge so that the mould can be filled quickly, keeping it full during the entire pouring operation and keeping the ladle lip close to the pouring basin.

Sprue. It is the vertical passage passing through the cope and connecting the pouring basin to the runner or gate.

The sprue cross-section may be circular, square or rectangular. The size of the sprue usually varies from 10 mm square for small work below 12 kg poured weight to about 20 mm square for heavy castings. The size of the sprue should be chosen with the following considerations :

The sprue should be small enough so that

(*i*) it can be kept full during the entire pouring operation.

(*ii*) the metal may not enter the mould cavity with high velocity causing splatttering and sutbulence.

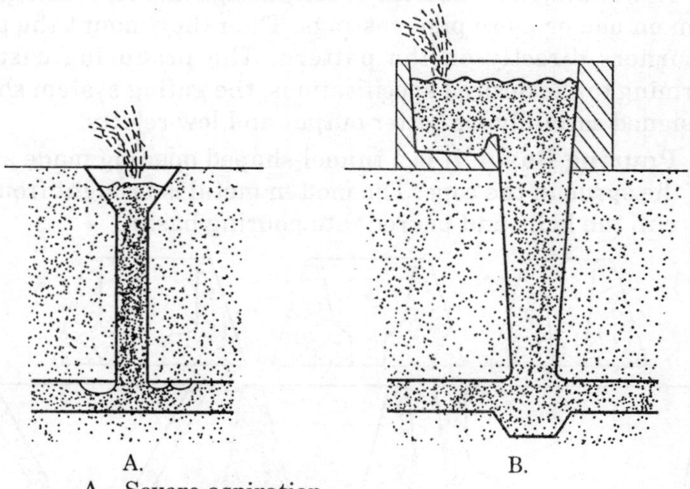

A. B.

A—Severe aspiration.

B—Negligible aspiration and turbulence.

Fig. 7.11. Effects of sprue design on metal turbulence.

Also the sprue should be large enough so that

(*i*) the mould cavity is filled completely without laps, seems or misruns.

(*ii*) a metal head is built up quickly to prevent mould gases from being aspirated into the metal.

If a single sprue is not sufficient for filling the large mould in the required time, two or more sprues and same number of ladles may be employed for pouring.

In order to avoid aspiration of air and metal damage, the sprues are generally tapered downward. If the cross-section of a sprue is uniform, severe aspiration occurs because as the metal descends the vertical sprue, its velocity increases. On the other hand, aspiration and turbulence are minimised if the sprue is tapered by an amount sufficient to assure that the metal lies firmly against the mould.

It is observed that there is severe apiration resulting turbulence in the metal, if the sprue is straight having sharp corners. On the other hand, aspiration is negligible with no turbulence, if the sprue is tapered, corners rounded, sprue-well used and dam type pouring basin made.

The base of sprue is usually made one and a half times wider and deeper than the runner. This deeper and widened cavity underneath the sprue is known as '*sprue well*'. It serves as a cushion to the falling weight of metal and absorbs its kinetic energy.

Runner. In case a mould contains more than one cavity, the common passage-way which supplies the metal to a number of cavities is called a '*runner*', and the branches from the runner to the respective mould cavities are known as '*ingates*'.

In large castings also, the molten metal is usually carried from the sprue base through a runner all round the periphery of the casting and distributed to several ingates for feeding to the main mould. The runner may be located either in the drag or in the cope depending on the shape of the casting, but it is generally preferred to have it in the drag.

In order to avoid aspiration and turbulence, the runner should be streamlined. The size of the runner is reduced in cross-section after each ingate by an amount equal to the ingate cross-section so as to obtain a flow of approximately equal metal volumes through each ingate.

Gates. The opening from the runner to the mould cavity is called *'gate'*. The size and location of gates is so arranged that (*i*) the moulds may be filled in quickly, (*ii*) cutting of the mould surfaces by the flowing metal is minimum, (*iii*) the cracks do not develop when the metal cools, (*iv*) they can be removed readily with out damaging the castings.

Gates are broadly classified according to the position in which they are located in the mould cavity :

(*i*) Top gates

(*ii*) Parting gates

(*iii*) Bottom gates

(*i*) **Top Gates.** In top gating, the molten metal is poured down the head or riser of the casting. The mould should be hard and strong enough to resist erosion by the dropping metal.

Advantages of Top Gating

(*a*) All the metal enters the casting at the top and so, the hottest metal remains at the top of the casting. Hence proper temperature gradients are formed and directional solidification towards the riser located on the top of the casting is achieved.

(*b*) The top gates themselves may be made serve as risers.

Precautions in Top Gatting

(*a*) To prevent loose sand and dross from entering the mould cavity and to allow the metal to fall in a small stream, a large size pouring basin is provided on the top of the sprue-cum-riser.

(*b*) For still better result, a strainer core is fitted in the pouring basin.

In case of light castings, wedge shaped gates referred to as *'wedge gates'* are provided. The finger gate is a modified form of wedge gate in which also the metal is allowed to reach in a number of streams.

For massive iron castings, where minimum weight of head is desired and also slag is to be checked from entering into the mould, *'pencil gates'* are used. *'Ring gate'* used a core, which breaks the dropping of the molten metal and at the same time retains the slag.

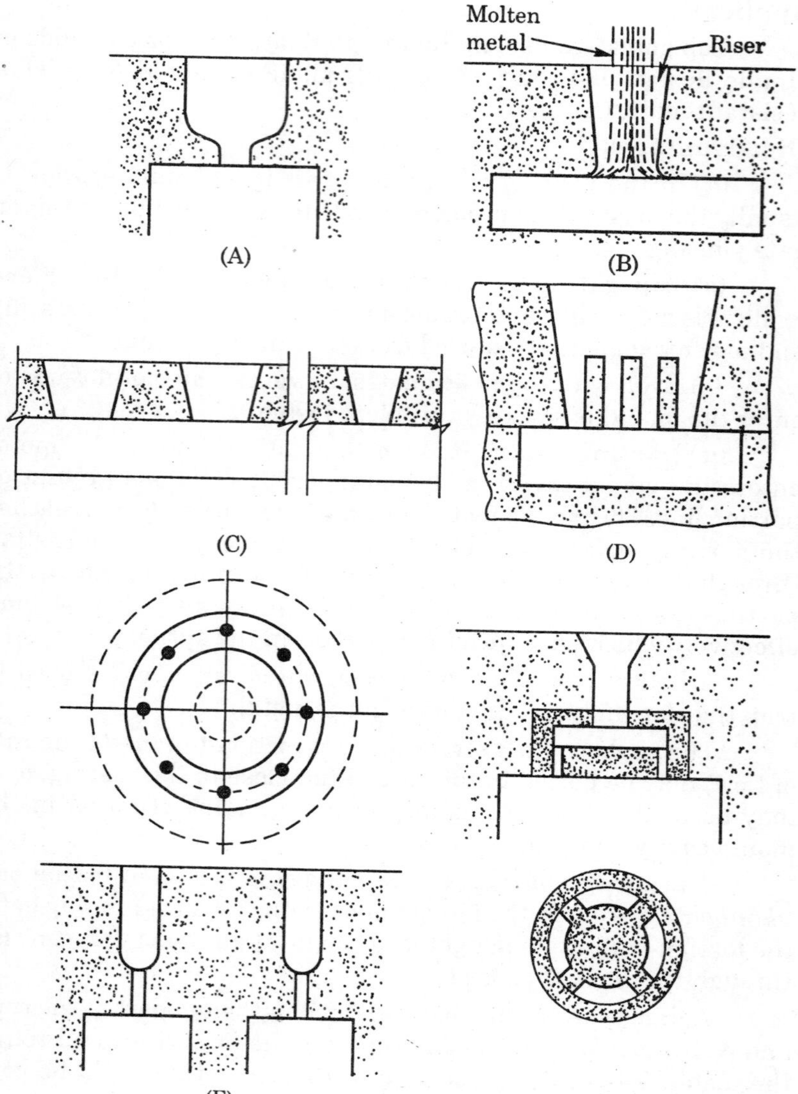

A–Top gate with pouring basin.
B–Top run gate.
C–Wedge gate.
D–Finger gate.
E–Pencil gate.
F–Ring gate.

Fig. 7.12. Types of top gates.

Application

Top gates are usually limited to relatively small moulds of simple design or to larger castings made in mould of erosion resistant material.

Disadvantages

(*a*) In the pouring of steel and cast iron, mould erosion is usually the most severe problem caused from the turbulence of top gate pouring.

(*b*) Top gating is not recommended for lighter, more oxidizable metals like aluminium and magnesium because drossing and air entrapment are caused from turbulent pourings.

(*c*) Even with top pencil gates, however, the metal tends to enter the mould is severely turbulent fashion.

(*ii*) **Parting line Gates.** In this gating system, the metal enters the mould cavity at the same level as the mould joint or parting line. The molten metal entering through the sprue, reaches the parting surface. Hence the sprue is connected to the casting through the gate in a horizontal direction. By providing gate at the parting line, *devices* can be used to trap any slag, dirt or sand effectively which pass with the metal down the sprue.

A hollow recess in the cope known as '*skimbob*' is used to trap the slag and foreign matter in the metal.

The choke, which serves as a restriction to control the rate of flow, may be placed in the gate either close to the casting, or it may be further away so as to prevent squirting of metal in the mould cavity and sand erosion.

The purpose of using a '*skimming gate*' is similar to that of a '*skimbob*' *e.g.*, to trap the foreign matter. In case of skimming gate, the foreign matter being lighter in weight than the metal, can rise through the vertical passage.

A dam type pouring basin formed in the top part of the cope and a strainer core are used to separate the impurities and refine the metal. When using a strainer core, the metal should be very fluid.

A '*shrink bob*' may be provided, if there is a tendency for shrinkage defect to occur near the ingate.

A dry sand core is sometimes used at the bottom of the sprue so as to prevent the sand from getting washed away.

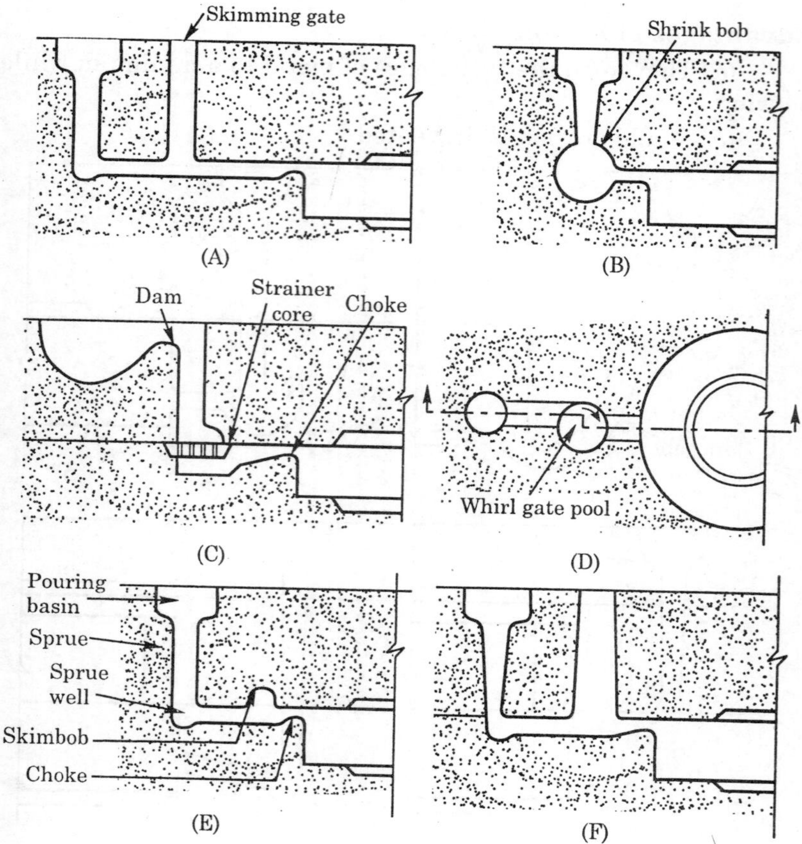

A–Skimming gate.
B–Parting gate with shrink bob.
C–Parting gate with dam type pouring basin.
E–Parting gate with skim bob.
F–Whirlpool gate.

Fig. 7.13. Types of parting gates.

Another effective device to trap, the slag etc., is to use a '*skimming gate with a whirlpool runner*'. Due to whirlpool action the slag comes to the centre from where it rises up in the skimming gate.

(*iii*) **Bottom Gates.** In this gating system, the molten metal flows down the bottom of the mould cavity in the drag and enters at the bottom of the casting. The metal is allowed to rise gently in the mould and around the cores.

Bottom gates are usually employed for large sized steel castings.

Advantages of Bottom Gates

(*a*) They keep the turbulence of metal to a minimum while pouring.

(*b*) Mould erosion is prevented.

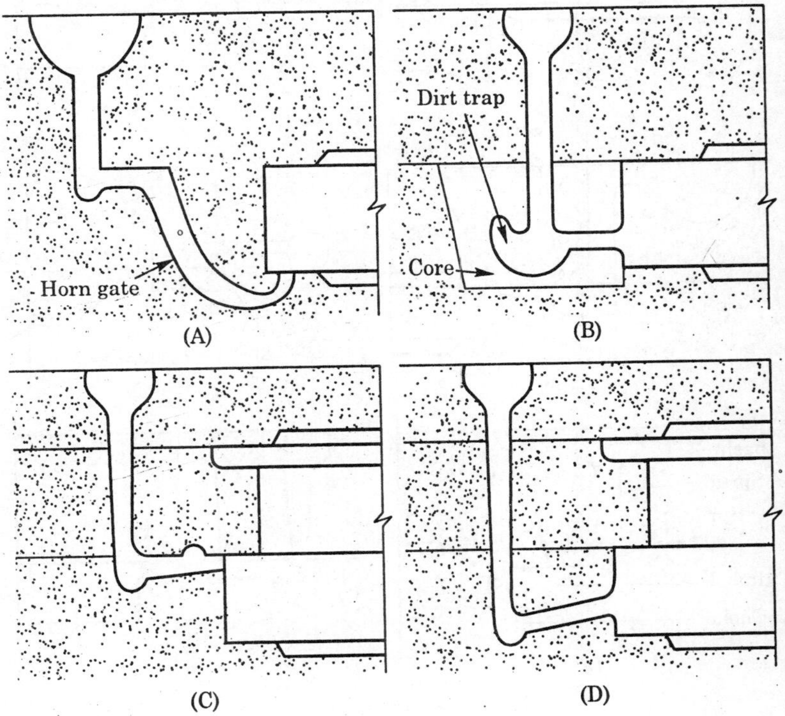

A–Horn gate.
B–Bottom gate with a dry sand core.
C–Bottom gate with skimbob and choke.
D–Bottom gate with draw-in runner.

Fig. 7.14. Types of Bottom Gates.

Disadvantages of Bottom Gates

(*a*) As the metal rises in the mould cavity, it continues to loose its heat and by the time it reaches the riser, it becomes much cooler. Thus, directional solidification is difficult to achieve.

(*b*) It is difficult to place the riser near the gate entrance where the metal is hottest, the place being referred to as '*hot spot*'.

Four Types of Bottom Gates are used

(*a*) *Horn type Bottom Gate* enables the mould to be made in two boxes only and thus the necessity of check, *i.e.*, the middle

flask is eliminated. The pattern for forming this gate is rammed in the drag and later drawn out by turning it out of the sand.

(*b*) *Bottom Gate using a dry sand core* at the bottom end of the sprue or down-gate. The passage through the dry sand core is curved at the bottom end to form a dirt-trap for slag, dirt etc.

It also enables the mould to be made in two boxes.

(*c*) *Bottom Gate with a skimbob* as in case of parting line gate along with a choke near the gate entrance is used to prepare the mould in three boxes.

(*d*) *Bottom Gate with draw-in type of runner gate* is also used to prepare the mould in three boxes. The taper in the gate is sloping towards the sprue. Thus, the pattern for the gate is also drawn into the mould cavity after the pattern for the casting has been drawn.

The gate is generally placed tangential on the mould cavity to impart a spinning and whirling action to the incoming metal. It tends to move the slag and scum to the centre from where it may ascend into the riser.

Gating Ratio. It is a term used to describe the relative cross-sectional areas of the components of a gating system.

Gating ratio is defined as the ratio of sprue area to total runner area to total gate area. For example, a gating system having a sprue of 6 sq cm cross-section runner of 18 sq cm cross-section and 4 gates, each of 4,5 sq cm cross-section will have a gating ratio of 1 : 3 : 3.

The gating ratios are classified as :

(*a*) *Pressurized system.* In this system, the proportions of sprue, runner and gate cross-sectional areas are so arranged that back pressure is maintained on the gating system by a fluid film restriction at the gates. The gating ratios like 1 : 2 : 1 or 4 : 3 : 2 produce a pressurized system, *i.e.*, the total gate area is not greater than the area of the sprue. This system is adopted for metals like steel, iron, brass etc.

Advantages of pressurized gating system. (*i*) Gating system is kept full of metal. The back pressure due to restriction at the gates tends to minimize danger of the metal pulling away from the mould walls with consequent air aspiration. If back pressure is sufficient, even untapered sprues may be kept full of metal.

(*ii*) When multiple gates are used, flow from each of the gates (if the gates are of equal area) is about equal.

(*iii*) Pressurized systems are generally smaller in volume for a given metal flow rate than unpressurized one. Thus, less metal is left in the gating system and casting yield is higher.

Disadvantages of pressurized gating system. (*i*) Severe turbulence may occur at junctions and corners unless careful streamlining is employed.

(*ii*) High velocities, with which the metal enters the mould cavity may result in additional severe turbulence there with consequent entrapment, dross formation and mould erosion.

Present foundry practice favours the use of mildly pressurized systems for ferrous metals, especially for cast iron. Brasses and bronzes are gated with either pressurized or unpressurized systems, depending on the individual shop and the alloy poured.

(*b*) *Unpressurized system*. In this system, the primary restriction to the fluid is at or very near to the sprue. The gating ratios like 1 : 3 : 3, 1 : 2 : 2 will produce an unpressurized system.

The system is adopted for light, oxidizable metals like aluminium and magnesium where the turbulence is to be minimised by slowing down the rate of metal flow.

Advantages of Unpressurized Gating Systems. (*i*) Lower metal velocity as compared with pressurized systems.

(*ii*) Large cross-sectional area of the runner and gates permits adequate flow rates at relatively low velocities, thus reducing (*a*) the turbulence in the gating system and (*b*) sprueing of the metal into the mould cavity.

Disadvantages of Unpressurized Gating Systems.

(*i*) Careful design is required to ensure that unpressurized systems are kept filled during pouring. Drag runners and cope gates aid in maintaining a full runner, but careful streamlining is essential to eliminate the separation effects and consequent air aspiration.

Tapered sprues with sprue wells are often employed. Streamlining of the junction between runner and gates is also recommended, with reduction in runner size at each gate.

(*ii*) To obtain equal flow multiple gates in unpressurized systems is difficult. To obtain uniform flow through all gates, careful design, including reduction of runner size after each gate, can be used.

(*iii*) Unpressurized systems require large runners and gates. Thus, casting yield somewhat reduced.

Elimination of slag and dross. Even the most carefully designed gating systems may have slag, dross, or air entrapped in the metal flowing through it for one or another reason. These foreign materials can originate in (*i*) the melting furnace or (*ii*) the ladle and be carried into the gating system. (*iii*) they can arise from faulty pouring ; or (*iv*) they can be produced in the gating system itself.

To prevent foreign materials in the flowing stream from reaching the casting, various steps taken to clean the metal as it passes through the runner system are :

(*i*) *By providing runner extension.* The first metal through a runner system is likely to be damaged by initial turbulence. Thus, the purpose of runner extension is to prevent this metal from reaching the mould cavity.

(*ii*) *By placing the runner in the cope and gates in the drag.* In this arrangement, foreign materials float to the surface of the flowing stream in the cope runner, while clean metal is tapped off the bottom of the runner to the castings.

Cope runners and drag gates are effective metal cleaners for metals (*a*) where dross (or slag) floats easily to the surface and (*b*) where a pressurized gating system is used.

Application. This type of system is most widely used for ferrous metals and some copper-base alloys. It is not much used for light metals where dross does not readily float out and where pressurized systems are usually undesirable.

(*iii*) For complete metal cleaning, *screens are added to the runner system e.g.,* perforated tin-plated sheet is used for this purpose. Such screens may be inserted in gating systems at the sprue base, in the runner or gates, or at the juncture between runner and gates.

(*iv*) *Strainer cores (disc-shaped sand and ceramic cores with small holes) are sometimes used* in place of metal screens, especially for metals other than aluminium and magnesium.

Solidification of Pure Metals

When pure metals, or nearly pure metal like low-carbon steels, solidify in a mould cavity, they do so by forming a solid skin which progresses inward until the entire casting is solid.

The process actually is quite continuous. As the casting solidifies, a '*pipe*' is formed primarily from solidification shrinkage. If billet walls are parallel, an elongated pipe may spread to the bottom ; this low-density area is called '*centre-line shrinkage*'.

The problem of risering is basically one of making solidification *'directional'*, so that all solidification shrinkage occurs in the riser, which is removed afterwards and remelted.

Rate of Solidification of Castings

Freezing rate has an important bearing on (*i*) the ability to eliminate solidification shrinkage in a casting *i.e.,* to produce directional solidification.

(*ii*) Such metallurgical factors as segregation and grain size.

In a sand mould, the rate at which a casting freezes is determined primarily by the ability of the mould to accept heat from the casting. If molten metal is poured against a flat mould wall heated only to room temperature, heat will flow into the mould, and a solid layer of metal will be deposited at the mould-metal interface.

As heat continues to flow, the thickness of this layer will increase with time. Heat flows from the hot portions to the colder portions of the system according to the following relation :

$$\frac{q}{A} = -k\left(\frac{\partial T}{\partial x}\right)$$

where $\frac{q}{A}$ = Rate of heat flow per unit area in kcal/hr m^2.

k = Thermal conductivity in kcal/hr m°C.

$\frac{\partial T}{\partial x}$ = Thermal gradient in units of temperature T and distance x.

Boundary temperature between liquid and solid metal is the freezing point of the metal, and heat of solidification is being liberated at this boundary. Rate at which the boundary moves is determined by how rapidly heat of fusion is being removed.

Useful conclusions from analytical treatment of the transient heat-flow :

(*ii*) *Solidification Rate.* If metal freezes against a large (flat) mould wall, and heat flow is normal to the mould surface, the thickness x of solid metal deposited will be proportional to the square root of time t.

i.e., $$x = K_1\sqrt{t}$$

(*iii*) *Solidification Time.* If geometrically similar castings of different sizes are poured into the same mould material, the time for complete solidification will be proportional to the square of their linear dimensions.

For comparing castings of different shapes, this relationship has been generalised into the form known as '*Chvorinov Rule*':

$$\text{Time} = K_2\ (\text{Volume/Surface area})^2$$

This relationship is an excellent engineering approximation. In actual castings, the rate of solid skin formation is affected by the shape of the casting. The solid skin builds upon flat surfaces roughly as the square root of time, but solidification is more rapid at external angles because heat is more easily dissipated at these points. Conversely, at internal angles solidification is slower. Also, shape of casting results in directional solidification from the thinnest section toward the heavier sections.

Solidification of Alloys. Pure metals freeze by forming a solid skin which grows progressively inward. Only in extremely pure metals, however, is the interface between the solid skin and the liquid metal a smooth wall. When even small amounts of impurities or alloying elements are present, they tend to be rejected by the solidifying metal at the liquid-solid interface.

These elements lower the melting point of the liquid adjacent the freezing wall and tend to inhibit further solidification. Freezing then continues by dendrites reaching out into unaffected liquid. The liquid-solid interface becomes jagged and minute pine-tree like crystals protrude into the liquid. In nearly pure metals, the dendrites do not protrude far. It is only in the very late stages of solidification, that the dendrites reach across the remaining liquid and interlock.

Low-carbon steels freeze very much like pure metals. As carbon content steel is raised, mushy zone (region whose temperature lies between liquidus and solidus) becomes wider. In higher carbon steels, cast in sand, the dendrites may reach into the extreme centre of the casting before appreciable solid skin forms.

Width of the mushy zone of solidifying casting depends on the solidification range of the cast alloy. Alloys which freeze over a large temperature range tend to have a wide mushy zone. Solidification range of steels varies from about 22°C for a 0.05% carbon steel to about 72°C for a 0.6 carbon steel.

Cast steels tend to have relatively steep temperature gradients during solidification (compared to other cast alloys) because of their high freezing temperatures and low thermal conductivities. Thermal gradients may be made even steeper by chilling (casting against a metal mould wall).

Most foundry alloys other than steel freeze with mushy zones even wider than that of high-carbon steel. These alloys generally

freeze over a fairly wide temperature range, and freeze with flatter temperature gradients than do similar steel castings.

Some cast iron, aluminium, magnesium alloys, and most brasses and bronzes freeze in sand moulds without forming any appreciably solid skin *e.g.*, in aluminium alloys, central portions of a casting are often more than 90% solid before the surface is completely frozen.

Grain structure of cast metals. When a hot molten metal is poured into a cold mould, the initial rate of heat extraction is very high. Liquid metal near the mould wall surface is often cooled below its freezing point (undercooled), and many fine equiaxed dendrites form in this narrow surface zone, termed the chill zone.

After initial thermal shock, these dendrites oriented most favourably grow perpendicular to the mould wall forming elongated or columnar dendrites. Pure metals, or metals which freeze with a very narrow mushy zone may have only these two types of grains, *i.e.*, (*i*) chill and (*ii*) columnar.

Metals which freeze with a wider mushy zone tend to '*nucleate new grains*' during late stages of solidification, in the region where liquid and solid co-exist. These new grains are equiaxed and the region where they appear is termed the '*Equiaxed Zone*'. Medium carbon steel may show all three type of grain structure, *i.e.*, (*i*) chill (*ii*) columnar, and (*iii*) equiaxed.

In cast irons and most non-ferrous alloys, the mushy zone is sufficiently wide and a columnar zone is seldom observed. Rather, fine exquiaxed grains tend to form throughout the casting. Addition of grain refiners also tends to reduce any tendency for columnar grains to form.

Risering

A hole cut or moulded in the cope to permit the molten metal to rise above the highest point in the casting is referred to as a '*Riser*'.

The useful purposes of providing the riser :

(*i*) It enables the pourer to see the metal as it is filled in the mould cavity. If the metal does not appear in the riser, it indicates that either there is some obstruction to the metal flow between the sprue and riser of the metal is insufficient for the mould cavity to be filled.

(*ii*) It helps in easy ejection of the steam, gas and air from the mould cavity while filling the mould with the molten metal.

(*iii*) It also serves as a feeder to feed the molten metal into the main casting cavity to compensate for shrinkage.

(*iv*) Using several risers in case of casting with thin sections imparts greater soundness.

The main requisites of a riser are :

(*i*) The riser must cover completely the sectional thickness which requires feeding.

(*ii*) For effectiveness, the riser must be the last part of the casting to solidify.

(*iii*) The design of the riser should be such that it establishes temperature gradient within the casting so that the casting solidifies directionally towards the riser.

(*iv*) The fluidity of the molten metal should be properly maintained so that the metal may penetrate the portions of the mould cavity which solidify in the end.

Directional Solidification. The molten metal in the mould as it cools down, solidifies and contracts in volume. This metal contraction takes place in three stages :

(*i*) Liquid contraction,

(*ii*) Solidification, contraction

(*iii*) Solid contraction.

(*i*) *Liquid Contraction* occurs when the molten metal cools from the temperature at which it is poured to the temperature at which solidification just commences.

(*ii*) *Solidification Contraction* occurs when the change of state from liquid to solid takes place, *i.e.*, when the metal loses its latent heat.

(*iii*) *Solid Contraction* occurs when the solidified metals cools from the freezing temperatures to the room temperature.

Out of the above three contractions for risering purposes, the last one is compensated by the contraction allowance of the pattern maker. The first one, *i.e.*, liquid contraction is generally negligible. But the second one, *i.e.*, the solidification contraction is large enough and should be considered during designing and positioning of risers.

All the parts of casting do not cool at the same rate due to varying sections, varying rate of heat loss to adjoining mould walls etc. So, some parts tend to solidify quickly than others. It gives rise to voids and cavities in certain regions of the casting. Such voids are filled up with liquid metal from the portion of the casting which

is still liquid. Thus solidification should continue progressively from the thinnest section which solidifies first towards the risers which should be the last solidify. The casting will be sound, without voids or internal shrinkages, if the solidification occurs in the above fashion. This process is known as '*Directional Solidification*', which is aimed at for producing sound castings.

It may not always be easy to achieve directional solidification in actual casting practice due to the factors like method of casting used, the shape and design of the casting etc.

In general the following ways are adopted for controlling directional solidification :

(*a*) The gating system should be designed and positioned properly.

(*b*) The risers should be designed and positioned properly.

(*c*) The thickness of certain sections of the casting may be increased by the use of padding.

(*d*) Exothermic materials in the risers or in the facing sand around certain portions of the casting may be used.

(*e*) Chills in the moulds may be used.

Design and Positioning of Risers

(I) Shape and size of riser. The most efficient shape of a riser of a certain size is that which gives a minimum of the heat loss, remains hot and keeps the metal in molten state as long as possible. The condition is satisfied when the riser is spherical in shape so that its surface area is minimum.

For the same volume of the riser the next best shape is a cylinder and the third is a square. As moulding a spherical riser is practically difficult, the best shape to be employed for the general run of castings is a cylinder.

As regards the height of the riser, the same should be tall enough so that any pipe formed in it may not penetrate the casting. The ratio of height to diameter usually varies from 1 : 1 to 3 : 2.

As regards diameter of the riser, the same is largely a matter of experience. To find out suitable riser diameter for a given casting, the empirical formulae derived by (*i*) Chvorinov, (*ii*) Caine, are used :

(*a*) *Chvorinov's Rule*. It states that the freezing time of a casting, *i.e.*,

$$t = \frac{1}{q^2}\left(\frac{V}{A}\right)^2$$

where q = solidification constant, depending on the composition of cast metal and the positioning of the mould cavity, *viz.*, along a vertical or a horizontal axis.

$\frac{V}{A}$ = ratio of volume of the casting to it surface area.

Values of $\left(\frac{V}{A}\right)^2$ and freezing time have been found out by actual experiments for different metals and alloys and for different cylinder diameters and the same enlisted in the hand books of cast metals.

For finding out suitable riser diameter for a given casting, its $\left(\frac{V}{A}\right)^2$ ratio is computed. A riser whose $\left(\frac{V}{A}\right)^2$ is little larger (10–15% larger) than that of the casting is chosen.

(*b*) *Caine's Method.* This method of finding the size of riser is based on the relative freezing time of the casting and the riser. It defines the relative freezing time to complete solidification as the ratio of surface area of casting ÷ volume of the casting : surface area of riser ÷ volume of the riser.

According to Caine, (1) if the casting solidifies infinitely rapidly, the feeder (riser) volume should be equal to the solidification shrinkage of the casting, and (2) if the feeder and casting solidify at the same rate, the feeder should be infinitely large. From this it significant that hyperbolic relationship exists between the relative freezing time and relative volume.

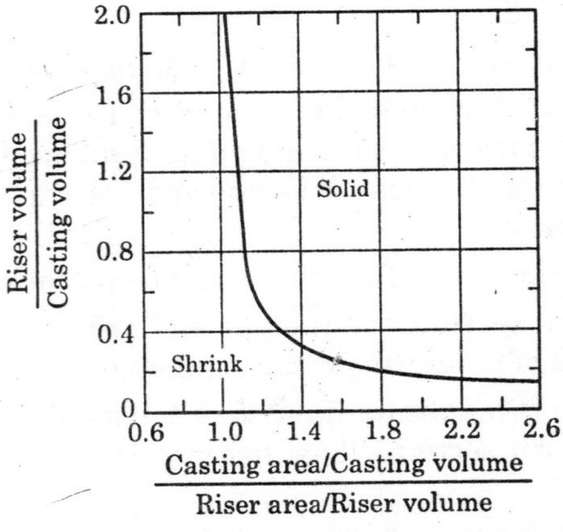

Fig. 7.15. Relative Riser and Casting Geometry for obtaining sound steel casting (After Caine).

Thus, relative freezing time X is given by

$$X = \frac{L}{Y - B} + C$$

where $$Y = \frac{\text{Volume of feeder}}{\text{Volume of casting}}$$

B = Relative contraction on freezing

L and C = Constants depending on the metal to be cast.

The values of the constants L and C, relative contraction B being given, and by assuming a certain value of riser diameter, X can be found out. Then, the values of X and Y are plotted on the graph. The curve known as '*Soundness Curve*' is drawn.

The value of riser size chosen above the soundness curve will be satisfactory and that below it will be unsatisfactory.

(II) Location of Riser. The riser should be loacted keeping in view

(*a*) the metal to be cast.

(*b*) design of the casting,

(*c*) feasibility of directional solidification.

The riser may be located either at the top or at the side of the casting.

For light metals, top risering is extensively used as it enables the benefit of the metallostratic pressure in the riser.

For most effective use, the number of risers has to be more than one. To minimise the shrinkage, their spacing should be carefully arranged.

In locating risers, it should be remembered that :

(*i*) Each casting should be carefully analysed for risering by a competent foundry engineer, and no compromise should be made with the requirements because location of risers influences quality and cost of castings.

(*ii*) Directional solidification must be maintained because :

(*a*) Heavy sections cannot be fed through thin sections without the use of insulating or heating pads.

(*b*) There is a definite limit to the distance a riser can feed even in a uniform section. This distance is often called '*Feeding Distance*'.

(*iii*) Gating through risers not only improves thermal gradients but also eliminates the need for cutting the gate and cleaning the entrance area.

(*iv*) Risers attached to flat open sections can be easily removed than those attached to curved sections.

(III) Type of Riser. Risers are classified as :

(*a*) Open Riser

(*b*) Blind Riser.

(*a*) **Open Riser.** In this, the upper surface is open to the atmosphere and is usually placed on the top of the castings or at the parting plane. The open riser seldom extends downwards into the drag, *i.e.*, below the parting plane. It drives the feeding pressure (1) from atmosphere, and (2) from force of gravity on the metal contained in the riser. As soon as the certain thickness of metal solidifies at the riser top, the atmospheric pressure becomes ineffective and the flow of metal from riser to the casting becomes difficult or stops.

(*b*) **Blind Riser.** It is surrounded by the moulding sand on all sides and is in the form of a rounded cavity in the metal placed at the side or top of the casting. It may be located either in the cope or in the drag.

In blind riser, the atmospheric pressure is completely kept out as this riser is closed from all sides. Due to the formation of vacuum in the blind riser, the pressure due to the force of gravity is also reduced.

In some improved blind risers, a permeable dry sand core is fitted at the top of the riser. Due to its permeable nature, atmospheric air is able to enter the riser and exert some pressure. The use of dry sand core reduces the chilling effect and slows down the solidifications of riser, thus making it more effective.

Artifical pressure is sometimes created to blind riser by putting some explosive substance in the cavity of riser. When the explosive comes in contact with the molten metal, it explodes and creates high pressure over the riser metal.

Use of Padding. If the directional solidification is not fully achieved with the method described above, padding is used.

Padding improves soundness of casting. When the casting is thinnest at points distant from the riser, freezing is complete in these regions first. Such sections are made gradually thicker toward

the riser so that freezing progress directionally, and each successive region to freeze is supplied with enough molten metal for feeding it properly.

The paddings consist of extra metal added to the original uniform section of the casting. The extra metal so added may be removed later on by machining or the casting can be designed with the tapered sections as integral, useful parts of the ultimate assembly.

Usually padding is an extreme expedient, as engineers do not like the added weight. However, in the long run, much is saved by making tapered designs the rule, especially for steel castings. Padding should be provided only after due consultation so as to determine how the casting is to be made, otherwise the taper may be placed in the wrong direction.

Use of Exothermic Riser Compounds. These days, the exothermic materials are used in risers for producing directional solidification by creating heat. They consist of oxides of metals like iron, chromium, nickel or copper and aluminium metal in powder form. Each cast metal requires exothermic material containing its own oxides.

It may be added to the surface of the molten metal in the riser just after pouring. Or, it may be added to the sand of riser walls. A chemical reaction takes place due to the contact with molten metal producing a large amount of heat. Thus, the metal in the riser gets superheated remaining molten for a longer time. Also it forms a refractory insulating top on the riser conserving the heat.

It may also be used as an insert in the mould at the desired position to help control directional solidification.

It may be moulded in the form of a core by mixing with water and baking it. Such exothermic core is inserted at the desired location. This core retains its shape after the reaction and provides heat insulation to the metal.

It may also be used by mixing it with facings and using this mixture around the desired portions of the casting.

Exothermic riser compounds not only prevent heat loss from the riser top, but also add some heat, and even add some molten metal to the riser. They are essentially mixtures of a metal oxide and aluminium. These, when placed on the metal in an open riser, the mixture react to give molten metal, heat and a slag insulator. With iron oxide and aluminium, the reaction is

$$4Fe_2O_3 + 8Al = 4Al_2O_3 + 8Fe + 2480°C \text{ heat}$$

Oxides of other metals, *e.g.*, copper, nickel, cobalt and manganese react similarly.

Use of exothermic riser compounds improves feeding efficiency by about 70%, and risers can be made about a third size of a normal riser. Short risers concentrate the heat at the casting-riser neck where it is needed to

(*i*) prolong feeding and

(*ii*) develop desirable thermal gradients in the casting.

Use of Insulation Pads and Sleeves for Risers. Plaster of Paris is an excellent insulator for non-ferrous castings made in sand moulds. Sometimes, sheet asbestos is used for insulating risers for magnesium castings. Plaster of Paris cannot be used with ferrous castings because sulphur or calcium sulphate reacts readily with iron at high temperatures.

For ferrous casting, fireclay-sawdust sleeves are sometimes used ; raw sleeve is fired before use to burn out the saw-dust and leave air cells. For top insulation, loose cellulose materials *e.g.*, rice hulls are used.

Use of Chills. The casting may consist of both thick and thin sections. The thin sections tend to solidify earlier than the thick ones. This difference in rate of cooling produces uneven shrinkage of part which in turn causes internal strains in the metal. If the cooling of thinner parts is also severe, it may even develop cracks. To solidify heavy sections more rapidly for compensating volumetric contraction, metal '*chills*' may be embedded in the area of larger sections.

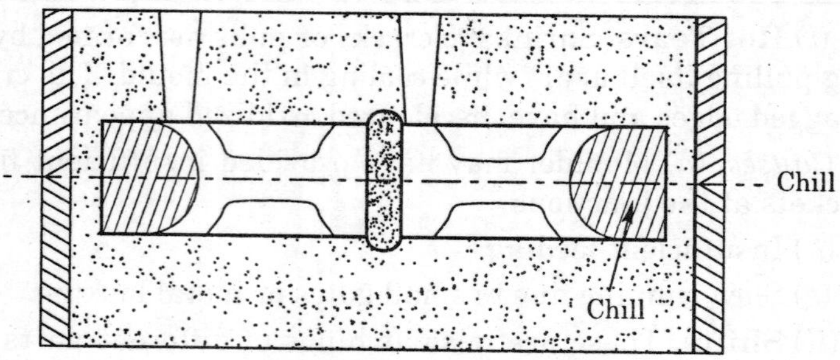

Fig. 7.16. Use of chills.

Chills are broadly of two types :

(*i*) External Chills (*ii*) Internal Chills

(*i*) *External Chills.* They are placed in the mould and become part of the mould walls.

They may be

(*a*) Direct External Chills

(*b*) Indirect External Chills

(*a*) Direct type external chill forms a part of the mould face which comes in direct contact with the molten metal.

(*b*) Indirect type external chill is embedded behind the mould wall so that it does not have any direct contact with the molten metal.

They are made in various shapes so that they may become part of the mould contour. They are made of metal like cast iron, steel, copper etc. Copper makes the most effective chill owing to its high heat conductivity and high specific heat.

Internal Chills. These are placed in the mould cavity and go into the casting when the metal is poured.

These chills may be in the form of a nail with a large head projecting out in the mould cavity. These may also be in the form of a helical spring with a straight shank. The shank is pushed into the sand wall with the chill in the form of spring projecting out into the mould cavity.

For internal chills, the metal should be the same as that being cast. The chills used should be of the proper and correct size. An undersized chills will not serve its purpose, whereas an oversized one will cause excessive chilling which tends to prevent directional solidification.

Defects Caused by Moulding, Core-Making and Gating

(*i*) **Hot Tears.** Shrinkage cracks or pulls are formed by the casting pulling itself apart while cooling in the mould. The cracks have jagged edges and have discoloured, oxidized appearance.

Causes. (*a*) Moulder may have provided insufficient fillets or brackets at the junctions

(*b*) Insufficient feeding.

(*c*) Slow running due to small gates or metal lacking.

(*ii*) **Shifts.** These are mismatchings of different parts of a mould at the joint lines.

Causes. (*a*) Use of under-size moulding box pins.

(*b*) Movement of the face of moulding sand during rolling over.

(*iii*) **Fins and Fash**

Causes. (*a*) Moulder raps the pattern excessively before withdrawing from mould.

(*b*) Moulder does not place sufficient weight on the top part of the mould.

(*c*) Parts of the mould not clamped tightly.

(*iv*) **Cold Laps or Misrun Castings**

Causes. (*a*) Gates too small.

(*b*) Too many restrictions in gating system.

(*c*) Pouring head too low.

(*d*) Metal lacking in fluidity.

(*e*) Faulty venting of moulds.

(*v*) **Crush.** It is a displacement of sand when mould is being closed.

Causes. (*a*) Carelessness on the part of the moulder.

(*b*) Excessive weighing of the mould.

(*c*) Cores too large.

(*d*) Core print too small.

(*vi*) **Swell.** It is a local displacement of the face of the sand by pressure of the fluid metal *e.g.*, local bulges.

Causes. (*a*) Soft ramming

(*vii*) **Sand Wash.** It usually occurs near the ingates as rough lumps on the casting surface.

Causes. (*a*) Soft ramming.

(*b*) Weak sand.

(*c*) Poor patterns *e.g.*, insufficient draft.

(*d*) Overbaked or insufficiently bonded cores.

(*viii*) **Scabs.** These are rough slightly-raised areas on the casting surfaces, often with some sand embedded in the scab.

Causes. (*a*) Uneven ramming.

(*b*) Slow or intermittent running.

(*ix*) **Sand Blow.** It is an excessively smooth depression on the outer casting surface.

Causes. (*a*) Moulding sand with high moisture and low premeability.

(*b*) Insufficient venting by moulder—defect sometimes called '*Air lock*'.

(*c*) Gating system faulty.

(*x*) **Core Blow.** It is an excessively smooth depression on the inner surface of a cored cavity or a gas pocket immediately above a cored cavity.

Causes. (*a*) Moulder may have forgotten to carry the vent from the core through the mould.

(*b*) Insufficiently backed cores or they may have packed up moisture after backing.

(*xi*) **Slag holes.** These are smooth depressions on the upper surfaces of castings. Usually occur near ingates.

Remedy. By inserting slag traps in the gating systems.

QUESTIONS

1. Give the basic requirements of a core sand? How it differs from moulding sand?
2. Explain various types of cores and give their specific uses.
3. Explain in a systematic manner the core making operation.
4. Cores are used (*i*) because they are essential (*ii*) to simplify moulding operations. Illustrate with suitable examples.
5. What are the tests carried out to determine the quality of a core sand mixture?
6. Show how the following sands differ from each other with respect to ingredients and properties :
   (*i*) Core sand
   (*ii*) Facing sand
   (*iii*) System sand
   (*iv*) Baking sand or filling sand
7. Explain how the hob spots of an intersection in a casting can be reduced or eliminated.
8. Describe how hot tears can be avoided by design and by moulding procedure.

8

Moulding Process

Moulding Process

Moulding processes are broadly classified as :

1. *Hand Moulding*–Used in piece and small-lot production foundry practice.

2. *Machine Moulding*–Used in large-lot and mass production.

Moulding processes are often classified according to :

1. Type of Material of Moulding, *viz.*
   - (*i*) Green sand moulds
   - (*ii*) Dry sand moulds
   - (*iii*) Loam moulds
   - (*iv*) Metal moulds
2. Method used, *viz.*
   - (*i*) Bench moulding
   - (*ii*) Floor moulding
   - (*iii*) Pit moulding
   - (*iv*) Sweep moulding
   - (*v*) Plate moulding.

Green Sand Moulding. If the mould is filled with molten metal while the sand is still in the moist state, the method used is known as '*Green sand moulding*'. Green sand is generally used for casting small and medium size mould.

Advantages. (*i*) Cost and delay involved in drying moulds are saved.

(*ii*) Larger output can be obtained from a given floor space. Green sand moulds, therefore, cost less and are used more extensively than any of the other types.

(*iii*) Green sand moulds are softer than dry sand moulds. This allows greater freedom in contraction when the castings solidify and cool.

(*iv*) For small depths, green sand-moulds are quite strong as the gases can escape from them.

Drawbacks. (*i*) Due to the presence of moisture, the moulds lack permeability and strength which give rise to defects like blow holes, gas holes etc., in castings.

(*ii*) The surface finish of the casting obtained from green sand moulds is not very smooth.

Table 8.1: Typical Sand Mixtures of Green-Sand Moulds

	Composition of Green Sand									
Purpose	*Floor sand*		*New dust*		*Coal sand*		*Carbon blacking*		*Talc (french chalk)*	
	Parts	*%*	*Parts*	*%*	*Parts*	*%*	*Parts*	*%*	*Parts*	*%*
Light work	6	8.0	1	13.4	$\frac{1}{2}$	6.6	—	—	—	—
General work	8	59.3	4	29.6	$1\frac{1}{2}$	11.1	—	—	—	—
Smooth finish	10	57.1	4	22.9	$1\frac{1}{2}$	8.6	$1\frac{1}{2}$	8.6	$\frac{1}{2}$	2.8

Principal Methods of Green-sand Moulding are :

(*i*) Open-sand method

(*ii*) Bedded-in method

(*iii*) Turn-over method.

(*i*) **Open-sand Method.** It is simplest form of green sand moulding, particularly suitable for solid patterns. For convenience in working and pouring, the entire mould is made in the foundry floor or in a bed of sand above floor level. Moulding box is not necessary and the upper surface of the mould is open to air. After proper levelling, the pattern is pressed in the sand bed for making mould. Pouring basin is made at one end of the mould, and the overflow channel cut at the sides of the cavity at the exact height from the bottom face of the mould for giving necessary thickness.

This method is mainly employed for simple castings with flat tops, *e.g.*, floor plates, grills, moulding boxes, grates and railings, weight etc., in which if the upper surface is rough, it does not matter.

(*ii*) **Bedded-in Method.** If the upper surface of a casting is not flat or is to be smooth, a solid pattern may also be moulded by '*bedded in method*' in which a cope, *i.e.*, a sand cover is necessary.

In this method, the pattern is hammered down or pressed to bed it into the sand of the foundry floor or in a drag filled partially with sand to form the mould cavity. The sand should be rammed close to the pattern carefully.

After smoothing the joint and spreading the parting sand, a cope is placed over the pattern. The cope is rammed up, runners and risers are cut and the cope box is lifted. Now the pattern is withdrawn, the surfaces of drag and cope moulds finished and cope replaced in its correct position for completing the mould.

(*iii*) **Turn-over Method.** This method is most suitable and very much used for solid as well as split patterns. One pattern-half is placed with its flat side on a moulding board, a drag is rammed and rolled over. The other pattern half and a cope box are placed in position. After ramming, the cope is lifted off and the two pattern halves shaken and withdrawn. Now the cope is replaced on the drag for assembling the mould.

Dry Sand Moulding. The method of making dry sand moulds is similar to that of making green sand moulds except that (*i*) different sand mixture is used, (*ii*) the mould surface is sprayed with molasses water, and (*iii*) all parts of the mould are dried in an oven (maintained at 150°–300°C until the moisture is driven off) before assembling it.

Advantages–(*i*) The casting prepared from dry sand moulds are very sound and free from defects.

(*ii*) Dry sand mould resist the shrinkage better and are more rigid and strong.

(*iii*) The castings have a better surface finish.

Drawbacks–Dry sand moulds are more expensive than green sand moulds on account of the baking operation.

Table 8.2: Typical Sand Mixtures of Dry Sand Moulds

Purpose	*Composition (parts)*		
	Floor sand	*New sand*	*Horse manure or saw dust*
Small and medium work	13	8	1
Ordinary heavy work	11	9	1
Extra heavy work	10	10	1

Dry sand moulds are often used for large work *e.g.*, engine blocks, engine cylinders, rolls of rolling mills, intricate castings and those requiring special smoothness, soundness and accuracy.

Skin-dried Moulding. When the moisture is dried from the surface layer of the rammed sand and to a depth of about 25 mm or more by heater or gas torches, the process is known as '*Skin-dried Moulding*'.

In a process the advantage of both dry sand and green sand moulding are obtained. Since the time required for drying is less than in case of dry sand moulding the method is less expensive.

Loam Moulding. Loam is sand clay milled with water to form a thin plastic mixture to the consistency of mud. This loam mortar is applied as plaster (6 to 12 mm layer) to the rough structure of the mould. The loam sand mould is constructed of porous brick cemented together with loam mortar. Cast iron plates and bars are used to reinforce the brick work which retains the moulding material. Loam moulds require adequate ventilation so as to open out pores in the otherwise compact, closely knit mass, by artificial means. For this, chopped straw or horse manure is mixed up with the loam sand.

A typical Loam-sand Mixture: (by volume)

Silica sand 22, Clay 5, Coke 10, Moisture 18-20%.

The rough structure of the mould is usually made of brick-work and exact shape is given by a rotating sweep around a central spindle, *i.e.*, by using sweep pattern. Loam moulds may also be prepared by using skeleton pattern and strickle made of wood. The surface of loam mould is blackened and dried before assembling it.

Loam moulding is used for large-sized castings where the use of regular moulding method in flasks will be too expensive and inconvenient *e.g.*, large cylinders, round bottomed kettles, chemical pans, large gears etc.

Table 8.3: Mould Sand Mixtures for Various Metals and Alloy Castings

Purpose	*Sand Mixture*	
1. Grey C.I. castings (35–100 kg)	Silica sand, AFS Fineness 60-75	... 500 kg
	Clay	... 40-42.5 kg
	Coal dust	... 35 kg
	Sawdust	... 4 kg
	Moisture	... 17-20 kg
2. Steel castings	Silica sand, medium grain	... 96%
	Bentonite	... 3.5 %
(*i*) Green sand moulds	Dextrine	... 0.5%
	Moisture	... 3-4%

(*ii*) Dry sand moulds	Silica sand, medium grain	... 94.5%
	Bentonite	... 5%
	Dextrine	... 0.5%
	Moisture	... 5-6%
3. Aluminium alloy casting,	Silica sand, AFS 140	... 77%
	Clay	... 15%
	Moisture	... 8%
(*i*) Natural sand Moulds	Green compressive strength	... 0.5 kg/cm^2
	Permeability AFS	... 15–20 cc/min
(*ii*) Synthetic sand moulds	Silica sand AFS Fineness 130	... 90.5–92.5%
	Bentonite	... 4–5%
	Moisture	... 3.5–4.5%
	Green compressive strength	... 0.55–07kg/cm^2
	Permeability AFS	... 25-30 cc/min.
4. Magnesium alloy Castings	Silica sand, AFS Fineness 65	... 88–90%
	Bentonite	... 4%
	Boric acid	... 1.5–2%
	Sulphur	... 1.5–2%
	Potassium fluoborate	... 0.5%
	Diethyl glycol	... 0.75–1.25%
	Moisture	... 2%
5. Facing sand mixtures for		
(*i*) Grey C.I. Castings	Silica, AFS Fineness 40-70	... 95%
	Bentonite	... 2–3%
	Dextrine	... 1–1.5%
	Corn flour	... 0.3–0.5%
	Moisture (*a*) 4–5% (for dry sand moulds) (*b*) 2.5–305% (for green sand moulds)	
(*ii*) Steel castings	Green sand mixture :	
	Silica, AFS Finess 40–60	... 96.4%
	Bentonite	... 1.5%
	Soda ash	... 0.04
	Dextrine	... 0.7%
	Moisture	... 3.5–4%
	Green compressive strength	... 0.45-05 kg/cm^2
	Permeability	... 260–300 cc/min.
(*iii*) Non-ferrous castings except magnesium	Green sand and dry sand moulds:	
	Silica, AFS Fineness 130 subangular grains	... 81.5%
	Bentonite	... 16%
	Graphite	... 2%
	Corn flour	... 0.5%
	Moisture	... 4–5%
	Green compressive strength	... 0.55–0.7 kg/cm^2
	Permeability AFS	25–35 cc/min.

Metal Moulds. When the impression or the mould is made of metal, it is known as *'Metal Mould'*. Metal moulds are employed for the production of large numbers of identical castings.

The processes which employ metal moulds are:

(*i*) Die-casting process

(*ii*) Permanent mould process

(*iii*) Centrifugal process.

Bench Moulding. Bench moulding applies chiefly to small sized castings which are light in weight and which can be easily handled.

In bench moulding, the moulds are prepared in moulding boxes or flasks placed at convenient height on a bench. Mould is prepared by the moulder while standing near the bench.

Methods of Bench Moulding

(*i*) Two-box moulding

(*ii*) Three-box moulding

(*iii*) Moulding with a false check

(*iv*) Plate moulding

(*v*) Stacked moulding

(*vi*) Odd side moulding.

(*i*) *Two-box Moulding.* It makes use of a moulding box or flask which is in two parts. The upper part and the lower part are called '*cope*' and '*drag*' respectively. The two part fitted with a suitable clamping and locating device. Clamping prevents the cope from

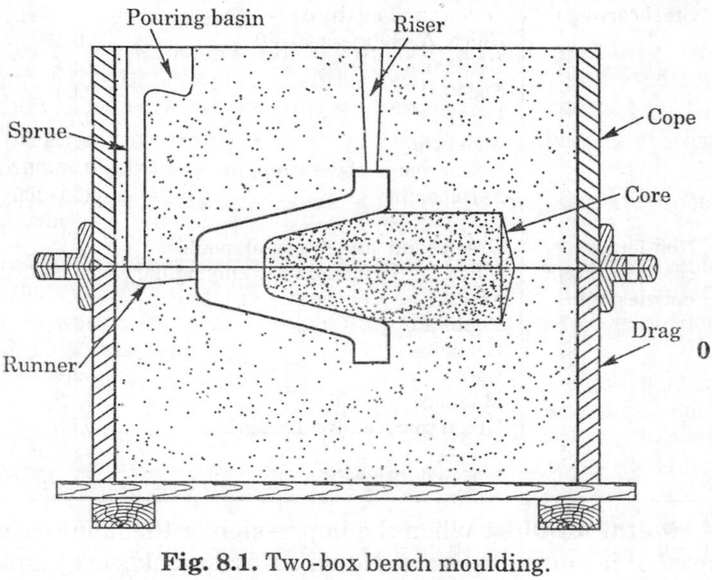

Fig. 8.1. Two-box bench moulding.

lifting due to the pressure of the molten metal while pouring. Locating device enables the two parts to maintain proper alignment at all times.

Moulding Procedure

(*a*) Place drag and pattern on the moulding board and ram sand in drag.

(*b*) Roll over drag on the board.

(*c*) Assemble pattern and place cope over the drag.

(*d*) Keep sprue-pin and riser pin in position, fill sand in the cope and ram.

(*e*) Vent mould, remove sprue and riser pins and part off mould.

(*f*) Withdraw pattern, clean mould cavity and cut gate in the drag.

(*g*) Place core in position.

(*h*) Reassemble and clamp mould to make it ready for pouring.

(*ii*) *Three-box moulding.* If the pattern is of flanged type, it will be inconvenient to prepare the mould in two boxes. To facilitate moulding work in such cases, three boxes are used instead of two and the pattern is used in two halves. Additional middle box is called '*cheek*'. All the three boxes are clamped with one another during pouring.

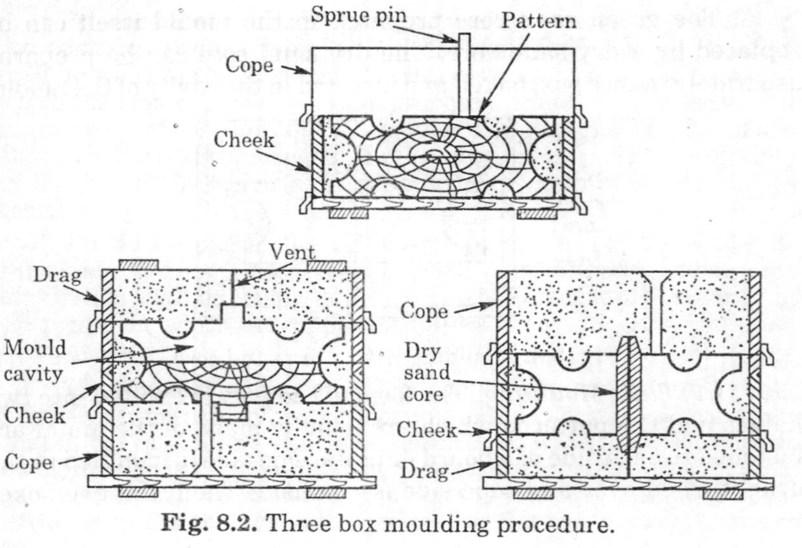

Fig. 8.2. Three box moulding procedure.

(*iii*) *Moulding with a false cheek.* The mould may be prepared in two parts with a green sand core often referred to as a '*false cheek*', if the set of three boxes cannot be made available.

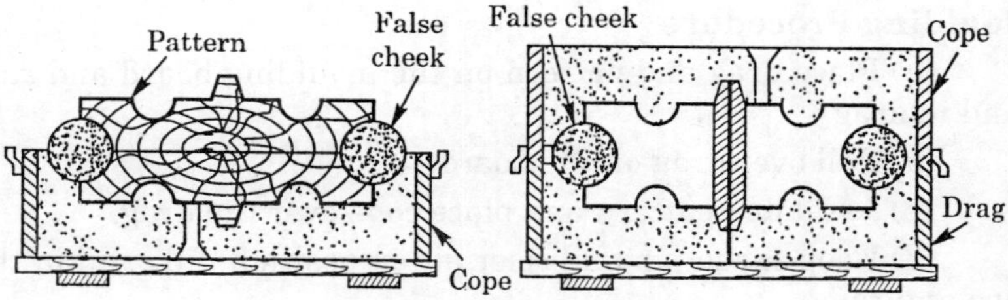

Fig. 8.3. Moulding with false cheek.

Moulding procedure

(*a*) First ram the cope half of the pattern in the cope.

(*b*) Roll over the assembly.

(*c*) Form the parting around the pattern in the cope.

(*d*) Prepare a false cheek with the green sand in the cavity so formed.

(*e*) Ram the drag over the false cheek.

(*f*) Draw the drag, remove the pattern and replace the drag again.

(*g*) Complete the mould by rolling over the assembly, drawing off the cope, removing the remaining pattern half and finally closing the mould.

The green sand core prepared in the mould itself can be replaced by a dry sand core. The dry sand core can be prepared separately in core box, baked and inserted in the cavity of the mould.

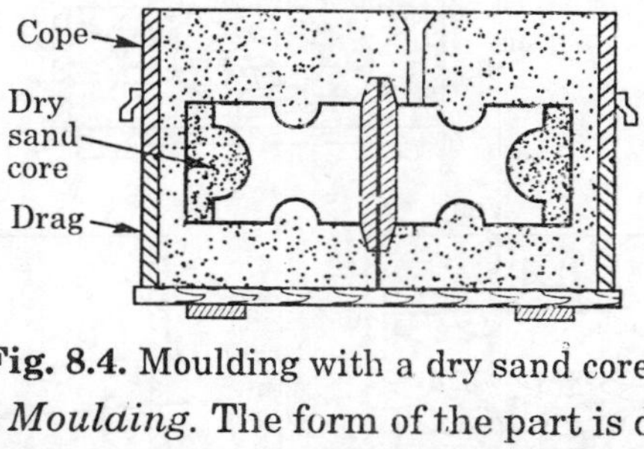

Fig. 8.4. Moulding with a dry sand core.

(*iv*) *Plate Moulding.* The form of the part is divided into two halves and the patterns which are usually made of the metal are fastened to each side of a board or plate. One side is moulded in the drag, turned over and cope side is moulded. Then, the two boxes

are separated and the board with patterns is removed. The moulded impressions match up on reassembling the two boxes and the mould is ready to be poured.

When a large number of fairly simple castings is required, their moulds are produced several at once by this process. This method is generally employed with moulding machines which ram the sand, like the pattern and roll over mechanically.

(*v*) *Stacked Moulding.* When a large number of small size casting is required, each having one flat surface, this method can be used. Both sides of one half of the mould can be made use of by stacking them so that the lower face of each part is a cope face and the upper face, a drag face. There will be a common passage for the molten metal running through the stock of the intermediate boxes.

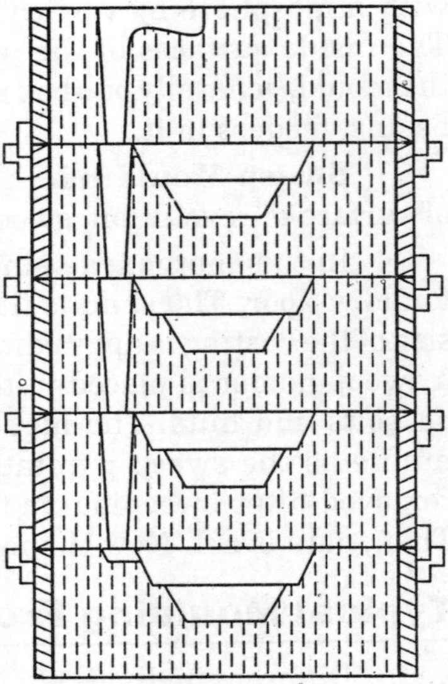

Fig. 8.5. Stacked moulding.

A number of parts can thus be cast in a single pouring operation.

(*vi*) *Odd side Moulding.* When the solid or one piece pattern does not have a flat face to rest on the moulding board and when it cannot be split conveniently, *'odd-side'* is first prepared in a box by moulding *'loose'*.

Floor Moulding. Very heavy castings or castings having considerable depth or area are moulded in the sand of the foundry floor in much the same way as green sand or dry sand moulding. Thus, the floor itself acts as the drag and this is covered with a cope or the mould is cast open.

Pit Moulding. In this method, moulds of large jobs are generally prepared in a pit dug in the foundry floor. This facilitates in lifting the pattern and casting the mould easily. The sand under the pattern is rammed by bedding-in because a pit which functions as a drag cannot be rolled over.

A coke bed is laid on the bottom of the pit. It is covered with straw and then a layer of sand is rammed and levelled. To provide an outlet for the escape of gases generated the coke bed is connected

with atmosphere by vertical vent pipes in the corners of the pit. The inside surfaces of the pit are lined with bricks. To complete the mould, generally one box is required for cutting runners, pouring basins, feeders in it.

Sweep Moulding. For moulding parts whose shape is that of surface of revolution, sweep moulding is employed.

In this method, a spindle with its base is well placed in the foundry floor. The sand is filled and rammed until the shape and size of the casting is approximately formed by the excavation. Then, a sweep holder is placed in the spindle and the sweep is fastened by bolts and nuts. The mould surface is produced by the sweep profile as the sweep is rotated about the spindle. The spindle is removed after sweeping and the mould is patched at the centre. Then, gate is cut. Now the mould is ready to be poured.

Typical Moulding Problems

Different methods of moulding given below illustrate certain types of moulding problems which may also be applied to more difficult and complicated patterns:

1. **False cope.** Making a false cope is a method very similar to making a bedded-in mould.

At first, the pattern is bedded into the cope, and a smooth parting surface is made. Now, drag flask is set on cope and rammed up as usual. Complete flask is then rolled over, and false cope is lifted off, leaving the pattern in place in the drag. The sand in the false cope is knocked out as the same has served its purpose. The real cope complete with gating system is then rammed up as usual.

False cope is used to obtain an irregular parting surface.

2. **Coping down.** This method of moulding is used for a pattern with the parting line not in one plane.

The pattern is first supported on a moulding board by placing a suitable wooden piece under the elevated end. Drag is set on the moulding board and rammed up. On rolling over the drag, irregular parting surface is formed to the parting line of the pattern. New parting surface is sloped gradually—this operation is known as '*coping down*' and is necessary so that the cope may be lifted off without dropping the sand projecting downwards. Now, this mould is completed as usual.

3. **Green-sand match.** If a number of castings are required from an irregular shaped pattern with the parting line not in one plane, coping down may be eliminated by using a '*green-sand match*'.

A green-sand match is made by first ramming up a drag and coping down to the parting line of the pattern. Green-sand match is now rammed up extra hard on this drag without sprue and riser pins. For supporting the pattern and automatically forming the irregular parting surface, green-sand match is retained.

Using a sand match saves much time which is otherwise necessary for coping down and forming a new parting surface on the first drag.

For more durability than ordinary sand other materials like plaster of Paris, portland cement, wood are used for making *'plaster of Paris match'*, *'portland cement match'*, *'follow board,'* respectively.

4. **Drawback.** When pattern is of such a shape that it cannot be drawn from the sand due to projection, *'drawback'* is employed to overcome this difficulty.

A cavity is dug out of the mould, well away from the pattern. The space behind the drawback must be greater than the width of the projection. A stiff paper is rammed up in the moulding sand to form a parting surface to the projection. Pattern can be withdrawn by sliding the *'drawback'*. After withdrawing the pattern, the drawback is brought back in its correct position and the space behind it is filled up with sand again.

5. **Using a loose piece.** If pattern cannot be withdrawn from the sand due to the projections, it can be drawn by making these projections as loose pieces.

Loose pieces are fixed to the pattern by means of pins, which are removed as soon as sufficient sand has been rammed round the loose pieces for holding them in position.

Now, mould is completed and main pattern is lifted out of the sand as usual. After this loose pieces the removed separately by skewer tool.

6. **Using a dry sand core.** A sheave wheel or a similar type of pattern is moulded by using a dry sand core for forming the groove in the pulley. A V-shaped dry sand core called a *'false core'* is placed in mould cavity to form the groove.

7. **Using a cover core.** A flat core used to cover cavity in a mould is known as *'cover core'*.

For example, pattern with a dovetail face at the top end, is placed upside down on a moulding board with a flat dovetail shaped cover core at each of the dovetail recesses.

Drag is set over the pattern, filled up with moulding sand and rammed. Drag is now rolled over so that dovetail face is at the top.

Cover cores are removed, pattern is withdrawn vertically upwards, and cover cores are replaced in the mould in their corresponding impressions.

Defects Caused by Moulding and Core-Making Materials

Materials used to make mould and core-sand mixtures are rammed to shape and air dried for a short time; flame or hot-air dried for a few minutes or hours, or the moulds and cores are dried or baked in an oven.

More defects occur in castings made in green sand because

(*a*) the rate of production is high.

(*b*) dried cores, metallic chills, studs and chaplets pick up moisture from the damp mould, and the defects result unless the moulds are cast within a short time or making and closing.

(*c*) as the compressive strength of the moist sand is less than 0.5 kg/cm^2, great care has to be taken to devise methods of gating that enable the sand to stand up to the flow of the molten metal.

Main Defects due to sand conditions are:

(*i*) **Blowholes.** These are smooth rounded holes visible on the surface of a casting. They may appear in clusters, or as in a core blow, there may be one large, smooth depression.

Causes: (*a*) High moisture, low permeability, excessive fine grains and gas-producing ingredients.

(*b*) Extra hard ramming.

(*c*) Improper venting.

(*ii*) **Drop.** It occurs when the upper surface of the mould cracks and pieces of sand fall into the molten metal.

Causes: (*a*) Low green strength, which can be improved by increasing the milling time, moisture or clay content.

(*b*) Low mould hardness.

(*c*) Using hot sand.

(*d*) Insufficient reinforcement.

(*iii*) **Scabs**

Causes: (*a*) Too fine a sand.

(*b*) Low permeability.

(*c*) High moisture.

(*d*) Uneven ramming of mould.

(*e*) Slow or intermittent running of molten over the sand surface.

(*iv*) **Pin-holes.** These are numerous, very small holes visible on the surface of the casting after it has been cleaned by shot-blasting.

Causes: (*a*) Sand containing too much moisture or gas-producing materials.

(*b*) Faulty metal.

(*v*) **Gas-holes.** These are the holes that appear when the surface of the casting is removed by machining, or when the casting is sectioned, *i.e.*, cut into sections.

Causes: (*a*) Faulty metal.

(*b*) Moist sand.

(*vi*) **Hot-tears (Pulls).** These are cracks having ragged edges.

Causes: (*a*) Excessive mould hardness from very hard ramming.

(*b*) High dry and hot strength. This can be reduced by using larger sand grains and reducing the amount of fines, clay and moisture.

(*vii*) **Dirt**

Causes: (*a*) Crushed mould.

(*b*) Sand wash.

(*c*) Low dry strength.

(*d*) Slag allowed to pass into the mould cavity.

(*e*) Dirty metal not thoroughly fluxed.

(*f*) Low green strength.

(*g*) Low moisture.

(*h*) Improper gating.

(*viii*) **Metal penetration and Rough surfaces:**

Causes: (*a*) High permeability.

(*b*) Large grain size.

(*c*) Low dry strength.

(*d*) Soft ramming.

(*e*) Poor plasticity.

Table 8.4: Defects in Castings

S.No.	Sand condition	Defects
1.	Moisture	High → Blowholes, pin-holes, gasholes, scabs, rough surfaces, hot tears.
		Low → Drops, sand wash.
2.	Permeability	High → Rough surface, metal penetration.
		Low → Blowholes, pin-holes, gasholes, scabs, dirt, and sand wash.
3.	Green strength	High → Scabs, rough surface, blowholes.
		Low → Drops, dirt.
4.	Dry strength	High → Hot tears,
		Low → Dirt, rough surface.
5.	Ramming hardness	High → Blowholes, hot tears.
		Uneven → Scabs
		Low → Dirt, rough surfaces.

Table 8.5: Remedy of Defects

S.No.	Variation required in Sand Condition	Remedy
1.	Decreased moisture	→ Use a stronger clay and reduce the fines.
2.	Low permeability	→ Ram harder, add fines, or use finer-grained sand.
3.	Higher permeability	→ Reduce percentage fines, use coarser sand and a better clay, ram softer, use less coal dust.
4.	Lower green strength	→ Ram softer, use less clay.
5.	Higher green strength	→ Ram harder, use a better or more clay, mix longer.
6.	Lower dry strength	→ Use less moisture and clay, reduce organic binders.
7.	Higher dry and hot strength	→ Use more water and clays, mix longer, ram harder, use stronger clay, add silica flour or iron oxide.
8.	Higher mould hardness	→ Ram harder, mix better, use better clay and uniform grain size sands.

Defect During Sand Mixing and Distribution

The greater the degree of mechanization and the greater the employment of synthetic sand, the more intensive must be the system of checking the batches of sand as they come from the mixers. Delivery of sand from overhead hoppers requires, so little effort from the moulders that there is tendency for them (*a*) to waste facing sand and (*b*) continue to use sand that is out of condition.

Each of the following factors, small in themselves and difficult to detect by the routine tests on small samples of sand, result in a gradual deterioration in the moulding quality of the sand:

(*i*) Mechanical plant wears very rapidly in the foundry *e.g.*, sieves wear, break and permit oversize pieces of sand to sand to pass through the broken mesh.

(*ii*) Rollers and ploughs wear and fail to maintain the correct mixing action in the stipulated times of mixing.

(*iii*) Aerators wear out and fail to deliver the sand in that fluffed-up condition that gives the best castings.

(*iv*) Dust-extractor pipes become choked, and the silt removed is restricted.

The moulder should be interested in the sand, and should assist his work mates in the mixing plant by reporting any variation in quality.

Moulder's Tool Kit

The hand tools used by a moulder are those manipulated by hand in the construction of a mould:

1. **Shovel.** It is used for mixing and tempering moulding sand for moving the sand from the pile to the flask. A clean, well-kept shovel is the badge of a careful workman.

2. **Riddle.** It is sometimes called a screen. It is a circular wooden frame with a wire mesh bottom.

It is used for removing foreign material, such as nails, shot metal, splinters of wood, etc., from the moulding sand.

The size of the openings in the mesh indicates the size of the riddle. A number eight riddle would be one having openings approximately 1/8 inch square.

3. **Bench Rammer.** It is a wooden tool used for packing the sand in the mould.

One end, called the peen, is wedge shaped and the opposite end, called the but, has a flat surface.

Bench rammers are usually made of maple that has been soaked in oil to preserve the wood.

4. **Strike-off Bar.** It is metal bar used to remove the surplus sand from the mould after the ramming has been completed.

A wrought iron or cast iron bar with a true edge is commonly used as a strike-off bar.

5. **Vent Wire.** It is a wire rod used for making openings called '*vents*' in the mould.

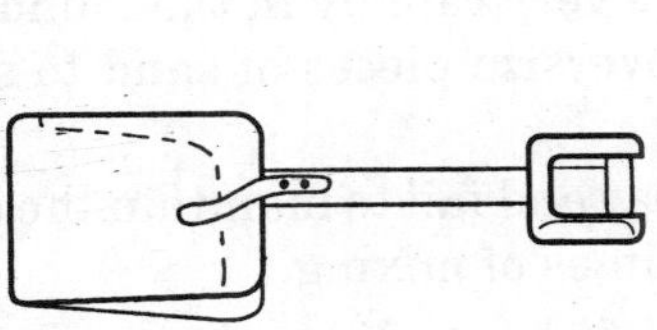

Fig. 8.6. Shovel.

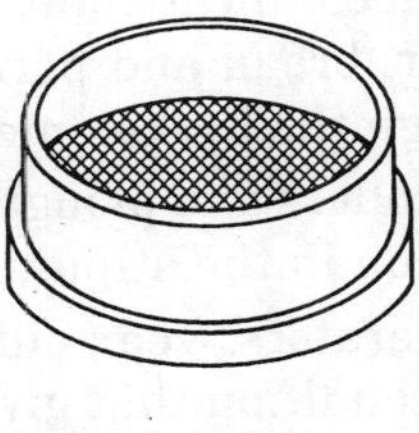

Fig. 8.7. Riddle.

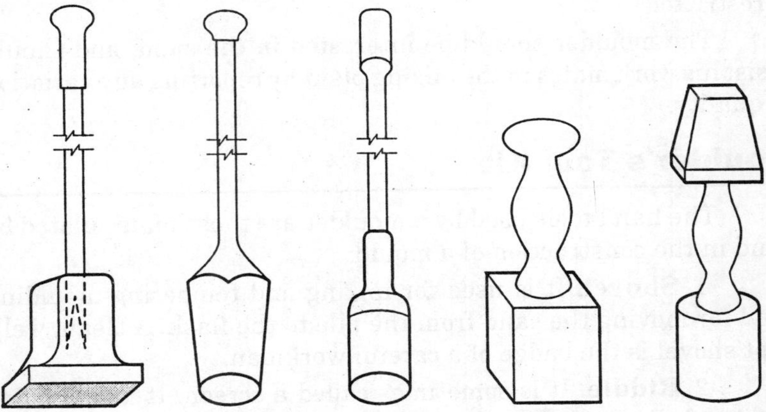

Fig. 8.8. A, B, C–Floor Rammers; D, E–Bench Rammers.

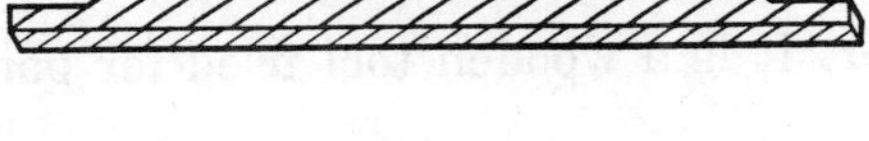

Fig. 8.9. Strike-off bar.

Fig. 8.10. Vent wire.

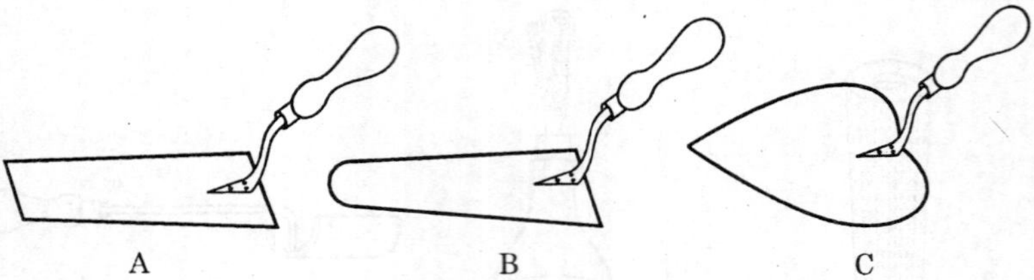

A — Square trowel.
B — Finishing trowel.
C — Heart-shaped trowel.

Fig. 8.11. Trowels.

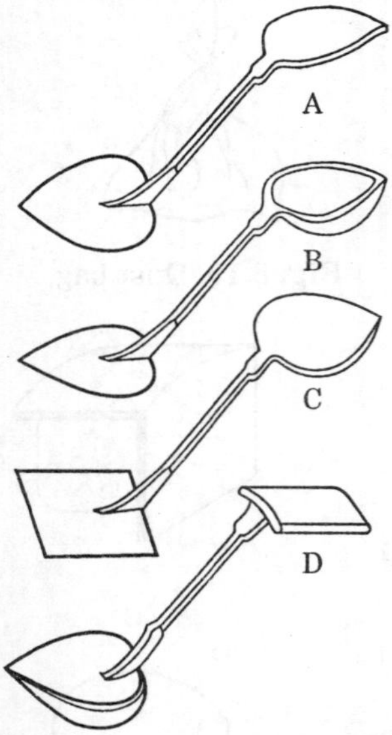

A— Heart and leaf.
B — Leaf and spoon.
C — Square and heart.
D — Spoon and bead.

Fig. 8.12. Sticks.

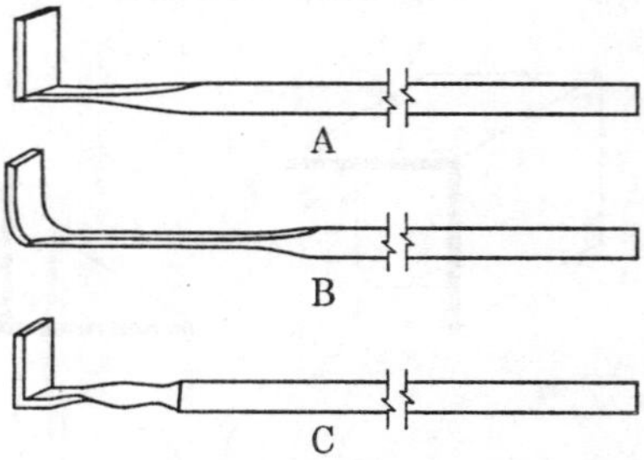

A — English cleaner or lifter.
B — Flange cleaner or lifter.
C — Scotch cleaner or lifter.

Fig. 8.13. Lifters.

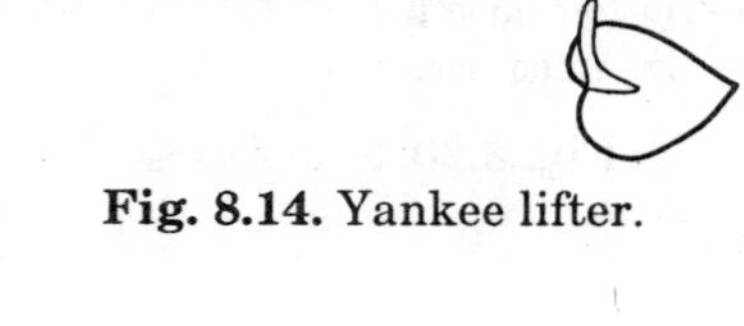

Fig. 8.14. Yankee lifter.

Fig. 8.15. Sprue pin.

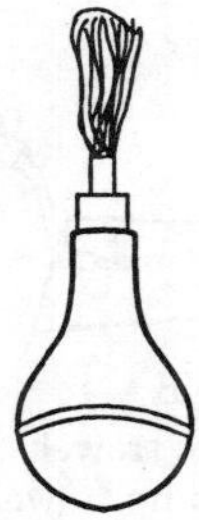

Fig. 8.16. Swap.

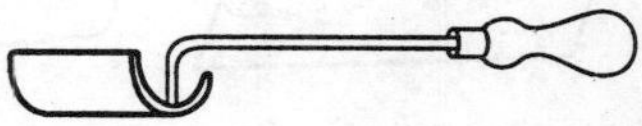

Fig. 8.17. Gate cutter.

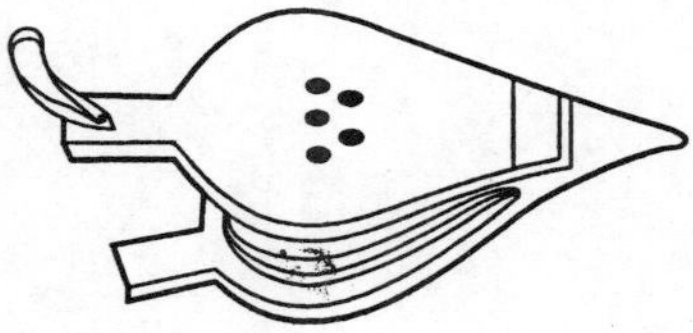

Fig. 8.18. Bellows.

Fig. 8.19. Dust bag.

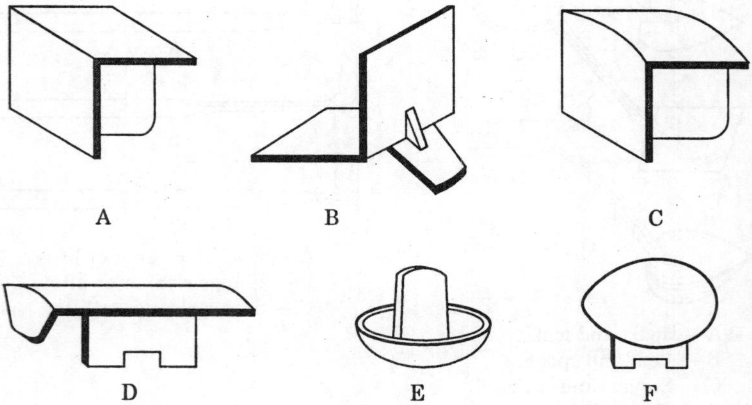

A — Inside square corner smoother.
B — Outside square corner smoother.
C — Half round.
D — Pipe smoother
E — Button smoother.
F — Egg smoother.

Fig. 8.20. Smoothers.

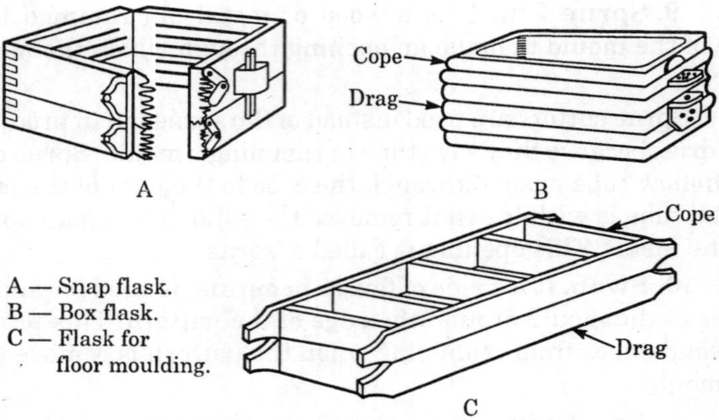

Fig. 8.21. Flasks or Moulding boxes.

Fig. 8.22. Gaggers for reinforcement in moulding boxes.

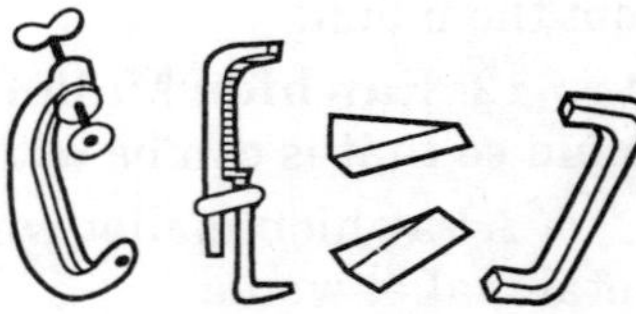

Fig. 8.23. Clamps for moulding boxes.

These vents permit gas and steam to escape from the mould during the pouring operation.

6. **Trowels.** These are used for making joints and finishing flat surfaces of a mould.

There are many different kinds of trowels, some of which are called finishing, square-end, heart, and spear.

The round-end finishing trowel is probably the most commonly used.

7. **Slicks.** These are small tools used for repairing and finishing moulds.

There are many types, some of which are oval spoon, heart and spoon, double spoon and double bead.

The type most commonly used is the oval spoon.

8. **Lifters.** These are used for patching deep sections of a mould and removing loose sand from pockets of the mould.

The Yankee lifter is the most useful in the average foundry.

9. **Sprue Pin.** It is a wood or metal pin rammed in the cope of the mould to make an opening through which the metal is poured.

Sprue cutters are used instead of the sprue pin in production foundries because they save time in ramming a mould. Sprue cutter is a hollow tube pushed through the cope to the joint of the mould. As the tube is withdrawn it removes the sand, leaving an opening for the metal. This opening is called a '*sprue*'.

10. **Swab.** It is made of flax or hemp and is used for applying water to the mould around the edge of the pattern. This prevents the sand edges from crumbling when the pattern is removed from the mould.

11. **Drawspike.** It is a sharpened piece of metal driven into the pattern. It holds by friction and is used for removing the pattern from the mould.

12. **Rawhide Mallet.** It is used to loosen the pattern in the mould so that is can be withdrawn without damage to the mould.

A rawhide mallet will not mark or deface the pattern as a metal mallet would.

13. **Gate cutter.** It is a piece of sheet metal used to cut the opening that connects the sprue with the mould cavity. This opening is called a '*gate*'.

14. **Bellows.** These are used to blow loose sand out of the mould. It is sometimes more satisfactory to use the bellows to blow out loose sand than to try to remove it with lifters or other tools.

The hand tools listed are used on all types of moulds, both large and small.

15. **Rapping Plate or Lifting Plate.** It is used to facilitate shaking and lifting of the pattern from the mould.

This plate is firmly attached to the pattern by long screws or by bolts in larger patterns. A draw spike is placed in the rapping hole by the moulder and the pattern rapped to loosen it. Then, draw screws are fixed into the screw hole on the plate and pattern lifted out.

16. **Pouring Weight.** It is a heavy plate of cast iron with an opening in the centre so that runner in the mould can be placed conveniently.

It is used on the top of a mould so as to give weight for preventing the pressure of the liquid metal from forcing the mould apart which may cause a run-out.

17. **Gaggers or Lifters.** These are iron rods bent at one end or both ends. These are used to reinforce sand in the top portion of the moulding box and for supporting hanging bodies of sand.

18. **Clamps.** These are used to hold the cope and drag of the completed mould together so that the cope may not float or rise when the metal is poured into the mould.

19. **Spirit Level.** Moulder uses it for ensuring that this sand bed, moulding box or table of moulding machine is horizontal.

20. **Moulding board and Bottom board.** These are smooth wooden boards. Flask and pattern are placed on moulding board while starting moulding. After turning over the mould, function of this board is over.

Mould is now placed on a similar board called a bottom board which acts as a support for the mould.

21. **Moulding Boxes.** Sand moulds are prepared in specially constructed boxes known as flasks, which give rigidity and strength to the sand.

Flasks are usually made in two parts, held in alignment by dowel pins. Top part is called the '*cope*' and the lower part the '*drag*'. If flask is made in three sections, the centre one is known as the '*cheek*'.

When production is large, metal flasks are used. When only a few castings are needed, wooden flask is economical.

In a foundry, different types of flasks are used:

(*i*) **Snap Flask.** It is made with a hinge on one corner and a lock on the opposite corner so that the flask may be removed from the mould before pouring. Advantage of snap flask is that many moulds can be made from a single flask for the same pouring.

(*ii*) **Tapered Slip Flask.** It is another removable type flask having rigid corners, its sides having smooth inside surface with 5° taper so as to allow removal of the flask upward.

(*iii*) **Box-Flask or Tight Flask.** It remains on the mould until the pouring operation is over. They are usually made of metal and very much suited to small and medium sized moulds.

(*iv*) **Wooden Moulding Box.** It is employed for large castings required in small quantity. Its side timbers are continued beyond the ends of the box forming two handles at each end for easy handling. They are held together by strong cross timbers, reinforced with bolts.

QUESTIONS

1. What do you mean by "green-sand" moulding? Explain any one method of green sand moulding.
2. Give the advantages and disadvantages of "dry sand" moulding. Describe loam moulding.
3. (*i*) What is bench moulding?

   (*ii*) Explain two box bench moulding method.
4. Describe in short:

   (*a*) Three box moulding method

   (*b*) Pit moulding

   (*c*) Sweep moulding.
5. Give the list of moulding tools with their uses.
6. Explain in brief various casting defects.

9

Melting Practice

Production of Pig Iron

Raw Materials for Production of Pig Iron

1. Iron, Ore *e.g.,* Hematite, Magnesite, Limonite, Siderite, Pyrite, etc.

2. Fuel, *e.g.,* Coal.

3. Flux, *e.g.,* Limestone or Dolomite.

1. **Iron ore.** Its large deposits are abundantly available in many parts of India, *e.g.,* Singhhum district, Bihar, Mayurbhanj, some other districts of Orissa, Madhya Pradesh, Mysore.

Following are the *common varieties of iron are:*

(*i*) **Hematite (Fe_2O_3).** It is known as '*Red ore*'. Its colour varies from bluish grey to dark red. It is chief ore in the world. It largely occurs in U.S.A., Brazil and China. It contains about 70% iron. Its specific gravity ranges from 4.9 to 5.3. Its reduction is more easy than other ores. Due to low phosphorus content (upto 0.5%) it can be reduced with acid refractories. Hence, it is sometimes referred to as '*Acid Ore*'.

(*ii*) **Magnesite (Fe_3P_4).** Its colour is steel grey. It occurs in U.S.A., Canada, Scandinavia and India (Tamil Nadu state only). It contains about 72-73% iron. Its specific gravity varies from 5.1 to 5.2. Its reduction is very difficult due to extreme hardness.

(*iii*) **Limonite ($2Fe_2O_3$. $3H_2O$).** Its colour varies from light brown to black. It largely occurs in France, Germany and South U.S.A. It contains about 60% iron with 14.5% water; hence also called '*Hydrated Hematite*'. It is not as hard as magnesite ore.

(*iv*) **Siderite ($FeCO_3$).** Its colour is grey. It occurs in Germany, England and Austria. It contains about 48% iron. It is a hard ore.

(*v*) **Pyrite (FeS_2).** It occurs in Italy. It is first reduced by burning off its sulphur content and converting it to iron oxide. Then iron oxide is further reduced to iron.

Impurities in Iron Ore. Iron ore contains 30 to 73% iron. The remaining are impurities comprising of rocky matter called '*Gangue*'. The main constituents of gangue are silica and alumina: others being $CaCO_3$ or $MgCO_3$, sulphur in the form of $CaSO_4$ or FeS_2, phosphorus in the form of $Ca_3(PO_4)_2$ or $Fe(PO_4)_2$, manganese etc.

Gangue content decreases the value of ore because:

(*i*) Iron produced per tonne of ore will be low.

(*ii*) Fuel and flux consumed per tonne of iron production will be high.

(*iii*) Handling cost per tonne of iron produced will be high.

$CaCO_3$ and $MgCO_3$ act as flux. Hence, their presence is advantageous since less amount outside flux will be required. Some ores provide sufficient fluxing themselves and no outside flux is required. Such ores are very valuable and are known as '*self-fluxing ores*'. Sometimes, self-fluxing ores are prepared by mixing suitable ores.

Sulphur and phosphorus present in iron ore in the form of $CaSO_4$ or FeS_2 and $Ca_3(PO_4)_2$ ore $Fe_3(PO_4)_2$ respectively exert very injurious effects on the properties of iron produced and should, therefore, be kept to a minimum. Sulphur (upto 1%) can be eliminated or appreciably reduced by using suitable fluxes. Phosphorus is reduced from pig iron only at the time of steel-making at a considerably high cost. Ores containing upto 0.05% phosphorus called '*Acid Ores*' are reduced by simpler and cheaper Acid Process. Ores containing above 0.05% phosphorus called '*Basic Ores*' are reduced and converted into steel by more expensive Basic Process.

Presence of manganese (1 to 1.5%) is desirable:

(*i*) to mitigate the injurious effects of sulphur as it forms manganese sulphide which is less harmful than iron sulphide.

(*ii*) to help in oxidising sulphur to SO_2 by enabling MnS to remain on the surface of the molten metal.

If manganese content is low and sulphur content high manganese is added externally in the furnace charge.

2. **Fuel.** Fuels for melting metals are coal, coke, gas, oil and electricity. Fuel is used for smelting in the blast furnace

(*i*) to supply necessary heat for melting,

(*ii*) to reduce the ore to pure iron by combining with oxygen of the ore.

Coke. The fuel generally used in blast furnace is hard coke. Coke is prepared by heating coking coal in a closed chamber at about 1100°C continuously for 2-3 days out of contact with air. The mass of coal swells up and becomes porous (porosity 40 to 50%) as volatile matter is expelled from its interior in the form of gases. The volatile matter is reduced to about 2 to 3%, the carbon content being 70 to 90% and the rest being ash. This mass called coke has crushing strength of 45 to 70 kg/cm^2. When struck, it gives a metallic sound and is light grey in colour.

Coke is used for crucible melting furnaces, cupolas and for the mould and core-drying stoves. There are two main types of coke:

(*i*) One used for heating mould and core stoves, and

(*ii*) Other a superior, hard type of coke used in cupolas and blast furnaces and, therefore, termed blast furnace coke.

While sulphur and ash contents of inferior coke need not be specially low, cupola coke must contain less than 1.0% sulphur to minimise the amount of sulphur absorbed by the molten iron. It should contain less than 10% of ash, because higher proportions need additional amounts of limestone to flux the impurities. Coke should be dry (with less than 0.2% moisture) and the best cokes contain over 90% fixed carbon.

A good blast furnace coke should possess the following properties:

(*i*) It must be sufficiently hard so that (*a*) it is not crushed easily by the weight of the charge (*b*) it is not disintegrated during its downward travel in the blast furnace.

(*ii*) It must have light heating value and low ash content.

(*iii*) It must be very dense so that it does not burn away in the upper region of the furnace before reaching the bosh where maximum heat intensity is required.

(*iv*) It must be porous to provide sufficient surface area to air for efficient combustion.

(*v*) It should be uniform in size. Not more than 5% of hard coke should have size less than 50 mm.

(*vi*) It should be free from impurities, *e.g.*, phosphorus, sulphur.

Table 9.1: Chemical and Physical Properties of Coke

S.No.	*Properties*	*Poor coke*	*Melting coke*
1.	Fixed carbon percentage	80.0	92.0
2.	Ash percentage	17.2	6.5
3.	Sulphur percentage	1.7	0.79
4.	Volatile matter percentage	1.0	0.4
5.	Moisture percentage	0.2	0.2
6.	Percentage small (less than 50 mm)	20.5	5.0
7.	Percentage drop (less than 50 mm after two drops of 2 m)	27.5	7.0

Hard coke is used for melting cast iron in cupola and non-ferrous metals in crucible furnaces.

Fuel for various melting furnaces:

(*i*) *Air furnaces* melting white iron for malleable-iron castings are fired with lumpy, bituminous coal of the long-flame type or with powdered coal, pulverized at a plant near the furnaces with pipes leading to special burners at the furnaces.

(*ii*) Pulverized coal or oil is the source of heat for *Air furnaces* and *rotary furnace* for melting cast iron.

(*iii*) Raw producer gas made from small size coal in adjacent gas making machines is used in the open *hearth-furnaces for* steel making.

(*iv*) Oil or the clean coal-gas from the town supply is often employed for firing small *crucible furnaces*.

(*v*) Electricity is an expensive but clean source of heat used in *low or high frequency induction melting furnaces* and the *arc furnace* operating at melting temperatures upto 1700°C.

Induction type electric furnaces can melt almost all foundry metals. Resistance heating furnaces are used for melting non-ferrous metals. Direct arc electric furnaces are used for melting cast iron, non-ferrous foundry metals and their alloys.

3. Flux. Indian ores require limestone (0.50 to 0.75) tonne per tonne of pig iron produced) as flux since they generally contain silica as the gangue. Sometimes dolomite (double carbonate of calcium and magnesium) is also used.

The objectionable impurities in the flux are sulphur and phosphorus, which should be kept to a minimum.

Flux is a low melting point material. When heated, it melts and combines with ash, viscous slag, sand metallic oxides, etc., making a fluid and easy flowing slag.

Slag being lighter, floats on the surface of the molten metal from where it can be easily skimmed, tapped or removed before pouring the metal into the mould. Slag protects the molten metal from furnace atmosphere.

Types of Fluxes

(*i*) *Limestone:* It is used in cupola when melting cast iron.

(*ii*) *Sodium carbonate:* It is used with limestone in cupola to give a slag which removes sulphur from C.I.

(*iii*) *Nitrogen, Helium and Chlorine*: These are used as gaseous fluxes in aluminium casting to remove dissolved hydrogen and entrapped dross.

Dross comprises of oxides of aluminium, magnesium silicon, copper etc., floating on the surface of molten aluminium or sink.

Fluxes separate molten metal and dross. For this, fluxes of some compositions of chlorides of aluminium and zinc are also used along with gaseous fluxes. Solid fluxes are easy to use than gaseous fluxes.

(*iv*) KCl, MgO, $MgCl_2$, CaF_2, $BaCl_2$ and $MnCl_2$: These are used as fluxes for melting magnesium alloys.

(*v*) *Charcoal:* It is used in copper alloy melting to prevent molten metal from oxidation. For cleansing the metal *i.e.*, for separating the metal from dross, some fluxes are commercially available.

Refractory materials. These are used to serve as *receptacles* for the molten metal. Crucibles, furnace sides and bottoms containing molten metal are made of refactories. Refractories are used for ladles to pour metal into the moulds. They constitute furnace walls and roofing, thus minimizing heat losses. Their main constituents are MgO, SiO_2; Al_2O_3 and their mixtures, newer ones being magnesia and zirconia. Hence, they should possess the following properties:

(*i*) They must not show any sign of fusion or softening below 1580°C.

(*ii*) They must be able to withstand thermal shock due to sudden changes in temperature.

(*iii*) They must be resistant to action of slags, abrasion and corrosion.

(*iv*) They should not get crushed under heavy pressure of the charge.

(*v*) They must be chemically inert.

(*vi*) They must have a low thermal coefficient.

(*vii*) If used for electric furnaces, they should have high electrical resistance.

(*viii*) They should not allow gases to permeate through them.

All the above requisites are not fulfilled by any of the refractory materials but some materials satisfy most of the above conditions.

Refractory materials are broadly classified as:

(*i*) Acid Refractories.

(*iy*) Basic Refractories.

(*iii*) Neutral Refractories.

(*i*) **Acid Refractories.** They are composed of silica, aluminium silicate or clay. Silica occur as quartzite. Dinas rock, sand and ganister in Gaya and Monghyr districts of Bihar.

Silica in pure state fuses at about 1710°C but when heated in contact with some basic material, it forms silicates.

Aluminium silicate occurs in the form of fire clay (Kaolin) containing about 10% water. It consists of 46% Al_2O_3 and 54% Si_2O_2. It fuses at 1775°C. It is found in India near Raipur, Rewa and Katni in M.P., in Kathiawar, certain districts of Bihar, Orissa and Tamil Nadu.

Other acid refractories are:

(*a*) silimanite containing 63% Al_2O_3 and 37% SiO_2 and fusion temperature 1900°C.

(*a*) corundum or alumina containing 100% Al_2O_3 and fusion temperature 2050°C.

(*ii*) **Basic Refractories.** Best basic refractory is magnesia (MgO) having fusion temperature 2800°C. It is costlier than silica or fire clay. It is found in Karnataka, Tamil Nadu and Orissa. It is used for furnaces which are to resist corrosive action of basic slags.

A cheaper substitute for magnesia is dolomite (a double carbonate of calcium and magnesium).

Pure Bauxite (Al_2O_3, $3H_2O$) has a highly refractory nature. But presence of many impurities lower its refractory value and its use is limited.

(*iii*) **Neutral Refractories.** The chief neutral refractories are graphite, chromite and zirconia. These are ideal refractory materials since :

(*a*) they neither combine with acids nor basics.

(*b*) they permit the use of both acid and basic processes.

Graphite occurs mixed with calcarious and silicious rocks in India, Siberia, Ceylon, England, Austria, U.S., Brazil. In India, it

occurs near Ajmer in Rajasthan, Travancore, Visakhapatnam, Kalamandi districts in Orissa. It fuses at about 3000°C.

Chromite is manufactured from chromite ores which are composed of 32% FeO and 68% Cr_2O_3. It fuses at 2180°C. Chromite ores occur in Singbhum district of Bihar.

Zirconia is composed of 100% zirconium oxide.

The use of neutral refractories is limited to special applications due to their high cost.

Selection of Refractories. The refractory is selected according to the specific properties required, *e.g.*,

(*a*) Chemical behaviour.

(*b*) Abrasion.

(*c*) Imperviousness.

(*d*) Thermal expansion.

(*e*) Electrical resistance.

The nature of refractory lining is kept same as that of the slag produced in the furnace.

Fire clay is found most suitable to withstand thermal shocks, *i.e.*, the furnace working intermittently.

Air blast. For proper combustion of the fuel, enormous quantity of air is required in the blast furnace. This air blast is supplied by gas blowing engines or steam turbo-blowers. It is preheated in stoves (heated by waste gases) before being introduced into the furnace.

Plant Layout for Production of Pig Iron

The complete plant for the production of pig iron mainly consists of the following :

(*i*) Blast furnace.

(*ii*) Dust catcher, gas washer etc., for cleaning blast furnace gases.

(*iii*) Gas blowing engines or steam turbo-blowers (driven by waste gases) for pumping the air to the blast furnace.

(*iv*) Blast stoves for preheating cold air blast coming from gas blowing engines and going to blast furnace.

(*v*) Appliances for sending required quantities of iron ore, fuel and flux to the furnace top.

(*vi*) Appliances for disposing off the slag.

(*vii*) Appliances for conveying pig iron produced.

(*viii*) Water pumping equipment for cooling blast furnace lining.

(*ix*) Power plant for generating electric power from blast furnace gases.

Blast Furnace

Working in brief. Ore, fuel and flux in required proportions are charged into the furnace at the top. Air blast is blown in through a number of pipes (tuveres) provided circumferentially around the furnace bottom. The air blast rises up through the descending charge. The gases of combustion move upwards, the liquid iron and slag formed collect in the bottom. Slag being lighter than iron floats over the latter. For tapping out slag and iron, slag spout and tapping spout are provided.

The capacity of blast furnace ranges from 250 to 1200 tonnes per day of pig iron. The process is continuous one which when once started runs for years.

Construction

(*i*) **Shaft or stack.** The furnace mainly consists of a tall structure about 30 metres high and 10 metres diameter at the widest section. It is made of two cones with their bases together ; the upper one being longer (known as stack or shaft). The height of the shaft is about three-fifths of that of the whole furnace. The stack diameter increases downwards gradually for allowing easy descent of the charge which expands due to increasing heat downwards.

The charge is introduced at the top of the stack (called throat) through a double cup and cone arrangement to prevent the blast furnace gases from escaping to the atmosphere.

The upper frustum is supported on 12 or 16 cast iron pillars all around the furnace.

(*ii*) **Bosh.** The lower frustum of cone is known as '*Bosh*'. It is much smaller in height, the hottest part of the furnace forming the main melting zone. Its diameter narrows down from about 10 to 8 metres in a vertical height of about 5 metres from junction with the stack. The bosh wall is inclined about 10 to 15° to the vertical axis.

(*iii*) **Well or hearth.** The bosh rests on a short cylindrical section called hearth or well. The well has same diameter as that of the lower end of the bosh. Its height is three-fourth to seven-eighth of its diameter. It serves as a vessel for collecting molten iron and slag. It rests on strong concrete foundation covered with several layers of fire bricks.

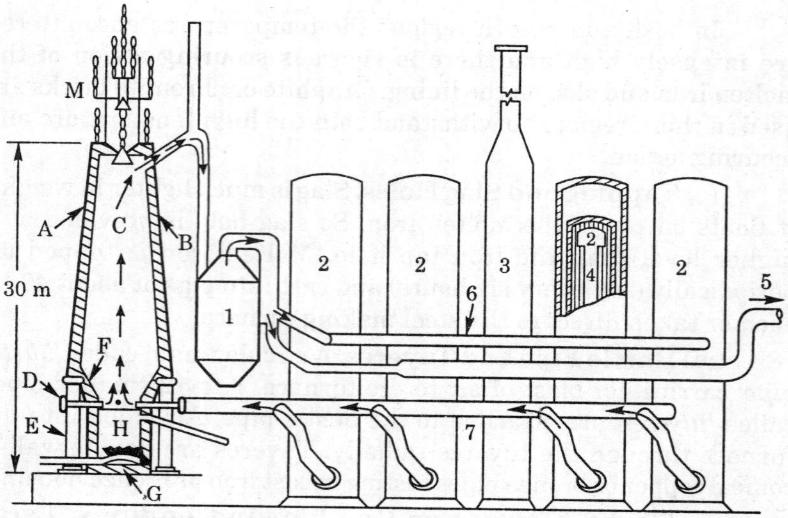

A—Outer steel shell
B—Refractory lining
C—Charge of iron ore, limestone and coke
D—Bustle pipe
E—Tuyeres or water-jacketed projecting nozzles of copper of bronze for forcing air blast.
F—Cooling tubes
G—Molten pig iron
H—Molten slag
M—Double cone and cup arrangement for feeding the charge without allowing the gases to escape.

1—Dust catcher which collects coke dust and other particles.
2—Cowper stoves.
3—Chimney.
4—Combustion chamber inside the stoves consisting of checkered brickwork for heating air.
5—Gas to blowing engines.
6—Gas for heating stoves.
7—Hot blast pipe.

Fig. 9.1. General arrangement of an iron-smelting Unit with a blast furnace.

(*iv*) **Lining.** Stack, bosh and hearth are lined with suitable thickness of refractory fire bricks.

In the stack region thickness is maximum due to wear and abrasion from solid charge being greatest there. The bricks used for stack are of high alumina.

In bosh and hearth regions the temperatures encountered are intensely high and there is vigorous scouring action of the molten iron and slag on the lining. Graphite or chromite bricks are used in these regions to withstand both the high temperature and scouring action.

(*v*) **Tapping and Slag Holes.** Slag is much lighter in weight. It floats on top of the molten iron. So slag hole is provided at a higher level than the iron tap hole. Molten iron is topped off periodically (say every six hours) and cast into pigs of about 40 kg each or taken direct to the steel making furnace.

(*vi*) **Bustle Pipe and Tuyeres.** A circular main called '*bustle pipe*' carries hot blast of air to the furnace. 8 to 12 smaller pipes called '*tuyeres*' are attached to the bustle pipe. Air is led into the furnace through the tuyeres radially. Tuyeres are double-walled conical copper or bronze pipes resting in cast iron or bronze housing.

(*vii*) **Turbo-blowers or Gas blowing engines.** Large quantities of air are supplied for combustion in blast furnace by means of turbo-blowers or gas blowing engines (upto 3000 H.P.) with a capacity of 1400 to 2000 cubic metres per minute.

(*viii*) **Blast stoves.** Air is preheated (to about 800°C) in heaters known as '*blast stoves*' before introducing in the blast furnace.

Advantages of preheating air

(*a*) It helps in producing a very high temperature inside the blast furnace resulting in a large saving of the fuel *e.g.*, coke required per tonne of pig iron using cold blast of air is about 8 tonnes whereas if air blast preheated to about 700°C is used, coke required per tonne of pig iron is hardly one tonne.

(*b*) Using preheated air acelerates the reduction process and melting down of the air.

(*c*) Even if air is heated by a separate fire, sufficient economy is found to be affected.

(*ix*) **Cooling system.** Continuous stream of cold water is circulated through numerous cooling boxes distributed in the bricks work to protect the walls of furnace, bosh and well regions against high temperatures. About 20 to 25 million litres of water per day are required for cooling a blast furnace.

For sending the charge to the top of the furnace, mechanically or electrically operated appliance is used. Different raw materials in measured quantities are carried in automatically operated hoppers or trolleys along an inclined plane from the base where the raw materials are first dumped from the wagons.

The slag which is periodically tapped off the furnace is first cooled and then carried away by suitable means to a distant place.

Chemistry of Blast Furnace. The temperature of the charge consisting of iron ore, coke and flux progressively rises and intensity of its reduction also increases as it descends from the throat towards the bosh. The whole furnace may be divided into the following four zones according to the reductions taking place at different sections :

1. Moisture Evaporation Zone. It is the space just below the throat. Only moisture content of the charge is removed in this zone as the temperature is low (about 200° to 400°C).

2. Iron Oxides Reduction Zone. The reduction of iron oxide (Fe_2O_3) is nearly complete in stages by first forming Fe_3O_4, then Fe_3O and finally Fe by the time, the charge descends by about 15 metres.

The intensity of reduction of carbon and carbon monoxide increases as the temperatures are higher:

At about 400° to 450°C:

$$2Fe_2O_3 + 6CO = 4Fe + 6CO_2$$
$$Fe + CO_2 = FeO + CO$$

At about 500°C to 600°C:

$$Fe + CO = FeO + C$$
$$3Fe_2O_3 + C = 2Fe_3O_4 + CO$$
$$Fe_3O_4 + C = 3FeO + CO$$

At about 650° to 700°C:

$$Fe_3O_4 + CO = 3FeO + CO_2$$

At about 700° to 750°C:

$$FeO + CO = Fe + CO_2.$$
$$CO_2 + C = 2CO.$$

In this zone, limestone also starts disassociating to form CaO and CO_2 and starts its fluxing action towards the end of this zone :

$$CaCO_3 = CaO + CO_2$$

3. Smelting Zone. Iron coming from the last zone in a spongy form tends to combine with carbon of hard coke in this zone (extending from about 15 to 22 metres from the top). This causes lowering in melting point, greater heat absorption and fusing at about 1350°C.

Also CaO combines with gangue (Al_2O_3 and SO_2) and slagging action is complete till the products reach the tuyere level. Main reactions taking place in this zone are :

$$CaCO_3 = CaO + CO_2$$

$CaO + Al_2O_3 + SiO_2$ = Silicates and Aluminates.

$MgCO_3 = MgO + CO_2$

$FeS + CaO + C = Fe + CaS + CO$

$Fe_3O_4 + C = 3FeO + CO$

$FeO + C = Fe + CO$

$3FeO + 4C = Fe_3C + 3CO$

$3Fe + C = Fe_3C$

$MnO + C = Mn + CO$

4. Zone of Complete Fusion. This zone comprises mainly the bosh portion. It is characterised by intense chemical reactivity, very high temperature and extremely reducing atmosphere.

In this zone, iron gets fully saturated with carbon, becomes superheated and is in a completely fused state when it reaches the lower end of bosh.

The molten iron along with the slag formed drops down and collects in the hearth or well. Slag being lighter floats over heavier iron.

Waste Gases from Blast Furnace. These are at a considerably high temperature (800–1200°C) as they pass out of the furnace. Their heat is utilized before letting them off to chimney. Before utilising, these gases are first passed through chambers called dust catchers and then through gas washers so as to separate the unrequired impurities like dust and coke particles.

(*i*) A great saving in power is affected by using the waste gases as fluid to run the gas-blowing engines of very large size and capacity. These engines compress and pump the air in the blast furnace.

(*ii*) Heat of waste gases is utilised by Cowper type blast stoves for preheating the cold air blast to about 800°C as it comes from the gas blowing engines. These stoves work on the regenerative principle of heating.

(*iii*) Blast furnace gases are also used in many cases for generating electric power in the gas-turbines. This results in a considerable saving fuel and overall economy in the production cost of pig iron.

Plast Stoves. They preheat the cold air blast as it comes from the gas blowing engines by utilising the heat of waste gases.

Cowper type stove working on the regenerative principle are usually used. They consist of tall cylindrical shells closed at the top and lined with fire bricks and filled with a chequer-work of firebricks.

Blast furnace gases heat the stoves for a period of 2-3 hours so that the brickwork attains an incandescent state. Now these gases are diverted to another set of stoves and cold air blast is introduced through these heated stoves. Thus, the brickwork heats the cold air to about 800°C before it is allowed to go to the blast furnace.

For one blast furnace, usually, three stoves are allocated so that while two of them are *'on gas'*, *i.e.,* heating the chequer work the third one is *'on blast'*, *i.e.*, heating the air because it takes twice the time for heating up a stove *'on gas'* as to exhaust it *'on blast'*.

Mechanically or Electrically operated Appliance for sending the Charge to the Top of the Furnace

The different raw materials in measured quantities are conveyed in automatically operated trolleys or hoppers along an inclined plane from the base where they are first dumped from the wagons.

The slag which is periodically tapped off the furnace is first cooled and then carried away to a distant place by a suitable means.

The molten pig iron tapped periodically is either poured and cast into *'pigs'* or taken direct to steel making furnace for refining. Pig iron is in a highly impure state and cannot be put directly into any practical use. During refining stage, other additional elements are also added up if desired, so as to eliminate or reduce a large proportion of impurities.

Production of Wrought Iron

Characteristics. (*i*) It is the purest form of iron, usually 99.5% pure iron.

(*ii*) Due to its very low carbon content, it is very malleable and ductile having a tensile strength of about 3000 kg/cm^2.

(*iii*) It can bend easily without cracking or fracture.

(*iv*) It has a fibrous texture when observed under a microscope. It is due to the inclusion of slag along with the filaments of pure iron.

(*v*) Presence of slag in it imparts it resistance to alternate bending stresses.

(*vi*) Besides high ductility and easy workability, it also has a high resistance to corrosion, easy weldability and high load carrying capacity.

Uses. It is largely used for manufacture of chain; draw bars, anchors, crane hooks, horse shoes bolts, nuts railway couplings pipes and pipe fittings, plates, sheets, boiler tube, etc.

Manufacture

1. Puddling process. Wrought iron is produced by removing most of the carbon, manganese, silicon, phosphorus and sulphur from pig iron by the process of what is called "*puddling*" in a reverberatory furnace. Maximum quantity of carbon present in wrought iron does not exceed 0.15%.

The furnace is rectangular in shape and has a chimney stack *K*, on one side. The fuel may be soft coal or coke, which is burnt in a grating *E* situated on the side opposite to that of the chimney stack *K*, and only the flames of the producer gas (CO) heat the metal in the shallow heart *B*.

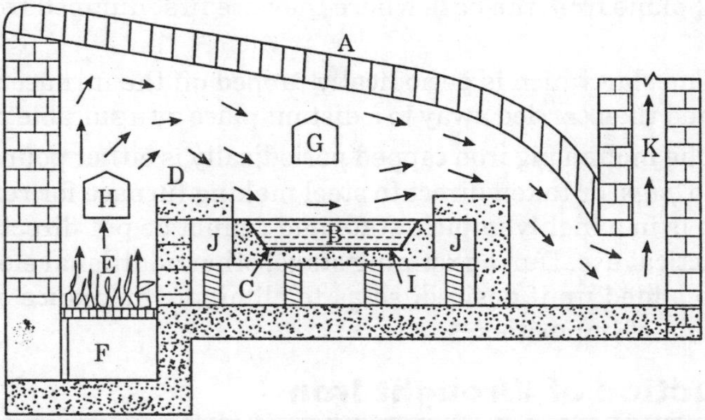

A—Roof of fire brick. B—Shallow hearth or bath.
C—Hearth lining. D—Bridge.
E—Grating. F—Ashpit.
G—Charging door. H—Fuel feeding door.
I—Bottom steel plates. J—Water jackets.
K—Chimney.

Fig. 9.2. Reverberatory furnace for puddling.

The bottom of the hearth consists of cast iron plates I, 38 mm thick, supported on dwarf brick walls which allow free circulation of air below the plates. The latter are, in consequence cooled. In addition to this, hollow casting *J* are provided on sides, through which water is circulated.

A lining *C* of molten slag is given with a top layer of rich iron ore before the charge of high grade pig iron is fed through the door *G*. The hearth is shaped like a saucer about 1.5 m by 1.2 m size. The flames from the grate *E*, which rise are diverted by the peculiar archshaped roof and concentrated on the hearth. The lining material acts as the oxidising agent and burns the impurities.

The operator puddles or stirs the contents of the hearth vigorously by a long bar and exposes them to flames of CO. When the metal has melted, balls of the pasty mass, each about 50 to 75 kg in weight are formed, which are like a sponge of white hot iron with the pores filled with molten slag. These are taken to the next process of shingling or squeezing.

Shingling or Squeezing Process. The balls are subjected to squeezing action, either under the blows of a power hammer or a squeezing machine (Fig. 9.3).

Squeezing machine consists of a thick steel cylinder with corrugations on the inside and another smaller cylinder with the corrugations on the outside surface, fixed eccentrically inside the outer cylinder.

As the inner cylinder rotates it pushes by means of the corrugations the balls introduced at one end. The eccentricity of the two cylinders causes the gap between them to be gradually reduced. The ball is progressively force into this gap and the molten slag is squeezed out of it as it passes out in the form of a '*bloom*' at the other end.

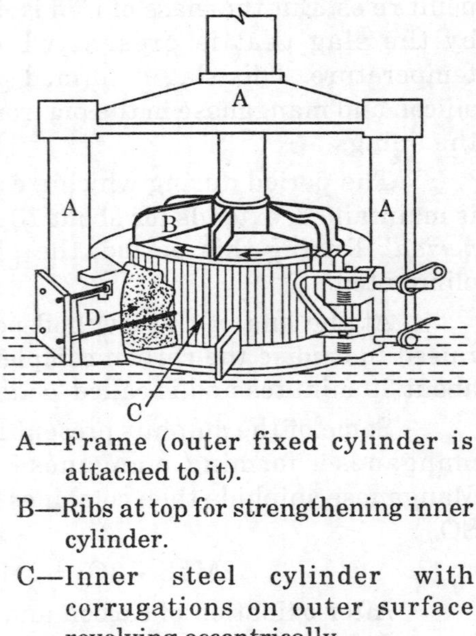

A—Frame (outer fixed cylinder is attached to it).

B—Ribs at top for strengthening inner cylinder.

C—Inner steel cylinder with corrugations on outer surface revolving eccentrically.

D—Wrought iron spongy balls.

Fig. 9.3. Squeezing or Shingling Machine (Outer cylinder front removed).

The bloom, still in white hot condition is passed through grooved rollers to form flat bars of 15 by 100 mm cross-section called '*muck bars*' or '*puddle bars*'. It still contains excess of slag. The bars are, therefore, cut and the pieces bundled together by wires

and several times reheated, welded and rolled until all, or practically all slag is removed and the metal assumes a perfectly fibrous structure inside. It is sometimes known as '*Double refined iron*'.

Chemistry of the process. A temperature of about 1200–1400°C at which the furnace is maintained, is not sufficient to melt pure iron. But owing to impurities present, the charge melts down readily taking about half an hour. The metal must then be stirred continuously for a period of 10 minutes to help the oxidation of silicon by the air passing over the charge.

Small amounts of iron ore are also thrown into the furnace to promote oxidation of carbon. As the carbon is oxidised, the melting point rises. But the mass of iron is prevented from becoming solid by the slag that is present which remains molten at that temperature. This slag is formed partly due to the oxidation of silicon and manganese in the pig iron and partly due to the wear of the lining.

The period during which a comparatively low temperature is maintained, extends for about 10 minutes and is called '*low boil period*'. During this period, the phosphorus content is almost eliminated.

At the end of the low boil period, furnace temperature is raised to oxidise the carbon completely. The period extends upto about 30 minutes and is called '*actual boil period*'.

Some of the sulphur present in pig iron also combines with manganese, forming manganese sulphide and join the slag. Manganese sulphide then combines with oxygen to form MnO and SO_2 :

$$2MnS + 3O_2 = 2MnO + 2SO_2.$$

After oxidation of carbon and other impurities, the mass of iron is left in a pasty form, which is then worked into balls. These balls are pulled out of the hearth by means of tongs for squeezing operation.

The quality of wrought iron produced by this puddling process is very high, but the process being very laborious, the iron so produced is much more expensive than steel.

2. **Aston or Byers Process.** In order to produce wrought iron in large quantities at a lower cost, this process was developed in the year 1925.

In this process, the pig iron is first melted in a cupola furnace and refining of molten metal is done in a Bessemer Converter. At

the same time, a quantity of iron silicate slag is prepared in an open hearth furnace.

Ther refined iron so made in the Bessemer converter is poured at pre-determined rate into a ladle containing the molten slag already prepared. The temprature of the slag being maintained several hundred degrees lower than the freezing point of the refined metal, the latter is rapidly solidified with the liberation of gases producing small globules of the metal which form a spongy mass on the bottom of the ladle containing the mixture.

After pouring the excess slag from the ladle, the remaining mass of iron and slag is taken to a press where some slag is removed. The rectangular block formed in the press is known as *'bloom'*. The hot bloom is immediately passed through rolling mills to produce wrought iron products of different shapes and sizes.

Table 9.2: Chemical Composition of Wrought Iron

(Per cent)

(Produced by Aston Process)

Carbon 0.02, Silicon 0.15, Manganese 0.03, Phosphorus 0.12, Sulphur 0.02, Slag 3.00, Remainder iron.

Characteristics and Uses of Steel Castings

Plain Carbon Steel Castings

Characteristic. (*i*) They contain 0.1–1.5% carbon whereas C.I. contains 1.8–4.2% C.

(*ii*) They are tough, ductile and easily weldable.

(*iii*) Solidification range for:

(*a*) Low carbon steels (0.1–0.25% C) is 1500–1435°C

(*b*) Medium carbon (0.2–0.5 %) is 1480–1220°C

(*c*) High carbon (0.5–1.5% C) is 1465–1180°C.

(*iv*) Their shrinkage is 1 to 2 mm in 100 mm.

Uses : They are used for:

(*i*) Ingot and pig moulds.

(*ii*) Rolling mill rolls.

(*iii*) Couplings, brake shoes, drawbars etc., in transportation.

(*iv*) Anchor chains, rudders etc. in marine works.

(*v*) Frames, gears, engine housings, cylinder blocks and heads etc., in automotive industry.

(*vi*) Frames, rotors, housings, base etc., in electricalindustries.

Alloy Steel Castings

Characteristics. (*i*) They contain more than 0.5% Si and 0.5% Mn.

(*ii*) They may contain Ni, Cr, Mo etc., also as alloying elements.

(*iii*) They possess sufficient abrasion and corrosion resistance.

(*iv*) They are more strong, tough and fatigue resistant and possess high yield point.

Uses. They are used for :

(*i*) Long span bridges.

(*ii*) Structural applications.

(*iii*) Components of small tankers, barges etc.

(*iv*) Earth-moving and agricultural machinery components.

(*v*) Transmission towers.

(*vi*) Railroad tyres.

(*vii*) Electric pole line fillings and hardware.

(*viii*) Components of ore boats.

(*ix*) Columns in high buildings.

(*x*) Coal bunkers.

Heat Resisting or High-temperature Steels

Characteristics. (*i*) They are meant for service at temperatures above 650°C.

(*ii*) They possess strength even at elevated temperatures.

(*iii*) They are of two types ; cast and wrought having different composition.

(*iv*) Selection of heat resisting steel for a particular purpose depends upon.

(*a*) Desired life of component.

(*b*) Nature of casting design.

(*c*) Frequency and range of temperature cycle.

(*d*) Fabrication of casting, if necessary.

(*v*) They can be cast in thicknesses of 4.5 mm and above. Machining allowance of 3 mm is given.

(*vi*) Most of machining operations are possible on them. For better results, rigid machines, slow feeds and deep cuts are necessary. Both high speed steel and carbide tipped tools can be employed. Water soluble cutting fluids should flood over the tool

and the workpiece. For this, sulpho-chlorinated petroleum oil with sulphur and about 8–10% fatty oil may be used.

(*vii*) Heat resisting steels are classified as:

(*a*) Iron chromium alloys, which contain 8–30% Cr, less than 7% Ni and have ferritic structure. They have good resistance to oxidation and sulphur atmospheres.

(*b*) Iron, chromium, and nickel alloys, which contain 19–32% Cr and 8–22% Ni and have austenitic structure. As compared to category I, they possess better temperature strength and may be used in oxidizing and reducing atmospheres.

(*c*) Iron nickel and chromium alloys, which contain 23–68% Ni and 10–23% Cr and has stable austenitic structure. They withstand rapid heating and cooling cycles and can be used upto 1150°C. They are not advisable to be used in sulphur bearing atmosphere.

Uses. They are used for:

(*i*) Power plant superheaters.

(*ii*) Cement kilns.

(*iii*) Glass making and oil refinery furnaces.

(*iv*) Processing equipments operating upto 1200°C.

(*v*) Heat treatment furnace components.

(*vi*) Steel mill economizers.

(*vii*) Missile, jet engine and gas turbine components.

Cast Stainless Steels

Characteristics. (*i*) Iron-Chromium and Iron-Nickel-Chromium alloys with a minimum 8% of alloying elements are called "*Cast Stainless Steels*". They are used in corrosive atmosphere at temperatures below 650°C.

Iron-chromium alloys contain 11.5–30% Cr and upto 4% Ni. They are:

(*a*) Highly resistant to oxidizing solutions.

(*b*) Used in chemical plants processing nitric acid and nitrates.

(*c*) Of two types; non-hardenable and hardenable.

(*d*) Resistant to erosion.

Iron-Chromium-Nickel alloys contain 15–30% Cr, 3–30% Ni and upto 0.2% C. In addition, may contain 2–3.25% Cu and 2–3.25% Mo.

(*ii*) An alloy for a particular use is selected depending on:

(*a*) concentration, pressure and temperature of corrosive environment.

(*b*) contaminants in the solution.

(*c*) fluid velocity.

(*iii*) They can be readily machined but cutting tool should not be work-harden the surface of the casting due to rubbing action.

For better results, slow feeds, deep cuts, rigid machines firm tool, flood lubrication and cooling are necessary.

Carbide tipped and high speed steel tools can be used.

Uses. They are used for:

(*i*) Chemical industries.

(*ii*) Pumps, valves, fillings, mixers, etc.

(*iii*) Soap industries.

(*iv*) Process equipments operating at 230–650°C.

(*v*) Pulp and paper industry.

(*vi*) Manufacturing explosives.

(*vii*) In atomic energy process.

(*viii*) Components for bleaching and dying in textile industry.

(*ix*) Food and beverage plants.

(*x*) Parts for manufacture of synthetic fibre.

(*xi*) Cryogenic applications.

Methods of Manufacturing Steel

For converting pig iron into steel, following methods can be used:

1. Cementation Process.
2. Crucible Process.
3. Converter Process.
4. Linz-Donawitz Process.
5. Open-hearth Process.
6. Electric Process.

Cementation Process. This process is very old one and was in use before the open-hearth and Bessemer processes were developed.

In this process, bars of wrought iron are arranged in a brick compartment of the furnace with charcoal between and around them. Furnace is heated to redness and maintained for 7 to 10 days at that temperature. The bars are then allowed to cool down.

During heating, the iron bars absorb carbon from the charcoal. The amount of carbon absorbed depends on the time and temperature. Outer layers of bars absorb more carbon than interior ones. Due to some air leakage into the compartment, carbon monoxide gas is formed which produces a short of blisters on the metal surface.

The bars so obtained are very heterogeneous in nature and their chemical composition is not certain. Their slag content also remains as such. However, the homogeneity can be increased to a certain extent by hammering and forging process.

Crucible Process. This process is also an obsolete one now but in the 17th and 18th centuries it was regarded as one of the producing finest quality steels.

It is actually a refining process for making steel of cementation process more homogeneous and uniform in structure. Steel pieces from cementation process are charged in the crucible kept in a furnace previously heated up. The pieces melt down in about an hour's time. The slag present in the metal comes to the surface and is skimmed off. The molten metal is poured into ladles or moulds.

Alloy steels were also made by adding suitable alloying elements in the charge along with the metal. These days, this process has almost been superseded by the electric furnaces.

Converter Process. Converter is a vessel in which molten pig iron coming from the blast furnace is poured. Through the molten pig iron, a strong blast of cold air is then blown which oxidises all the impurities in the metal.

These converters are classified according to the method used for passing the air blast as:

(*i*) Bottom blown or Bessemer converter.

(*ii*) Side blown or Tropenas converter.

Bottom Blown or Bessemer Converter Process. Bessemer converter consists of a pear-shaped steel shell about 3 metres in diameter and 5.4 metres height with a lining of fire clay or other highly refractory silicious material for acid or basic melting. The cylindrical shell can be rotated about a horizontal axis by means of two trunnions. One of these trunnions is hollow and cold air is led through it to the wind box or wind chamber which is finally distributed to several tuyeres made of fire clay.

As air enters the tuyeres, its pressure is about 2 to 2.5 kg/cm^2. This pressure is sufficient to prevent the molten metal from running down into the air box.

The converter is usually filled only about one-tenth full holding nearly 14 tonnes of metal and its mouth is kept eccentric so as to hold the charge when in horizontal position and prevent the metal from being ejected during the blowing operation.

The tuyere bricks get corroded due to the action of molten metal and slag. So they require periodical renewal say, after every 20 heats. The bottoms of the converters are, therefore, usually made detachable. The renewal is very easy and takes about 15 minutes as previously made bottoms are kept ready in stock for replacement.

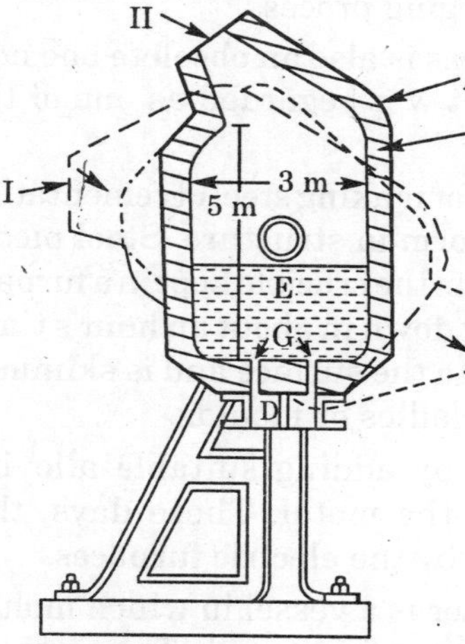

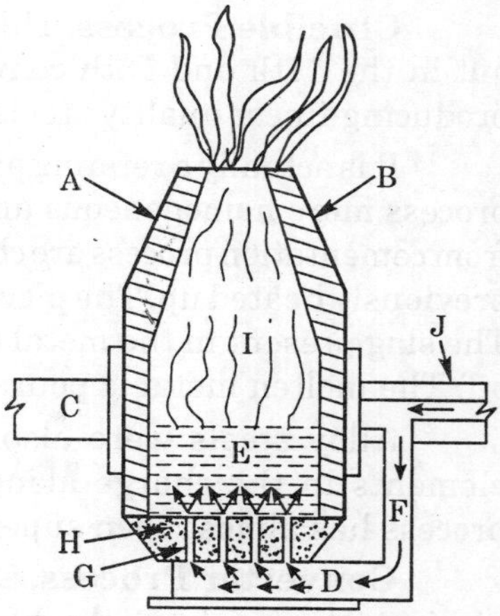

A–Steel shell, B–Refractory lining, C–Trunnion
D–Air box in the bottom, E–Pig iron, F–Air dust,
G–Tuyeres, H–Removable bottom, I–Flames,
J–Hollow trunnion.

I–Charging position.
II–Working position.
III–Tapping position.

Fig. 9.4. Bessemer Converter. **Fig. 9.5.** Converter in action.

Process. From the blast furnace, the molten pig iron is brought in ladles of about 60 to 80 tonnes capacity and transferred first to reservoirs of 1000 to 1500 tonnes capacity. Small quantities of molten metal (about 12 tonnes at a time) are taken from reservoir to the converter and poured into it when it is in horizontal position.

Air blast under a pressure of 2 to 2.5 kg/cm^2 is turned on and the converter is swung to vertical position. Fine streams of air are blown through the tuyeres into the molten metal for about 10 minutes, thus oxidising almost all impurities.

Now, converter is returned to horizontal position air blast is shut off and recarburisers and deoxidisers in necessary quantities are added to obtain steel of the desired composition.

Operation. The whole operation of Bessemer converter may be divided into three periods:

(*i*) **Slag period.** During this period, the molten pig iron is poured into the converter and the blast is started. Oxygen of the blast combines with silicon and manganese. Oxidises them to SiO_2 and MnO forming slag. Short, dull red flame with dense born clouds of smoke is produced. Due to this oxidation the temperature rises. Slag period extends for 4 minutes.

(*ii*) **Boil period.** Boiling takes place during this period due to oxidation of carbon to CO and CO_2. The flame is very long and luminous yellow about 10 metres high on the top of the converter. Boil period extends for 6 minutes.

(*iii*) **Finishing period.** When oxidation of carbon is complete, the boil period ends, the flame gradually gets shortened and the carbon content is reduced to about 0.04%. During this period, the actual carbon content may be judged by observing the size and colour of the flame. Finishing period extends for about 2 minutes.

The amount of heat required during these operations does not come from any external source but it is made available from the oxidation reactions themselves. The oxidation of silicon produces a large proportion of heat, which is mainly responsible for raising the temperature to about 1700°C. Silicon is thus an important and essential element in this case.

If silicon content in the charge is too low, the metal blows cold. This will require addition of additional silicon in the form of ferrosilicon. If silicon content in the charge is too high, the metal blows very hot. This will require addition of extra scrap iron to reduce the temperature.

The metal obtained at the end of the finishing operation is almost free from the impurities including carbon. To get the required content in the composition of steel, the carbon is added subsequently in the form of coke.

Gases in the metal, Deoxidation and Degasification of the metal. The metal contains dissolved gases and oxygen in it. If these are allowed to remain, they may cause blow holes in the metal. The metal has, therefore, to be degasified and deoxidised.

Deoxidisers consist of silicon, manganese, aluminium, etc. in the form of ferrosilicon (66% silicon), ferromanganese (80%

manganese, 7% carbon), spiegeleisen (20% manganese, 6% carbon) or other suitable compounds. These deoxidisers and recarburizers are either added to the converter after completion of oxidation or more commonly placed in the bottom of ladles.

Acid and Basic Bessemer Processes. The Bessemer process may be either of acid or basic type according to the nature of refractory lining used in the furnace.

(*i*) **Acid Bessemer Process.** In acid process, the slag produced is acidic in character. So, the impurities like sulphur and phosphorus are not reduced at all, *i.e.*, they remain as such in the steel produced. For making steel by this process, it is, therefore, essential that the original pig iron must be low in both sulphur and phosphorus.

Although sulphur content can be reduced in the blast furnace by proper control, phosphorus remains unaltered. Thus, in acid process, pig iron from ores containing low amount of phosphorus (usually below 0.05%) can only be used.

The silicon content present in the metal should be high (not less than 1%) so as to produce the required amount of heat during the blowing period. For production of steel by Acid Bessemer process, a suitable composition of pig iron may be : Silicon 1–1.5%, phosphorus 0.05–0.1% (max.), manganese 0.5%, suphur 0.08%.

(*ii*) **Basic Bessemer Process.** Acid process cannot be employed when the phosphorus content of iron ore or pig iron is high. For such irons, therefore, basic process is employed.

In basic process, lime is added to the slag to make it basic. This lime acts as a flux and helps in reducing phosphorus from the iron. The lining is made of some basic material like dolomite or magnesite so as to prevent its corrosion from the basic slag.

Silicon content of these irons should be basically low since high silicon tends to attack the basic lining and requires greater amount of flux for producing slag.

In basic process, necessary heat is supplied by the oxidation of phosphorus, which is the chief heat producer. Phosphorus must, therefore, be high (about 2%). High phosphorus is generally accompanied by a high sulphur content. So, manganese should also be high for taking care of high sulphur.

For steel making by Basic Bessemer process, a suitable composition of pig iron may be:

Silicon 1% (max.), phosphorus 2%, manganese 1%, sulphur 0.15% (max.).

In this process, the charge consists of molten pig iron and flux. The flux (*e.g.*, lime) is partly added in the beginning to take up the SiO_2 produced and the remaining added during the boil period to reduce phosphorus. Total amount of lime added may be 15–20% of the weight of pig iron.

In this process, the converter is somewhat larger in size because the amount of slag produced is larger. Also, this process requires somewhat longer time for completion than the acid one.

Side-blown Tropenas Converter Process. In this process the air blast is blown from the sides at a pressure of about 0.3 kg/cm^2 across the surface of the molten metal instead of being blown through the bottom.

The method of operation is practically similar in both cases except that reactions are slower in the side blown type. When the reactions are complete, the end point is also less sudden. Hence, possibility of over-blowing of the metal is less.

Deoxidisers and degasifiers are added by throwing them into the molten and blown iron. They are not placed in the ladle in the process.

Table 9.3: Comparison between Acid and Basic Processes

Acid Bessemer Process	*Basic Bessemer Process*
1. Operation is easier.	Due to danger of rephosphorization higher skill required.
2. Lining is less expensive and more durable.	Lining is more expensive.
3. Converter size is smaller.	Converter size is larger.
4. Handling costs are lower.	Handling costs are greater.
5. Slag produced is less.	Slag produced is greater.
6. Process is cheaper as operation is shorter.	Process is expensive as operation takes longer time and requires the use of lime.
7. More expensive grade of ore having lower phosphorus content is required.	Cheaper ores containing high phosphorus can be used.

Linz-Donawitz Process (L.D. Process). It is a modified and a refined form of the older Bessemer process first developed in Austria in the year 1953. In India, it has recently been used at Rourkela Steel Works for production of flat, plates and sheets.

This process is much simpler and more efficient than the basic Bessemer one. It does not use any tuyeres, windbox or detachable bottom.

Instead of using an air blast and blowing it from the bottom or sides, this process makes use of a jet of pure oxygen (99.5% pure) at a pressure of 8 to 11 kg/cm^2 which is introduced through a water-cooled nozzle pipe called '*lance*' at a very high speed. Lance is suspended vertically into the converter with its nozzle end about 75 to 90 cm above the bath.

During charging and emptying, the lance will not obstruct as it is of removable type. As the oxygen gas leaves the conical nozzle and strikes the bath, and intensely high temperature of about 2500°C is produced. At this high temperature, the oxygen reacts violently with silicon, manganese and carbon present in the molted metal producing large amounts of oxides. Due to the intense heat, sulphur and phosphorus are also effectively reduced.

Advantages. (*i*) Steels produced by this process, known as L.D. steels are superior in properties to those produced by the converter or open hearth process because they are almost free from nitrogen.

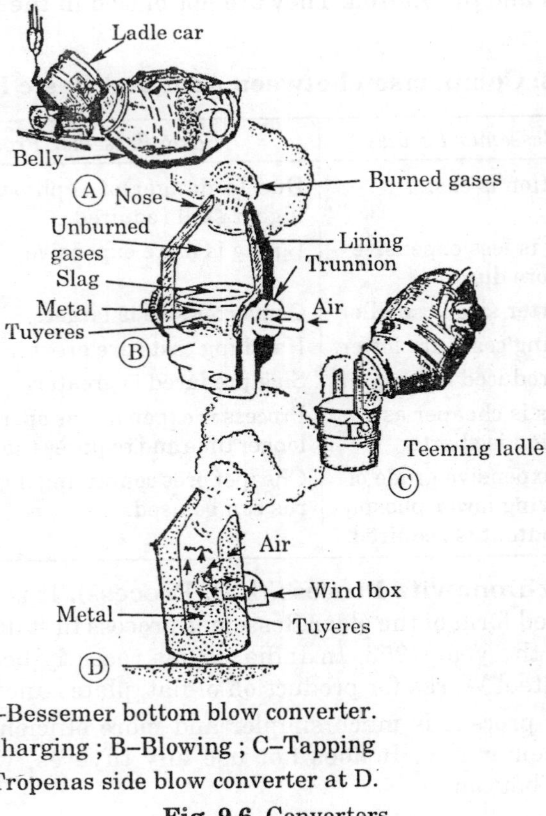

(1)—Bessemer bottom blow converter.

A–Charging ; B–Blowing ; C–Tapping

(2) Tropenas side blow converter at D.

Fig. 9.6. Converters.

(*ii*) Although an additional plant for generating highly pure oxygen is required, this process is more economical due to simplicity and rapidity of operation.

(*iii*) Indian raw materials which are rich in phosphorus and sulphur are particularly suited to this proces for steel making.

Open Hearth Process. It is based on the regenerative principles of heating, *i.e.*, very high temperatures required for steel making are obtained by preheating the gaseous fuel and air by the outgoing products of combustion.

Construction. Open hearth furnace consists of a shallow hearth about 12 metres long, 4.5 metres wide and 50 cm deep lined with a highly factory material (acid or basic) depending upon the kind of metal charged and the type of steel to be made. A slightly arched roof of refactory brick and brick side walls supported heavy metal stays are provided.

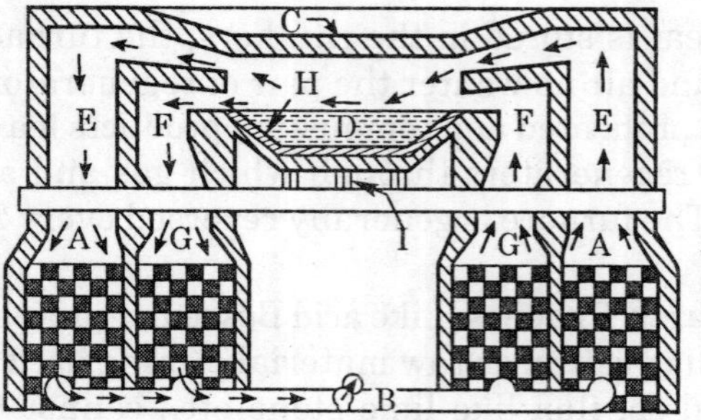

A, A – Hot air regenerative chambers.
B – Gas and air pipe.
C – Fire brick lining.
D – Molten metal bath.
E, E – Air ducts.
F, F – Gas flues.
G, G – Gas regenerative chambers.
H – Hearth lining.
I – Steel girders.

Fig. 9.7. Siemens-Martin Regenerative Open-hearth Furnace.

Several charging openings are located on one side of the furnace for convenience in loading the metal charges. The tap hole is located on the opposite side. The combustion chambers, located at each end, are used alternately during the melting process. The furnace is heated by burning gas and air that has been heated before it enters the combustion chamber.

Regenerative chambers are located below each end of the furnace. These chambers are filled with fire brick laid in a checkerboard pattern to absorb the heat from the gases discharged from furnace hearth. This heat will be returned to the incoming gas and air when the flow is reversed. Waste gases are exhausted into the atmosphere through a stack after they have passed through the regenerative chamber.

The flame is directed over the top of the metal to prevent oxidation. The metal is heated by indirect radiation from the roof and direct radiation from the flame. Tests are made during the

melting process to determine the condition of the metal. When the process has been completed, the metal is tapped into ladles to be poured.

Working. Gaseous fuel used may be producer gas, natural gas, coke oven gas or a mixture of coke oven gas and blast furnace gas.

Gas and air flow through one of the pair of regenerators and absorb heat from them. These are then led through the uptake flues into the hearth and get ignited there. Products of combustion produced by ignition sweep over the bath containing molten pig iron and transfer their heat to it.

The combustion products then leave the furnace through the ports on the other side, pass through the other pair of regenerators transferring most of their heat to the checker bricks and finally escape through the chimney to the atmosphere.

When sufficient heat is stored in the checkers, the furnace is reversed, *i.e.*, the gas and air now enter the pair of regenerators on the other side, become preheated and combustion products leave the hearth by ports and regenerators through which gas and air was passing previously. The furnace is generally reversed every 20 to 30 minutes.

(*a*) **Acid Open-hearth Process.** Like acid Bessemer process, it requires low phosphorus pig iron as raw material. Lining used is for silica or fire clay and so, flux like lime stone etc., cannot be used, for reducing phosphorous and sulphur. These impurities, therefore, cannot be removed by this process.

For steel making, this process is rarely used as the corresponding acid Bessemer process is much more simpler and economical.

Basic Open-hearth Process. For producing steel from high phosphorus pig irons this process is employed. Lining is of some base material like dolomite, magnesite etc. and so flux like limesone can be used for reducing phosphorus and sulphur.

The hearth may either be of fixed or tilting type for the metal to flow out easily. Its capacity varies between 100–200 tonnes. It is made of fire bricks at the bottom, covered by magnesite bricks upon which another layer of calcinied magnesite mixed with basic open-hearth slag is put.

The furnace charge consists of solid or molten pig iron, scrap, iron ore (for affecting oxidation) and limestone as a flux.

The ports should be designed at such an angle that (*i*) the gases do not directly impinge on the bath and also (*ii*) the roof may not be unduly heated. To prevent excessive oxidation of the metal and permit good mixing, the air port is usually placed above the gas port.

Advantages of Open-hearth Process over Bessemer Process. (*i*) The temperature and the composition of the bath are under much better control as the ore acts as an oxidising agent and heat is applied externally.

(*ii*) This method has greater flexibility as greater variety of raw materials can be employed.

(*iii*) Due to addition of ore and scrap, it gives a much increased output from the same among of pig iron.

(*iv*) Basic open-hearth process permits the use of any pig iron. It can eliminate phosphorus completely whereas in Bessemer process, there are limitations.

(*c*) **Duplex Process or Special Open-hearth Process.** It consists of using an acid Bessemer converter in conjunction with a basic open-hearth furnace.

Advantages. (*i*) High silicon and high phosphorus pig iron can be converted into good steel by this method.

(*ii*) It increases the life of open-hearth furnace as there is no silica present which may react with the lining.

(*iii*) It also considerably reduces the time of open-hearth heat and labour.

Electric Process of Steel Making. The first large scale application of electric heating to metallurgical practice was allowed by the advent of electric furnaces some sixty years ago. Since then, the electric furnaces have been a boon to the steel industry because:

(*i*) more accurately controlled higher temperatures can be obtained.

(*ii*) the charge may be exposed to atmosphere which will not contaminate the metal.

Limitation of Electric Process. Electric furnaces are mostly used for high quality steel production usually alloy steels and tool steels due to high cost of electric power.

For smelting and remelting two types of electric furnaces generally used, *viz.,* arc furnaces and induction furnaces have been described in the next article.

Oxygen Process of Steel Making. High nitrogen content of Bessemer steel is a disadvantage for certain cold forming applications. In recent years, modified pocesses have been developed, in which oxygen replaces air. As already discussed, in Austria, L.D. Process converts low-phosphorus pig iron into steel by top blowing with an oxygen lance using a basic lined vessel.

To avoid excessive heat, scrap or ore is added. High quality is produced with low hydrogen and nitrogen (0.002%). (*i*) A further modification of the process is to add lime powder to the oxygen jet (*O.L.P. Process*) when higher phosphorus pig iron is used.

(*ii*) **Kaldo (Swedish) Process** uses top blowing with oxygen together with a basic lined rotating (30 r.p.m.) furnace to get efficient mixing. Use of oxygen allows simultaneous removal of carbon and phosphorus from pig iron. Lime and ore are added.

(*iii*) **German Rotor Process** uses a rotary furnace with two oxygen nozzles, one in the metal and one above it.

(*iv*) **Use of Oxygen with Steam in the Traditional Basic Bessemer process** is also now widely used to produce low nitrogen steel.

These new techniques produced steel with low percentages of N, S, P, which are quite competitive with open-hearth quality.

Vacuum Melting and Casting for Steel Making is also gaining ground for special alloys. Vacuum largely removes hyrogen, atmospheric and volatile impurities (Sn, Cu, Pb, Sb), reduces metal oxides by C–O reaction and eliminates effects of atmospheric contamination. The clean metal produced is of a consistent high quality, with good properties in transverse direction of rolled products.

Table 9.4: Classification of Steel Castings

1. *Carbon Steel Castings:*
   (*i*) Low carbon (less than 0.20 per cent).
   (*ii*) Medium carbon (0.20 to 0.40 per cent).
   (*iii*) High carbon (over 0.40 per cent).
2. *Alloy Steel Castings :*
   (*i*) Low alloys (special alloying elements less than 8 per cent).
   (*ii*) High alloys (special alloying elements over 8 per cent).

Chemical Composition of Medium Carbon Steel Castings (per cent).

Carbon 0.2 to 0.4, Manganese 0.5 to 1.

Silicon 0.2 to 0.75, Phosphorus 0.05 max.
Sulphur 0.06 max., Remainder iron.

QUESTIONS

1. What is meant by "acid refractories" and "basic refractories"? Give examples for both. Why this distinction is important in steel melting?

2. Explain the effect of the following in cupola melting:
(*a*) Coke-bed height.
(*b*) Iron coke ratio
(*c*) Air flow rate.

3. Give the merits and demerits of acid and basic linings in a cold blast cupola.

4. Describe how would you specify a cupola? Explain with a neat sketch the cupola operation.

5. (*a*) Explain the various combustion reactions in a cupola having the blast at room temperature.
(*b*) How these reactions can be affected if a hot blast is substituted?

6. Discuss the practice adopted for melting aluminium base alloys with special reference to the following:
(*a*) Melting furnace
(*b*) Grain refinement
(*c*) Fluxing and digasification of melt.

10

Remelting Furnaces for Casting

Generally, the metals which are obtained either from the blast, furnace, steel making furnaces or other non-ferrous smelting furnaces, are not cast directly into the desired shapes of articles or components due to the following reasons :

(*i*) The metals so obtained are not always in a sufficiently refined state that can be directly cast.

(*ii*) From practical point of view also it is difficult to pour the huge quantity of molten metal in the moulds of different shapes and sizes.

The metals which are obtained from the smelting furnaces are first cast into some regular forms like the pigs or ingots. These forms are remelted in foundries for casting the required components.

For remelting purpose, one of the following furnaces may be used :

(*i*) *Crucible furnace :*

(*a*) Pit-type coke-fired furnace

(*b*) Tilting type or Bale out type gas–or oil-fired-furnace.

(*ii*) *Electric furnace :*

(*a*) Direct-arc type

(*b*) Indirect-arc or Induction type.

(*iii*) *Open hearth furnace.*

(*iv*) Air furnace or Reverberatory furnace.

(*v*) Cupola furnace.

(*vi*) *Converter :*

(*a*) Bottom blown or Bessemer Converter

(*b*) Side blown or Tropenas Converter.

Table 10.1 : Principal Processes used for Remelting and Refining Pig Iron

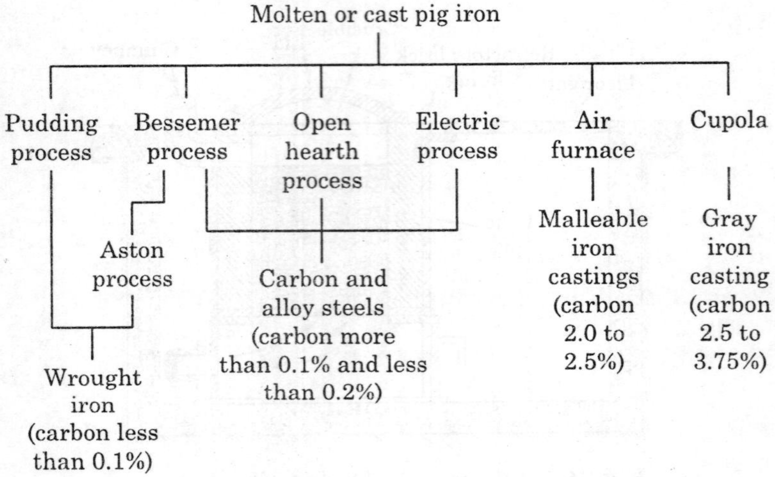

Principal Difference between Cast Iron, Steel and Wrought Iron is Carbon Content

Cast Iron.........	carbon more than 2.0%
Steel.........	carbon less than 2.0%, but more than 0.1%.
Wrought Iron.........	carbon less than 0.1%.

Crucible Furnaces

For small foundries, the crucible furnaces are very convenient because the operation is intermittent and various alloys are handled in small quantities.

For melting the metal, it is put in a heated crucible which acts as a melting pot. The crucible is made of clay and graphite by moulding into a standard shape and size. Its size is specified by a number ranging from 1 to 400. The crucible number represents its approximate holding capacity in kg, of aluminium. For other metals, the capacity of a crucible may be determined by multiplying its number with the ratio of their densities (metal : aluminium).

According to the fuel used for heating the charge, that crucible furnaces are classified as under :

(*i*) **Pit-type coke-fired crucible furnace.** This furnace is installed in a pit so is referred to as '*pit type*'. It essentially consists of a cylindrical steel shell lined with refractory fire bricks on the

inner side. It is closed at the bottom with a grate and covered at the top with a removable lid. The metal to be melted is put in the crucible which is embedded in the burning coke.

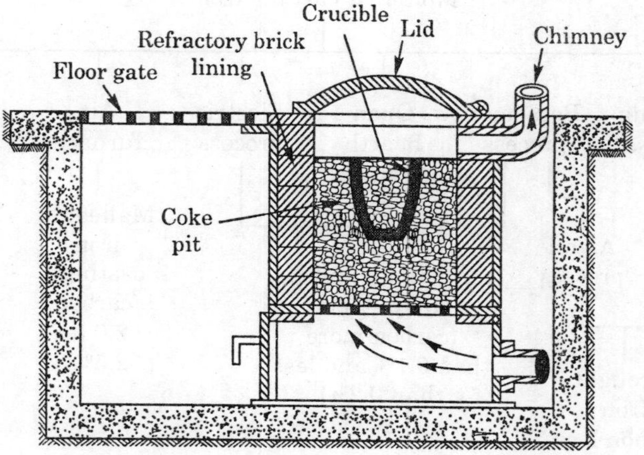

Fig. 10.1. Pit-type coke fired crucible furnace.

It is most commonly used for melting non-ferrous metals like aluminium, brass, bronze etc., owing mainly to :

(*a*) its low cost of installation,

(*b*) cheap fuel, and

(*c*) easy operation.

Working. A deep bed of coke is kindled and allowed to burn until a state of maximum combustion is attained. Some coke is removed from the top and the crucible is lowered into the furnace. The coke is again added surrounding the crucible on all sides. The metal is then charged in the crucible and lid is replaced to facilitate the chimney draft. Forced draft is generally available from a blower, which is used to help in rapid combustion of the coke. When the metal melts and reaches the desired temperature, the crucible is taken out by means of special long handled crucible-tong and carried away for pouring into the moulds.

(*ii*) **Tilting type oil or gas-fired crucible furnace.** In this furnace, oil or gas is used as a fuel for heating the crucible. The furnace is cylindrical shaped lined inside with fire bricks. The flame produced by the combustion of oil or gas with air is allowed to sweep around the crucible and heat it uniformly.

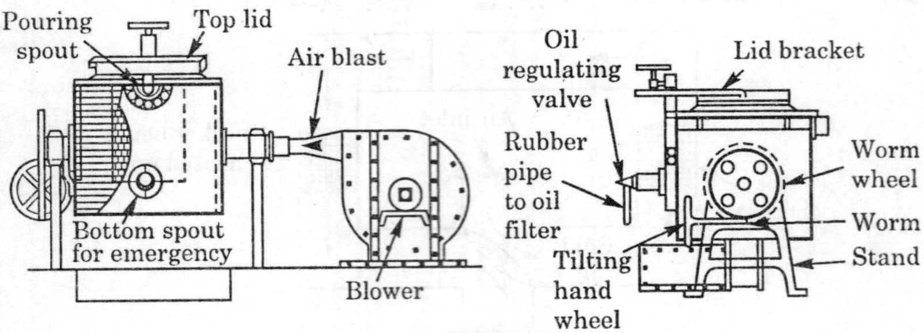

Fig. 10.2. Tilting type oil-fired crucible furnace.

Atomised fuel oil or gas is fed through a manifold. It enters the furnace tangentially where it ingnites and swirls upwards between the refractory lining and the crucible. The metal is charged in the crucible through the opening in the centre of the head.

Modern gas and oil fired furnaces are equipped with :

(*a*) automatic proportioning device which produces a neutral flame by regulating the fuel-air ratio.

(*b*) thermostatic device for controlling temperature.

(*c*) regenerative system of heating for economy in gas-fired furnaces.

These furnaces are generally of bale out type or tilting type.

(*a*) The bale out or lift out furnaces are of fixed type but unlike the pit type, are installed on the floor. In order to take out the metal, the crucible is lifted out of the furnace by means of long-handled crucible tongs.

(*b*) The tilting type furnaces are raised above the floor level, mounted on two pedestal trunnions and rotated by means of a geared hand wheel, a hydraulic ram or in case of large sized furnaces rotated by power. The tilting gear is generally designed so that the furnace tilts on a central axis.

Advantages of gas-or oil-fired furnaces over the coke-fired ones :

(*a*) As soon as the metal is ready, the supply of oil or gas can be stopped. It can also be varied while working according to the requirements. Thus, there is no waste of fuel.

(*b*) Better temperature control.

(*c*) Saving in floor space.

(*d*) Less contamination of metal.

(*e*) No stocking is needed. Hence saving in labour.

(*f*) In a given time, output is greater due to higher efficiency.

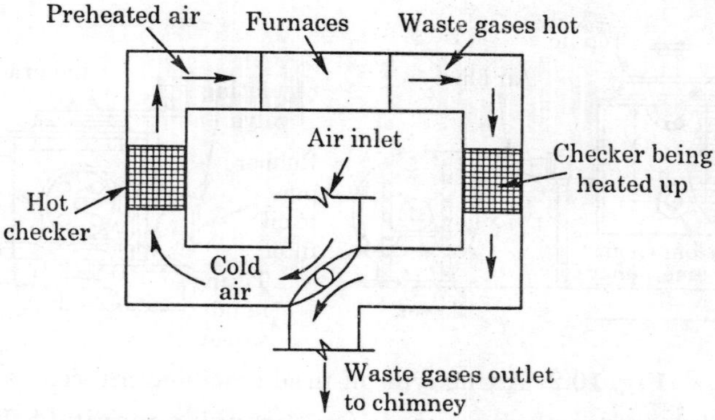

Fig. 10.3. Regenerative heating of air for gas fired crucible furnace. (Waste hot gases from furnaces being utilised for preheating supply air)

Electric Furnaces

Both arc and induction type electric furnaces can be used for remelting purposes. Although adaptable equally well for both ferrous and non-ferrous metals, electric furnaces are mainly used for producing highest quality steels (tool steels, stainless steels), grey irons, brasses due to their high cost of operation.

Usually, these furnaces are worked in conjunction with cupola and Bessemer converter, thus the processes used are known as :

(*i*) Duplexing Process.
(*ii*) Triplexing Process.

(*i*) **Duplexing Process.** In this process, the iron is more economically melted in a cupola and refined in the electric furnace.

(*ii*) **Triplexing Process.** In this process, the iron is melted in a cupola, converted into steel in a Bessemer converter and then transferred to electric furnace for altering, adjusting or improving its properties.

In this process, the function of electric furnace is to maintain a constant supply of molten metal at a constant temperature for continuous pouring.

The application of these furnaces mainly depends on the quality of metal desired and the cost of electric power. The high quality product is due to the following facts :

(*a*) A precise control of temperature is possible.

(*b*) The atmosphere produced by the arc is free from any deletrious effect.

(*c*) Metal composition can be closely controlled.

Types of Electric Furnaces. Three types of electric furnaces used for melting are :

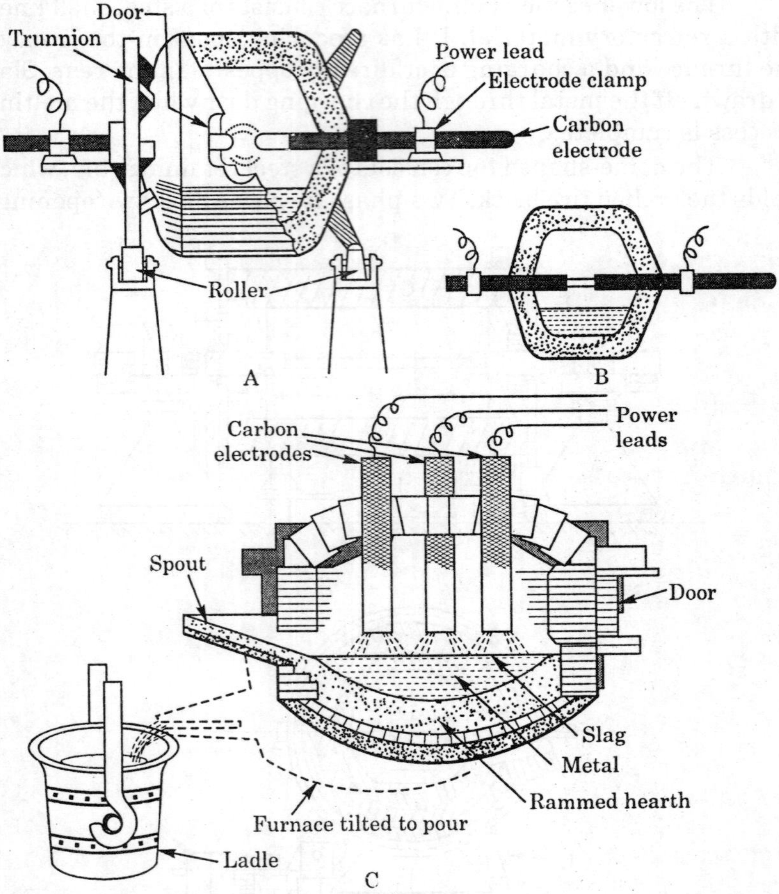

A–Indirect Arc Furnace "*Rocking Arc*".

B–Resistance Unit.

C–Direct Arc Furnace "*Three-phase*"

Fig. 10.4. Electric Arc Furnaces.

(*i*) Direct arc electric furnace.

(*ii*) Indirect arc electric furnace.

(*iii*) Induction electric furnace.

(*i*) **Direct arc electric furnace.** The direct arc furnace is cylindrical in shape, with a bowl-shaped bottom. The top consists of a dome-shaped fire brick cover. The furnace is mounted on two

bearings fastened to its side. These bearings are mounted in trunnions assembled on a concrete base.

The lower section of the furnace consists of a steel shell lined with a refractory material. It has a pouring spout in the front of the furnace and a charging door directly opposite in the rear. Slag is drawn off the metal through the charging door when the melting process is complete.

The dome-shaped top consists of a steel retaining ring, which holds the arched fire brick. Two-phase furnaces have two openings

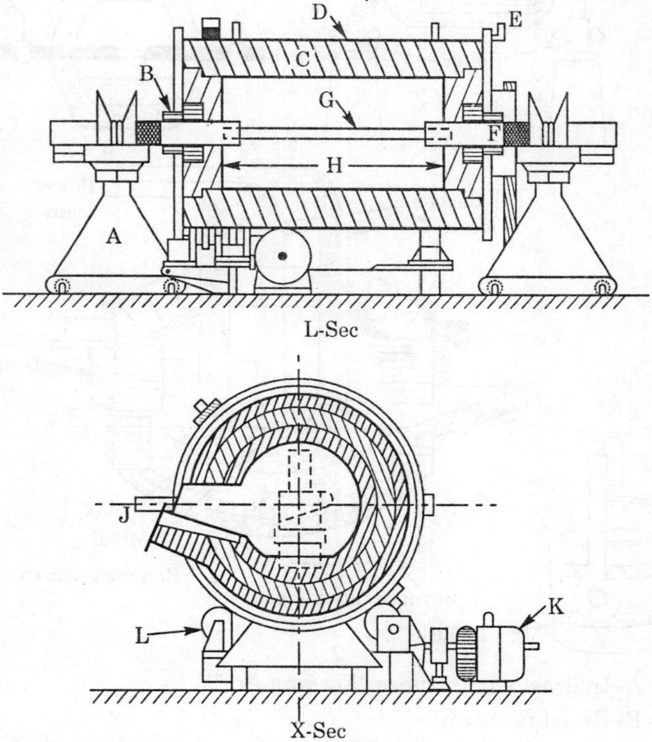

A–Movable carriages.	B–Sealing rings.
C–Lining and insulation.	D–Body.
E–Detachable flanged ends.	F–Graphite resistor holders.
G–Resistor.	H–Metal level.
J–Pouring spout.	K–Tilting and rocking gear unit.
L–Rollers.	

Fig. 10.5. Rocking resistor furnace heated by the passage of electric current through the horizontal resistor rod. Resembles Indirect rocking arc furnace. Suitable for melting special cast irons, bronze and other copper alloys.

in the roof, and three-phase furnaces have three. These openings permit the electrodes carrying the electric current to the furnace to be raised and lowered during the melting process. The electrodes carried on horizontal arms that are raised and lowered mechanically on vertical posts attached to the furnace body. The electrode glands or guides, placed on top of the furnace roof, are water cooled. The charging door flame is also water cooled to resist the action of the intense heat. The size of the furnace to be installed in a foundry is governed by the maximum molten metal demand of that shop.

Direct arc furnaces are lined with either acid or basic linings, depending upon the class of metal melted and the type of castings produced. The acid lining is used for high quality steels and grey or white iron. The basic-lined furnace is used for carbon, alloy and manganese steels.

Furnace Operation. The furnace is preheated by placing short pieces of electrode on the hearth and lowering the carbon electrodes until they form an arc. The mechanical operating switch starts motors, which raise the electrodes slowly until the electric arc breaks. The motors reverse automatically, lowering the electrodes to form another arc. The process is repeated until the furnace is thoroughly heated.

The arc creates the heat, which is retained by the refractory lining. When the preheating process has been completed, the electric current is shut off. The small pieces of electrode in the furnace are removed. The charge of metal that is to be melted is carefully proportioned, weighed and placed on the hearth of the furnace. The electric current is turned on, and the electrodes lowered to form an arc upon contact with the metal. The controls are set to cause the electrodes to raise and lower automatically, making and breaking the electric arc, which creates the heat necessary to melt the metal.

Silica sand and lime placed on top of the metal charge melt to form a liquid slag over the metal. The slag covering the molten metal is removed from the furnace when the melting process has been completed. The metal is transferred from the furnace to the moulds in refractory-lined ladles.

The furnace is drained of all metal and a refractory material is used to make repairs to the side walls and hearth.

The direct arc furnace is also used for duplexing metal, *i.e.*, liquid metal tapped from the cupola furnace is poured into the heated electric furnace. The temperature of the furnace is raised

and other elements are added to the molten metal to make an alloy. This heating process may also be used as a medium for removing or burning out undesirable elements in metal charge.

The use of the direct arc furnace is desirable for melting and refining all grades of steels and irons where careful control of composition and temperature of metal is required.

Specifications. The most commonly used type of direct arc furnace is the Heroult furnace. It is built in sizes ranging from 2 to 6 metres diameter and capacity ranging from 1 to 125 tonnes. The average unit has 50 to 70 tonnes capacity, about 5 metres diameter and 25 mm steel shell encasement. The power input of the transformers used to supply the current varies from 150 to 40,000 kVA.

Advantages. The main advantages claimed by the direct arc electric furnace are as under :

(*a*) It affords to attain high purity in the metal as the electric arc is greatest commercial source of heat without any risk of contamination.

(*b*) The rate of heat applied can be closely controlled.

(*c*) The thermal efficiency is high (above 70%).

(*d*) The atmosphere above the molten metal in the furnace can be easily controlled.

(*e*) Steel can be made direct from pig iron and steel scrap.

(*f*) Alloying elements *e.g,* nickel, chromium, tungsten etc., can be recovered from the scrap.

(*ii*) **Indirect Arc Electric Furnace** (Fig. 10.4 and 10.5). The indirect arc furnace is a single-phase electric furnace. It differs from the direct arc furnace in that the electrodes do not come in contact with the metal but form an arc above it. The furnace is rocked mechanically during the melting cycle, insuring a thorough and complete mix of the metal.

Rocking electric furnace is built in the form of a hollow cylinder or drum mounted in a horizontal position or rollers. The rollers are part of the supporting frame that is mounted on a brick or concrete base.

The shell of the furnace is steel plate with a refractory lining and has three openings, one electrode port at each end a charging door opening midway between. The spout is built into the charging door, which is clamped in place during the pouring operation.

The furnace is roked mechanically, clockwise and counter clockwise, on its horizontal axis. The arc of rotation is adjustable from a minimum to a maximum angle.

The electrodes are adjusted manually at the start and operate mechanically during the melting period.

The metal is charged into the furnace through the charging opening. Pig metal is placed on the bottom, underneath the electrodes. The scrap metal is placed on top of the pig and is banked to the front and rear of the electrodes.

When the electric current is turned on, the heat from the electric arc melts the scrap first, forming a pool on the bottom of the furnace. The rocking action is started, and the molten metal picks up heat as it washes over the hot refractory lining and conveys the heat to the heavier metal that is still unmelted. The charge is, therefore, heated by radiation from the arc and conduction from the lining. The high thermal efficiency thus obtained results in lower power consumption.

Advantages. The indirect arc rocking type furnace has the following advantages :

(*a*) The rocking action prevents excessive water on the furnace lining because no part is unduly exposed to the extreme heat radiated from the arc.

(*b*) The lining surface is submerged regularly beneath the bath, dissipating the absorbed heat to the molten metal and causing rapid and efficient melting.

(*c*) The non-oxidising atmosphere of the furnace permits careful control of the metal composition without the use of special slags.

(*d*) The mechanical mixing caused by the rocking action insures a uniform composition of the metal.

The rocking type indirect arc furnace is simple to operate and control and is particularly useful when low-priced scrap metals are to be used to produce high-test iron.

(*iii*) **High Frequency Induction Electric Furnace.** The coreless induction furnace is built on the principle of an air transformer whose primary is a helical coil of water-cooled copper tubing and whose secondary is the charge of metal to be melted. A high frequency current of 1000 to 3000 cycles is supplied by a motor generator set or an electric generator set. By induction, secondary currents called eddy currents are produced in the crucible charge.

These currents flow due to the potential difference between various parts of the charge and the resistivity of the metal causes current losses which are dissipated to heat energy therby melting the metal. In ferrous metals showing magnetic property, the loss due to hysteresis produces extra amount of heat.

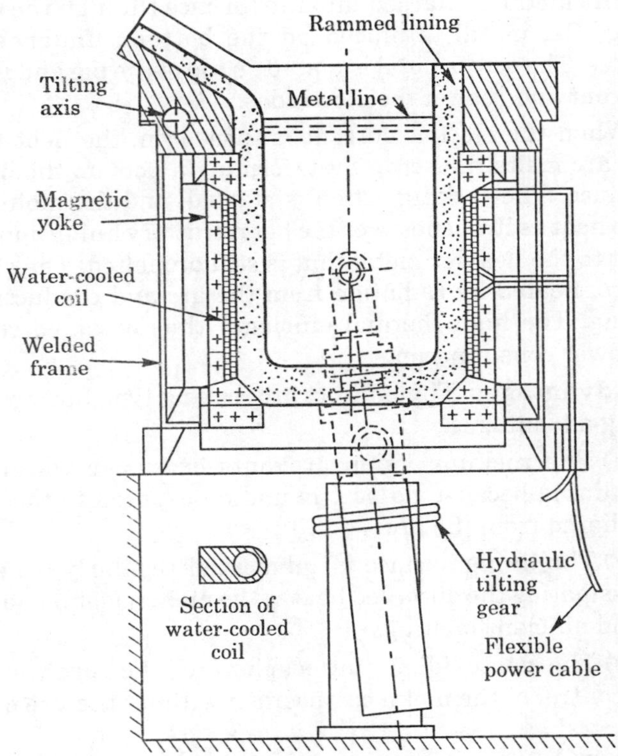

Fig. 10.6. High frequency induction electric furnace.

Furnace capacity varies from 0.3 to 6 tonnes and electric consumption 700 to 1000 kWh per tonne of steel.

Operation of the Induction Furnace. A weighed charge of metal is placed in the furnace. High-frequency current passing through the primary coil induces a secondary current in the metal charge, heating it by resistance. The heat is developed in the outer part of the charge and is carried to the centre by conduction. When the metal starts to melt, it forms a pool in the bottom of the furnace.

A stirring action occurs in the molten metal, causing it to wash against the unmelted metal, transferring heat to it and therby speeding the melting process. The stirring action also insures a

thorough mixture of the metal resulting in uniformity of the finished product. The stirring action is controlled by the power input.

When the metal is melted and the desired temperature is obtained, the electric current is shut off. The furnace is tilted forward to empty the molten metal into ladles to be conveyed to the moulds for pouring.

The furnace lining must be carefully checked and the cracks sealed to prevent any leak of molten metal, which would damage the copper coil. When the furnace is shut down, the water in the copper coil continues to circulate until the furnace is properly cooled.

The induction furnace can be controlled to melt rapidly or slowly. It is particularly adaptable for melting metals that must be free of contamination from carbon and for alloying metals that must be thoroughly and completely mixed.

Air Furnace

It is essentially of open-hearth type, *i.e.*, it works on the principal of reverberatory furnace. The unit is fired at one end only, using powdered coal for fuel; air for combustion may be preheated in regenerators as described under open hearth furnace.

Fuel bituminous lump coal is pulverized by high speed rotary crushers and blown into the furnance as fine dust. Oil may also be used as fuel. The product of combustion are drawn across the metal charge and out a draft stack.

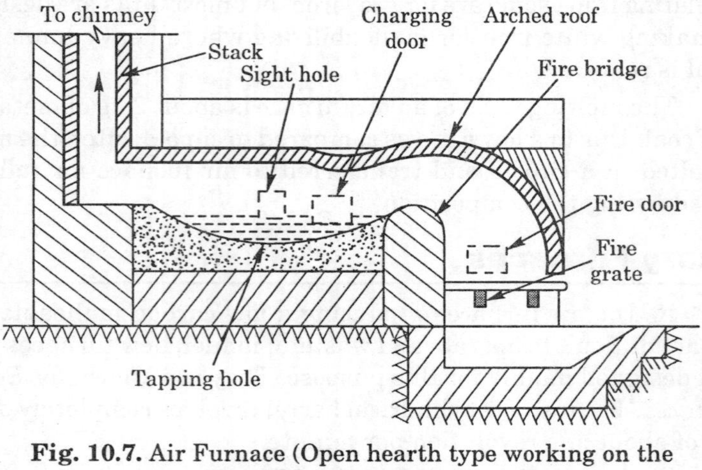

Fig. 10.7. Air Furnace (Open hearth type working on the principle of reverberatory furnace).

Charging. Air furnaces are charged by removing sections of the arch roof, called *'bungs'*, and dropping the scrap, pig iron, or other ingredients through the hole ; the bungs are then replaced and sealed with clay.

Construction and Working. The fire box, in which the heat is created, is separate from the hearth or melting chamber. The chimney, located at the end of the furnace opposite the fire box, draws the flame over the fire bridge through the melting chamber. For stirring, skimming etc., suitable openings are provided in the side wall.

The flame and hot gases heat the walls and roof of the furnace. The metal charge lying on the furnace hearth is melted and superheated by the heat radiated from the roof and side walls of the furnace.

The fuel and metal are not in direct contact during the melting process. A small amount of sulphur may be absorbed by the metal from the hot gases passing through the furnace.

Tests can be made during the melting process which result in careful control of the metal. When the metal reaches the proper temperature and composition, the furnace is tapped and the metal drawn off into ladles for pouring.

The size of the hearth for a 20 tonnes capacity air furnace may be about 8 metres length and 2 metres width.

Applications. Air furnaces are used in the foundry chiefly for melting iron ; some are for grey iron, but most units are designed for making white iron for malleabilizing where heavy tonnage of metal is required.

The melting ratio of an air furnace is about 2 kg of metal per kg of coal. Due to a low ratio as compared to cupola, often the metal is melted in a cupola and transferred to air furnace for refining and adjusting the composition.

Rotary Furnaces

As the air furnaces producing a low-carbon malleable cast iron are difficult to operate and wasteful in fuel, new furnaces have been designed mainly for this purpose. They are known as *'Rotary Furnaces,'* because the cylindrical barrel revolves completely at the rate of about one revolution per minute.

Their capacity ranges from 1 to 50 tonnes, there being a single burner at one end of the barrel ; they are fired by oil or pulverized coal. High-temperature flame melts and superheats the charge in

the barrel ; the waste gases passing out at the other end of the barrel are directed through a series of recuperator tubes on their way to the chimney. Fans or blowers direct the incoming cold air over the outer surfaces of these tubes to enable the air to pick up heat which would be otherwise wasted up the chimney.

The temperature of the air arriving at the pulverized fuel burner is adjusted by dampers to suit the volatile content, moisture content and state of fineness of the powdered coal. Air to fuel ratio can be adjusted, and by burning powdered coal without excess air a high temperature can be obtained without any oxidation of iron.

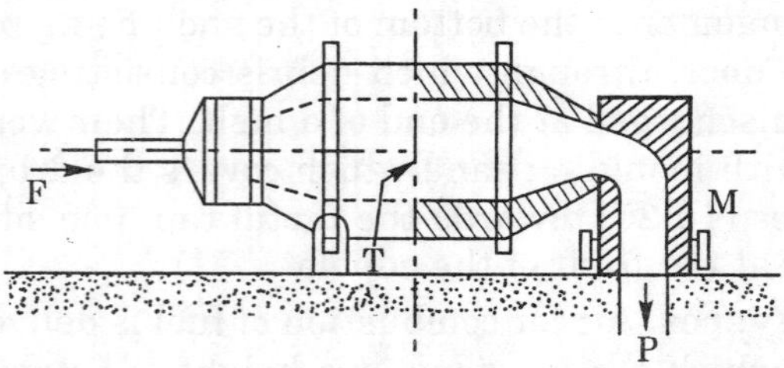

F–Fuel and air to burner T–Tapping spout
M–Movable exhaust box P–To preheater

Fig. 10.8. Rotary furnace with recuperator.

Such a furnace will produce molten grey iron as cheaply as a cupola furnace can. Molten metal can be held in the furnace until a sample has been analysed and composition of both corrected.

In addition to being given rotary motion, the furnace body can be tilted on an angle of 45° to bring the mouth level with a charging platform so as to speed up the charging operation. Rapid transference of heat from rotating refractory lining to molten metal enables the melting to be out by 50% in comparison with a stationary furnace using a similar burner.

Cupola Furnace

Introduction. The cupola is the standard unit of the iron foundry. Cupola melting is generally considered the cheapest method for converting cold scrap metal or pig iron to usable molten iron. The features of the cupola are essentially those of a typical blast furnace, well known for use in converting iron ore to pig iron.

Fuel for the cupola is preferable a good-grade, low sulphur coke. Anthracite coal or carbon briquettes may also be used.

The furnace is charged at frequent intervals with proportioned amounts of coke, limestone, and metal (pig iron, scrap steel or scrap iron).

Melting can be continuous over long periods of time, or intermittent, as required.

Description. (*i*) **Shell.** It consists of a vertical, cylindrical shell made of 6 to 12 mm thick boiler plate riverted or welded together and lined inside with acid refractory bricks and clay. Refractory bricks and clay used for cupola lining consist of silica acid (SiO_2) and alumina (Al_2O_3). Cupola diameter varies from 1 to 2 metres with a height of from 33 to 5 times the diameter.

(*ii*) **Foundation.** The shell is mounted either on a brickwork foundation or on steel columns. Most modern cupolas use steel column arrangement ; the bottom of the shell being provided with drop bottom door, through which debris consisting of coke, slag, etc., can be discharged at the end of a melt. Their working bottom is built up with moulding sand which covers the drop doors. This bottom slopes (1 : 20) towards the metal tap-hole situated at the lowest point at the front of the cupola.

(*iii*) **Tuyeres.** Air for combustion of fuel is delivered through the tuyeres which are provided at a height of between 0.6 to 1.2 metres above the working bottom. Total area of the tuyeres should be 1/5 to 1/6 of the cross-sectional area of the cupola inside the lining at tuyere level. Tuyeres have usually a size 50 × 150 mm or 100 × 300 mm. Some cupolas are provided with tuyeres in one row, others have two or more rows.

(*iv*) **Wind belt.** The air is delivered to the tuyeres from a wind belt which is a steel plate duct mounted on the outer shell of the cupola.

(*v*) **Blower.** A high pressure fan or a blower supplies the air at the wind belt through a blast pipe. A valve is provided in the blast pipe to control the supply of air. The blast pressure varies from 265 to 350 kg/m^2 in small, low cupolas to 150 kg/m^2 in large tall cupolas.

(*vi*) **Volume meter.** It is sometimes installed to know the volume of air passing. The amount of air required to melt one tonne of iron depends upon the quality of coke and coke-iron ratio.

In a cupola, assuming that a 10 : 1 ratio of iron to coke is used, about 850 cubic metres of air are required to melt one tonne of iron. Higher volumes of air will be required for lower fuel ratios.

(*vii*) **Slag-hole.** It is located at a level about 250 mm below the centres of the tuyeres.

(*viii*) **Charging hole.** It is provided through which metal, coke and flux are fed into the furnace. It is situated 3 to 6 metres above the tuyeres, according to the size of the cupola.

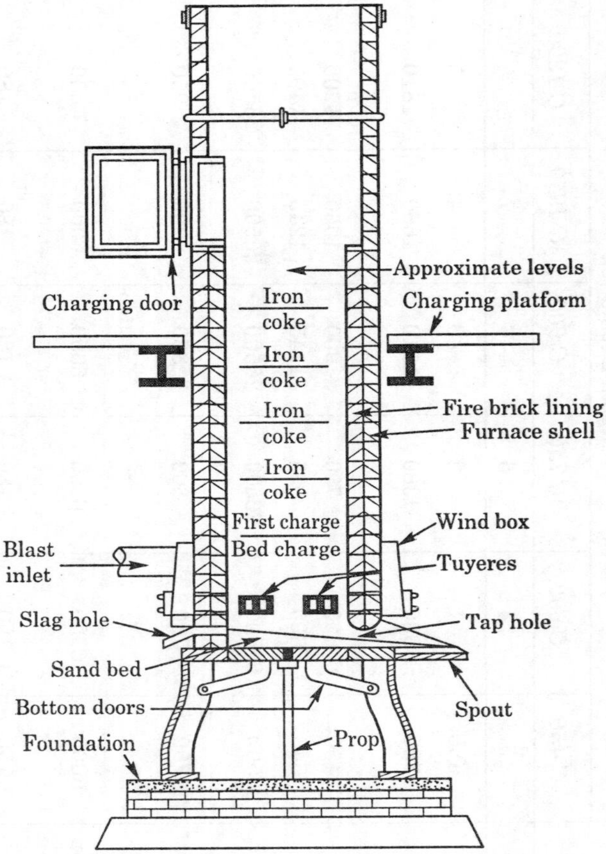

Fig. 10.9. Section through a Cupola Furnace.

(*ix*) **Charging platform.** It is a large platform or stage usually surrounding the cupola at the level of about 0.3 metre below the bottom of the charging door.

(*x*) **Chimney or Stack.** The shell is usually continued for 4.5 to 6 metres above the charging hole to form a chimney.

Zones in a cupola. The entire shaft of the cupola is divided into four sections :

(*i*) Crucible zone. (*ii*) Melting zone.

(*iii*) Charging zone. (*iv*) Stack zone.

(*i*) **Crucible zone.** It is between top of the sand bed and bottom of the tuyeres. The molten metal accumulates here. It is also called the '*well*'.

Table 10.2 : Indian Standard Specification for Cupola Furnace for Grey Cast Iron

(I.S. : 5032–1975)

S.No.	Characteristics	Cupola Desination					
		C 450	*C 600*	*C 750*	*C 900*	*C 1950*	*C 1200*
1	2	3	4	5	6	7	8
1.	Nominal capacity (tonnes/hour)	0.5	1	2	3	4	5
2.	Shell diameter (inside, (mm)	780	930	1360	1510	1660	1810
3.	*Diameter lining inside, (mm)*						
	(*i*) Below charging door	450	600	750	900	1050	1200
	(*ii*) Above charging door	540	690	995	1145	1245	1495
4.	Wind chamber, cross-sectional area (mm)	26500	26500	26500	26500	26500	26500
5.	Height of centre line of tuyeres from base plate below the sand bottom, (mm)	700	750	800	850	900	950
6.	Distance between charging door top and stock zone end point (mm)	6000	6000	6000	6000	6000	6000
7.	Height of centre line of tap hole from base plate (mm)	150	150	180	180	180	180

8.	Height of centre line of slag hole from base plate, (mm)	450	450	480	480	480	480
9.	*Shell plate thickness, (mm)*						
	(*i*) Below charging door	5	5	8	10	10	12
	(*ii*) Above charging door	5	5	6	6	6	
10.	Diameter of air inlet pipe, (mm)	150	200	250	300	400	450
11.	*Air consumption*						
	(*i*) Pressure, (mm, water gauge)	600	600	600	600	600	600
	(*ii*) Volume, (m^3/min.)	16–18	22–25	45–50	70–75	85–90	105–110
12.	Numbers of tuyeres	4	4	6	6	8	8
13.	Area of each tuyere, (mm^2)	13000	13000	15000	15000	20000	20000

(*ii*) **Melting zone.** It starts from the first layer of iron above the coke bed. It is between 300 to 900 mm above the bed charge. Iron melts in this zone. Highest temperatures developed in this zone of complete combustion of the coke reach 1600° to 1700°C.

(*iii*) **Charging zone.** From the top of the melting zone, it extends upto the charging door. Charging materials are fed in this zone of cupola furnace. They are preheated in this zone before coming to the melting zone.

(*iv*) **Stack zone.** It extends from above the charging zone to the top of the cupola. The gases generated within the furnace are carried to the atmosphere by this zone.

Cupola Operation

(*i*) **Preparation of cupola.** The slag and refuse on the lining and around the tuyeres from the previous run are cleaned. Any bad spots or broken bricks are repaired with a mixture of fire clay and silica sand or ganister.

As soon as the patching of the lining is complete, the preparation of the sand bottom in the cupola is begun. The bottom doors are raised and held in this position by metal props. The bottom sand is introduced through the main hole and is rammed well around the lining and across the intersection of the bottom doors. This sand layer in the bottom is built up to a height of 100 to 200 mm. The surface of the sand bottom is sloped from all directions towards the tap hole so that at any time the molten metal may be drained completely.

An opening of about 35 mm diameter is provided for the removal of the slag and a tap hole of about 20 mm diameter is formed. Before firing, the cupola should be thoroughly dried.

(*ii*) **Firing the cupola.** A fire of kindling wood is ignited on the sand bottom. When the wood burns well, coke is dumped on the well from above making sure that the coke begins to burn too. Coke is then added to a level slightly above the tuyeres and the air blast is turned on at a lower blowing rate than normal for igniting the coke.

As soon as red spots begin to show over the top of the fuel bed, additional coke is introduced into the cupola to a height of 700 to 800 mm above the upper row of tuyeres. For determining the height of the coke bed, a measuring rod prepared to indicate the distance from the sill of the charging door to the top of the coke bed, is used.

Firing is done $2\frac{1}{2}$ to 3 hours before the molten metal is required.

(*iii*) **Charging the cupola.** As soon as the coke bed is built up to the correct height and ignited uniformly througout, pig iron and scrap may be charged. The proportion of this scrap is ordinarily from 25 to 50% of the total weight of the metal poured. 2 to 4% ferro-manganese is used as deoxidiser when considerable steel scrap is used along with pig iron.

Coke and pig iron are charged in alternate layers until the cupola is full. The weight of the metal charged should be from 10 to 15% of the hourly output of the cupola. The thickness of the layers should be kept about 150 to 200 mm.

In addition to charging iron and coke, a certain amount of *limestone* (the flux used to form the cupola slag) is added above the first metal charge. besides limestone, fluorspar (CaF_2) and soda ash (Na_2CO_3) are also used as fluxing materials. A flux removes the impurities in the iron and protects the iron from oxidation. The reaction between the lime and silica introduced into the cupola reduces the melting point of the slag and increases its fluidity. Limestone added consitutes about 2 to 3% of the metal charge by weight of 25% by weight of the coke charged.

Table 10.3 : Ratio of Metal Melted to Coke Charged

S. No.	*Class of work*	*Metal to Coke Ratio*
1.	Charge with 50–76% steel scrap	6 : 1 to 8 : 1
2.	Low-phosphorus iron for high duty and automobile castings	7 : 1 to 9 : 1
3.	Medium-phosphorus iron for engineering casting	8 : 1 to 10 : 1
4.	High phosphoric iron for light casting	10 : 1 to 12 : 1
5.	High-phosphoric iron for fairly heavy castings	11 : 1 to 14 : 1
6.	Charge with more than 75% steel scrap	12 : 1 to 15 : 1

Note : More commonly a ratio of 10 : 1 is kept which means that 1 tonne of coke is required to melt 10 tonnes of iron.

(*iv*) **Soaking of iron.** After the furnace is charged fully, it is kept as such for about 45 minutes. The charge gets slowly heated up since the air blast is kept shut during this time. This caused the iron to get soaked.

(*v*) **Opening of air blast.** At the end of the soaking period the air blast is opened. The top hole is kept closed with a plug called '*bot*' till the metal melts and sufficient metal is accumulated.

As melting proceeds, the contents of the charge move gradually downwards. The rate of charging should be equal to the rate of melting so that the furnace is kept full throughout the heat.

(*vi*) **Pouring the molten iron.** When sufficient metal collects in the hearth above the sand bed, the slag hole is opened and the slag is run off preferably into a bogie for easy removal. Then, the bot from the tap hole in removed. Molten metal coming out of the spout is collected is ladles and is carried to the moulds for pouring. The same procedure is repeated until all the metal is melted and the operation is over.

(*vii*) **Closing the cupola.** At the end of the operation, the blast is shut off and the prop is knocked down so that the bottom plates swing open. The remains inside the furnace come out and drop on the floor. These remains are then quenched and removed from underneath the cupola.

Generally, cupolas are run continuously as arc blast furnaces, but are worked only for such periods as may be required. At most of the foundries, the melting period does not exceed 4 hour. But, cupolas can be operated continuously for 10 hours or more.

Output or capacity of a cupola. It is defined as "*the tonnes of molten metal obtaind per hour of the heat*". It depends upon—

(*i*) The cross-section of the cupola.

(*ii*) The intensity of coke consumption.

'*Intensity of coke consumption*' means '*the tonnes of the coke bruned per equare metre of the cross-sectional area of the cupola in unit time*'. An efficient cupola is expected to melt 5860 to 8300 kg per hour for each square metre of cross-section of the cupola.

Air requirements for cupola. For complete combustion of the fuel in the furnace, about 2 cubic metres of air is required per kg of coke at 1.079 kg/cm^2 and 15°C

If the metal-fuel ratio, *e.g.*, $\dfrac{\text{Amount of metal melted}}{\text{Amount of coke burnt}}$ is 8 : 1, which is considered to be a normal figure, coke required per tonne of iron $= \dfrac{1000}{8} = 125$ kg.

Thus, the volume of air required per tonne of iron melted = $2 \times 125 = 250$ cubic metres approximately.

Allowing for 5% leakage of air in the pipe line, generally, the air supplied is in little excess *viz*, about $250 + 250 \times 0.05 = 250 + 12.5 = 262.5$ cubic metres.

Pressure of air supplied to cupola. Depending on the size of cupola, type of iron melted and compactness of the charge, the pressure of air supplied to cupola may vary from 25 to 40 cm or water for small and medium sizes and 40 to 75 cm for large size furnaces.

Inside diameter of cupola. The amount of coke that can be burnt and the amount of iron that can be melted per unit time are determined by the inside diameter of cupola.

It is seen that 14 cm^2 of cupola plan area burn about 1 kg of coke per hour. Thus a cupola having a capacity of 5 tonnes per hour will require 5 × 1000/8 = 625 kg of coke per hour, assuming a metal : fuel ratio of 8 : 1. The plan area required will, therefore, be equal to 625 × 14 cm^3 = 8750 cm^2.

The internal diameter

$$= 2\sqrt{\frac{8750}{\pi}} = 2\sqrt{\frac{8750}{22} \times \frac{7}{1}}$$

$$= 2 \times 52.77 = 105.54 \text{ cm.}$$

Problem. *A blower supplies 90 cubic metres of air per minute to a cupola. If the air required to melt one tonne of metal is 835 cubic metre per hour, calculate the capacity of the cupola.*

Solution. Amount of air reaching the cupola per hour (allowing 5% as leakage in the pipe line)

$$= \frac{90 \times 60 \times 95}{100} = 54 \times 95 \text{ cubic metres per hour.}$$

If the capacity of the cupola is M tonnes per hour.

Amount of air required will be = 835 × M cubic metres.

Therefore, 835 × M = 54 × 95, or $M = \frac{54 \times 95}{835} = 6.145$ tonnes per hour of say 6 tonnes per hour.

Calculation of cupola charge. For controlling the specifications of the cast iron produced by the cupola furnace, it is necessary to estimate the proportion of the contents of the charge particularly that of pig iron and scrap. Several grades of pig iron and scrap are usually available to the foundryman. These grades have to be suitably combined in a most economical manner so as to achieve a desired composition of the cast metal.

Melting loses. During the remelting operation, the various impurities in metal undergo chemical changes. Allowances are, therefore, given for their loss or gain while making up the charge.

(*i*) **Carbon.** As the metal passes through the incandescent coke, it absorbs carbon from the latter. The absorption of carbon depends upon the following factors :

(*a*) Initial carbon content.

(*b*) Size of coke

(*c*) Temperature.

(*d*) Time allowed for the molten metal to remain in the cupola.

A gain of 0.15% carbon may be expected with properly controlled melting conditions.

(*ii*) **Silicon.** During the melting operation silicon tends to get oxidised and lost. Under well controlled and normal working conditions, a loss of 10% silicon is expected. Under abnormal conditions, the loss may be as high as 30%. Thus, to achieve a certain silicon content in the casting :

Either (*a*) the original charge taken must be richer in silicon by the amount expected to be lost ; or

(*b*) silicon may be added externally in the from of ferrosilicon to the laddle containing molten metal for compensating the loss.

Granulated charge of ferro-silicon is added to the stream of molten metal during tapping from the cupola into the laddle. This gives a uniform distribution and homogeneity all over the metal.

(*iii*) **Sulphur.** Sulphur content also tends to increase, like carbon due to absorption of the same from coke. Gain in sulphur depends on

(*a*) the sulphur content of coke.

(*b*) iron-coke ratio.

(*c*) manganese content in the charge.

(*d*) flux used during melting.

Gain in sulphur is generally assumed to be about 0.03 to 0.05%.

(*iv*) **Manganese.** It tends to get lost during melting along with silicon. This loss varies from 15 to 20% of the manganese present in the charge.

To get a certain manganese content.

Either (*a*) the initial charge taken must be richer in manganese or (*b*) external additions may be made in the form of ferromanganese.

(*v*) **Phosphorus.** Its content does not change appreciably. Its percentage remains nearly the same.

(*vi*) **Iron.** It tends to get oxidised and lost during the melting operation. The loss is generally quite small varying from 3 to 4%.

Computing Charging Mixture. The method adopted is based mostly on trial and error :

(*i*) A certain mixture is arbitrarily chosen by experience.

(*ii*) Considering the loss and gain of various constituents, the analysis of the cast metal is estimated.

(*iii*) If it does not conform to the specifications desired, the necessary changes are made in the mixture and the analysis is again checked up.

(*iv*) This is repeated till the desired composition of the cast metal is obtained.

Problem. *The typical raw materials available in the foundry have the following percentage composition :*

	Carbon	*Silicon*	*Manganese*	*Phosphorus*	*Sulphur*
Pig Iron No. 1	*3.5*	*2.5*	*0.72*	*0.18*	*0.016*
Pig Iron No. 2	*3.5*	*3.00*	*0.63*	*0.12*	*0.018*
Cast Iron scrap	*3.4*	*2.30*	*0.50*	*0.20*	*0.030*
Returns from foundry	*3.3*	*2.50*	*0.65*	*0.17*	*0.35*

The above materials are used in the following proportions :

Pig Iron No. 1–15%; Pig Iron No. 2–30%; Returns–35%; New scrap 20%.

Estimate the probable analysis of the cast metal.

Solution. Assuming that 1000 kg of iron are needed and will be fed into cupola.

(*i*) **Carbon content.** Some carbon is oxidised, but the same amount is picked up from the fuel.

Pig Iron No. 1	$1000 \times 0.15 \times 0.035 =$	5.25 kg
Pig Iron No. 2	$1000 \times 0.30 \times 0.035 =$	10.50 kg
New scrap	$1000 \times 0.20 \times 0.034 =$	6.80 kg
Return from foundry	$1000 \times 0.35 \times 0.033 =$	11.55 kg
		34.10 kg

$$\text{The final percentage of carbon} = \frac{34.1}{1000} \times 100 = 3.41$$

(*ii*) **Silicon content.** The silicon content can be expected to be reduced 15% by oxidation.

Pig Iron No. 1	$1000 \times 0.15 \times 0.025 =$	3.75 kg
Pig Iron No. 2	$1000 \times 0.30 \times 0.030 =$	9.00 kg
New scrap	$1000 \times 0.20 \times 0.023 =$	4.60 kg
Return	$1000 \times 0.35 \times 0.025 =$	8.75 kg
		26.10 kg

$$\text{The final percentage of silicon} = \frac{26.1 - (26.1 \times 0.15)}{1000} \times 100$$

$$= 2.2185$$

(*iii*) **Manganese content.** The manganese content can be expected to be reduced by 20%.

Pig Iron No. 1	$1000 \times 0.15 \times 0.0072 =$	1.080 kg
Pig Iron No. 2	$1000 \times 0.30 \times 0.0063 =$	1.890 kg
New scrap	$1000 \times 0.20 \times 0.0050 =$	1.000 kg
Returns	$1000 \times 0.31 \times 0.0065 =$	2.275 kg
		6.245 kg

$$\text{The final percentage of manganese} = \frac{6.245 - (6.245 \times 2)}{1000} \times 100$$

$$= 0.4996.$$

(*iv*) **Phosphorus content.** The phosphorus content lost in cupola is negligible.

Pig Iron No. 1	$1000 \times 0.15 \times 0.0018 =$	0.27 kg
Pig Iron No. 2	$1000 \times 0.30 \times 0.0012 =$	1.36 kg
New scrap	$1000 \times 0.20 \times 0.0020 =$	0.40 kg
Returns	$1000 \times 0.35 \times 0.0017 =$	0.595 kg
		1.625 kg

The final percentage of phosphorus

$$= \frac{1.625}{1000} \times \frac{100}{1} = 0.1625.$$

(*v*) **Sulphur content.** In melting almost no sulphur is lost by the iron. But, about 4% of the sulphur in the coke is picked up by the metal.

Pig Iron No. 1	$1000 \times 0.15 \times 0.00016 =$	0.0240 kg
Pig Iron No. 2	$1000 \times 0.30 \times 0.00018 =$	0.0540 kg
New scrap	$1000 \times 0.20 \times 0.00030 =$	0.0600 kg
Returns	$1000 \times 0.35 \times 0.00035 =$	0.1228 kg
		0.2605 kg

Assuming a coke to iron melting ratio of 1 to 10 and a coke with a sulphur content of 0.50%, we have

$$\frac{1000}{10} \times \frac{0.5}{100} = 0.5 \text{ kg of sulphur}$$

pick up $4\% = 0.5 \times 0.04 = 0.02$ kg.

The final percentage of sulphur

$$= \frac{0.26 + 0.02}{1000} \times \frac{100}{1} = \frac{0.28}{10} = 0.028.$$

Hence, probably analysis of cast metal is total carbon 3.41%, silicon 2.22%, manganese 0.5%, phosphorus 0.163%, sulphur 0.028%.

Problem on Coke Bed Charge. *Diameter (d) of cupola is 780 mm. Height (h) of groove i.e., location of high temperature zone is 1300 mm. Determine the weight (W) of bed charge, assuming density (w) of coke to be 500 kg/m³.*

Solution. Weight of bed charge,

$$W = \frac{\pi}{4} (d)^2 . h.w = \frac{\pi}{4} \times (.78)^2 \times 1.3 \times 500 \text{ kg}$$

$$= 310.6 \text{ kg. } \textbf{Ans.}$$

Problem. *In the above problem, if one-tenth of bed charge is burnt at a time regularly; each such layer covered by metal charge, find the weight of regular charge of coke.*

Solution. Weight of regular charge

$$= \frac{1}{10} \times 310.6 = 31.06 \text{ kg. } \textbf{Ans.}$$

Or

$$= \frac{\pi}{4} (0.78)^2 \times 0.13 \times 500 = 31.06 \text{ kg. } \textbf{Ans.}$$

Problem on Melting Ratio. *A cupola 780 mm in diameter has a melting ratio of 8 : 1. How much iron is melted per hour ? Assume melting rate to be 0.5 kg/hour/cm². Determine the weight of coke consumed per hour.*

Solution. (*i*) Iron melted/hour

$$= \frac{\pi}{4} d^2 \times \text{melting rate}$$

Melting rate $= 0.5$ kg/hr/cm², $d = 78$ cm.

$\therefore$ Iron melted/hour $= \frac{\pi}{4} (78)^2 (0.5)$ kg/hr.

$$= 2390 \text{ kg/hour. } \textbf{Ans.}$$

(*ii*) As melting ratio is 8 : 1, coke consumed per hour

$$= \frac{2390}{8} = 298.75 \text{ kg/hr. } \textbf{Ans.}$$

Heat balance for cupola associated with cupola zones

Heat Input. (*i*) Heat in the coke *i.e.*, calorific value (*ii*) Oxidation of carbon, iron, silicon, and manganese in combustion zone, (*iii*) Heat in the blast of preheated air due to its temperature (more purposeful in hot blast cupola).

Heat output. (*i*) Preheating, melting and superheating of metal, (*ii*) Limestone calcination, (*iii*) Slag formation, its melting and superheating, (*iv*) Evaporation of moisture in the air blast, (*v*) Sensible and latent heat in the chimney gases, (*vi*) Radiation heat losses from cupola shell.

Efficiency of cupola

$$= \frac{\text{Heat utilized in preheating melting and superheating}}{\text{Heat input due to heat in the coke + heat evolved due to oxidation of C, Fe, Si and Mn + Heat in the air blast.}} \times 100$$

Efficiency of a cupola varies from 30 to 50%.

Selection of Furnace

For foundry operations, all types of metal-melting furnaces can be used. However, foundry requirements are sometimes unique and one or another type of furnace may be best for a particular operation :

(*a*) Open-hearth furnaces are desirable in large foundries requiring 10 to 200 tonnes of molten metal at one time.

(*b*) An electric-arc furnace may prove best in a smaller jobbing shop, where 1 to 15 tonnes of metal may be needed at frequent intervals.

(*c*) An induction furnace will give best all-round performance in still another foundry requiring only 125 kg to 1 tonne of alloys of various special compositions.

Table 10.4: Furnaces for Melting Common Metals and Alloys

Grey Iron	*Steel*	*Non-ferrous Metals*
Cupola furnace Electric furnace Direct arc furnace Indirect arc furnace Induction furnace Air furnace	Open hearth furnace Convertor Electric furnace	Crucible furnace Reverberatory furnace Electric furnace

Factor affecting the choice of type of furnace :

(*i*) Considerations of initial cost.

(*ii*) Relative average cost of repair and maintenance.

(*iii*) Cost of operation.

(*iv*) Availability and relative cost of various fuels in the particular locality.

(*v*) Cleanliness and noise level in operation.

(*vi*) Melting efficiency, in particular the speed of melting.

(*vii*) Degree of quality control required in respect of metal purification or refining.

(*viii*) Composition and melting temperature of the metal, *e.g.*, a cupola is normally used for cast iron melting but seldom, if ever, for aluminium or magnesium melting.

(*ix*) Personal choice or sales influence.

Table 10.5 : Fuels and Furnaces for Melting Metals and Alloys for Foundry Work

S. No.	*Fuel*	*Form of fuel*	*Metal melted*	*Furnace used*
1.	Coal	Powdered bituminous Anthracite lump Briquettes	Cast iron Cast iron Cast iron	Air furnace Cupola Cupola
2.	Coke	Sized lump	Cast iron Non-ferrous	Cupola Crucible furnace
3.	Oil	—	Non-ferrous Iron, Steel	Crucible furnace Open-hearth
4.	Gas	—	Non-ferrous Iron, Steel	Crucible furnace Open-hearth

5.	Electricity	Direct arc	Cast iron, Steel	Single, two and three phase electric arc furnace
		Indirect arc	Cast iron, Non-ferrous	Rocking arc furnace
		Resistance	Non-ferrous	Rocking arc furnace
		Induction	All metal	Tilting or lift induction furnace

Metal-pot Furnaces. The metal pot is usually made of cast iron or steel. It is preferred for melting those alloys which have relatively low melting points, *viz* ; alloys of aluminium, magnesium, antimony, zinc, lead cadmium and tin.

The metal-pot is supported by its rim in a stationary furnace which is fired by oil or gas fuel. The products of combustion do not come in contact with the metal as they are discharged through a flue.

Converters. They cannot be used for direct melting purposes but are used for making steel from molten pig iron as already referred.

For steel casting, pig iron along with suitable scrap is first melted in cupola furnace. Then, the molten iron is transferred to the converters, where the excess carbon along with other constituents is eliminated and pure iron in an oxidised form is obtained. Now, depending on the composition and properties of steel required, suitable deoxidisers and re-carburisers are added. Molten steel from these converters is then taken into ladles and poured into the moulds.

Both, bottom-blown and side-blown type converters are used for steel casting. They provide a very easy means for getting molten steel to any required specifications.

For high degree of refinement and precise control of composition, the molten metal from these converters can be transferred to electric furnaces. This process is then called "*Triplex Process*."

Ladles

They are containers used for moving or conveying the molten metal from the furnace to the pouring area. The molten metal from the cupola or furnace is commonly run into a large receiving ladles from which it is distributed to smaller pouring ladles.

Depending upon the method of carrying them, the various types of ladles are :

(*i*) **Hand type ladle.** It is the most commonly used ladle in a foundry shop. It resembles a bucket with a removable, long handle shank. It normally holds 15 to 30 kg of metal.

(*ii*) **Shank ladle or bull ladle.** It is handled by two men. It holds 30 to 150 kg of metal.

(*iii*) **Bottom pouring ladle.** Large castings of the floor and pit type are poured with this ladle. It is widely used in steel foundries. It may also be used for pouring cast iron.

(*iv*) **Tea pot ladle.** It is used for small and medium-sized mould.

Advantages of bottom-pouring and tea pot ladles

Both of these have a built-in spout which allows the metal to be taken from the bottom and does not disturb the slag forming on the top. The floating slag is thus controlled. So, they are also called "*self-skimming ladles*".

Ladle handler. It is a mechanical device which enables one man to handle and pour with large ladles. It is hung from a monorail making it easy to be removed.

Lining of ladles. The inside of the ladle bowl is lined generally with about 25 mm thick layer of fire clay. Large ladles require a thicker lining.

Fire clay is mixed by adding the right amount of water to mix it into a so-called "*mud*". It is then plastered on the inside of the ladle and allowed to dry.

Pouring the Molten Metal

(*i*) It should be carefully controlled.

(*ii*) It should be done continuously and at a uniform rate until the mould, gates and risers are full.

(*iii*) The temperature of the metal must be just right. If it is too hot, the hot gases will produce blow-holes ; if it is too cold, the metal will solidify permaturely and will not fill the entire cavity.

(*iv*) Temperature are easily checked with an optical pyrometer. After a sufficient period of experience, one can visually judge the temperature of the metal with remarkable accuracy.

(*v*) An assistant should skim back the floating slag with a skimming bar during the actual discharge of the ladle into the mould.

Scum or slag present on the top of molten metal must not be allowed to enter the mould. Otherwise, slag pockets may form in the casting.

Some General Principles of the Melting Practices

Carried out in the various melting furnaces :

(*i*) Foundry melting operation usually involves much more than simply adding enough heat to a solid metal to liquefy it. To avoid damage to the furnace refractories in charging and melt-down operations, care must be taken.

(*ii*) Melting operation, particularly the slag condition (in case slag is used) and the furnace atmosphere, should be controlled carefully so that alloying elements are not lost and the metal does not dissolve unwanted impurities.

(*iii*) Often the metal is alloyed during melting by addition of other metals.

(*iv*) If undesirable impurities are present in the initial charge, or are absorbed during melting, they should be removed by refining.

One type of refining, the removal of gaseous impurities, is usually termed '*Degassing*'.

(*v*) At the end of melting operation, metals are sometimes inoculated to improve their final solidification structure. Incoulation treatment alters the metallurgical microstructure *viz*., refines the grain and produces ductile iron.

Metals and Alloys Used for Melting

Quality of castings is often influenced by the selection of melting stock for the charge :

1. Non-ferrous alloys are nearly always melted from :

(*i*) primary or secondary ingot, and

(*ii*) foundry returns *viz*., gates, risers and scrap castings from previous operations.

For adjusting the alloy composition :

(*a*) if the melting point of the elements is sufficiently low, pure alloying elements are added, and

(*b*) if the melting point of an alloying element is too high, a lower melting point master alloy (alloy of element and base metal *viz*., copper plus 15% phosphorus, or aluminium plus 5% titanium) is used for making the charge addition.

Table 10.6 : Copper-Zinc-Tin Casting Alloys

S. No.	*Name*	*Cu*	*Sn*	*Zn*	*Pb*	*Ni*	*Si*	*Mn*	*Al*	*Fe*	*Use*
1.	Red brass	90	—	10	—	—	—	—	—	—	Hardware
2.	Yellow brass	70	—	30	—	—	—	—	—	—	Tubes, catridges
3.	Leaded red brass	85	5	5	5	—	—	—	—	—	Machinery castings
4.	Leaded yellow brass	72	1	24	3	—	—	—	—	—	Plumbing fixtures
5.	Tin bronze	88	8	4	—	—	—	—	—	—	Ship, hardware, bearings
6.	Bell metal	80	20	—	—	—	—	—	—	—	Bells
7.	Bearing bronze	83	7	3	7	—	—	—	—	—	Machine bearings
8.	Silicon bronze	95	—	—	—	—	4	1	—	—	Machine castings
9.	Manganese bronze	62	15	31	1	—	—	1.5	1.5	1.5	High strength parts
10.	Aluminium Bronze	78	—	—	—	5	—	3	10	4	Corrosion resisting parts
11.	Nickel silver	65	4	6	5	20	—	—	—	—	Diary and boundary

Also sometimes alloying elements are added from a salt of the element *e.g.*, a flux like titanium chloride.

2. Cast iron is made from :

(*i*) pig iron,

(*ii*) iron and steel scrap, and

(*iii*) foundry returns.

Alloying elements are generally added as master alloys of iron plus the alloys element (ferro-alloys). It is economical to use ferro-alloys as compared with alloying with pure metals.

Primary ingot is prepared from commercially pure metals by refineries known as *smelters*.

Secondary ingot is a remelt of scrap metals sorted, melted and alloyed by refiners to approximately the composition required by the foundryman for his castings.

Scrap may consist of obsolete, worn, or broken machinery flashings from razor blades and other wrought object, etc.

Refining

The removal of unwanted impurities from the metal bath in the melting operation is known as '*Refining*'.

The general types of impurities that may be present are :

(*i*) Dissolved gases

(*ii*) Dissolved non-gaseous elements, and

(*iii*) Suspended oxides and inclusions.

In *non-ferrous melting*, pig is generally purchased of the proper chemical composition for casting. No attempt is made in the foundry to remove dissolved impurities except dissolved gases. Dissolved gases are removed by one of the degassing techniques.

Removal of entrapped oxides and inclusions from non-ferrous metals like aluminium and magnesium alloys is often necessary. These alloys easily form solid oxides, known as '*dross*'. The dross tends to remain suspended in the melt. Either (*a*) sufficient time is allowed for dross particles to float to the surface in the furnace and ladle, or (*b*) they are fluxed from the metal by stirring a reactive salt flux into the bath.

Refining in the ferrous foundry, particularly the steel foundry, is more extensive than in the non-ferrous shop :

1. In the case of *steel*, two general types of melting practices are used :

Table 10.7 : Aluminium—Base Sand Casting Alloys

S.No.	*Name*	*Al*	*Cu*	*Fe*	*Si*	*Mg*	*Mn*	*Ni*	*Use*
1.	Al-Cu (heat treatable)	93	5	1	—	—	—	—	Engine castings
2.	Al-Cu	92	8	—	—	—	—	—	Miscellaneous
3.	Al-Si	95	—	—	—	—	—	—	Machine castings
4.	Al-Si (heat treatable)	93	1	0.5	5	0.5	—	—	Leak pryo of casting
5.	Al-Cu-Si	92	4	1	3	—	—	—	Good strength
6.	Al-Mg	95	0.15	0.2	0.2	4	0.5	—	Cooking utensiles
7.	Al-Cu-Mg-Ni	93	3.5	—	—	1.5	—	2	Pistons, Bearings

Table 10.8 : Magnesium—Base Sand Casting Alloys

S. No.	*Name*	*Mg*	*Al*	*Zn*	*Mn*	*Use*
1.	Mg-Al-Mn	95	4	—	0.2 min	Low stress castings
2.	Mg-Al-Mn	91	8	—	0.2 min	Tough, leakproof castings
3.	Mg-Al-Zn	90	6	3	0.2 min	General castings

(*i*) **Acid Practice.** Acid melting uses acid refractor and acid slags in contact with the metal. Such refractories and slags are high in SiO_2 content and low in CaO and MgO. Dissolved gases and suspended non-metallics are removed, oxidizable impurities are partially or completely removed, and carbon composition is adjusted.

Phosphorus and sulphur contents are not, however, affected. Since these impurities are harmful to the mechanical and casting properties of steel, acid melting requires an initial charge low in these elements.

(*ii*) **Basic Practice.** Basic melting uses refractories and slags of relatively high CaO and MgO content. It possesses the metallurgical advantages of acid melting. In addition, sulphur and phosphorus may be reduced to any desired level by proper control of many variables, particularly the concentration of lime and iron oxide in the slag. A lower and cheaper grade of scrap as charge material can, therefore, be used in basic melting.

2. In the case of *cast iron*, the acid cupola permit close control of carbon and silicon contents, but does not remove sulphur or phosphorus.

For mass production of ductile iron (a more pure grade of cast iron with low sulphur), sulphur is eliminated by :

(*i*) melting in a basic cupola.

(*ii*) melting in a basic electric furnace, or

(*iii*) melting in an acid cupola and adding desulphurizing compounds in the ladle or forehearth.

Desulphurisation in the ladle may be accomplished by :

(*i*) Pouring over a sodium oxide slag, or

(*ii*) Injecting powdered desulphuriser *viz*., calcium carbide, by blowing the powders (with an inert gas) into the metal through a tube immersed in the melt.

Phosphorus removal is not ordinarily accomplished in the cupola. Hence, for the cupola, melting practice, high phosphorus charge materials are avoided.

Both phosphorus and sulphur may, however, be removed by a double slag electric furnace operation.

Gases in Cast Metals

Effect of Gases in Cast Metals. Gases are almost universally more soluble in liquid metal than in solid metals. As

metals freeze and cool, dissolved gases tend to form *'gas holes'*. The gas holes may be in the form of large *'blowholes'*, *'finer pinholes'*, or still finer *'microporosity'* depending on the amount of gas present and on the manner in which the metal or alloy freezes.

The gas holes in their various forms are quite detrimental to :

(*i*) mechanical properties,

(*ii*) pressure tightness, and

(*iii*) the surface finish of machined or cast surfaces.

Molten metal should, therefore, be free of all dissolved gases before it is cast.

Gases dissolve in metals not as molecules (*e.g.*, CO_2, H_2, etc.) but as elements (*e.g.*, C, H, O, etc.). On solidification ; the elements recombine to form molecular gases which in turn form *'gas holes.'*

Table 10.9 : Elements which dissolve in Various Metals and Precipitate on Solidification to Form Voids

S. No.	*Metal*	*Element dissolved*	*Gas evolved on solidification*
1.	Iron	C, N, O, H	CO_2, CO, H_2O, N_2, H_9
2.	Copper	S, C, O, H	SO, SO_2, CO, CO_2, H_9O, H_2
3.	Aluminium	H	H_9
4.	Magnesium	H	H_2

Hydrogen is soluble in all metals to a greater or lesser extent and is usually the greatest trouble maker. At high temperatures, it is quite soluble in the liquid alloy, Gas solubility decreases as the temperature decreases causing gas porosity in the castings.

Prevention of Gas Absorption

Sources of Gas Absorption. (*i*) In the furnace, from the atmosphere and from wet charges.

(*ii*) In the furnace or ladles, from incompletely dried linings or wet tools.

(*ii*) In passing through air from furnace to ladle or from ladle, to mould.

(*iv*) In the mould, from moist atmosphere or excess moisture or volatile hydrocarbons in the mould materials.

Precautions against gas absorption. (*i*) Melt under slags or protective atmospheres or in a vacuum.

(*ii*) Keep dry all the items coming in contact with the metal.

(*iii*) Melt and pour at temperatures as low as possible to minimise gas solubility.

(*iv*) Handle (skim, stir or reladle) the metal as little as possible.

Water vapour, hydrogen and oxides of carbon (CO and CO_2) are responsible for most pinholes in castings. To prevent gas absorption entirely is usually impractical as some hydrogen gas is nearly always present in molten metals unless they are melted in vacuum.

Gas Removal or Degasification of Metals

Absorption of dissolved gases may be reduced by

(*i*) Removing the gas or gases, or

(*ii*) Removing or isolating one or mode of the components of the gas.

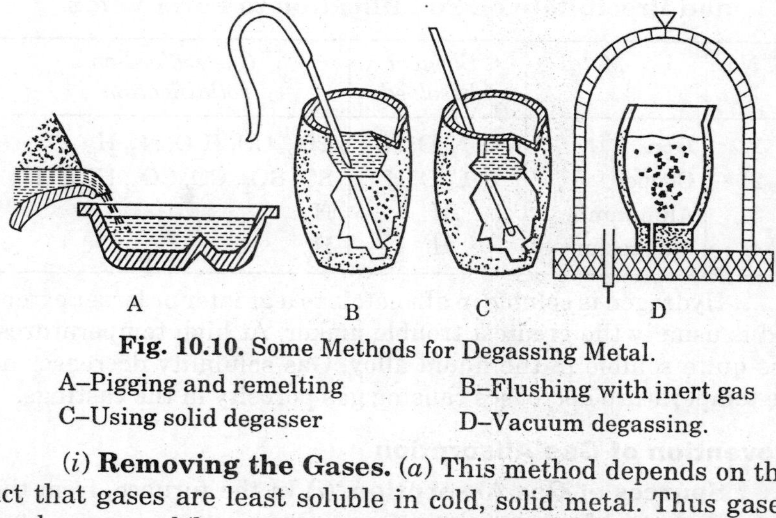

Fig. 10.10. Some Methods for Degassing Metal.

A–Pigging and remelting B–Flushing with inert gas
C–Using solid degasser D–Vacuum degassing.

(*i*) **Removing the Gases.** (*a*) This method depends on the fact that gases are least soluble in cold, solid metal. Thus gases may be removed '*by a sequence of melting, freezing, and remelting.* Except in special cases, however, this method is too expensive and time consuming to be used in practice.

(*b*) More common techniques of gas removal rely on the fact that the amount of gas dissolved in a molten metal depends on the pressure of that gas above and around the metal.

In case of diatomic gases (*e.g.*, H_2, O_2 or N_2) the amount dissolved at any particular temperature may be expresed by the

equation : $V = K\sqrt{P}$

where V = volume of diatomic gas dissolved

P = pressure of the gas above and around the metal

K = a constant.

The equation shows that, if hydrogen is completely removed from the atmosphere around a melt, any hydrogen gas dissolved will tend escape.

Thus *melting and pouring under a vacuum* is one method. This is also a very expensive method for obtaining gas-free castings.

(*c*) **Vacuum Degassing.** It combines the advantages of vacuum melting with the economy of air melting. The metal is melted in air and then placed in an evacuated chamber for degassing before pouring. Pouring takes place in the open atmosphere.

(*d*) **Flushing with an inert gas.** It is the most common method of removing gas employing the principle described above. Inert gas is bubbled directly through the metal ; the pressure of the dissolved gas (usually hydrogen) within each inert gas bubble is zero and any dissolved gas migrates readily to the bubble where it collects and is flushed from the metal baths.

For degassing metals like aluminium and magnesium, inert gases like chlorine, nitrogen or argon are used. These inert gases are simply piped from storage tanks through graphite tubes directly into the metal baths.

Sometimes *solid degassers* are also used as a source of inert gas *e.g.*, a solid compound like C_2Cl_6 held beneath the melt surface decomposes to give the flushing action.

In steel making practice, the CO from the carbon boil (FeO + C = Fe + CO) acts as an inert gas to flush hydrogen from the metal.

(*ii*) **Removing or isolating one or more of the components of the dissolved gases.** This method also minimises the gas porosity.

(*a*) In steel making, after the carbon boil has progressed to the point desired, it is blocked by adding silicon or aluminium to the bath to tie up one of the reagents of the CO gas

$$3FeO + 2Al \longrightarrow Al_2O_3 + 3Fe$$

(*b*) Phosphor-copper is added to copper-base alloys to tie up dissolve oxygen. Phophorus combines with dissolved oxygen to form a solid, P_2O_5, which floats out of the bath, and prevents the oxygen from combining with any dissolved hydrogen to form water vapour.

Foundry Refractories

Refractories (heat-resistant materials) are the backbone of the foundry. They form the crucibles and furnace bottoms which contain metal during melting. They comprise of the furnace walls and roof which reduce heat losses and contain gases. Molten metal is carried in refractory ladles and poured into refractory moulds. Refractories are the common requirement of all processes carried out at elevated temperatures.

Foundry refractories are usually, but not always, oxides of elements (MgO, SiO_2, Al_2O_3 and mixtures of these and others). Research has resulted in tremendous improvement in the servicability of traditional refractory materials. A wide range of entirely new refractory material has been created *e.g.*, magnesia from sea water and zirconia.

Classification of Refractories

Refractories for foundry use classified on a chemical basis are :

(*i*) Acid Refractories

(*ii*) Basic Refractories

(*iii*) Neutral Refractories

Acid refractories are oxides of metalloids, *e.g.*, SiO_2 and P_2O_5, and basic refractories are metal oxide *e.g.*, MgO and CaO. In foundry, the best-known acid refractory material is silica (SiO_2) and basic one is magnesia (MgO).

Acid refractories are not used in contact with basic refractories to avoid erosion and weakening of a refractory structure. For the same reasons, basic slags are commonly used only with basic refractories, and acid slags with acid refractories. In cast iron and steel foundries, acid slags are used when sulphur and phosphorus lamination from the molten metal is not necessary, but, when these impurities must be removed, basic slags are essential.

Refractory Raw Materials

Over half of all refractories used are obtained from ores of essentially pure silica (quartzite), or from ores that are mainly compounds of silica and alumina (fire clays and similar clays).

Formerly, Magnesia (MgO) was, obtained by calcining (heating) magnesite, $MgCO_3$. At present, large quantities of MgO are also obtained by chemical treatment of magnesium bearing brine.

Chrome (Cr_2O_3) is obtained from chrome ore of widely varying purity and used in the impure form.

Table 10.10 : Typical Compositions of Silica and Basic Bricks

(Per cent)

S. No.	*Type of Brick*	*Silica (SiO_2)*	*Alumina (Al_2O_3)*	*Lime CaO*	*Magnesia (MgO)*	*Iron oxide Fe_2O_3*	*Chromic oxide (Cr_2O_3)*	*Other Oxides*
1.	*Silica*: (overall range)	95–97	0.2–1.2	1.8–3.5	–	0.3–0.9	–	0.05–0.3
2.	*Basic* :							
	Chrome	2–6	15–33	–	14–19	11–17	30–45	1–2
	Fosterite	33–39	–	–	47–55	9–11	–	3–4
	Magnesite	3–6	0.4–2.0	1–5	85–95	0.5–4.0	–	0.5–1.0

Some refractories are now being produced chemically from essentially pure elements or compounds *e.g.*, silicon carbide (SiC) is produced by high temperature reaction of silica with carbon.

Various special refactories, or *'super refactories' e.g.*, beryllia, thoria, etc., are produced for specific purposes by other special leaching, chemical and thermal methods.

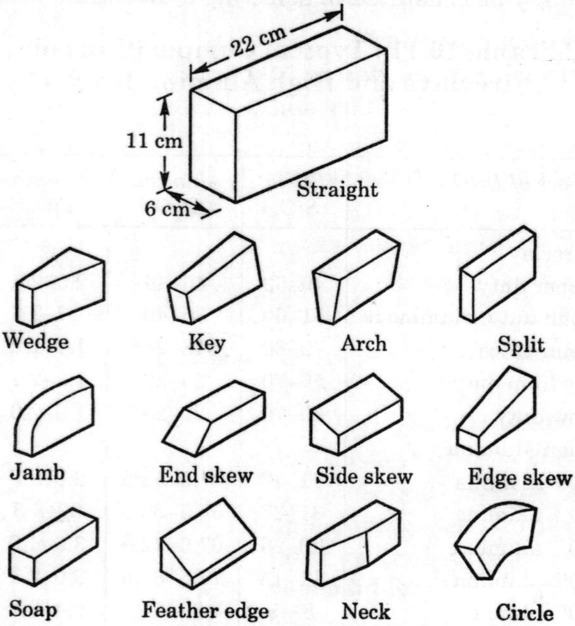

Fig. 10.11. Standard Shapes of Refractory bricks.

Forms of Refractories and Refactory Materials

After mining or chemical production, and calcining if necessary, refractory raw materials are crushed, ground and sized. They are then mixed with other materials as desired for use, or are fabricated into shapes *e.g.*, bricks or blocks.

Refactories are used in many forms to suit the special needs *e.g.*, prefabricated shapes, mortars, coatings, plastic mixes and castables.

Most melting and other furnaces require brick masonry construction and are lined or built up with prefabricated shapes. Such bricks are commercially available in a wide variety of sizes and shapes ranging from square blocks to keys, wedges and arches (Fig. 10.11).

Acid, basic, or neutral bricks of widely varying chemical and physical properties are readily obtainable.

In brick construction, a refactory mortar is generally used to bond the brick work into a solid unit on firing, and to provide a cushion between the irregular surfaces of the bricks. Many special compositions of mortars are available in which chrome, silicon carbide, silica and alumina are used. The manufacturer of a brick should usually be consulted in selecting a mortar.

Table 10.11 : Typical Compositions of Fireclays and High Alumina Bricks

(Per cent)

S. No.	*Types of Bricks*	*Silica (SiO_2)*	*Alumina (Al_2O_2)*	*Titania (TiO_2)*	*Other oxides*
1.	Fireclay				
	Super duty	49–53	40–44	2.0–2.5	3–4
	High duty, aluminous	51–60	35–40	1.7–3.3	3–6
	Semi-silica	72–80	18–24	1.0–1.2	1.5–2.5
	Medium duty	57–70	25–36	1.3–2.1	4–7
	Low duty	60–70	22–23	1.0–2.0	5–8
2.	High alumina :				
	50% alumina	41–47	47.5–52.5	2.0–2.8	3–4
	60% alumina	31–37	57.5–62.5	20–3.3	3–4
	70% alumina	20–26	67.5–72.5	3.0–4.0	3–4
	80% alumina	11–15	77.5–82.5	3.0–2.1	3–4
	90% alumina	8—9	82–91	0.4–0.8	1–2
	99% alumina	0.5–1.0	98–99	Trace	0.6

Table 10.12 : Fusion Temperatures of Some Important Refractories

S. No.	*Type of Refractory*	*Approx. Fusion Temperature (°C)*
1.	*Acid :*	
	(*i*) Silica (SiO_2)	1700
	(*ii*) Alumina (Al_2O_3)	2050
	(*iii*) Aluminium silica (Al_2O_3–46%, SiO_2–54%)	1780
	(*iv*) Sillimanite (Al_2O_3–63%, SiO_2–37%)	1900
2.	*Basic :*	
	Magnesia (MgO)	2800
3.	*Neutral :*	
	(*i*) Graphite	3000
	(*ii*) Chromite	2180

After completing brick and mortar construction, the mortar is sometimes thinned with water and used as coating for the face of the refractory walls.

(*i*) to seal the joints further,

(*ii*) to protect the wall from destructive elements in the furnace or,

(*iii*) to patch worn linings of furnaces.

Applications of Various Types of Refractories in Furnace Construction

1. Refractories in the Acid and Basic cupola

(*i*) Bottom	Moulding sand.
(*ii*) Tapping	Fire brick.
(*iii*) Melting Zone :	
(*a*) Acid cupola	High duty fire brick.
(*b*) Basic cupola	Magnesite chrome brick.
(*iv*) Stack	Medium duty fire brick.

2. Open-hearth steel furnaces

(*i*) Working hearth	Rammed on fritted dolomite grain.
(*ii*) Lacking	Dolomite or magnesite brick.
(*iii*) Sub-hearth	Fire brick.
(*iv*) Spout	Fire brick covered with ganister.
(*v*) Slag pockets	Second quality silica bricks.

Table 10.13 : Characteristic Properties of Refractory bricks

S. No.	*Type*	*Class*	*Characteristics*
1.	High Alumina	99% alumina	(*i*) High refractoriness, increasing with increasing alumina content.
		90% alumina	(*ii*) High mechanical strength at high temperatures.
		85% alumina	(*iii*) Excellent to fair resistance to spalling.
		80% alumina	(*iv*) Greater resistance then fireclay brick to corrosion by most basic slags and fluxes.
		70% alumina	
		60% alumina	
		50% alumina	
2.	Fire clay	Super duty	(*i*) Stability of volume and high mechanical strength at high temperature.
			(*ii*) Excellent resistance to thermal spalling.
			(*iii*) Fair resistance to highly acid slangs.
			(*iv*) Lower resistance to basic slags.
		High duty	(*i*) Relatively good spalling resistance and thermal insulation value.
		Medium duty	(*ii*) Fair resistance to acid slags and fluxes.
		Low duty	(*iii*) Lower resistance to basic slags and fluxes.
		Semi-silica	(*i*) Rigidity under load at high tempertures.
			(*ii*) Resistance to structural spalling.
			(*iii*) Volume stability.
			(*iv*) Resistance to penetration and attack by volatile alkalies or fumes.

S. No.	*Type*	*Class*	*Characteristics*
			(*v*) High temperature of incipient vetrification.
3.	Silica	Super duty Conventional	(*i*) High refractoriness and resistance to abrasion. (*ii*) High mechanical strength at high temperatures. (*iii*) Thermal conductivity at high temperatures appreciably greater than that of most high-duty fireclay bricks. (*iv*) High resistance to corrosion by acid slags. (*v*) Fair resistance to attack by oxides of lime, magnesia and iron. (*vi*) Readily attacked by basic slags and fluorine. (*vii*) Not subject to thermal spalling above 650 °F. (*viii*) Poor resistance to thermal spalling at low temperatures.
4.	Magnesite	Fired 88–90% magnesia More than 90% magnesia chemically bonded, metal-encased	(*i*) Extremely high refractoriness and high thermal conductivity. (*ii*) Great resistance to corrosion by basic slags. (*iii*) Poor resistance to slags containing high silica percentages. (*iv*) Chemically bonded and metal encased bricks have resistance to spalling.
5.	Chrome	Fired	(*i*) High resistance to corrosion by basic and moderately acid slags and fluxes. (*ii*) Generally, basic slags do not adhere to chrome brick. (*iii*) Iron oxide is absorbed and causes a damaging expansion. (*iv*) Thermal conductivity lower than that of magnesite but higher than that of fireclay.

S. No.	*Type*	*Class*	*Characteristics*
6.	Magnesite chrome	Chemically bonded	(*i*) Mechanical strength and stability of volume at high temperatures.
		Chemically bonded	(*ii*) Excellent resistance to spalling.
		metal-encased	(*iii*) High resistance to corrosion by basic slags.
		Fired	
7.	Chrome-magnesite	Chemically bonded	(*i*) Mechanical strength and stability of volume at high temperatures.
		Fired	(*ii*) Excellent to good resistance to spalling.
			(*iii*) High resistance to corrosion by basic slags.
8.	Forsterite	Fired	(*i*) High refractoriness.
			(*ii*) Excellent strength at high temperatures.
			(*iii*) Marked resistance to corrosion by alkali compounds.
			(*iv*) Fair resistance to most basic slags.
			(*v*) Attacked by acid slags.

(*vi*) Ends (below roofing)	Silica or chrome magnesite brick.
(*vii*) Doors	Fire brick.
(*viii*) Side walls	Silica or chrome-magnesite brick.
(*ix*) Roof	Silica brick.
(*x*) Blocks (below roofing)	Chrome-magnesite brick.
(*xi*) Checker arches	Silica brick.
(*xii*) Cheker chambers	Fire brick or silica brick.
(*xiii*) Checker filling	Fire brick or silica brick.

3. Induction Furnace for Ferrous Melting

(*i*) Bottom	Fire brick
(*ii*) Lining	
Acid	Rammed magnesite.
Basic	Rammed magnesite.
(*iii*) Former	Asbesto or steel.

4. Direct arc Furnaces for Ferrous Melting Acid

Acid

(*i*) Sub-hearth	Silica brick.
(*ii*) Working hearth	Silica sand or ganister.
(*iii*) Spout	Fire brick covered with ganister.
(*iv*) Side walls	Silica brick.
(*v*) Roof	Silica brick.
(*vi*) Changing arch	Silica brick.
(*vii*) Door	Medium alumina fire brick.

Basic

(*i*) Sub-hearth	Magnestic or dolomite brick.
(*ii*) Working hearth	Grain magnesite or dolomite.
(*iii*) Spout	Fire brick covered with ganister.
(*iv*) Side walls	Magnesite, chrome-magnesite or dolomite brick.
(*v*) Roof	Silica brick.
(*vi*) Charging arch	Silica brick.
(*vii*) Door	Medium alumina firebrick.

5. Ladle Refractories for Iron and Steel

(*i*) Lining	Silica, Fire, clay, or High alumina fire clay.

(*ii*) Nozzle, Stopper, Rod covers } High alumina fire clay.

6. Refractories in the Non-ferrous Foundry

Most non-ferrous metals which are cast in appreciable quantities are less reactive than iron, or melt at a much lower temperature.

Table 10.14 : Melting Points of Important Casting Alloys and Alloying Element

S. No.	*Alloy / Element*	*Melting Point*	
		°F	*°C*
1.	Tungsten	5450	3050
2.	Platinum	4500	2483
3.	Nickel	2900	1595
4.	Monel metal	2500	1370
5.	Manganese	2400	1315
6.	Silicon	2600	1430
7.	Gold }	1950	1065
8.	Copper }		
9.	Gun metal }	1850	1010
10.	Bronze }		
11.	Silver	1800	970
12.	Aluminium bronze	1700	926
13.	Red trass	1650	896
14.	Brass	1500	815
15.	Yellow brass	1400	760
16.	Aluminium	1300	705
17.	Antimony	790	421
18.	Zinc	775	411
19.	Lead	620	326
20.	Bismuth	518	270
21.	Tin	512	266
22.	Grey cast iron	2400–2000	1315–1095
23.	White cast iron	2550–2065	1400–1130
24.	Malleable C.I.	2550–2065	1400–1130
25.	Ductile C.I.	2150–2050	1175–1120

26.	*Plain carbon steel*		
	(*i*) Low carbon	2730–2615	1495–1435
	(*ii*) Medium carbon	2695–2590	1480–1420
	(*iii*) High carbon	2670–2160	1465–1180
27.	Low alloy steels	2730–2280	1495–1250
28.	Aluminium alloys	970–1255	520–680
29.	Magnesium	1200–1205	650–654
30.	Magnesium alloys	860–1200	460–650
31.	Chromium	3350	1845
32.	Molybdenum	4750	2620
33.	Zirconium	3326	1830
34.	Thorium	3346	1840
35.	Bismuth	520	270
36.	Arsenic	1497	810

Hence, refractory problems in melting these alloys are not nearly as great as in the melting of steel. Ordinary cast non-ferrous alloys include alloys of nickel, copper, aluminium, magnesium, zinc and others in lesser amounts.

Electric Furnaces (for non-ferrous metals)

(*i*) Induction Furnaces (*ii*) Electrical-resistance Furnaces	Lined with standard monolithic linings for either acid or basic materials, or prefired crucibles.
(*iii*) Direct-arc Furnaces (for copper and nickel) — Hearth, Side walls	Magnesite
Roofs	Magnesite chrome, Silica, or Alumina silica.
(*iv*) Indirect Furnaces	High-alumina firebrick

Gas or Oil-fired Crucible Furnaces

(*i*) For most non-ferrous metals	Prefired crucibles for fire clay, fire clay-graphite, magnesite, silicon carbide.
(*ii*) For copper-base and aluminium base alloy.	Fireclay-graphite, silicon carbide crucibles.

Silicon carbide crucibes have considerably longer life than clay graphite. Their higher thermal conductivity permits more rapid

melting. They are of course, more expensive than claygraphite crucibles.

(*iii*) For magnesium and zinc alloys	Crucibles of cast iron or stamped steels.
(*iv*) For aluminium alloys	Cast iron or steel crucibles with proper refractory washes.

Temperature Measurement of Furnaces and Metals

In all melting practices and in a number of different situations, some equipments are necessary for measuring temperatures. A scientific and reliable method of measuring temperatures is by an instrument called *'Pyrometer.'*

Two types of pyrometers are commonly used :

1. Thermo-electric Pyrometers.
2. Optical Pyrometers.

1. **Thermo-electric Pyrometers.** These may be employed at any temperature (*a*) up to about 1200°C for those made of *'base-metals'* and (*b*) to 1500°C for *'noble-metals'*.

(*i*) **Base metal couple** is made from (*a*) nickel chromium wire with nickel aluminium wire for temperatures upto 1200°C and (*b*) nickel chromium with constiantan wire upto 800°C.

Base metal couples oxidise more readily than noble-metal couples. They have, therefore, much shorter life.

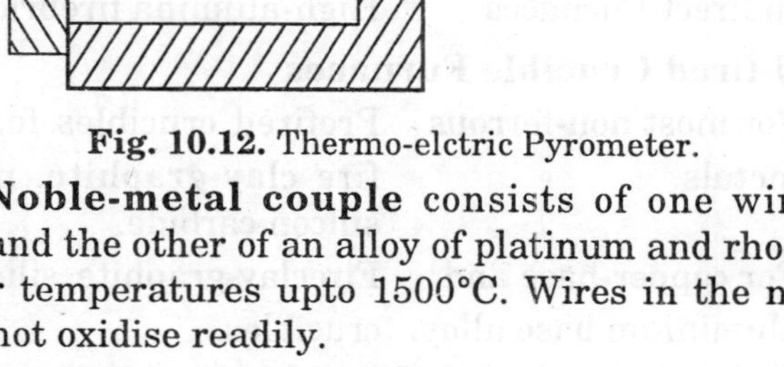

Fig. 10.12. Thermo-elctric Pyrometer.

(*ii*) **Noble-metal couple** consists of one wire of pure platinum and the other of an alloy of platinum and rhodium. This is used for temperatures upto 1500°C. Wires in the noble-metal couple do not oxidise readily.

Operation of Thermo-electric Pyrometers is based on the principle that when two wires of different metals are joined to

form a complete electric circuit, and one junction is at a higher temperature than the other, an electric current flows in the circuit.

The magnitude of the current depends upon the metal used and the temperature difference of the junctions.

In the practical application of this principle, an electric meter is connected to two wires which are welded together to form the hot junction. The two wires which form the junction are known as '*thermocouple*'.

The three essential parts of a thermo-electric pyrometer are :

(*i*) Thermocouple,

(*ii*) Galvanometer, and

(*iii*) Wires which lead from thermocouple to galvanometer.

The galvanometer is so calibrated that instead of indicating electrical units, it reads in degrees of temperature.

2. **Optical Pyrometers.** For measuing the temperature of a final bed or other body which may be at or above a red heat thermocouple is frequently not the best means either because,

(*i*) the temperature are too high, or

(*ii*) the position is inaccessible.

Under such circumstances, optical pyrometers are used. These may be employed at any temperatures upto about 4000°C. They are frequently used by steel smelters for ascertaining the furnace temperature while melting steel.

Principle. It compares the intensity of light being emitted from the furnace with that of some standard source. This instrument is calibrated so that it reads in degree of temperature, instead of in units of electric current.

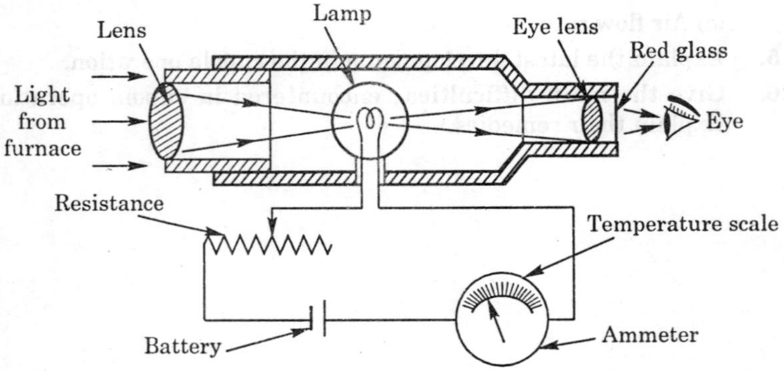

Fig. 10.13. Optical Pyrometer.

Operation. The telescope is sighted on the hot object and focussed. The lamp filament will then be seen against the red-hot background. Current is supplied to the filament from a battery through an adjustable resistance and is gradually increased until the tip of the filament just disappears into the background.

When too much current passes through the lamp filament, it appears as a bright line upon a darker background. It is due to the fact that the excess current makes the filament glow more brightly than the hot body.

With insufficient current, it appears as dark line on a lighter background.

When the current is correctly adjusted, the tip of the filament merges into and becomes indistinguishable from the background. At this moment, the current is read on an ammeter which is calibrated to give temperature readings.

QUESTIONS

1. Describe the relative merits and demerits of acid and basic livings in a cold blast cupola.
2. How would you specify a cupola? Explain with a neat sketch the cupola operation.
3. Describe the various combustion reactions in a cupola having the blast at room temperature. How these reactions will be affected if a hot blast is substituted ?
4. Discuss the influence of the following in cupola melting :

   (*a*) Coke-bed height

   (*b*) Iron-coke ratio

   (*c*) Air flow rate
5. Explain the latest developments in the cupola operation.
6. Give the main difficulties ; encountered in cupola operation ? Explain their remedies.

11

Casting

Advantages of Casting

Casting possess has a large number of characteristics which make them very useful in modern equipments used for construction, transportation, agriculture, communication, power and in industry. Cast metals are required in various shapes and sizes in large quantities for making machines and tools which provide the comfort for the modern civilisation.

Other metal shaping processes *e.g.*, hot working, forging, machining, welding stamping etc., are of course necessary to meet the tremendous variety of needs. However, certain advantages are inherent in castings and casting processes which render them superior to all other methods.

Advantages of casting and casting processes are broadly classified :

(*i*) Design advantages of castings.

(*ii*) Advantages of the casting process.

(*iii*) Metallurgical advantages.

Design Advantages of Castings

By casting the metal can be shaped to almost any configuration with slight limitation on size, accuracy and intricacy :

(*i*) **Size.** In fact, casting is the only method to produce massive objects in one single piece. Castings weighing as much as 200 tonnes and as small as a wire of 0.05 mm diameter and 50 mm length can be produced.

(*ii*) **Intricacy.** Intricate shapes having complex surfaces inside or outside which may be very difficult or impossible to machine forge or fabricate can be usually cast *e.g.*, hydraulic transmssion components, automotive motor blocks, etc.

(*iii*) **Saving in weight.** Large saving in weight can be affected as the metal can be placed exactly where it is required ; thus it reduces cost. Weight saving also affects an increase in efficiency of transportation and reduced transport charges.

(*iv*) **Prototypes.** In the production of prototype or models required for creating new design, the casting process is extremely useful.

(*v*) **Service Requirements and Casting Alloy.** Castings possess the complete range of mechanical and physical properties available in metals. Thus, they fulfil a large majority of service requirements.

Almost all requirements of properties *e.g.*, mechanical stresses, wear resistance, hardness, strength weight ratio, endurance, heat and corrosion resistance electrical and thermal conductivity, electrical resistance and appearance etc., can be supplied by casting alloys. There are some alloys which can only be cast to shape as they can not be worked mechanically.

Advantages of Casting Process

(*i*) **Mass production.** For mass production work metal casting process is unexcelled. Casting can be produced in large numbers rapidly at low cost *e.g.*, part required in automotive industry, agricultural implements, home appliances, transportation and construction.

(*ii*) **Dimensional accuracy.** Castings can be made in wide range of dimensional tolerances and surface finish. Tolerances of ± 0.025 mm to – 3 mm on a dimension can be obtained depending on the selection of material, casting process and design. Similarly surface finish from 25000 down to 500 micro mm can be obtained.

(*iii*) **Machining.** In certain casting methods, a marked reduction or sometimes complete elimination of machine is possible. Cam surfaces gear teeth, threads etc., can often be cast which may require no further machining.

Metallurgical Advantages

(*i*) **Fibrous structure.** When rough metals are worked, inclusions of non-metallic impurities are strung out in the direction of working and so the fibrous structure results in marked directional properties.

In cast metals, the inclusion are more or less randomly distributed during the solidification process. Hence cast alloys

usually do not exhibit any fibring or directionally of properties, except under unfavorable solidification conditions.

(*ii*) **Grain size.** Although mechanical working of wrought metals breaks up the coarse grains and promotes fine grain size, many casting possess grain size, not greatly different from those of the former. The grain size developed during freezing of the casting is retained by most of the non-ferrous alloy.

(*iii*) **Density.** Cast alloys and wrought alloys of the same chemical composition and heat treatment usually have the same density, when both are fully sound.

From the above facts, it is seen that metal casting is one of the most versatile methods for shaping metals.

Table 11.1: Flow Sheet of Typical Metal Casting Operations

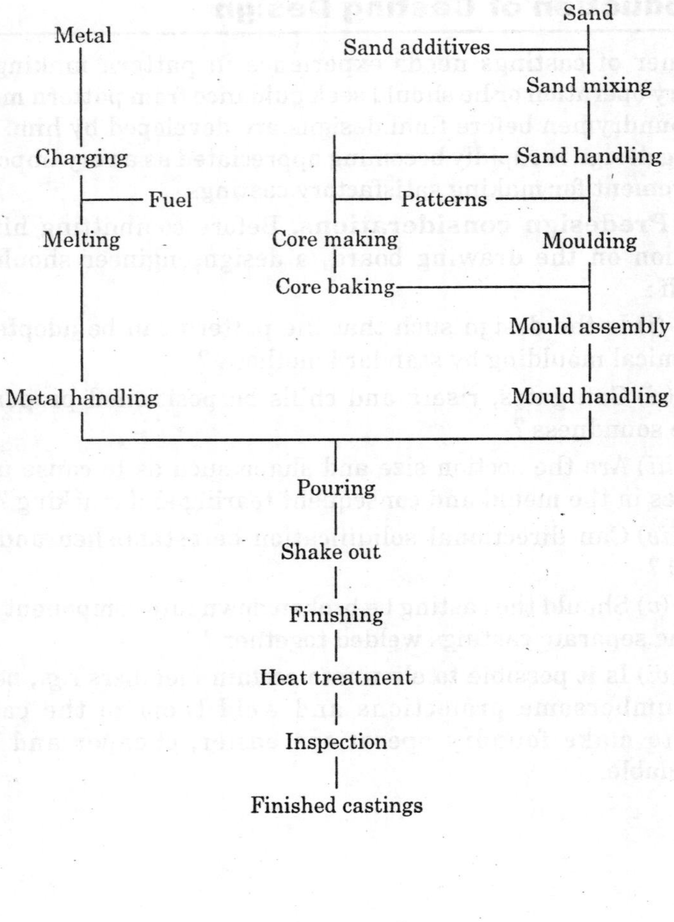

Inherent Weaknesses in Castings result from certain characteristics associated with the solidification process. These include ;

(*i*) Shrinkage
(*ii*) Segregation
(*iii*) Gas porosity, and
(*iv*) Low hot strength.

Casting defects that are more directly the result of poor moulding or foundry practice, rather than inherent in the solidification process, include :

(*i*) Cold shuts
(*ii*) Dirt spots
(*iii*) Fins
(*iv*) Misruns
(*v*) Penetration
(*vi*) Scales
(*vii*) Swells
(*viii*) Washes, etc.

Introduction of Casting Design

Designer of castings needs experience in pattern making and foundry operation or he should seek guidance from pattern makers and foundrymen before final designs are developed by him. Good casting design is rapidly becoming appreciated as a very important requirement for making satisfactory castings.

Predesign considerations. Before committing himself to action on the drawing board, a design engineer should ask himself :

(*i*) Is the design such that the pattern can be adopted for economical moulding by standard methods ?

(*ii*) Can gates, risers and chills be positioned properly to insure soundness ?

(*iii*) Are the section size and shape such as to cause undue stresses in the mould and consequent tearing and cracking ?

(*iv*) Can directional solidification be established and controlled ?

(*v*) Should the casting be broken down into component parts and the separate castings welded together ?

(*vi*) Is it possible to eliminate certain members *e.g.*, bosses, and cumbersome projections and weld them to the casting later to make foundry operations easier, cheaper and more dependable.

Design for Minimum Casting Stresses

Ferrous castings are particularly susceptible to external cracking or tearing in the mould because :

(*i*) Total contraction is high due to high pouring temperatures.

(*ii*) At critical temperatures, hot strength and ductility are low.

These defects may be caused

(*i*) By influences external to the casting, or

(*ii*) By inherent characteristics.

(*i*) The important *external influence* is the effect of the mould, which may restrain normal contraction and cause cracks tear or warpages, stresses can be reduced (*a*) by moulding expedients, or (*b*) by design considerations.

If casting is large, and of complex shape it is desirable to cast two or more sections and weld them together. To prevent tearing small tie bars are used in critical areas. To reduce stress slightly, straight members like spokes of wheels may be curved.

(*ii*) Stresses arising from *inherent conditions* are

(*a*) those due strictly to design and

(*b*) those peculiar to the composition of the metal.

Thin sections of castings cool and contract much faster than heavier members. If much members are attached rigidly, high stresses develop. As the small members cool and shrink they are restrained by larger, slower-cooling sections. Thus, small members may either tear to relieve the stresses or deform (warp) plastically without tearing.

Metal composition influences tearing tendencies in atleast three ways :

1. By the inherent strength and ductility at critical temperatures.

2. By the existence and extent of solid transformations.

3. By the presence of impurities *e.g.*, sulphur at grain boundries.

In general, plain low-carbon steel resists tearing better than alloy steels and grey irons are less susceptible than alloy irons. In iron and non-ferrous castings, tearing is usually more a matter of design than of composition.

Design for Directional Solidification

For sound castings, temperature gradients in solidifying casting must be properly controlled. The various design considerations are discussed in order for easy understandings.

(*i*) **Heavy sections cannot be fed through light sections.** Various component parts or members of castings are joined in *L, Y, T, X,* or *V* fashion. Junction of each is a reign of larger mass of metal. The metal at the centre of such region is a hot spot which solidifies last. Usually, it is neither convenient nor economical to place a riser at this point.

Designer should therefore, attempt to limit junctions to as few as possible. If limiting the number of junctions is not possible, it is advisable to cast in segments and join them together later by welding or bolting.

(*ii*) **If possible, sections should taper towards riser.** Casting soundness obtained by natural solidification is proportional to the degree of tapering allowed. Cylindrical castings are difficult to make sound by static methods. They are best made sound by centrifugal casting.

(*iii*) **Horizontal flat surfaces are not desirable.** Castings with flat surfaces are particularly difficult to make because—

(*a*) it is hard to prevent centre line shrinkage, as temperature gradients are not favourabe, and

(*b*) slag, dross, and other impurities lighter than metal tend to collect on the upper flat surfaces.

Wherever possible, it is advisable to have curved surfaces or to make castings so that flat surfaces are either vertical or inclined to the horizontal.

(*iv*) **Isolated hot spots must be avoided.** Small pockets or cores of sand surrounded by metal reduce the rate of cooling as compared to more open regions. Such isolated regions are likely to shrink or tear without special means for feeding or chilling.

Design for Metal Flow

Minimum section thicknesses for sand castings depend on the metal composition.

In average sand foundry practice :

(*i*) For very small castings of grey iron, aluminium, magnesium and copper-base alloys, thickness should not be less

than 3 mm. For larger castings of these metals, thickness should not be less than 4.5 to 6 mm.

(*ii*) Iron with 0.5 to 1% phosphorus used for stove plates, household, radiators etc., may have thicknesses upto 1.5 mm.

(*iii*) Steel castings, is small, should never be less than 6 mm in thickness, and if large, less than 12 mm.

New casting methods specially developed greatly extend the field for thinner castings.

Cast-weld Design

Cast-weld structures have many advantages :

Tendency of a casting to warp or tear is proportional to its length and complexity. Separating a casting into parts and welding components together, or welding forgings and casting together enhances the versatility of all the fabricating processes.

The use of cast-weld structures is increasing rapidily as this method of fabrication is more economical than all welded construction.

Design for Low Pattern Cost and Minimum Manipulation

The problems of pattern making should be understood at least, before design is fixed, so as to determine if anything can be altered to make pattern construction more economical. Practical experience is the best guide as it is not possible to formulate rigorous rules.

Design determines the number of operations needed to make moulds and cores and to assemble them for a casting. Core making and core setting are expensive operations. Much can be done on the drawing board to minimise the number and complexity of cores needed. Design engineer should follow his creations through all steps to the final casting, and make design changes whether such changes favourably affect the cost and quality of the final product.

Safety Factors in Casting Design

Design engineers usually employ excessively high factors of safety, as high as 3 to 1, which can often be decreased.

The mechanical properties of sound castings, properly made from well-melted metal, are comparable to those of wrought metals. Comparisons often made between forgings and castings on the basis that cast parts are more liable to failure, is not favourable.

With latest inspection methods available and improved foundry practice, there is no need to employ a faulty casting. A capable foundry engineer knows very well whether a particular casting is likely to be equivalent to its wrought counterpart.

Model Making as an Aid to Casting Design

Even the best trained foundry engineer may miss the important details of design when he makes casting with the help of blue print only. If complicated castings are made as an accurately scaled wood or plastic model, trouble and money can be saved for producer and consumer alike.

By making and studying a model of the job to be done—

(*i*) Many costly design changes and casting repairs can be eliminated.

(*ii*) Areas of potential shrinkage and tearing can be predicted.

(*iii*) Gates and risers can be judiciously placed without trial and error.

(*iv*) Money-saving changes in pattern construction can be spotted before making working patterns.

If necessary, a model-sized casting can be made, and cut up for inspection to determine potential casting problems.

By making sectional models, each part of the casting can be studied and important decisions arrived at. For model work, transparent plastics are excellent.

Scope and Position of Foundry Industry in India

Foundry industry is the basis to the development of heavy industries set up in India. At present, a very large number of foundries are engaged in the production of iron, steel and non-ferrous castings in the various parts of the country.

Current requirements of steel castings alone have been estimated to be about 80,000 tonnes. A heavy foundry set up at Ranchi at a cost of about 130 crores have capacity of 45,000 tonnes of steel castings and 40,000 tonnes of grey iron castings. Foundries attached to the steel plants at Bhilai, Durgapur, Rourkela, Heavy Electricals Ltd., Bhopal, Mining Machinery Project, Durgapur, Hindustan Machine Tools, Banglore (now it is Bengaluru), and Chittranjan Locomotive Works have an additional capacity. Under the current Five Year Plan, a total capacity of about 150,000 tonnes of grey iron castings and 100,000 tonnes of steel castings is expected to be available.

In view of such rapid developments, efficient and economic operation of foundries carries considerable importance. Increasing demand for castings of close tolerances and intricate design has brought about a tremendous growth of foundry industry in India and needs due consideration to the basic requirements, *e.g.*, selection, testing and controlling of foundry sands and their mixtures so as to have desired specification in the castings.

Previously, Indian foundries had no technical data on the indigenous resources of foundry sand. They experienced considerable difficulties in proper planning and rational utilisaton of indigenous sands. Sometimes back, the National Metallurgical Laboratory, Jamshedpur undertook a comprehensive nation-wide survey and published the results in the form of monograph. These findings can be used to advantage by all the foundries in the country.

Casting Processes

Pouring the molten metal into a previously made mould (which contains an impression of the shape of the casting desired) is known as '*Casting*'. Casting Processes are classified according to—

(*i*) the material used for making moulds, and

(*ii*) the methods used for feeding the molten metal into the moulds.

Sand Casting

It is the most common of all casting processes and is employed for producing the largest proportion of castings in the foundry. As already described, the sand for moulding purposes is suitably mixed and prepared.

Green sands are more generally used for small and medium-sized castings due to their ease of working and low cost.

Dry sands consist of the moulding sand with suitable additives and binders. They are used for castings of high quality, *e.g.*, good surface finish and soundness. In this case, moulds are prepared from specially prepared sand. Their surfaces are sprayed with molasses and water. Then, they are dried in an oven for driving off the moisture.

Loam sand moulds are used for very large size casting of regular shape. They are made from moulding sand, clay and bricks.

Sand casting processes have already been described in details in previous chapters.

Recent Treads in Foundry Practice—Special Casting Methods

Castings from various types of sand moulds probably have fewer limitations than those produced by any other processes. All metals may be cast in sand moulds. There is no restriction as to size.

However, sand moulds are single-purpose moulds, being completely destroyed after the metal has solidified. Quite obviously, the use of a *'permanent mould'* would effect considerable saving in labour cost. In this field, particularly in the die casting of non-ferrous alloys, great strides have been made :

Table 11.1 : Summary of Various Special Casting Methods

1. Casting in Metallic moulds :
   (*a*) Gravity or Permanent-mould casting.
   (*b*) Slush casting.
   (*c*) Pressed or Corthias casting.
   (*d*) Die casting.
      (*i*) Hot-chamber machines,
      (*ii*) Cold-chamber machines.
2. Casting in Non-metallic moulds :
   (*a*) Centrifugal castings.
      (*i*) True centifugal,
      (*ii*) Semi-centrifugal,
      (*iii*) Centrifugal.
   (*b*) Precision castings—
      (*i*) 'Lost wax' method,
      (*ii*) Plaster moulds,
      (*iii*) Mercast process,
      (*iv*) Shell Moulding.
   (*c*) CO_2 mould-hardening process.
   (*d*) Moulds of wood, rubber, paper etc.
3. Continuous Casting :
   (*a*) Reciprocating moulds,
   (*b*) Raw casting,
   (*c*) Stationary moulds,
   (*d*) Direct sheet casting.

Methods of Casting in Metallic Moulds

Permanent moulds are made of metals capable of withstanding high temperatures. They are recommended only when many

castings are to be produced because of their high cost. For large castings and alloys of high melting temperatures, permanent moulds are impractical. But, for small and medium sized non-ferrous castings manufactured in large quantities they can be used advantageously.

Gravity of Permanent Mould Casting

This method consists of filling a metal mould as in sand casting. No pressure is used except that obtained from the head of metal in the mould. Therefore, it is also known as *'Gravity Die Casting'*.

The process is used successfully for both ferrous and non-ferrous castings, although the latter do not present so many problems because of their lower pouring temperatures.

Mould Construction and Operation

Permanent moulds are generally made of dense, high duty cast iron *viz.*, Mechanite or steel. Moulds are made in two parts which can open or close in alignment in a horizontal plane. The parting surface is usually in all vertical plane.

The hollows or cavities in the interior are formed with grey iron or steel cores. Two types of cores used in permanent moulds are :

(*i*) **Fixed Cores.** These cores can be withdrawn with the mould and are fastened to the mould body.

(*ii*) **Movable Cores.** These cores are separate from the mould. They are drawn before parting the mould.

These cores are withdrawn as soon as the metal starts to solidify by means of :

(*a*) Rack and pinion mechanism

(*b*) Screw mechanism

(*c*) Hydraulic mechanism.

The moulds being metallic, the heat of the molten metal is removed very rapidly and the metal shrinks very fast, leaving an air space between the mould surface and casting. This air space protects mould material from the effect of heat.

The two halves of the mould may be mounted on a sliding carriage where one half is fixed on one side and other half is movable along a horizontal bed.

The simplest type of permanent mould hinges at one end of the mould with provision for clamping the halves together at the other.

In large-scale production, a number of moulds are placed on a rotating table where various operations are performed automatically as the moulds pass through different stations.

The cycle of events consists of pouring, cooling and ejecting the casting, blowing out the moulds, coating them, and, in some cases, setting the cores.

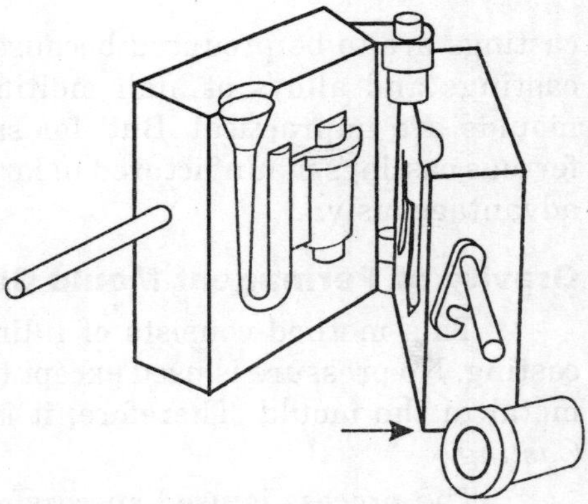

Fig. 11.1. Permanent Mould Casting Process. (Solidified casting with gate and metal core shown in left half of the mould with completed casting in the front.)

After solidification, the casting tend to cling to one of the mould halves and may not come out on its own accord. Spring-loaded ejector pins operated manually or automatically are used to eject the casting from the mould. Ejector pins are provided in one of the two halves in which the casting tends to cling.

Gating, risering and venting problems are same as in sand casting. Depending on where the junction of sprue and mould cavity is desired, the gates may be top, bottom or side type. Shallow channels about 0.15 mm deep are made in the parting surfaces for venting purposes.

Thickness of mould walls usually varies from 20 to 25 mm. Ribs and flanges are provided on the outer surfaces for strengthening the mould. Moulds are usually coated with a refractory wash and then lamp black, which reduces the chilling effect on the metal and facilitates the removal of the casting. Castings are frequently removed before they are completely solidified to prevent cracks which may develop as a result of shrinkage strains.

Advantages. (*i*) Permanent moulds produces castings free from sand with good surface finish.

(*ii*) Castings are capable of maintaining tolerances ranging from 0.0625 to 0.25 mm.

Disadvantages. (*i*) High initial cost of equipment.

(*ii*) High cost of mould maintenance.

Applications. Permanent mould casting is especially adopted to the quantity production of small and medium-sized

castings *e.g.,* aluminium pistons, cooking utensils, refrigerator parts, electric irons small gear black etc.

Slush Casting

It is a method of producing hollow castings in metal moulds without the use of cores. The mould is filled with molten metal and held stationary until a thin sking of solid metal freezes against the mould walls. The mould is then inverted and the unfrozen metal run out from the casting. A thin-walled casting results, the thickness depending on the chilling effect from the mould and the time of the operation. The casting is removed by opening the halves of the mould.

Precautions (*i*) The mould should not be inverted too sharply or air will be excluded as molten metal chokes the cavity ; a partial vacuum will be formed, and the still weak solid skin of the casting will collapse at its weakest point.

(*ii*) The casting must be made of a relatively pure metal, as most alloys do not form a strong solid skin.

Applications. For some castings *viz.*, statuary work, only the external features of the casting are important.

Since such castings are not meant for engineering use, uniformity of wall thickess is not an important consideration.

Owing to its obvious drawbacks, this method is used only on a limited scale for low melting point alloys like zinc or load. It can be used for objects, in which dimensional accuracy is not important *e.g.,* ornamental objects, statuettes, toys and other novelties, *i.e.*, only for a limited amount of art and decorative work.

Slush casting of metals corresponds to slip casting techniques used by ceramists to make ceramic bodies. Parts cast in this fashion are either painted or finished to represent bronze, silver, or other more expensive metals.

Pressed or Corthias Casting

This method of casting developed in France by Corthias resembles both the gravity and the slush processes but differs some what in the manner in which the operation is performed.

A definite amount of metal is poured into an open-ended mould and a close-fitting core is forced into the cavity, causing the metal to be forced into the mould cavities with some pressure. The core is removed as soon as the metal sets, leaving a hollow thin-walled casting.

Applications. This process is limited in the use mainly to ornamental casting of open design.

Die Casting (Pressure Die Casting)

Die casting refers to the forcing, by pressure of molten metal into a metal die or mould. The term *'die'* used in this process implies a metallic mould which is filled under pressure. The pressures, which range from 6 to 3000 kg/cm^2 are maintained unit solidification is completed.

Die Casting Dies

The dies resemble the common type of permanent mould, which consists of two halves arranged to open and close with a vertical parting. On a die casting machine, one die half, called the cover die is stationary. The other die half, which moves for the opening and closing is known as the *'ejector die'*.

Characteristic of Die Metal

Die casting dies are usually made of an alloy steel having the following characteristics :

(*i*) It should be dimensionally stable.
(*ii*) It should have high resistance to heat.
(*iii*) It should not get soldered to the cast alloy.
(*iv*) It should resist erosion.
(*v*) It should have high wear resistance and toughness.

Die cavities are made with great accuracy usually by machining process. Dies for both the hot and cold-chamber machines are similar in construction because there is little difference in the method of holding and operating them. The life of these dies depends on the metal cast and may range from 10,000 fillings, if brass castings are made, to several millions if zinc is used.

Vents and small overflow wells are provided on one side of a die (*i*) to facilitate the escape of air and (*ii*) to catch surplus metal that has passed through the die cavity. In spite of this provision, there is certain amount of flash metal which is trimmed off in the finishing operation *e.g.*, grinding or blanking (press shearing).

For large or complex castings, a single-cavity die is used. If the quantity of casting to be produced is large and they are relatively small in size, a multiple-cavity die can be used. A combination die is one that has two or more cavities, each of which is different.

Most dies are provided with channels for water cooling to keep the die at correct temperature for rapid production.

Dies (*i*) for tin and lead alloy casting, dies are made of carbon steels without that treatment,

(*ii*) for zinc, aluminium and magnesium, dies are of heat treated hot-alloy steel,

(*iii*) for copper-base castings, heat treated special alloy steel dies are used.

Dies are provided with a separate mechanism for moving the ejector plate or movable cores. Methods used for closing and locking the dies are :

(*i*) **Straight hydraulic clamping.** With this mechanism, live pressure backs up the die at all times when it is closed. In this method, hydraulic pressure on the die is maintained throughout.

(*ii*) **Hydraulic and mechanical toggle clamping.** With the mechanism, the die is closed by the hydraulic pressure and piston movement in the hydraulic cylinder causes simultaneously the toggle links to be straightened so that they close the die with a great force.

(*iii*) **Mechanical clamping.** This mechanism relies wholly on the mechanical arrangement for closing and loking the dies. It does not make use of any hydraulic pressure.

Design Considerations in Die Casting

During the design of die casting dies, the following points should be kept in view in addition to the considerations given for sand casting design :

(*i*) Die casting should be so designed that the cost of flash removal is minimum.

(*ii*) Non-refractory nature of the dies should be kept in view.

(*iii*) Artificial means of venting are essential to have sound castings free from porosity.

(*iv*) As the die can not be destroyed and disintegrated at will, the runners and risers should be so located that they facilitate the removal of the casting.

(*v*) Proper type of cores should be provided. Extra long cores should be avoided. Cores should have the simplest possible shape and yet produce the desired results.

(*vi*) Undercuts requiring movable cores or loose pieces should be avoided, if possible.

Types of Die Casting Machines used for feeding the metal into the dies under pressure are :

(*i*) Hot Chamber Submerged-plunger type.

(*ii*) Cold Chamber type.

(*iii*) Air-blown or Goose-neck type.

Hot Chamber Submerged-plunger Type Die Casting Machine (Fig. 11.2). It consists of a suitable furnace for melting and holding the metal. Submerged below the surface of the molten metal *E*, plunger *C*, operates within a cylinder *B*. When the plunger is raised, it uncovers an opening or port in the cylinder wall, through which the metal enters, filling the cylinder.

The operation, the pluger is forced downwards pneumatically or hydraulically, closing the opening and then forcing the confined metal up through a suitable channel and nozzle into the die *G*. After a predetermined time, the plunger is again raised, allowing the molten metal in the channel and nozzle to drop back. The die is opened and the solidified die casting is ejected.

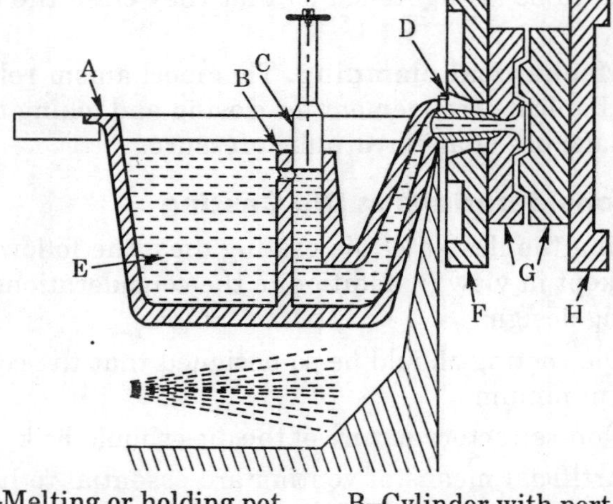

A–Melting or holding pot. B–Cylinder with port.
C–Injection plunger. D–Nozzle.
E–Molten metal. F–Fixed press platen.
G–Die bocks. H–Moving press platen.

Fig. 11.2. Hot Chamber submerged plunger type die-casting machine.

Metal injection speeds and pressures are controllable to suit different metals and castings. To attain uniformity and maximum speed of operation, a predetermined and automatically controlled

cycle for various operations should be used. Operator is however required to remove the casting from the die, inspect and sometimes lubricate it.

Applications. This machine is primarily used for zinc and has a capacity of 4.5 kg per shot, with an injection pressure of 1500 kg/cm^2.

Limitations. Hot chamber machines are used with low-melting alloy because of :

(*i*) Machine difficulties encountered at high temperatures.

(*ii*) The increased corrosion of the machine parts.

(*iii*) Since many metals have an affinity for iron, only those casting alloys, which do not attack the immersed metal parts are used. Alloys of zinc, tin and lead are particularly recommended for these machines.

(*iv*) Die casting of brass, aluminium and magnesium requires higher pressures and melting temperatures. Hence, a change in the melting procedure is necessary. These metals are not melted in a self-contained pot, since the life of the pot would be very short.

Cold Chamber Type Die Casting Machine

The cold chamber process has been explained schematically in the figure as applied to the manufacture of a cup shaped piece.

The molten metal, which may be an alloy of zinc, aluminium, copper, magnesium, lead, or tin, is ladled from the melting pot into a pouring slot in the main pressure chamber [Fig. 11.3 (*a*)].

A close fitting plunger is rammed forward by hand or pneumatic action. This confines the metal against the die opening and actually squirts it into the die at pressures of 400 to 1500 kg/cm^2 and higher [Fig. 11.3 (*b*)].

Because most die castings are of thin section (usually 3 mm or less), solidification is extremely rapid. After the casting is solid, the die halves are opened and cores are withdrawn [Fig. 11.3 (*c*)].

Finally ejector pins automatically forces the casting out of the cavity [Fig. 11.3 (*d*)].

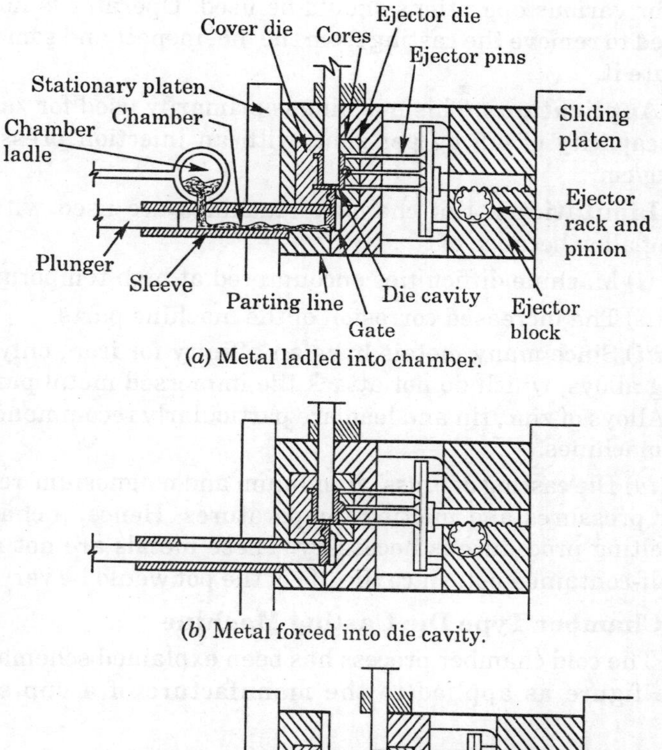

(*a*) Metal ladled into chamber.

(*b*) Metal forced into die cavity.

(*c*) Die opened, cores withdrawn.

(*d*) Casting and excess metal ejected.

Fig. 11.3. Die casting, cold-chamber Machine.

These machines are fully hydraulic and semi-automatic. After the metal is ladled in, the rest of the operations are automatic. Aside from the ladling procedure, the operation of the machine is the same for hot-chamber machines.

The manufacture of brass die castings is a comparatively recent achievement. Difficulties of rapid oxidation of steel dies due to high temperatures involved have been largely overcome.

(*i*) by improvement in die metals and

(*ii*) by casting at as low a temperature as possible.

A machine developed in Czechoslovakia, known as Polak machine, has been used successfully for the production of brass die castings. This machine is designed to use metal in a semi-liquid or plastic state to permit operation at lower temperatures than those used for liquid metal. To protect the dies further from overheating, water is circulated through plates adjacent to the dies. Metal is maintained under close temperature control and is ladled by hand to the compression chamber. The pressure used in this machine is 700 kg/cm^2. 100 to 200 shots per hour can be made, depending on the machine size.

Air-blown or Goose-neck Type Die Casting Machine

The principle of the goose-neck machine is shown in Figure 11.4. Pressures usually do not exceed 45 kg/cm^2. Machine may either be

(*i*) operated by air actuated ram or

(*ii*) operated by direct air pressure.

The bottle being of goose-neck type, it can be tilted about trunnions from air blowing position to filling position and *vice versa*. The metal can thus be inserted into the bottle simply by filling the bottle.

The machine is much simpler in operation and construction than the plunger type as there are no moving parts like plunger etc. It however requires greater attention of the operator since the work is mostly of the manual type. These days, the air-blown type is being replaced by the hot chamber type due to a much higher rate of production of the later and its easy adaptability for mass production.

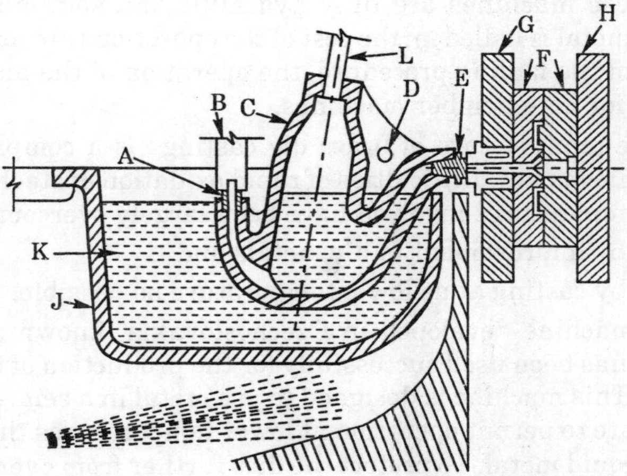

A–Filling nozzle. B–Sealing abutment.
C–Goose-neck bottle. D–Trunnion.
E–Nozzle. F–Die blocks.
G–Fixed press platen. H–Moving press platen.
J–Melting and holding pot. K–Metal.
L–Compressed air inlet.

Fig. 11.4. Air blown type Die Casting Machine.

Advantage of Die Casting

(*i*) Very high rates of production are possible *viz.*, in cold chamber type 75 to 150 per hour and in hot chamber type 300 to 350 per hour.

(*ii*) Close dimensional control can be maintained. In zinc, a tolerance of ± 0.075 mm upto 25 mm size and ± 0.25 mm for each additional 25 mm can be easily achieved.

(*iii*) Thin sections can be cast. Under favourable conditions minimum thickness cast are about 0.5 mm for zinc and 0.875 mm for aluminium.

(*iv*) Surface finish of 1250 micro-mm R.M.S. can be obtained. Hence, appearance is improved and finishing operations are minimised.

(*v*) Details can be reproduced successfully with a high degree of precision.

(*vi*) Die casting dies retain their accuracy and usefulness for a long time. Dies for zinc alloys may produce as many as 5 million castings.

(*vii*) For mass production die casting is very economical due to elimination of machining and mould making resulting in saving of labour and time.

(*viii*) Because of the uniformity in wall thickness less material is required in die casting than in sand casting.

(*ix*) There are no possibilities for sand inclusions and a strong dense metal structure is obtained.

Disadvantages of Die Casting

(*i*) High cost of the equipment and dies used requires sufficiently large quantities to compete economically with other processes. For die casting, minimum economic quantity is considered to be about 20,000.

(*ii*) There is a rapid decrease in the life of the dies as the metal temperature increases.

(*iii*) In some cases, there is an undesirable chilling effect on the metal.

(*iv*) Metals having a high coefficient of contraction must be removed from the mould as soon as possible because of the inability of the mould to contract with the casting.

(*v*) There are certain limitations in the shape of die castings and the process is not adapted to the production of large castings. So far, the maximum size cast is 100 kg in zinc and 30 kg in aluminium.

(*vi*) Die castings usually contain some porposity due to the entrapping of air.

(*vii*) Die casting has, to a large extent, been limited to low melting non-ferrous alloys.

With a gradual improvement of heat-resisting metals for dies, this process can now be used for numerous alloys.

Die-Casting Alloys

(*a*) **Zince base alloys.** Over 75% of die castings produced are the zinc base type. The purest grades of commercial zinc 99.90%, known as Special High grade, should be used, since impurities like lead, cadmium, tin cause serious casting and aging defects.

Applications. Zinc alloys are widely used in the automotive industry and for other high-production markets *e.g.,* washing machines, oil burners, refrigerators, radios, phonographs, television, business machines, parking meters, small machine tools, etc.

Table 11.3 : Zinc-Base Casting Alloys

S. No.	*Al*	*Cu*	*Mg*	*Zinc*
1.	4.1	0.1 max	0.04	Remainder
2.	4.1	1.0	0.04	Remainder

(*ii*) **Aluminium base alloys.** Many die castings are made of aluminium alloys because of their lightness in weight, resistance to corrosion, high electrical conductivity, ease of applying surface finishes and good machinability. Compared to zinc alloys, however, they are slightly lower in physical properties and more difficult to die cast. Their melting temperature is around 1185°F.

Generally, the cold-chamber process is used in casting because molten alloys of aluminium attach steel if kept in continuous contact with it. Although more expensive to operate than the air-in jet type, it has advantage of producing sounder casting.

Table 11.4 : Aluminium Base Die-Casting Alloys

S. No.	*Cu*	*Si*	*Mg*	*Al*	*Uses*
1.	—	12	—	Remainder	Large intricate castings with thin sections.
2.	—	5	—	Remainder	General purpose and permanent mould casting.
3.	3	—	—	Reminder	High strength, ductile and corrosion resistance.
4.	3.5	9	8	Reminder	Good machinability, physical properties and casting characteristics.

Silicon increases hardness and corrosion resistance.

Copper improves mechanical properties slightly.

Magnesium increases lightness and impact resistance.

(*iii*) **Copper-base Alloys.** Die castings of brass and bronze present more problems in pressure casting because of their high casting temperatures (1600 to 1900°F). Heat-resisting alloy steel dies are used to reduce their rapid deterioration. Cost of brass die castings is, therefore, comparatively higher.

Copper-base alloys, due to their high temperatures are melted in an auxiliary furnace and ladled to the plunger-type cold-chamber machine.

Copper-base alloys are extensively used in miscellaneous hardware, electric machinery parts, small gears, marine aircraft and automotive fittings, chemical apparatus etc. Where high strength, corrosion resistance are important.

Table 11.5 : Copper-Base-Die-Casting Alloys

S. No.	*Cu*	*Si*	*Sn*	*Pb*	*Zn*	*Uses*
1.	57	—	1.5	1.5	40	Yellow brass alloy having good machinability and casting characteristics.
2.	65	1	—	—	34	General purpose.
3.	81	4	—	—	15	High strength, hardness and wear resistance.

(*iv*) **Magnesium-base Alloys.** Magnesium is alloyed principally with aluminium but may contain small amounts of Si, Mn, Zn, Cu and Ni. Its alloys are the lightest in weight of all the die-cast metals, being about two-thirds the weight of aluminium alloys. Their corrosion resistance is inferior to that of the other die-casting alloys.

The principal die casting alloy of magnesium having good casting characteristics (casting temperature 1200–1300°F), mechanical properties and excellent machinability contains Al 1%, Zn 0.5%, Mn 0.13%, Si 0.3% max, Cu 0.3%, Ni 0.03%, Mg the reminder. To minimise corrosion Cu and Ni should be kept very low. Melting crucible is hooded, keeping the metal covered by a non-oxidising atmosphere.

Magnesium-base alloys are extensively used for aircraft, motor and instrument parts, portable tools, textile machinery, household appliances etc.

(*v*) **Lead base Alloys.** Pure lead melts at 621°F. When alloys with about 16% antimony, it melts at about 470°F. Antimony is the principal alloying element ; its percentage ranges from 9.25 to 16.

Principal die-casting alloy of lead containing Ph 80%, Sb 15%, Sn 5%, Cu 0.5% is used mainly as a bearing material for moderate loads ; other applications being weights, battery parts, X-ray shields, non-corrosive metal parts etc.

Presence of tin increases fluidity, hardness, strength and thus improves its bearing characteristics. Use of lead compounds for die casting is limited due to their toxic effect upon workmen.

(*iv*) **Tin base Alloys.** As far as mechanical properties are concerned, they are in about the same category as the lead alloys, but they are high in price. Tin alloys are high in corrosion resistance well suited for use in contact with food and beverages. Also, they have excellent bearing properties, and can be within remarkable close dimensional tolerances.

In most tin alloys Sb 4 to 16% and Pb upto 19% is common. Where die casting remains in contact with food or beverages, use of lead is eliminated. Tin alloys can also be used for low-cost jewellery, pewter etc. Their low melting point and low solidification shrinkage promotes long die life.

Use for tin-alloy die castings is very limited because die casters cannot afford the risk of contaminating zinc alloys with tin.

Methods of Casting in Non-metallic Moulds

Each mould material has its own temperature limitations as to the kind of metal for which it is suitable. In many cases, non-metallic moulds are used in precision casting.

Centrifugal casting is included under this heading although castings are made by this process in both metal and non-metallic moulds.

Centrifugal Casting

'It is the process of rotating a mould while the metal solidifies, so as to utilize centrifugal force for positioning the metal in the mould. The metal is forced against the walls of the mould with much greater pressure than that obtained by static pressure in ordinary sand casting. Greater detail on the surface of the casting is obtained, and the dense metal structure has superior physical properties. This method is particularly suited to castings of symmetrical shape.

Methods of Centrifugal Casting are classified as :

(*i*) True centrifugal Casting

(*ii*) Semi-centrifugal Casting

(*iii*) Centrifuging.

(*i*) **True centrifugal Casting** is used for pipe, liners and symmetrical objects which are cast by rotating the mould about its horizontal or vertical axis. Metal is held against the wall of the

mould by centrifugal force and no core is required to form a cylindrical cavity on the inside. This method is illustrated by the casting machine shown in Fig. 11.5, designed for the production of steel or cast iron pipe. The amount of the metal poured into the mould controls the wall thickness of the pipe produced.

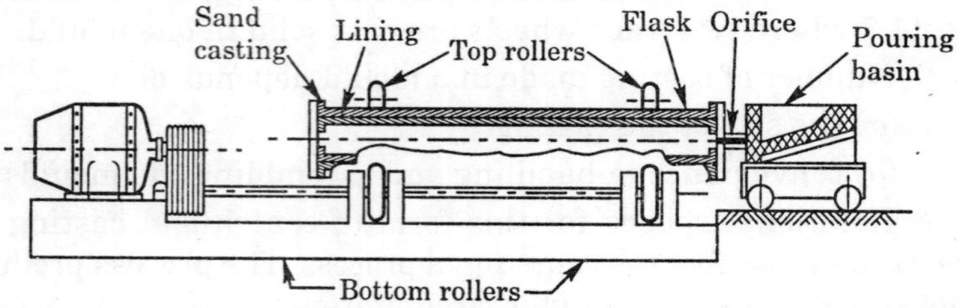

Fig. 11.5. Centrifugal Casting Machine for casting cast-iron or steel pipes.

Figure 11.6 shows another example of true centrifugal casting. It illustrates two methods which may be used for casting radial engine cylinder barrels. Horizontal method of casting is similar to the process followed in casting pipe lengths ; the inside diameter being a true cylinder requiring minimum machining.

In vertical casting, the inside cavity takes the form of a paraboloid : the slope of the sides of the paraboloid depending on the speed of rotation-paraboloid 'A' represents a higher rotational speed than paraboloid 'B'. For reducing the inside diameter difference between the top and bottom of the cylinder, spinning speeds for vertical casting are higher than that for horizontal.

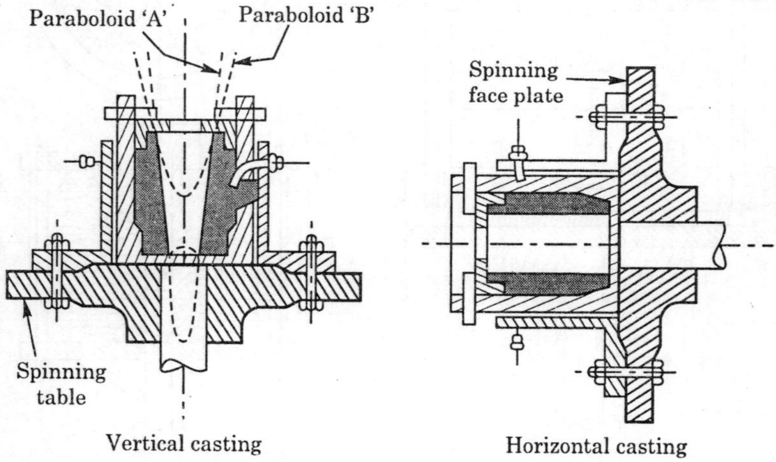

Fig. 11.6. True Centrifugal Method of casting radial-engine cylinder barrels.

(*ii*) **Semi-centrifugal Casting** is rotating the mould about its vertical axis. In this method, the centre of the casting is usually solid. The centre cavity is machined out later or is formed by the metal passing down around the outside of a core.

This method often used in stack moulding, is illustrated in Fig. 11.7 where two track wheels are cast solid in one mould.

Number of casting made in a mould depends on :

(*a*) the size of the casting.

(*b*) convenience in handling and assembling the moulds.

Rotational speeds for this form of centrifugal casting are lower than those for true centrifugal process. The process produces a dense structure at the outer circumference where it is needed, while the centre metal is machined out.

(*iii*) **Centrifuging.** In this method, several casting cavities are located around the outer portion of a mould. Metal is fed to these cavities by radial gates from the centre of the mould. Mould cavities are filled under pressure from the centrifugal forces of the metal as the mould is rotated. Either single or stack mould can be used.

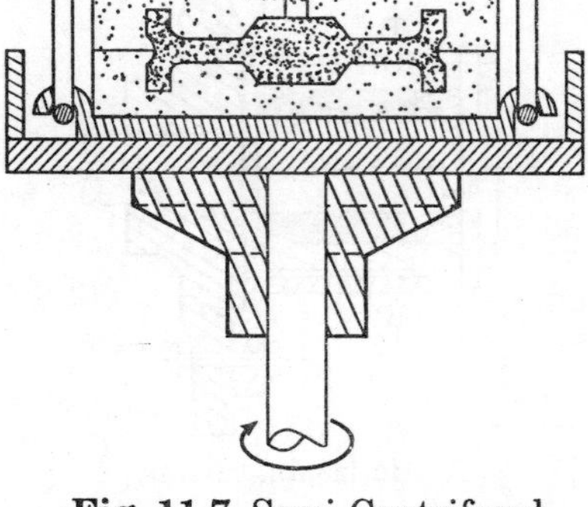

Fig. 11.7. Semi-Centrifugal Casting Process.

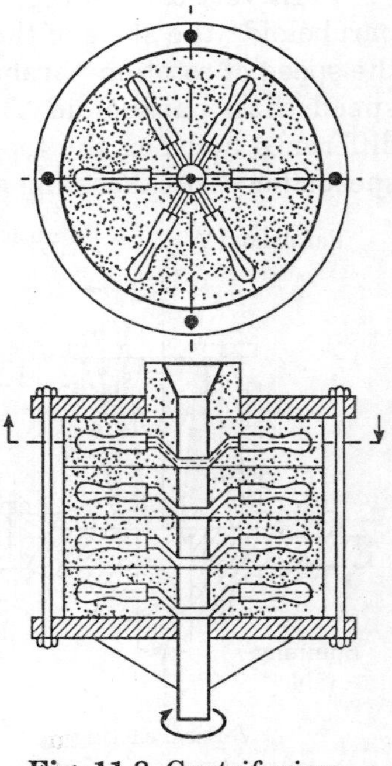

Fig. 11.8. Centrifuging Process.

This method is not limited to symmetrical objects. It can produce castings of irregular shape *e.g.*, bearing caps, small brackets, etc. Dental industry has used this process for casting gold inlays for many years.

For miscellaneous centrifugal castings, average rotational speed is 200 surface metres per minute. For cast iron pipe, the speeds may be as high as 400 surface metres per minute. Rotational speed depends on :

(*a*) the kind of mould used (whether sand or metal).

(*b*) the manner of rotation (whether horizontal or vertical),

(*c*) the size of casting,

(*d*) the kind of metal being cast.

Too great a speed may result in surface cracks caused by high stresses set up in the mould.

Advantages of Centrifugal Casting

(*i*) It is more economical than other methods.

(*ii*) Cores in cylindrical shape and risers or feedheads are eliminated.

(*iii*) Castings have a dense metal structure with all impurities forced back to the centre where frequently they can be machined out.

(*iv*) Because of the pressure exerted on the metal, thinner sections can be cast than would be possible in static casting.

(*v*) Any metal can be cast by this process.

Disadvantages of Centrifugal Casting

All castings cannot be made centrifugally since there are definite size and shape limitations.

Precision Casting Processes

(*i*) **Investment of 'Lost wax' casting.** This process derives its name from the fact that the wax pattern used in this process is subsequently melted from the mould, leaving a cavity having all the details of the original pattern.

Procedure. One or more master patterns of steel or brass are first prepared. These patterns are raplicas of the part to be cast. Using these patterns, a bismuth-alloy or lead-alloy split mould

is cast. The mould is properly finished and gated. Mould is then ready for use in forming the wax patterns.

In the forming operation, the mould is held in a water cooled ice, and heated wax is injected into it under considerable pressure. Sometimes, thermoplastic-polystyrene resin is used in place of wax. Upon solidification, the wax patterns are removed from the mould. Wax patterns are now ready for final assembly.

Several patterns are usually assembled with necessary gates and risers by heating the contact surfaces to a correct temperature (wax welding) with a hot wire by electrical resistance. The patterns are than ready to be placed in a metal flask and surrounded by a refractory plaster. This is done by pouring into the flask a finely ground refractory material, thinned by some mixing agent as alcohol or water.

The general procedure is to dip or spray the pattern first with a fine silica-flour mixture to insure a smooth surface on the castings, and then to fill the flask with a coarser plaster-mixture. After the plaster sets, the mould is placed upside down and heated in an oven for several hours to melt out the wax and to dry the mould. The final casting can be produced by gravity, vacuum, pressure, or centrifugal casting.

Pressures ranging from 0.25 to 2 kg/cm^2 are generally used in the casting operation. When the mould has cooled, the plaster is broked away. After cutting of gates and feeds, the castings are finally cleaned by grinding, sand blasting, or other finishing operations.

Advantages of 'Lost wax' Casting

1. Intricate forms having undercuts can be cast.
2. An excellent detail and a very smooth surface finish on casting is obtained with no disfiguring parting line as found on castings made by cope and drag methods.
3. Dimensional accuracy is good.
4. Certain unmachinable parts can be cast to preplanned shape.
5. It may be used to replace die casting where short runs are involved.

Disadvantages of 'Lost-wax' Casting

1. The process is expensive.
2. It is limited to small castings.
3. It presents some difficulties where cores are involved.

Applications. Unmachinable and unworkable alloys for such used as turbine blades, jet nozzles, gun and machine parts, and parts for household and other appliances can be cast.

(*ii*) **Plaster-mould casting.** Plaster of Paris (gypsum, or $CaSO_4 \cdot nH_2O$) is used for casting silver, aluminium, magnesium, copper, and alloys of these metals, particularly brass and bronze. Gypsum may be used as an investment casting, or for cope and drag moulding.

In plaster casting, copes and drags are made and a parting line is established as in ordinary sand casting. For preparing plaster for use, 100 parts of plaster are added to 160 parts water and stirred to creamy consistency.

The slurry is poured over a carefully made match plate-type pattern, usually of metal. The mould is vibrated slightly to insure plaster's filling all small cavities. In a few minutes at room temperature, the mixture develops an initial set and pattern can be removed.

Copes and drags may be made simultaneously on separate lines and dried in ovens held at 400–800°F (200–425°C) until all free and combined moisture is removed. Mould sections are very fragile and require care in assembling.

Dimensions can be held to an accuracy of about 0.08 to 0.1 per cm. Casting surfaces are excellent, often requiring neither machining nor grinding.

Since plaster moulds possess very low permeability, care must be taken to remove all combined water, and avoid absorption of moisture after baking. The moulds are not permanent. They are destroyed when the castings are removed.

Patterns are made of a free-machining brass and are held to a close tolerance. They are assembled on bottom plates of standard size flasks (usually 250 × 450 × 75 mm and 300 × 50 × 100 mm). Before receiving the plaster, they are sprayed with a parting compound.

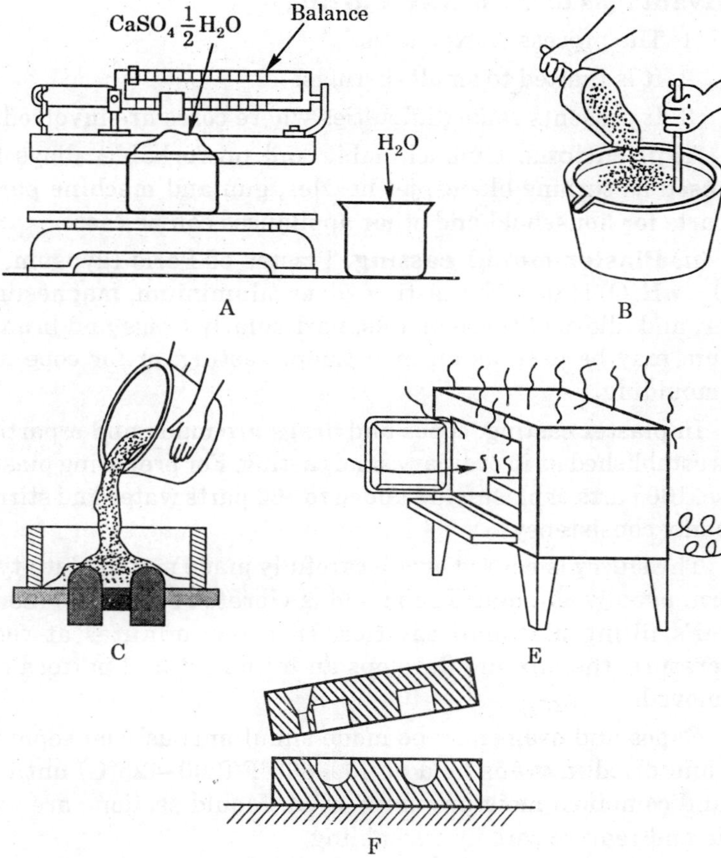

Fig. 11.9. Plaster casting process.

A—Metal casting plaster and water are weighed.

B—Gypsum is added to water and stirred to creamy consistency.

C—Prepared plaster is poured over greased match plate or pattern in flask.

D—When plaster has set, it is removed from the match plate and the steps A through D are repeated for the other half of mould.

E—Mould halves are placed in oven and thoroughly dried.

F—Finally cope is set on drag for pouring.

In addition to having adequate porosity, plaster moulds have the necessary structural strength for casting, plus enough elasticity to allow some contraction of the metal during its cooling.

Advantages

1. High degree of dimension accuracy (a tolerance of ± 0.125 mm).

2. Smooth surface finish.

3. Because of the low thermal conductivity of plaster, the metal does not chill rapidly, and very thin sections may be cast.

4. There is little tendency towards internal porosity in plaster mould castings. Hence, no sand or other inclusions.

5. The process competes more successfully with die casting using high temperature alloys like brass rather than metals like zinc and aluminium.

6. At high temperatures, metal moulds have a relatively short life. With plaster moulds, which are used only once, the temperature is no problem.

Limitations. Plaster moulds are suitable only for non-ferrous alloys having casting temperatures not much over 1150°C ; although plaster has proved to be an excellent mould material for yellow brass, certain bronzes and aluminium alloys.

Applications. The wide variety of small castings made by this process includes miscellaneous airplane parts, small gears, cams handles, pump parts, small housings, and numerous other intricate castings.

(iii) **Mercast process or moulds from mercury patterns.** This process utilizing frozen mercury has been developed for the production of castings.

Procedure. A metal mould or die is first made of the part to be cast with necessary gates and sprue hold. When assembled and ready for pouring, it is partially immersed in a cold bath and filled with acetone, which acts as a lubricant. As the mercury is poured into the mould, the acetone is displaced. Freezing takes place in a liquid bath held at around – 25°C and is complete in about 10 minutes.

Patterns are then removed from the mould and inverted in a cold ceramic slurry by repeated dippings until a shell about 3 mm thick is built up. Mercury is melted and removed from the shell at room temperature. After a short drying period, it is fired at a high temperature resulting in a hard permeable form. The shell is then placed in a flask, surrounded by sand, preheated, and filled with metal. Casting is usually done by the centrifugal method.

Advantages

1. Castings produced by this method are accurate in detail have a smooth surface, and for small castings, maintain a tolerance of 0.02 mm per cm.

2. Both ferrous and non-ferrous metals can be cast by this process, the maximum pouring temperature being around 1650°C.

Limitations. Wide commercial use of this process is limited by the high cost of the castings.

(*iv*) **Shell moulding process.** In this process, the mould is made up of a mixture of dried silica sand and phenolic resin, formed into thin, half mould shells which are clamped together for pouring as illustrated by the series of sketches in the figure.

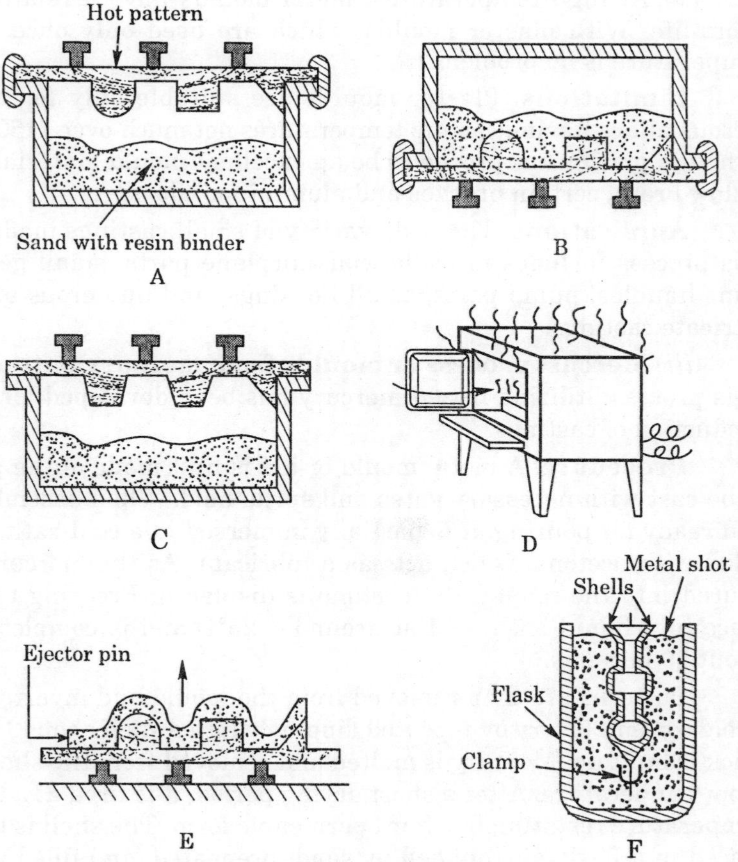

Fig. 11.10. Shell Moulding Process.

A – Heated metal pattern is clamped to *'dump box'* containing sand mixed with thermo-setting plastic resin.

B – Box and pattern are inverted. Heated pattern melts resin next to it.

C – When box and pattern are heated, a thin shell of resin bounded sand is retained on the pattern.

D – Pattern with shell is placed in oven and heated to cure resin bond.

E – Shell is stripped from pattern by means of ejector pins.

F – After half of mould has been made, shells are clamped together and placed together in flask. Metal shots or coarse sand is poured around shells, and shell mould is ready to receive molten metal.

Procedure. The sand, free from clay, is first mixed with either urea or phenol formaldehyde resin (thermo-plastic) and the mix then put into a dump box or blowing machine.

A metal pattern must be used since it is preheated to a temperature around 230°C. It is sprayed with a silicon release agent before being placed on top of the dump box. The box is then inverted, causing the sand mix to drop on the pattern. It is held there for 15 to 30 seconds before returning to its original position.

The pattern, with a thin shell of sand, 3 to 4.5 mm thick, adhering to it, is then placed in an oven and the shell cured half to one minute until it is rigid.

The shell is finally removed from the pattern by ejector pins and the mould halves assembled with clamps, resin adhesives, or other devices. They may then be put in a flask, supported against one another, or by some backing material such as shot or gravel. Some are poured while they are resting flat on the floor with a weight on top.

Advantages

1. Close tolerances (0.02 to 0.05 mm per cm) and reduction in machining allowances.

2. Low cleaning costs.

3. Smooth surfaces.

4. Little moulding skill is necessary.

5. Sand requirements are low ; only about 10% of the green sand moulding and no box parts are needed.

6. It can be readily adopted to automatic mechanisation.

7. Greater production from a given floor space.

Disadvantages

1. The process requires metal patterns since heat is needed to soften the resin. Hence high pattern cost.

2. Fairly expensive equipment for making and heating the moulds.

3. Resin is an expensive binder.

4. Little of the sand can be economically reclaimed.

5. Since the silica sand used is fine and dry, adequate dust extraction equipment must be installed to avoid any danger from silicosis.

6. Only castings upto about 12 kg weight can be cast.

Applications. Most metals can be cast by this process but the castings are usually small not exceeeding 12 kg. The largest field of application is with stainless steel and copper alloys and to a lesser extent grey cast iron and malleable iron. Low carbon steels cast in shell moulds are liable to show depression in the upper surface of the casting.

(*v*) **Carbon Dioxide Mould Hardening Process.** This process of hardening moulds and cores using CO_2 and a sodium-silicate liquid base binder has been widely used in Europe for some time. It is now being used in many foundries in this country because of its inherent advantages and the rapid speed with which it hardens the sand.

The process consists of thoroughly mixing clean, dry silica sand with 3.5 to 5% sodium-silicate liquid base binder in a muller. It is now ready for use and may be packed in flasks and core boxes by standard moulding machines, core blowers, or by hand.

The sand should be free from moisture and clay. In some cases, other ingredients like coal dust, pitch, graphite or wood floor may be added to improve certain properties like collapsibility.

When the packing is complete, CO_2 is forced into the mould or core at a pressure of about 1.5 kg/cm^2 for a period normally measured in seconds. The reaction which takes place can be broadly represented by the following equation :

$$\underset{\text{Sodium silicate}}{Na_2O \cdot SiO_2 . xH_2O} + \underset{\substack{\text{Carbon}\\\text{dioxide}}}{CO_2} \longrightarrow \underset{\substack{\text{Sodium}\\\text{carbonate}}}{Na_2CO_2} + \underset{\text{Silica gel}}{SiO_3 \cdot xH_2O}$$

The silica gel, which is formed, hardens and acts as a cement to bound the sand grains together.

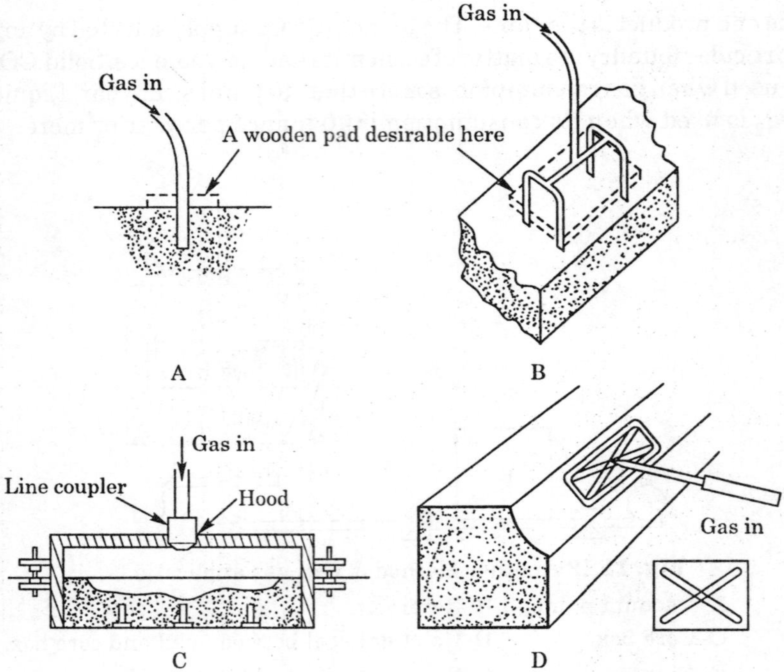

Fig. 11.11. CO_2 Mould-hardening Process
(Four Simple Methods of Gas Application)
A–Single Probe B–Muliple Probe
C–Hood D–Rubber Pad.

CO_2 Gas and its Application. The method of introducing the gas is important to the success of the process. It must be simple, rapid, and uniform throughout the sand mass, and not cumbersome to apply.

The time to harden a small or medium size body of sand ranges from 15 to 30 seconds. Overgassing is wasteful resulting deterioration of the sand. The best practice is to under-gas rather than over-gas and to allow the sand mass to harden further in the atmosphere. Such a course is the most economical in gas consumption and gives strong mould and cores with a good shelf life.

For small cores a gasketed, funnel-shaped head can be placed over the core box. Larger moulds are hardened (*i*) by placing a hood over the mould, (*ii*) by running small tubes into the mould, or (*iii*) by introducing the gas into a hollow, vented pattern.

Carbon dioxide gas can be supplied in cylinders, in the solid state and, when consumption is large, in bulk liquid form. In each case,

the end product is the same. The means of CO_2 supply selected by any particular foundry is a matter of economics and convenience. Solid CO_2 is used when gas consumpion is more than 10 tonnes per year. Liquid CO_2 is used when its cousumption is 40 tonnes per year or more.

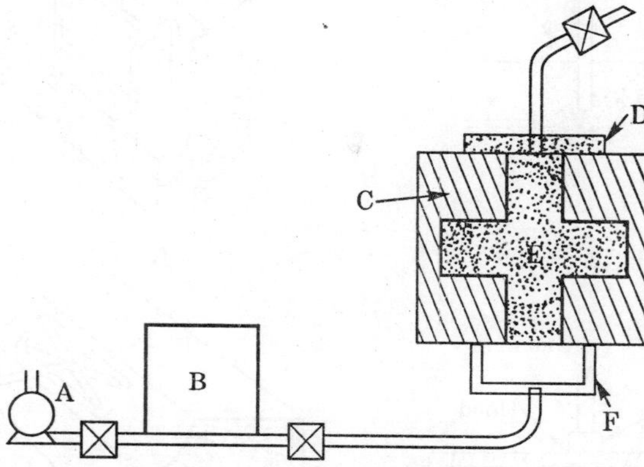

Fig. 11.12 Another Method of CO_2 gas application.

A–Vacuum pump. B–Reservoir.
C–Core box. D–Gas tight seal between pad and core box.
E–Core. F–Gas tight seal on face of core box.

To avoid interrupted supply and wastage of gas in the foundry, the gas in the cylinder must have its pressure reduced in stages by means of a number of suitable reducing valves. If the drop from cylinder pressure to working pressure is allowed to take place in one stage, the fall in temperature is sufficiently great for solid CO_2 to form in the gassing tube. Standing a cylinder in 15 to 20 cm of water helps to maintain the temperature of the gas.

Table 11.6 : Chemical Analysis of CO_2 Process Cores gassed for varying periods of time

	Casting time (Seconds)						
	0	*15*	*30*	*45*	*60*	*180*	*360*
CO_2 content precent	0.01	0.350	0.338	0.357	0.338	0.450	0.412
Na_2CO_2 percent	—	0.640	0.660	0.615	0.570	0.490	0.380
$NaHCO_3$ percent	—	0.050	0.100	0.170	0.220	0.350	0.390
Percent binder reacted	—	57	62	62	65	65	65

Some of the simple methods of gas application shown in Fig. 11.11 aim to pass gas through the rammed mix, an other method of gas application aims evacuation of the air in the pores of the rammed mass and replacing it with CO_2 which will quickly react with the binder present. The latter method represents the ideal to aim at although for small quantities it may not be practicable. Gassing can be effective only if the air present in the pores of the rammed mass is replaced by gas. Provision must therefore be made for the escape of this air, together with precautions to prevent gas from escaping along the easiest path, leaving certain regions of the core or mould ungassed.

Carbon Dioxide Mixes

Most of the common foundry sands have proved satisfactory. The sand used should be clean and preferably dry and free from clay. Other additives made to the basic mix are designed to improve surface finish. Prominent among these are pelleted pitch, wood flour and graphite. Such additions rarely exceed 1%. They also aid collapsibility *i.e.*, facility with which the core can be removed from the casting.

Table 11.7 : Some Typical CO_2 Process Mixes (Per cent)

Clean dry silica sand %	*Binder %*	*Other Additions %*	*Applications*
94.5–95.5	3.5	Pitch 1 or coal dust 2	Moulds and cores for steel, cast iron and copper alloys
86	4	Natural sand 10	Moulds for steel, C.I. and copper alloys when gassing is done after withdrawing the pattern
94	5	Pitch 1	For copper alloy moulds. Dressing not required
96	3	Wood flour 1	Moulds for aluminium alloys
4.5	3.5	Wood flour 1	Cores for aluminium alloys

The paddle-type mixer is most suitable for this process. The order of addition should be sand, carbonaceous addition and binder. Mixing should be complete with 4 to 5 minutes. Over-mixing should be avoided since.

(*i*) this raises the temperature,
(*ii*) reduces the water content, and
(*iii*) may lead to friability after gassing.

Table 11.8 : Recommended Sand Mixture Proportions for CO_2 Process (By weight in kg)

S. No.	*Purpose*	*Washed silica sand*	*Zircon sand*	*Iron oxide*	*Sea coal*	*Sodium silicate*
1.	Heavy grey C.I. :					
	(*i*) Moulds	100	–	1–2	–	4–5
	(*ii*) Cores	100	–	1–2	2	4–5
2.	Light Grey C.I. :					
	Moulds and Cores	100	–	1–2	–	3–4
3.	Heavy steel casting moulds	75	20	2–5	–	4–5
4.	Light steel castings	100	–	2	–	4–5
5.	Bronze castings	100	–	–	–	4–5
6.	Aluminium alloy	100	–	–	–	3–3.5

The green compression strength of the standard CO_2 mix is about 75 gm/cm^2. It can be increased to about 225 gm/cm^2 by the addition of a suitable additive *e.g.,* ball clay, sulphite clay or natural clay bonded sand. The compression strength of gassed CO_2 compacts varies from 15 to 30 kg/cm^2, depending upon the standing time after gassing. For oil sand and shell moulding-mixes, compression strength is about 90 kg/cm^2.

Cores possessing thin projections and narrow necks may be difficult to handle when made by the CO_2 process, and it is not always either practicable or desirable to remedy this by increasing the number of strengthening devices.

Collapsibility of cores on occasions gives rise to some difficulties which may be overcome by

(*i*) working with the smallest addition of binder,

(*ii*) making an addition of a carbonaceous material (the most common being pelleted pitch) which chars at the casting temperature,

(*iii*) making the core hollow, *i.e.*, in shell form.

Pattern and Core Boxes for CO_2 Process

Both wood and metal patterns can be used with CO_2 process mixes. Normal patterns varnishes on wooden patterns are attacked by the alkaline binder, causing. Good results can be obtained by using an alkaline resistant cellulose varnish or a silicone-base lacquer ; although both are expensive. It must be borne in mind that since gassing is normally carried out before the removal of the pattern or core box, any roughness or undercuts will cause serious sticking because of the inability of the mould or core to yield. Rubbing the pattern or a core with graphite often aids withdrawal.

Dimensional Tolerances CO_2 Process

As compared to shell moulding process, it is not possible to be so precise about the dimensional tolerances possible with the CO_2 process. Where CO_2 process is used as a substitute for shell moulding, the tolerances should approach those obtainable with that process, provided a fine sand is used. Where it is used as a substitute for dry sand moulding, the dimensional tolerances possible should be at least as good as those obtainable with dry sand.

If a mix is made using a coarse sand, a dressing must be used but this will introduce inaccurancies and give an inferior result. Close tolerances can therefore only be held if gassing is carried out before the pattern or core box is withdrawn.

Main Advantages of CO_2 Process

(*i*) Pattern withdrawal is easier since the moulds may be hardened before withdrawing the pattern.

(*ii*) Rush orders can be quickly hardened.

(*iii*) More number of castings can be produced in a factory working on three shifts with a given number of core boxes.

(*iv*) Overnight baking of the mould is not needed.

(*v*) Heavy mould of lathe beds and other castings need not be carried to the even and back to the pouring place. This results in economy of labour and considerable reduction in cranework.

(*vi*) While pouring, the sand does not flow with the metal.

(*vii*) Accurate castings with sharper corners can be made.

(*viii*) Surface finish on the castings is improved.

(*ix*) Operation is speedy.

(*x*) No core baking equipment is involved.

(*xi*) Core plates are not necessary.

(*xii*) Semi-skilled labour can be used.

(*xiii*) Cores may be stored for longer periods of time.

(*xiv*) A uniform sand may be used for production of both moulds and cores.

(*xv*) Cores can often be made hollow, with a consequent saving in binder.

(*xvi*) Use of core irons and other strengthening devices can be eliminated or at least reduced in complexity because the core need not leave its box in the green state.

(*xvii*) Damaged cores are easily patched.

(*xviii*) Chills can be incorporated without fear of the core sagging.

(*xix*) Stoving can be avoided, with all the saving in time, stove capacity, floor space and fuel.

(*xx*) Many of the advantages listed for cores apply to moulds.

(*xxi*) Only a facing of CO_2 mix, 5 to 7.5 cm thick against the face of the pattern can be used. This economizes in binder.

Limitations

(*i*) Due to the use of binders and additives etc., the sand mixture becomes costly to use. Sodium silicate itself is also quite expensive.

(*ii*) Lack of any cheap method for recovery of the spent sand. This hinders adoption of the process for moulding but presents no problem for core making where reclamation of oilsand is not normally practised.

(*iii*) Tendency of sand with a silica-base binder to air-harden to some extent if kept a long time.

(*iv*) Poor collapsibility of moulds and cores will sometimes give trouble, but with proper additives this can be eliminated.

Applications. The primary application of the CO_2 process for moulding is a substitute for dry sand moulding, the elimination of stoving being the principal attraction. The process is used for the production of :

(*i*) large moulds from wooden patterns ;

(*ii*) small repetition castings to a high standard of surface finish and close dimensional tolerance, so acting as substitute for shell moulding.

(*iii*) cores for the jobbing foundry using wooden core boxes.

(*iv*) repetition small cores either by hand method or, preferably, by blowing.

The process is suitable for all common casting alloys. A very wide range of casting size is possible with the process. At present, the principal applications lie in the manufacture of moulds and cores for steel, iron and copper alloy castings, and the sand cores used in large quantities in the production of aluminium alloy castings by the gravity-die process.

(*iv*) **Continuous Casting.** The process consists of continuously pouring molten metal into a mould, which has the facilities for rapidly chilling the metal to the point of solidification, and then withdrawing it from the mould.

Experimental work and research has proved that there are many opportunities for saving in the continuous casting process of metals. Following processes are typical of those in use or in the process of development.

1. Reciprocating Mould Process of Continuous Slab Casting. In this process, a reciprocating water-cooled copper mould is used, the down stroke being synchronized with the discharge rate of the slab. Molten metal is poured into the holding furnace and is discharged to the mould through a 12 mm tube at the rate of 10,000 kg per hour. Molten metal is distributed across the mould from a submerged, horizontal crosspiece, the level of the metal being held constant at all times.

Pouring rate of molten metal is controlled by a needle valve through the top of the holding furnace. As the metal becomes chilled in the lower part of the mould, it is discharged at a constant rate and enters the withdrawing rolls. These are synchronized with the downward movement of the mould and are mounted just above a circular saw which cuts the slab to required lengths.

Brass slabs produced by its process are further processed, by cold rolling, into sheets and strips.

2. Asarco Process for Continuous Cast Shapes. This process differs from other continuous processes in that the forming die or mould is integral with the furnace and there is no problem of controlling the flow of metal. Metal is fed by gravity into the mould from the furnace as it is continuously solidified and withdrawn by the rolls below.

An important feature of this process is the water-cooled, graphite-forming die, which is self-lubricating, has excellent thermal stock resistance and is not attacked by copper-base alloys. The upper end, being in the molten metal, acts as a riser and compensates for any shrinkage which might take place during

solidification, while simultaneously acting as an effective path for dissipating evolved gases. There dies are easily machined to shape. products may be produced from 10 mm to 130 mm in diameter. Multiple production from a single die permits casting the small section rods.

To start the process, a rod of the same shape as that to be cast is placed between the drawing rolls and inserted into the die. This rod is tipped with a short length of the alloy to be cast. As the molten metal enters the die, it melts the end surface of be rod, forming a perfect joint. Casting cycle is then started by the drawing rolls and the molten metal is continuously solidified as it is chilled and withdrawn from the die.

When the casting leaves the furnace, it ultimately reaches the sawing floor where it is cut to desired length while still in motion. A tilting receiver takes the work and drops it to a horizontal position and from there it goes for inspection and straightening operations.

For phosphorized copper and many of the standard bronzes, the process has proved successful. Alloy compositions may be produced with satisfactory commercial finish as rounds, tubes, squares, or special shapes. Physical properties are superior to permanent-mould and sand castings.

3. **William Continuous Casting Process for Steel.** This process, developed for continuous casting of carbon and alloy steels, utilizes thin walled brass moulds having cross-sectional areas upto 280 square cm. These moulds are preferable oval in cross-section.

A small stream of metal is poured into the mould from an electric holding furnace a rate controlled by the metal level in the mould. The mould must necessarily be constructed of a material having a high heat conductivity and one which is not easily wetted by the liquid metal.

Rapid mould cooling is essential for the success of this process, and results in :

(*i*) Improved mould life.

(*ii*) Less segregation.

(*iii*) Smaller grain structure, and

(*iv*) A better surface.

Actually the metal next to the mould wall solidifies only a few centimetres below the top surface ad shrinks slightly from the mould sides. As the cast section leaves the cooled mould, it passes

through a section that controls the rate of cooling and then to the drawing and straightening rolls.

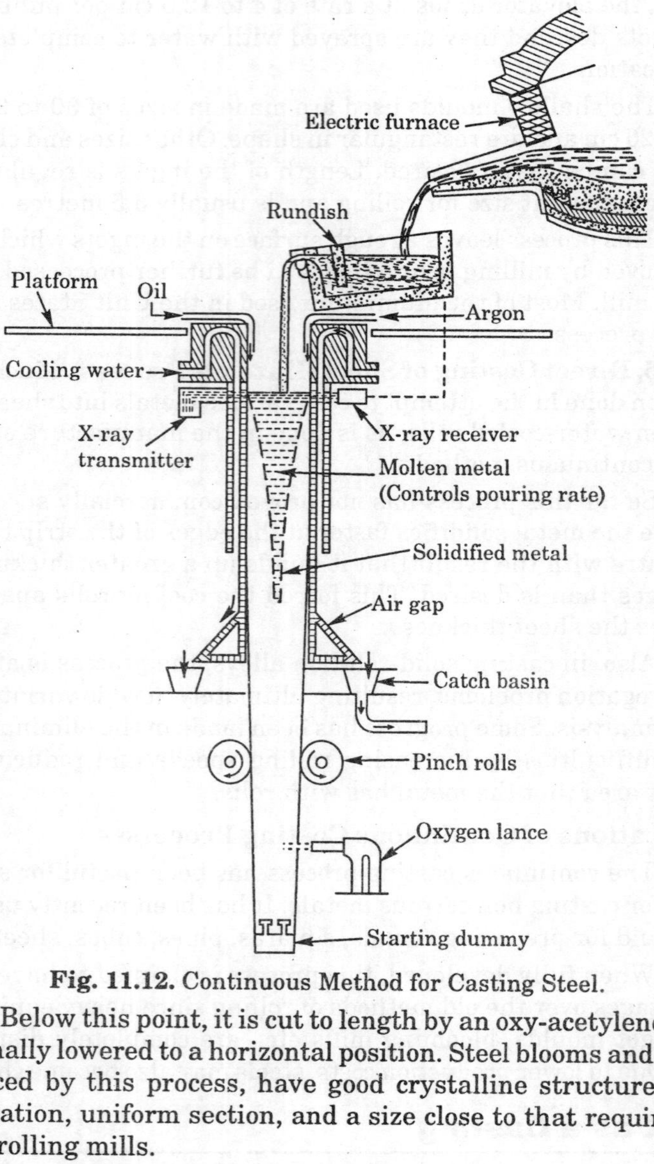

Fig. 11.12. Continuous Method for Casting Steel.

Below this point, it is cut to length by an oxy-acetylene torch and finally lowered to a horizontal position. Steel blooms and billets produced by this process, have good crystalline structure, little segregation, uniform section, and a size close to that required for many rolling mills.

4. Alcoa Direct-Chill Process for Continuous Casting of Aluminium Ingots. This process consists of pouring molten aluminium from a holding furnace through a refractory trough into

shallow, stationary moulds, the bottoms of which rest on a hydraulic elevator. When the metal at the bottom of the mould becomes chilled, the elevator drops at a rate of 4 to 12.5 cm per minute. As the ingots descend they are sprayed with water to complete their solidification.

The shallow moulds used are made in sizes of 30 to 90 and 30 by 120 cm and are rectangular in shape. Other sizes and circular shapes can be cast if desired. Length of the ingots is regulated to give a convenient size for rolling and is usually 3.5 metres.

This process leaves a rough surface on the ingots which must be removed by milling before they can be further processed in the rolling mill. Most of the aluminium used in the Unit States is cast by this process.

5. Direct Casting of Sheet (Hazelett Process). Much work has been done in the attempt to cast various metals into sheet form between water-cooled rolls, as is done in the manufacture of glass by the continuous method.

So far this process has not proved commercially successful because the metal solidifies faster at the edges of the strip than at the centre with the result that it builds up a greater thickness at the edges than is desired. This forced the cooling rolls apart and changes the sheet thickness.

Also, in casting solid-solution alloys, the process is affected by segregation problems, resulting ultimately in wide variations of metal analysis. Some progress has been made in the elimination of these difficulties by increasing rolling speeds and reducing the contact area that the metal has with rolls.

Applications of Continuous Casting Processes

The continuous casting process has been useful for several years for casting non-ferrous metals. It has been recently used for steel, and for preparing rounds, squares, pipes, tubes, sheets, etc.

When fully developed, this process is claimed to have many advantages over the old methods of rolling since heavy equipment like ingot moulds, blooming mills etc., are completely dispensed with. Due to lower production costs, steels may also become cheaper.

Ingot as a Casting

Ingots are castings made in relatively simple shapes, and designed for subsequent fabrication by working (rolling, forging etc.). Moulds into which these ingots are cast are usually made of

metal (cast iron, steel, or copper) ; seldom is an ingot of this type made in a sand mould.

So-called pigs (ingots of pig iron and non-ferrous metals) designed for remelting purposes are made in large quantity in both sand and metal moulds ; their shape and size vary widely and are not particularly important consideration since the pigs only need be in convenient form for handling as melting stock.

Ingot moulds may be made with thin water cooled walls. But nearly all are of massive construction and depend upon (*a*) mass, (*b*) thermal conductivity, and (*i*) specific heat of the mould to chill the cast ingot at the proper rate. For small ingot moulds, graphite is relatively fragile and most suitable. It has the advantage of not heat checking at the mould-ingot interface as readily as metal.

Steel ingots are divided *according to internal structure* into the following types :

(*i*) Rimming ingots.
(*ii*) Semi-killed ingots.
(*iii*) Killing ingots.

Externally they must be identifies as :

(*i*) Flat sided square or rectangular.
(*ii*) Fluted.
(*iii*) Rippled or corrugated.
(*iv*) Bottle-neck.

According to their method of casting as :

(*i*) Big-end-up.
(*ii*) Big-end-down.
(*iii*) Top poured.
(*iv*) Bottom poured.

Requisites of an Ingot Mould. (*i*) Ingot moulds are usually made of cupola, a blast-furnace, the approximate composition is 3.5% carbon, 1% silicon, 0.9% manganese, 0.2% phosphorus, and 0.07% surphur.

(*ii*) Mould must be heavy to extract-enough heat from large ingots to prevent welding at the interface and to freeze the ingot at the proper rate so that an outside skin quickly forms and pulls away from the mould wall.

(*iii*) Flat-sided moulds are ideal for rolling, Rippled or corrugated moulds increase freezing rate through their relatively greater surface area. Fluted mould provides a crystal structure less prone to cracking during initial forging operations.

(*iv*) Large ingots must be tapered liberally and mould surfaces kept clean to prevent transverse tearing of the ingot as it settles in the mould. At all costs, tearing of ingots must be prevented.

Ingot Structures

A 'Rimmed Ingot' is one made from under de-oxidized steel *i.e.*, steel which continues to evolve carbon monoxide gas in the mould after pouring. The term *'rimmed'* is developed from the orderly deposition of blowholes along the outer rim of unkilled ingots. The state of deoxidation of a steel is gauged respectively in the order of increasing completeness by the shop terms unkilled, semi-killed and killed. Usually all three types are top-poured if ingots are large.

The elements responsible for degree of rimming, or conversely degree of deoxidation, are carbon and oxygen : they may or may not combine into carbon monoxide gas. Amount of carbon present in molten bath can be controlled in the furnace during refining process. For a given carbon content, oxygen can be controlled by addition of deoxidizers which react with some or all of the oxygen to form insoluble oxides. A typical reaction is

$$2Al + 3FeO = Al_2O_3 + 3Fe.$$

Such deoxidizers, in order of increasing effectiveness, are manganese, silicon and aluminium.

Piping. A layer of solid metal forms round the ingot walls, contraction occurs, resulting in fall in the level of the liquid. Successive layers of solid form, each accompanied by a fall in the liquid level, the fall increasing as the volume of liquid decreases. In this manner, a central cavity is formed, known as the *'Primary Pipe'*.

With the ingot mould used narrow-end-up, a conical volume of metal still remains liquid after the top portion of the ingot is solid. Solidification of this metal will give rise to further cavities, known as *'Secondary Piping'*.

'Secondary piping' can be prevented by using the mould *'wide-end-up'* since the shrinkage is counteracted by the feeding down of molten metal from the top, the region last to solidify *'Primary piping'* can also be reduced by using a brick-lined top on the mould, in which the metal remains molten for a prolonged period, and consequently *'feeds'* the ingot.

During rolling of steel, the portion of the billet containing primary pipe is discarded, but secondary piping still remains.

Although the cavities are closed up by rolling, their surface may not be welded together and are liable to open up again when steel is quenched, thus constituting a dangerous flaw in good quality steels. Such steels are, therefore, cast in mould wide-end-up fitted with a brick head.

Chemical Haterogeneity—Segregation. It is found that the composition of castings and particularly of metal ingots is not uniform throughout and that the concentration of impurities and sometimes of alloying components is greater in certain parts of the ingot than in others. This subject is particularly important in steel production owing to large ingots (upto 200 tonnes) used.

Molten steel contains soluble impurities *e.g.,* sulphur, phosphorus and soluble alloying elements together with insoluble impurities or slag particles in suspension. Those elements which lower the freezing-point *e.g.,* sulphur, phosphorus, carbon, manganese and silicon, collect in the last portions to solidify. This separation of various substances into different places in the ingot is called *'Segregation'* and can be *classified* as follow :

(*i*) **Interdendritic Segregation.** It is caused by concentration of impurities or alloying components between arms of the dendrites. On annealing, carbon diffuses and becomes uniformly distributed, but phosphorus and non-metallic inclusions are only slightly affected.

(*ii*) **Normal Segregation.** In case of steel ingots, it is the concentration of sulphur, phosphorus and carbon in the centre and upper portions of the ingot. It is largely associated with the pipe and is mainly removed when this is discarded. Direction of flow of metal during feeding is in the V-form.

(*iii*) **Inverse or Segregation.** It is the concentration of fusible elements near the outer zones of an ingot. In extreme cases of inverse segregation, exudation occurs on the surface of bronzes, particularly those containing lead (tin sweat).

In *'killed steel'* this type of segregation occur about midway between the centre and the outside, in the form of an *'inverted V'*.

(*iv*) **Ingot Corner Segregation.** It is the entrapping of impurities at the junction of two sets of crystals growing from the sides and bottom of the mould.

(*v*) **Gravity Segregation.** It occurs when the primary crystals differ in density from the liquid *e.g.,* rising of cuboids in tin-antimony alloy.

Seams, Rokes, Shells, Laps in Steel Ingots. In order to get good properties, the ingots should be cast at as low a temperature as possible. It is just as important that the metal should be sufficiently fluid to prevent semi-solid skin forming on the surface as the metal level rises in the mould.

Periodically, the liquid metal bursts through the oxidised skin and covers it. When rolled, a '*Seam*' is formed. Smaller defects starting from the surface, but due to similar causes, are called '*Rokes*'.

A defect, somewhat similar to roke, is caused by poor roll design or by rolling at a low temperature. The metal spreads to an extent greater than the designed pass and forms fins on the opposite sides of the bar, which in subsequent passes are lapped over to give the '*Lap*'.

Splashes of oxidised metal on the mould surface, particularly near the bottom, appear as scales or '*shells*' on the ingot after it is stripped.

Surface defects mentioned above tend to cause cracks during heat-treatment and have a harmful effect on the fatigue and other properties of the material. These can be revealed by macro-examination.

Non-ferrous ingots are usually subject to dross and dirt inclusions at the surface and are frequently surface scalped. Internally, they are often prone to segregation of alloying elements.

QUESTIONS

1. Discuss the use of chills chaplets, exothermic materials and risers in making castings. Explain with suitable examples.
2. Explain various factors affecting the rate of solidification in a metallic mould.
3. Write short notes on :
   (*a*) Blind Risers
   (*b*) Padding
   (*c*) Heuver's circles.
4. What are the various methods employed to trap dross and dirt in the gating of castings ?
5. Explain the various method for improving the efficiency of risers.
6. Why is it necessary to achieve directional solidification in castings? Explain.

12

Casting Defects

Introduction

Casting defects are usually not an accident. They occur because some step in the manufacturing process is not properly controlled. Melting, casting and solidification of metal comprise many intricate operations, and perfect control is difficult. It is not surprising that castings are afflicted with a greater variety of defects than the products of other fabricating methods.

To study defects rather than sound castings seems a negative approach to learning. However, it is important to producer, designer, consumer, and engineer that the defects occuring in castings be recognised and their origin (causes) and control (remedies) be properly understood.

Surface Imperfections

1. Surface Roughness. Surfaces of castings are sometimes *'rough'* or *'pebbly'* because :

(*i*) the moulding sand is too coarse, or

(*ii*) the pouring temperature of the metal too high, or

(*iii*) penetration of metal between and around sand grains.

In steel casting, a surface reaction occurs at the mould-metal interface causing roughness unless properly controlled. The reactions are the oxidation of the iron of the steel and subsequent combination of the oxide with silica to form fayalite :

$$2Fe + O_2 = 2FeO$$

$$2FeO + SiO_2 = 2FeO\ SiO_2 \text{ (fayalite)}$$

In magnesium casting, *'burning'* (oxidation) at the mould-metal interface cause a black, roughned casting surface. It is prevented by adding inhibiting agents *e.g.*, sulphur, boric acid, or ammonium fluoborate to the moulding sand.

2. Pinholes. Surface reactions sometimes cause subsurface porosity or pinholes. In aluminium alloys containing more than about 1% magnesium, a reaction between magnesium of the alloy and the water vapour of the mould tends to occur :

$$Mg + H_2O = MgO + H_2 \text{ (gas)}$$

Hydrogen-filled pinholes at the surface are the result.

Some copper-base and other alloys are subject to similar defects unless proper precautions are observed.

In steel castings subsurface pinholes may result from incomplete deoxidation of the molten metal.

3. Scabs and Buckles. These defects usually appear in cope surfaces of castings. A '*buckle*' is a relatively extensive overlapping of metal *i.e.*, a layer of metal is separated from the casting proper by a layer of sand which has sheared from the cope surface. '*Buckles*' and '*scabs*' are alike in appearance, the only difference is that scabs are relatively small. In other words, scabs are relatively small patches of sand at the surface of the casting.

Causes. (*i*) Usually these defects are caused by cope surface becoming preheated too rapidly by radiation from the rising metal.

Non-uniform expansion of sand at and immediately behind the cope surface, caused by rapid preheating, develops stresses sufficient to shear layers of sand from the cope surface. These sheared layers then extend into the mould cavity and surrounded by rising metal.

(*ii*) Development of high gas pressure in a region of too low permeability can also produce excessive stresses in the cope and cause scabbing.

(*iii*) Scabs are also caused by the falling in, or the erosion, of a portion of the mould.

Remedies. Buckles and scabs may be prevented :

(*i*) by using sands with high hot-plasticity or low expansion characteristics, or

(*ii*) by using an expansion buffer *e.g.,* wood flour mixed with sand. Wood flour burns and leaves space for surface sand grains to expand without shearing from the mould.

(*iii*) They may be minimized by rapidly filling the mould.

4. Surface Laps, Seams, and Cold Shots. They occur in casting with relatively light sections where two surfaces of flowing metal meet and do not fuse properly. They can be distinguished by clean appearance and lack of sand or other impurity to account for poor surface finish.

In *'cold shots'*, small shot-like spheres of metal are almost distinct from the casting.

Causes. These defects result from pouring metal too cold.

Remedies. These defects can usually be prevented :

(*i*) By using higher pouring temperatures.

(*ii*) By using streamlined sprues to give smoother flow.

5. Entrapped Air, Dross and Slag Inclusions. They are usually found on the cope surfaces of the castings.

'Entraped Air' is recognised as small, internally oxidised holes just beneath the cope surface.

It is found more frequently in aluminium and magnesium casting.

'Dross' and *'Slag Inclusion'* are oxides or other reaction products of the metal being cast. Slag may be other non-metallics from the melting operations.

Causes. These defects are caused by improper control of :

(*i*) Melting and pouring.

(*ii*) Gating design.

(*iii*) Moulding sand practice.

Remedies. (*i*) To prevent slag or dross inclusions entering from the laddle, they should skimmed before pouring or teapot or bottom-pouring laddles should be used.

(*ii*) Pouring basins should be employed so that any slag or dross entering from the ladle with rise and not pass into the runner system.

(*iii*) Runner system should be designed to exert additional skimming action on the flowing metal. Streamlining the runner system will minimize any tendency to entrap air or form dross or slag inclusions during pouring.

(*iv*) Careful control of mould permeability and gas content reduce danger of entrapping air of mould gases and minimize any tendency to form dross from mould-metal reactions.

6. **Sand spots.** They appear as small irregularly shaped depressions in the finished casting. They may be spaced randomly or gathered in clusters where the impurities have been collected at one or more vortices developed by the metal. Sand spots sink or float depending on the density of the metal cast. They may also become entrapped by growing dendrities along the side walls of the casting.

Causes. Sand spots are caused—

(*i*) By the metal washing particles from the runner system or mould walls.

(*ii*) By excess turbulence in the gating system.

(*iii*) By spuring of metal into the mould.

(*iv*) By poor moulding sand properties.

Remedies. Various defects can be eliminated by controlling foundry practices, *e.g.*, moulding practice, gating system, melting practice etc.

Defects Resulting from Incomplete Feeding

Many of the more prevalent defects of castings result directly from solidification shrinkage. Figure 12.1 shows typical defects due to shrinkage :

1. **External imperfections.** The most prevalent type is localized cavities appearing at unfed hot spots in the casting *viz.*, depressed regions on cope and upper surfaces.

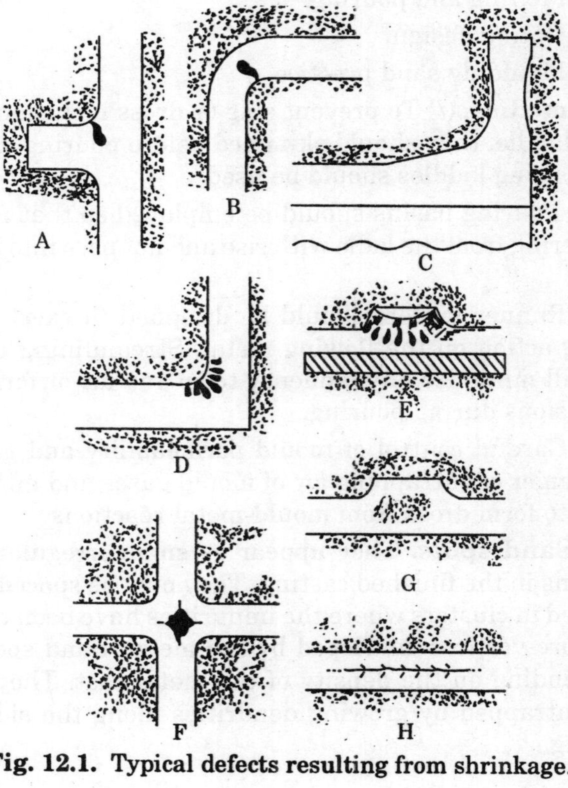

Fig. 12.1. Typical defects resulting from shrinkage.

Whenever feeding is grossly inadequate, internal unsoundness is usually indicated by some external imperfection, *e.g.*,

(*i*) wall punctures,

(*ii*) deforms by dishing at the weakest point,

(*iii*) elongated wormholes appearing at the riser base, at internal angles, on cope surfaces,

(*iv*) defects resembling collections of dross where cope surfaces are wrinkled and drawn inward,

(*v*) small voids appearing to be pinholes.

2. **Internal imperfections.** Gross shrinkage, centre-line shrinkage, microporosity are internal manifestations of solidification shrinkage :

(*i*) **Cross shrinkage** is a localized cavity most likely to occur in isolated sections called *'Hot Spots' i.e.*, the last regions of the cavity to solidify.

(*ii*) **Centre line shrinkage** is narrow, more or less continuous void sometimes found along the centre line of castings with extensive plate like sections. It may actually be in a continuous line or may appear as a line of fine shrinkage chevrons (zig-zig) with the tips pointing away from the main direction of feeding.

This defect is found only in alloys like steel which freeze over a relatively narrow temperature range.

(*iii*) **Interdenritic shrinkage (Microporosity).** Alloys that freeze over a wider temperature interval tend to exhibit this defect when improperly fed.

Causes

(*a*) Improper feeding

(*b*) Dissolved gases.

Remedies

(*a*) Adequate degassing

(*b*) Directional solidification to produce sound castings.

3. **Internal hot tearing.** *'Internal hot tears'* are radially disposed discontinuities inside castings, more commonly steel castings, which can be disclosed non destructively only by radiography. The discontinuties resemble external hot tears except that they are radial rather than roughly parallel (Fig. 12.2).

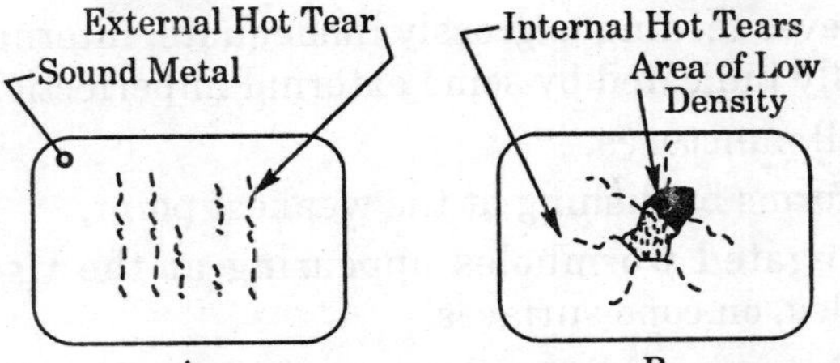

Fig. 12.2. Appearance of External and Internal Hot Tears on Radiographic Film.

The tears emanate from a low-density area, giving the radiograph an octopus-like appearance.

Cause

(*i*) Contraction stresses

(*ii*) Inadequate measures to give mould relief.

Remedies. Cure for internal hot tears is improved feeding.

Gas Porosity

Miscroporosity, centre-line shrinkage and gross porosity (resembling gross shrinkage) may be caused :

(*i*) By gases dissolved in the metal during melting and pouring.

(*ii*) By solidification shrinkage.

Voids in a well-fed section may be caused by gas. Rounded voids with smooth walls are generally due to gas called '*Gas Porosity*'.

Angular voids, perhaps with dendrite arms protruding into the voids, are usually caused by imperfect feeding.

Fine microporosity observed occasionally in non-ferrous castings may be due to both—

(*i*) Gas content,

(*ii*) Metal shrinkage.

Remedies. Methods of eliminating gas porosity are described in Chapter 10 under '*Methods for Degassing Metal*'.

External Hot Tears, Cold Cracks, and Warpage (Figs. 12.3 and 12.4).

1. **External hot tears** are jagged, roughly parallel tears generally visible to the unaided eye but usually found by X-ray, magnetic powder, or Zyglo testing.

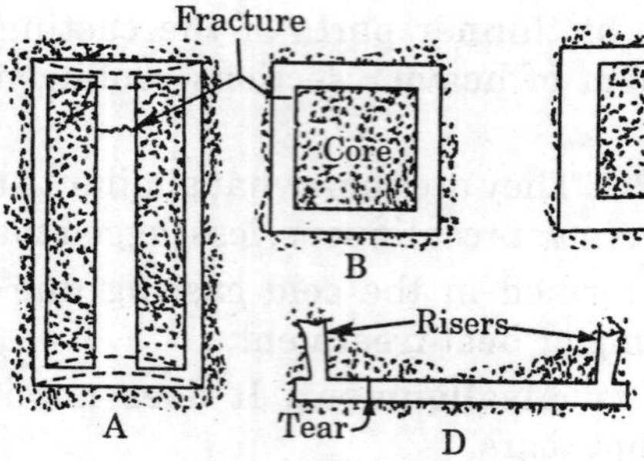

Fig. 12.3. Typical Examples of hot tears and casting stresses.
A to C–Effects of casting stresses due to poor collapsibility of cores.
D–Part of casting between two risers rigidly held or sand between them rammed too hard.

Tears are often deep and are formed by surface rupture near the temperature at which the casting is completely solid. Figure 12.2 A shows appearance of an external hot tear on a radiographic film.

Causes

(*i*) External hot, tears, cold cracks, or warpage may occur if castings do not contract relatively freely in the mould as they cool from solidification temperature to room temperature :

(*ii*) Stresses developed in the casting by resistance of the mould (Fig. 12.4 A and B).

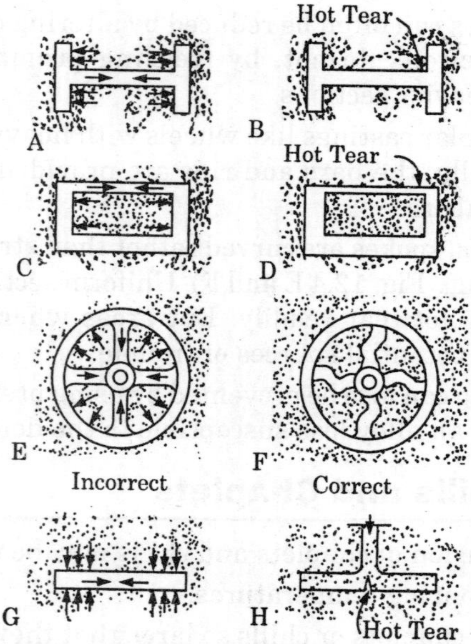

Fig. 12.4. Hindered contraction in solidifying castings.

(*iii*) Resistance of thinner parts of the casting to normal contraction upon them of heavier sections cooling more slowly (Fig. 12.4 C and D).

2. **Cold cracks.** They are somewhat similar to external hot tears. Usually a '*cold crack*' is continuous, less jagged than hot tears.

Cause. It is formed in the cold casting due to stresses imposed during cooling or heat treatment.

3. **Warpage** is misalignment. It does not involve any discontinuities like hot tears.

Causes. Stresses set up by conditions of—

(*i*) Cooling,

(*ii*) improper design or,

(*iii*) mould resistance.

Remedies for external hot tears, cold cracks and warpage—

(*i*) By increasing collapsibility of moulding sand by adjusting its composition.

(*ii*) By placing chains, or relieving blocks in the mould at critical regions so that they can be removed at the proper time to allow the casting to contract.

(*iii*) By using coke or other filler which is less resistant than sand.

(*iv*) Stresses can often be reduced by altering casting design, so that thin sections do not, by freezing prematurely, resist contraction of heavier sections.

(*v*) In circular castings like wheels with heavy spokes which tear longitudinally, the bars and rips are provided to strengthen the weaker members.

Sometimes, spokes are curved rather than straight to reduce warping or tearing (Fig. 12.4 E and F). Uniform sections of castings (Fig. 12.4 G) do not tear readily. But areas where sections join (Fig. 12.4H) are potential sources of trouble.

(*vi*) Tearing can also be prevented by using preheated moulds, or by employing an alloy less susceptible to the defect.

Unfused Chills and Chaplets

Causes. Poor fusion of chaplets and chills may be due to—

(*i*) Low pouring temperatures.

(*ii*) Use of chaplets or chills so large that they cool the metal before surface fusion can occur.

Blows from chaplets and chills may be due to—

(*i*) moisture,

(*ii*) other contamination *e.g.*, oil, dust ;

(*iii*) oxide accumulated on the chills or chaplet before or after it is placed in the mould ;

(*iv*) external chills sometimes cause surface blows by similar contamination.

Remedies

(*i*) By choosing and using internal and external chills and chaplets wisely.

(*ii*) External and internal chills and chaplets should have clean, roughened surface, such as can be imparted by sand blasting. This reduces blows and causes metal to lie quitely against external chills and to fuse with internal chill and chaplets.

Moulding Defects

1. **Sand spots** are caused by—

(*i*) Inadequate control moulding sand properties.

(*ii*) Carelessess in finishing the mould.

(*iii*) Use of damaged pattern equipment.

2. **Oversize castings,** are caused by—

(*i*) Improper moulding.

(*ii*) Rapping a pattern too hard when removing it from the mould.

(*iii*) Excessive allowance in the pattern for metal shrink.

(*iv*) Sand rammed too soft.

3. **Mismatch, lifts and shifts.** A mismatch is a slight displacement of the cope half of the casting with respect to the drag half.

Mismatch is caused by loose pins on the flask.

Lifts and shifts are caused due to cope or core misplacements.

(*i*) **Fins** are a thin metal flash at the parting line of the mould or core halves. They are readily removed in the cleaning operation.

Other defects in castings :

1. **Blow holes** caused by—

(*i*) The sand being too wet.

(*ii*) Low temperature of the mould.

(*iii*) Hard ramming.

(*iv*) Improper venting.

2. Honeycombing or sponginess is an external defect consisting of a number of small cavities in close proximity.

Causes

(*i*) Dirt or '*scurf*' held mechanically in suspension in the molten metal.

(*ii*) Imperfect skimming in the ladle.

(*iii*) Poor metal.

3. Sand holes found on external surface or inside the casting.

Causes

(*i*) Loose sand washing into the mould cavity and fusing into the interior of the casting.

(*ii*) Rapid pouring of the molten metal.

4. Swelling—

Cause. Defective ramming of moulds.

5. Poured short—

Cause. Insufficient metal at one pouring.

6. Internal air pockets—

Causes

(*i*) Pouring boiling metal.

(*ii*) Rapid pouring of the molten metal in the mould.

Defects Caused by Moulding, Core-Making and Gating

1. Hot Tears. Causes (*i*) Shrinkage cracks, or pulls, are formed by the casting pulling itself apart while cooling in the mould. The cracks have jagged edges and have discoloured, oxidised appearance.

(*ii*) Moulder may have provided insufficient fillets or brackets at the junctions of sections or have used insufficient feeding.

(*iii*) Slow running on account of small gates or metal lacking in fluidity.

2. Shifts. These are mismatchings of the different parts of a mould at the joint lines.

Causes. (*i*) By the use of undersize moulding-box pins.

(*ii*) By movement of the face of the moulding sand during rolling over.

3. Fins and Flash along the joint lines of castings.

Causes. (*i*) When the moulder raps the pattern excessively before withdrawal.

(*ii*) If moulder does not place sufficient weight on the top part of the mould.

(*iii*) If the moulder fails to see that the parts of the mould are tightly clamped.

4. Cold Laps or Misrun Castings-Causes. (*i*) If the gates are too small.

(*ii*) When there are too many restrictions in the gating system.

(*iii*) When the pouring head is too low.

(*iv*) When metal lacking in fluidity is used.

(*v*) Faulty venting of the moulds.

5. Crush is a displacement of sand when the mould is being closed.

Causes (*i*) Carelessness on the part of the moulder.

(*ii*) Excessive weighting of the mould.

(*iii*) Cores too large.

(*iv*) Core prints too small.

6. Swell is a local displacement of the face of the sand by the pressure of the fluid metal.

Causes. These local bulges are often caused by soft ramming.

7. Sand wash usually occurs near the ingates as rough lumps on the surface of a casting. It appears on the upper surface of the casting as rough holes or depressions.

Causes (*i*) Soft ramming.

(*ii*) Weak sand.

(*iii*) Poor patterns.

(*iv*) Insufficient draft on patterns.

(*v*) Sand wash from cores overbacked or insufficiently bonded.

8. Scabs are rough slightly-raised areas on the surfaces of castings, often with some sand embedded in the scab.

Causes. (*i*) Uneven ramming.

(*ii*) Slow or intermittent ramming.

9. Sand blow is an excessively smooth depression on the outer surface of a casting.

Causes (*i*) By moulding sand with high moisture content and low permeability.

(*ii*) Insufficient venting. The defect is called '*Air lock*'.

(*iii*) Faulty gating system if defect occurs near the ingate where the incoming metal impinges on small area of sand.

10. Core blow is an excessively smooth depression on the inner surface of a cored cavity or a gas pocket immediately above a cored cavity.

Causes. (*i*) Moulder forgets to carry the vent from the core through the mould.

(*ii*) Moulder uses cores insufficiently baked or having picked up moisture after baking.

11. Slag holes are smooth depressions on the upper surfaces of castings. They usually occur near the ingates.

Remedy. By inserting slag traps in the gating system.

Defects caused by mould drying and core baking. Unsatisfactory baking of dry-sand moulds causes more unsightly defects on castings than occur with a green-sand mould. A pocket or layer of moisture collecting under the impervious layer of mould paint on the surface of the mould will cause the sand and paint to scab and peel, with the result that the castings how unsavoury sand washes, scabs and blowholes.

Beads of moisture gathered on metal chills, denseners or chaplets, are converted with explosive voilence to steam when the molten metal flows over the metallic surfaces. Blow-holes caused by the reaction are frequently deep-seated, and the casting has to be scrapped.

Underbaking of oil-sand cores causes more defects than overbaking. Organic compounds are not fully converted or polymerized, and this condition is more liable to absorb moisture from the atmosphere or from green-sand moulds in which cores are placed. Low strength of underbaked cores permits the surface of the cores to be washed away, so that the defects caused may range from core blows and blowholes, to core sand washes.

Overbaking of an oil-sand core is readily detected on account of dark colour and friable nature of its surface. if such cores are used, they are not strong enough to resist the flow of molten metal and the defects such as sand washes, rough surface, metal penetration, and undersized holes are caused.

There is little danger of over-drying of clay-bonded moulding and core sands because with modern fuel economy, moulds are closed as soon as they are thoroughly dried.

Under-drying results steam condensing on the surface of the mould and chill, etc., causing sand blows, core blows, scabs, etc., which mark the casting appearance.

Defects caused during closing and pouring the moulds

1. Shift or mismatching of the cope and drag at the mould joint.

Cause. By use of loose box pins in moulding or closing operation.

2. Misrun casting is one in which metal fails to fill the mould.

Cause. Interrupting the flow of metal from ladle or using molten metal too cold.

3. Cold laps (or cold shuts) occur in castings where two streams of metal fail to join.

Cause. Insufficient temperature of molten metal.

4. Crush

Causes. (*i*) By a displacement of sand while closing the mould.

(*ii*) Weight on the top of the mould too heavy.

(*iii*) Core print too small for the core.

5. Gas-holes near the surface of heavy sections of castings.

Cause. (*i*) Presence of hydrogen, etc., in the molten metal.

(*ii*) Ladles fired at a low temperature.

(*iii*) Evolution of steam alloys hydrogen to be absorbed by the molten metal.

Defects caused by the molten metal

1. Misruns

Cause. Mould cavity not completely filled.

2. Cold shuts. Metal fails to join along a line which looks like a crack.

Causes. (*i*) Bye metal which is too cold and sluggish

(*ii*) Interrupted pouring.

(*iii*) Bye contamination of metal by impurities which reduce the fluidity of the metal or introduce inclusions that interfere with proper coalescene of molten metal in the mould.

(*iv*) In pouring aluminium bronze, drops of metal that become separated from main stream during pouring become surrounded by a film of alumina that causes a cold shut.

3. Excessive penetration. Excessive burning into the sand of the mould or cores giving a rough surface.

Causes. (*i*) In copper base alloys and cast iron, excessively fluid metal results from a high phosphorus content or high casting temperatures.

(*ii*) In heavy steel castings, penetration of metal into the core sand is caused by high casting temperatures.

4. Rough surfaces. Shallow pits on upper surfaces, particularly near the ingates of castings.

Causes. (*i*) Slag-holes are caused by slags and fluxes too fluid to be restrained by slag traps in pouring basin and in gating system, and by careless skimming and pouring.

(*ii*) Dirty scrap in the charge.

5. Tin or Lead sweat. Surface of copper base is covered with a discontinuous, thin layer of metal, containing a higher content of tin than the parent alloy.

Lead sweet occurs in high leaded copper-base alloys in spots and lumps.

6. Shrinkage cracks and hot tears. Cracks with oxidised walls and following a jagged path.

Cause. By too low pouring temperature. Iron castings leak under pressure if cast at low temperatures.

Remedy. Low sulphur content prevents the formation of hot tears.

7. Weak or discontinuous structure. A very coarse structure with minute fissures between the large crystals.

Cause. In copper base alloys, presence of silicon or aluminium and a high pouring temperature produce a coarse, dendritic (tree-like crystals) discloured fracture.

8. Gas porosity, gas-holes, sponginess. Small gas bubbles under the skin of castings. Gas-holes occur in heavy sections, and are round and bright, free from oxide tint.

Cause. (*i*) In non-ferrous melting, presence of hydrogen or sulphur dioxide in the metal, absorbed from the furnace atmosphere or from oil or water in the charge.

(*ii*) An excessively high pouring temperature and damp ladles.

9. Irregular composition. The composition falls outside the specification limits.

Causes. (*i*) Use of unknown scrap.

(*ii*) Mixing of different types of foundry scrap.

(*iii*) Careless weighing of rich-alloy additions.

(*iv*) Pick-up of carbon from the resinuous bond in the moulding sand by very low carbon steel castings.

10. Unmachinable edges of grey-iron castings. Silicon content of grey iron is a critical factor because if it is too low, the thin portions of the castings may be white and difficult to machine.

Defects caused by wrong fettling operations. These fall into two classes :

(*a*) Defects that should be discovered and remedied by the works inspection system.

(*b*) Defects not apparent until the customer machines or uses the castings.

Some examples of unsatisfactory fettling operations :

(*i*) Sand not properly removed from pockets and cavities, particularly when oil is to be circulated.

(*ii*) Sand and scale not properly removed from surfaces to be machined.

(*iii*) Distorted castings or castings bent in heat treatment improperly straightened.

(*iv*) Failure to smooth the rough chisel marks.

(*v*) Incipient cracks caused by rough handling or too heavy grinding or brittle castings.

(*vi*) Failure to reheat heavily machined castings in order to relieve internal stresses.

(*vii*) Heads burned off too low. These must be built up again with weld metal.

(*viii*) Heads burned off too high, leaving too much metal for the customer to remove in his machining operations.

(*ix*) Heads burned off too near the casting may cause cracking in hard alloys.

(*x*) Failure to anneal or normalize steel castings after burning off the riser leads to difficulties in machining, and may cause failure through cracking in service.

(*ix*) Unsatisfactory welding repairs are caused by failure to explore a defect fully before starting welding. Or, a faulty welding

technique permits the formation of slag inclusions in the weld or cracks around the edges of the weld.

Defects caused by faulty heat treatment. Such defects can be minimised by the following ways :

(*i*) Control of initial heating operations to avoid cracking of brittle castings.

(*ii*) Maintenance of specified soaking temperatures for the metal composition.

(*iii*) Careful stacking of the castings to prevent undue distortion taking place while the castings are in a semi-plastic state at the heat-treatment temperature.

(*iv*) Controlling the rate of cooling to achieve the desired results.

(*v*) Taking care not to crack the castings by cooling too rapidly.

(*vi*) Provision of a furnace atmosphere that is not determinantal to the surface appearance of the castings.

(*vii*) Small castings distorted in heat treatment may be rectified by cold straightening under hydraulic presses, steam hammers or even with sledge hammers, if made in ductile metals.

(*viii*) Brittle castings, and heavy tough castings too strongly built to be cold straightened, are straightened while they are hot.

(*ix*) Medium size castings may be withdrawn from the furnace and hot straightened under a press, etc., while weights are placed on large castings to cause them to sag to a controlled amount in the furnace. In such instances, the supports must be carefully arranged and rigid so that the required amount of straightening is obtained.

FETTLING OR CLEANING OF CASTINGS

Introduction to Fettling or Cleaning of Castings

Whatever type of mould is used, castings will require cleaning and trimming before passing them on for machining, or other operations. Amount of work to be done depends on :

(*i*) The size of castings.

(*ii*) Types of alloys used.

(*iii*) The care and degree or accuracy given to the production of the mould and core.

The noise and dusty atmosphere associated with fettling shops gives the casual observer an impression that this phase in production requires little or no skill. This is entirely wrong because it is the finish produced by the fettler which either definitely enhances or entirely mars the saleability of a foundry's products.

In many foundries making repetition light castings *e.g.*, switch gear etc., the work of the fettler is limited to removing runners and risers and cleaning off any adhering sand. In heavier and more intricate castings, more work is necessary to remove cores, flash metal at joints and surface imperfections.

As temperature rises progressively from white metal alloys to cast steel, the refractoriness of the mould must be improved. Generally, the higher the metal melting point, the greater the surface roughness of the castings. Thus, the heavier castings in grey and malleable cast iron and cast steel call for the most work in fettling.

Fettling is not a precision operation like machining. The main function of fettling department is

(*i*) speed in removing all unnecessary metal.

(*ii*) the production of a reasonably smooth finish.

Removal of Sand

After a casting arrives at the fettling department, the first job is to remove any sand which adheres from the mould and cores.

Method of removing sand depends on

(*i*) Size of the casting

(*ii*) Intricacy of the casting.

If design in fairly simple, it will be sufficient to rape with a hammer followed by wire-brushing or shot blasting. If design is more intricate, it takes longer to remove cores and their grid or wire reinforcements. Although a wide range of castings are made in green sand moulds, cores are more usually dried. Dried sand if artificially bonded, does not break easily. At the same time dry sand moulds and cores usually strip well, *i.e.*, once the sand is removed, casting surface requires little cleaning.

On heavy intricate castings, if only picks and bars are employed, cleaning becomes very laborious. Pneumatic picks are, therefore, used to some extent. These have the disadvantages.

(*i*) they are weighty,

(*ii*) considerable dust is created by their exhaust.

However, water sprays in conjunction with penumatic pick are used to overcome dust problem.

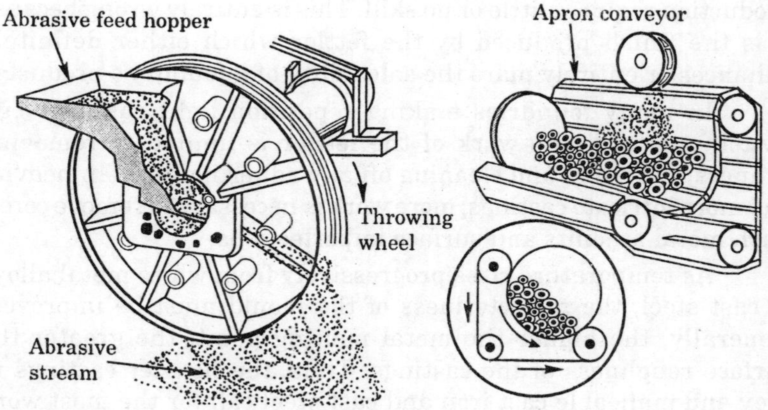

Fig. 12.5. Mechanical Blast Cleaning (Wheelabrator system).

Modern automatic units for smaller castings rotate or tumble the casting under the grid blast. Figure 12.5 illustrates one such unit where abrasive is mechanically blasted into castings which are being tumbled on an apron conveyor.

Three types of blast cleaning in common use are :

(*i*) **Air Blasting.** A high pressure stream of air propels and (sand blasting) or shot (shot blasting) against the casting surface.

(*ii*) **Water Blast Cleaning.** Water is used instead of air, to propel sand.

(*iii*) **Mechanical Blasting.** Rapidly rotating paddles mechanically hurl shot or sand on the surface of the casting (Fig. 12.5).

Wet Process of Cleaning

This process has always been attractive, because it offers promise of elimination of the dust problem. The operation has been proved to be completely successful and accepted as a standard method of cleaning.

There have been various stages in the development of this '*wet process*'. One such plant embodies a gun which is easily handled by one man. It projects a fine stream of water and sand against the casting at a pressure of 775 kg with a velocity of about 5 km per minute. The quantity of water used is about 115 litres per minute, carrying with it upto 32 kg of sand per minute.

Heavier equipment (Fig. 12.6) is available which includes a gun working with water at 900 kg pressure and delivering 225 litres per minute. This gun is operated mechanically from outside the chamber. It is mounted in a carriage which can be moved the entire length of the room and vertically as may be required.

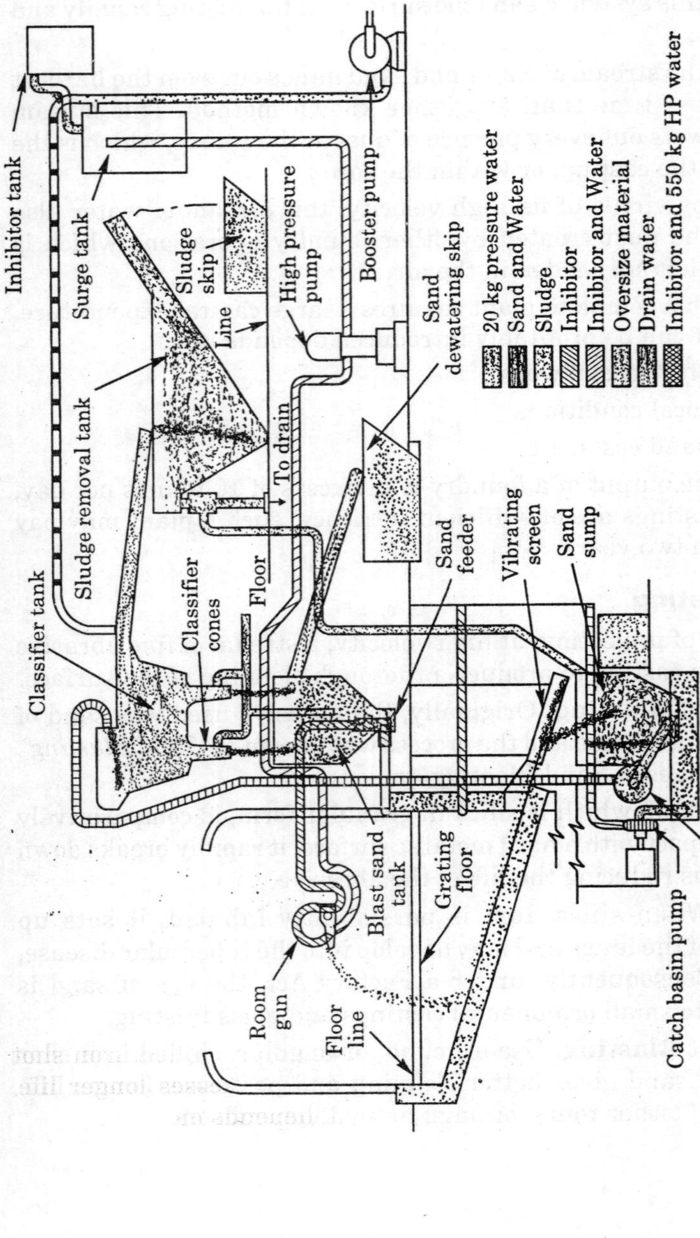

Fig. 12.6. Hydraulic Casting Cleaning Plant (Arrangement showing circulation of materials).

The gun swivels in the carriage in a cone of more than 90°. All the motions are controlled by two levers outside the room actuated hydraulically and electrically. No special abrasive is required, as the sand cleaned from the castings is quite suitable. It is claimed that

(*i*) this system cleans the surfaces of the casting rapidly and throughly ;

(*ii*) the stream of water and sand mines out even the hardest cores in less time than any other known method. This stream instantly wets out every particle of dust at the source, which is the surface of the casting, or within the core ;

(*iii*) by virtue of its high velocity, this stream of water also removes the dust created by other foundry operations which is otherwise left suspended in the air.

Such a complete plant requires a large capital expenditure. Whether it can be profitably introduced depends upon

(*i*) the class of work ;

(*ii*) local conditions ;

(*iii*) sand costs, etc.

If the output of a foundry is in excess of 10 tonnes per day, and the castings are of sufficient intricacy, such a plant may pay for itself in two years.

Shot Blasting

It consists of projecting, at high velocity, a stream of fine abrasive against the casting to produce a thorough cleaning of the surface.

Sand Blasting. Originally, the abrasive used was sand of fairly large grain size and the process was known as '*Sand Blasting*'. Disadvantages of Sand Blasting are :

(*i*) Sand, which is silica in granular form, is comparatively soft. On impact with a hard metallic surface, it rapidly breaks down in size, thus reducing the life of the abrasive.

(*ii*) When silica dust is persistently inhaled, it sets up irritation of the lungs and may develop into the tubercular disease, silicosis. Consequently, under a Factory Act, the use of sand is restricted to small ornamental castings and glass frosting.

Shot Blasting. Use of round, or angular, chilled iron shot in place of sand gives better cleaning and possesses longer life. Selection of either round or angular shot depends on

(*i*) the finish desired and

(*ii*) the material to be treated. The round shot is generally restricted to the shot blasting of non-ferrous castings.

In recent years, considerable developments have taken place in the form and nature of the abrasive. Chopped steel wire and steel grit are claimed to be economical because of their long life and are coming into more general use.

For propelling these abrasives, many designs of machines are used. Each has a particular and useful application. All of them fall under one of these two heading :

(*i*) Pneumatic, or (*ii*) Airless.

Pneumatic-type Shot Blasting Machine

Principle. A stream of shots falls into a chamber through which compressed air is passing. It is then carried along a flexible pipe to a suitable nozzle through which the stream is directed against the surface to be cleaned.

Air pressure is usually 1.5 to 2 kg/cm^2 for grey iron and non-ferrous castings, and upto 6 kg/cm^2 for cast steel. After striking the casting the shot, together with disloged material, falls through the perforated floor of the cleaning machine. Sand and shots are then separated by a screen and suction dust extraction system. Thus, cleaned shot is ready for use again, so as to carry on the blasting continuously.

Classification of Shot blast Equipment

(*i*) Direct pressure system

(*ii*) Gravity system

(*iii*) Suction feed system.

(*i*) **Direct Pressure System.** Air and abrasive are combined in and discharged from a sealed container through a single nozzle.

(*ii*) **Gravity System.** Abrasive is delivered by gravity to the blasting gun. Air enters the gun body through an air jet, and combining with the abrasive, drives it out through a discharge nozzle.

As diameter of air jet is half of that of the discharge nozzle, expansion takes place. Thus the pressure of the air at discharge is lower than the indicated gauge pressure, although the full force of the air is exerted in the abrasive discharge.

(*iii*) **Suction or Syphon System.** A gun is used as in the gravity feed system. A portion of the air energy is exerted for lifting

the abrasive to the gun, so that the force of the abrasive discharge is not as intensive as in other systems.

The machine may take one of the two forms according to the size of castings to be cleaned :

(*i*) **For small work.** A barrel rotating on a horizontal axis into which the castings are placed, is convenient. The shots are applied through nozzles at either end. As the barrel slowly rotated, the castings, tumble about and thus expose each face in turn to the action of shot.

(*ii*) **For larger work** (having a large surface area to weight ratio), a table rotating on a vertical axis is most commonly used. The table is virtually divided into two halves : one-half enclosed in a chamber in which the shot blast can be applied, the other half exposed for loading and unloading.

Work to be cleaned is placed upon the slowly revolving table. It passes through rubber curtains into the cleaning chamber, where it comes under action of the blast through a series of overhead jets. Area of table inside this chamber is effectively covered by the abrasive blast by using a cam motion to traverse the jets through which the abrasive is projected. It is arranged so as to accelerate the movement of the nozzles as they come to the centre of the table for ensuring the speed of jets travel to be in correct proportion to the table diameter at any time.

Work leaving the blast chamber again passes through a rubber curtain. It is then ready to be removed, or turned over for exposing fresh surfaces to the blast.

For casting over 250 kg, a special room is provided in which the shot-blast operator works. He must be provided with protective clothing, including a helmet with an independent air supply for breathing. He directs the stream of abrasive for flexible pipe having a nozzle made from hard, wear-resisting metal.

The system applied to *barrel and rotary table types of machines* consists of a mechanism for abrasive cleaning. It uses centrifugal force of a high-speed impeller, in place of compressed air to propel shot against surfaces to be cleaned. Main advantages of this system are :

(*i*) Because no compressed air is used, it is possible to eliminate air compressors requiring large electric motors, pressure tanks, nozle control valves, mixing tanks and air receiver tanks.

(*ii*) Cleaning is extremely fast.

(*iii*) In case of barrel type, loading and discharge arrangement enables conveyors to be used with advantage for feeding the work to and from the mechaine.

(*iv*) Barrel and rotary types of machines posses sound mechanical design and efficiency, with adequate protection of bearing against dust, and a completely dust-tight cleaning chamber to prevent air pollution.

Examples of Barrel and Rotary types of machines are :

(*i*) Barrel-type Centrifugal Cleaning Machine in which shot is directed on to the casting by means of an impeller.

(*ii*) Rotary-table Shot-blasting Machine using an airless system of hot propulations and incorporating a dust-collection system.

(*iii*) Hexagonal type of Tumbling Barrel for cleaning castings.

Tumbling in Barrels

The essential difference between shot blasting and plain tumbling is in the speed of operation. Shot-blasting performs the cleaning in few minutes, while tumbling takes possibly 30 minutes to an hour to do it. Plain tumbling is considerably slower than shot-blasting in producing a clean surfae, but possesses some *advantages* :

(*i*) Prolonged tumbling about the castings gives a burnishing effect by rubbing against each other, and the small, hard, star-shaped pieces of cast iron added to the charge.

(*ii*) A considerable amount of flash metal is also broken off. Hence, any subsequent grinding and chipping are appreciably ruduced.

Applications. In fact, economics decides as to which process ; shot-blasting or plain tumbling is considered superior. But in small foundries, the tumbling barrel provides the simpler and cheaper means of cleaning.

Tumbling barrels may be hexagonal, square or circular in cross-section and revolve on a horizontal or inclined axis at approximately 0 to 15 r.p.m. A dust exhaust system should be fitted.

Removal of Gates and Risers

After removal of adhering sand or refractory by one or another of the preceding techniques, gates and risers are removed from the casting. A wide variety of methods are available for accomplishing this, including chipping, flogging, shearing, sawing, abrasive wheel cutting and flame cutting etc.

1. **Chipping Hammers.** These are air-driven hammers with a chisel as the working tool. They ar very versatile, but are subject to high human equation in efficiency of operation. Their cutting efficiency is greatly affected by the following factors :

(*i*) The sharpness of the cutting bit.

(*ii*) The way it is ground to shape.

(*iii*) The material of which it is made.

(*iv*) The way it is held against the work by the operator.

(*v*) Keeping the cutting tip wet with oil means as much as 40% improvement in operation.

Applications. Chipping hammers are useful for low and medium carbon steel and copper-base castings where hardness and ductility are suitable to the process.

Hard, brittle alloy like cast iron respond to the correct cutting angle or inclination of the chisel to the face of the work (about 60°). Greater the care taken in moulding and core making, the less the chipping required to remove metal fins at joints. In fact, the fettler is sometimes expected to exercise the genius of a sculptor for rectifying the mistakes of foundry and pattern making.

For thin intricate work, hand hammer and chisel are widely employed. Use of pneumatic hammer usually results in speeding-up of operation, smaller chip and much smoother surface. Pneumatic hammers are made in a number of sizes to a variety of designs. But, all operate on an air pressure of about 6 kg/cm^2 and deliver from 1200 to 1800 blows per minute with a consumption of between 0.5 to 1 cubic metre of free air per minute.

Description. Essential feature of penumatic hammer is a compact and simple operating mechanism. High-speed blows are delivered by a sliding piston on to the shank of the chisel. To reduce vibration and fatigue to the operator, the tool is free from recoil and light in weight. All parts subject to wear are easily renewable. Maintenance and lubrication are carried out daily. A trigger-operated needle valve controls the force of th blows.

Generally, the chisels have round and hexagonal shanks and are located in sockets. Cutting edge hardness of chisels should be about 560 Brinell.

Using pneumatic chisels produces dust. Equipment *viz.*, a chisel sleeve moulded in abrasion-resisting rubber is now available to draw this dust away at the source. Fine dust is drawn up through two pairs of ducts moulded in the sleeve. One pair takes the dust

from the front edge of the chisel and the other pair removes the dust from the lower edge. The ducts lead to a branch tube to which is connected a 10 mm bore plastic hose. Sleeves operate on a vacuum of 12.5 cm mercury passing a volume of 0.25 cubic metre of air per minute. Small dust collector units operated by a compressed air ejector or by an electrically driven exhauster serve an installation of upto eight fettling chisels.

2. **Flogging.** For more brittle materials, gates and risers are more easily removed by striking with hammer or sledge. The operation is known as '*Flogging.*'

3. **Shears** are heavy, matching steel jaws worked past one another by a flywheel and cam assembly.

Applications. Shears can only be used on materials softer than the shear blades. Thus, their use is limited to.

(*i*) malleable iron, soft and medium hard steel, bronze, brass, aluminium and magnesium ;

(*ii*) small work.

When adaptable, they are fast and economical. They are often used in malleable iron foundries for removing the stub left when gates are broken from the casting.

4. **Sawing.** It is carried out mainly on non-ferrous castings in a variety of ways according to circumstances :

(*i*) *Ordinary hacksaw* is suitable for very small foundries, but for large number of castings it is too slow and laborious.

(*ii*) For large number of castings, a *power-driven band saw,* of conventional design performs the operation more speedily. By virtue of greater control which can be exercised, it allows closer cutting, and consequently less waste of metal in subsequent grinding.

In die-casting foundry, a band saw is essential for removing gates and risers. In band saw practice, the tooth size and speed are important factors. Modern machines are generally made to give flour or eight speeds.

(*iii*) Foundries handling small bronze and brass castings where gates and other wastes are small enough often prefer the *grit cutter* or *power-driven shear.* It offers certain advantages over band saw *viz.*, greater robustness and less maintenance.

(*iv*) *Abrasive Cut-off Wheels* are used whenever metals are too hard to be cut by saw, and where flame cutting or chipping is not feasible *viz.*, for parting off risers in steel and tough non-ferrous metals.

The machine consists of a motor-driven high-speed abrasive disc from 30 to 50 cm in diameter and 3 mm thick, running at a peripheral speed of 3000 to 5000 metres per minute. The wheel is mounted on an arm which can be swivelled vertically to effect the necessary cutting-off.

It is not economical for small castings owing to the time required for clamping.

5. **Flame Cutting.** Removal of large feeding heads on heavy steel castings is a difficult problem. On gears and other circular castings, they may be parted off in a lathe. On irregular shaped castings, an oxy-acetylene cutting torch is usually employed.

Castings are first shot blown. Particular care is taken to remove any sand at the neck of each head to be cut off. If any mould-facing material burns on the casting surface, it must be removed with hammer and chisel so as to avoid slag formation.

Flame gouging and flame scarfing, for removing excess metal are adaptations or flame cutting. Tipe are accordingly curved to accommodate the work.

Applications. Flame scarfing and gouging are much used :

(*i*) for removing surface defects from ingots,

(*ii*) for removing riser pads,

(*iii*) for cleaning away penetrated sand, and

(*iv*) for preparing castings for welding.

Limitations. Flame cutting is not commonly used on small castings, or on castings that would be damaged by the heating effect of the torch.

Local application of so much heat as that used in flame cutting sets up strains in a casting. These strains may cause warping, or in intricate designs cracks. Local hardening takes place around the edge cut by the flame. Castings are, therefore, annealed at about 860°C to relieve these stresses and normalize the structure.

Size of cutting torch and tip, together with the amount cf gas which should be used, are available from the accumlated experience of the makers of this equipment.

A *development* used in steel fettling shops after cutting off risers with oxy-acetylene torch involves the use of a carbon electrode to arc on the riser giving very localised melting. Molten steel is blown with compressed air and riser trimmed down very nearly to contour of the casting with much less effort than trimming with a pneumatic chisel.

6. **Pickling (Chemical Cleaning).** Castings may be placed in a vat containing a weak solution of acid to remove the sand and scale. Acids used are sulphuric and hydrofluoric for cast iron, and nitric, or a mixture of nitric and sulphuric for brass.

Sulphuric acid attacks metal and in doing so loosens any adhering sand. Hydrofluoric acid attacks the sand alone, and therefore, although somewhat slower in action, is usually preferred. A commonly used acid solution is one part of 48% hydrofluoric acid and 25 parts of water.

Tanks holding the acid are lined with lead or other suitable acid-resisting material. To neutralize the acid remaining on the castings when they are removed from the pickling process, further tanks containing alkaline solutions and finally, hot water must be provided. The whole process should be carried out in an open-sided or well-ventilated building to reduce the irritation of the fumes which are given off.

Finish Cleaning

After removing gates and risers, castings are given one or more finishing operations. These are performed.

(*i*) to smooth the gate and riser areas of the casting ;

(*ii*) to remove any excess metal remaining on the casting ;

(*iii*) to improve surface finish or appearance.

Preliminary metal removal is obtained by grinding. An abrasive grit of about 25 to 80 mesh is bonded into the shape of a grinding wheel or onto an abrasive belt of canvas. Wheels and belts are available in a variety of different shapes, sizes, grits, grit sizes and binders. The right combination for a given application is chosen.

Grinding machines are either portable or stationary. Portable machines are usually used only for large castings. In softer metals, rotary files (*i.e.*, hardened steel grinding wheels) are sometimes used instead of grinding.

If a smooth surface finish is desired ; castings may be polished, brushed or buffed after grinding :

(*i*) **Polishing** is usually performed with an abrasive belt machine. It is similar to abrasive belt grinding except that a finer grit (80 to 400 mesh) is used.

(*ii*) **Brushing** employs rotary wire of fibre brushes that remove burns and grinding marks.

(*iii*) **Buffing** is used to obtain an exceptionally high lustre on cast surfaces. It employs wheels of '*buff*' (usually discs of muslin

sewn together) called *'mops'*. A very fine abrasive mixed with a grease binder is rubbed on the wheel face.

Unless castings are brushed or buffed, they are usually given a final blast cleaning or tumbling to remove dirt and grease, and smooth any remaining grinding or polishing marks. In blasting, a sand or shot grid which is sufficiently fine, should be used otherwise the operation may actually increase the roughness of the as-cast surface.

For castings with very fine as-cast finish (*viz.*, investment or plaster moulding) grits such as rise hulls, ground corncobs, or ground walnut shells are used in the blasting operation.

Safety and Hygiene in Cleaning Room

Dangers associated with the various fettling operations can be reduced by providing safety appliancs, proper education of personel, by poster, etc.

(*i*) Safety shoes with toe protectors should be worn to protect the feet against injury from falling castings.

(*ii*) When grinding or chipping castings or when operating sand blasting equipment, safety goggles should always be worn.

(*iii*) When grinding castings or when using moving machinery, gloves should not be worn.

(*iv*) Lifting or moving loads beyond one's capacity should not be attempted. Help from other workers should be taken or mechanical equipment should be used.

(*v*) Properly fitted clothing suitable for the job being done should be worn.

(*vi*) When working in a dusty atmosphere, an approved type of respirator should be worn.

(*vii*) Safeguards from any machine should not be removed. They are installed for out protection.

(*viii*) An emery wheel which is not running true should not be used.

(*ix*) Castings should be ground on the face of the emery wheel and never on its side so as to present its damage and explosion.

(*x*) When chipping castings, a screen should be placed in position to prevent metal chips from striking fellow workers.

(*xi*) No work should be done on castings suspended from a crane. They should be set on the floor or on a solid bench.

(*xii*) Acids for pickling etc., should be handled with great care, special tongs and tilting devices are provided for safety.

(*xiii*) In preparing pickling baths, acid should be added to water slowly. Water should not be added to acid.

(*xiv*) Every fettling shop should be provided with a adequate dust collection system for the grinding machines tumbling barrels and shot blast equipment *e.g.*, combination of a cylone for heavy particles and linen ; filters for fine particles. These dust collectors should be regularly cleaned.

(*xv*) Fettling shops are affected by the provisions of '*Iron and Steel Foundries Regulations*' under the heading '*Dust and Fumes*'.

All dressing or fettling operations shall be carried out in a separate room suitably partitioned off and effectively ventilated.

From the above, it is evident that fettling is an important operation. Like moulding and core making, it requires skill and dexterity if the product of the foundry is to have best appearance and ever-increasing saleability.

QUESTIONS

1. Explain in short the casting defects directly attributed to the moulding sand used for steel castings.
2. Differentiate between :
   (*a*) Blow holes and pin holes
   (*b*) Rat tail and Buckle
   (*c*) Cold shuts and Misruns.
3. Explain how hot tears can be avoided by design and by moulding procedure.
4. Describe with sketches how the hot spots of an intersection in a casting can be eliminated or reduced.
5. State the effect that sharp corners have on :
   (*i*) Moulding (*ii*) Moulding erosion
   (*iii*) Stress concentration (*iv*) micro structure.
6. What do you mean by fettling? Give its functions.
7. Explain in short the various methods of fettling.
8. Describe Pneumatic-type Shot Blasting Machine for cleaning the casting.
9. Explain in brief the various methods of Gates and Risers removable from the casting.
10. Give the list of precautions to be taken in the cleaning shop of casting in a foundry.

13

Inspection of Castings

Purpose of Inspection

Purpose of inspection of a casting is to determine the presence of internal as well as external defects and provide complete knowledge of the extent of such defects. Sometimes, a casting possessing a very good surface finish and excellent appearance from outside is found to have internal flaws on machining of pressure testing.

It is, therefore necessary to provide such method of inspection which may show the condition inside the casting and reveal the extent of the faults and their probable effect upon its final serviceability. Defects in the casting have already been explained in Chapter 12.

Methods of Inspection

They are broadly classified as :

(*i*) Destructive Methods of Inspection.

(*ii*) Non-destructive Methods of Inspection.

In *Destructive Method*, a specimen sample out of a given lot of castings is sectioned into two or more parts on a metal band saw. It is then examined for internal flaws and defects.

Limitations of Destructive Method

(*i*) Accuracy of locating a defect obviously depends on the judgement of the inspector who is to anticipate the real location of the defect.

(*ii*) Selected specimen casting may not be really a representative of all the lot and many defective castings may be accepted.

(*iii*) There is practical limitation to the number of pieces that can be taken for sectioning.

Method of destructive inspection is, therefore, less recommended unless as a means of checking accidental defects which often occur in large lots despite exercising all care during the process.

In *Non-Destructive Methods,* the casting retains its final shape, dimensions and usable state. These methods can disclose the presence and true location of the defects in the casting without destroying it.

Non-Destructive Methods in regular use are :

(*i*) Visual Examination.

(*ii*) Sound or Percussion Test (Ring Tests of Vibration Tests).

(*iii*) Impact Test.

(*iv*) Pressure Test.

(*v*) Magnetic and Fluorescent Powder Inspection.

(*vi*) Radiographic Examination.

(*vii*) Electrical Conductivity Test.

(*viii*) Penetrants of Chalk Testing.

(*ix*) Supersonic Test.

(*x*) Weight or Displacement Testing.

(*xi*) Chemical Analysis.

(*xii*) Metallographic Test.

(*xiii*) Mechanical Testing.

(*xiv*) Hardness Testing.

Visual Examination

This is the oldest and most commonly used method. The success of other lately developed methods also depends on visual inspection. The method usually consists of examining the surface of the casting with the unaided eye, a magnifying lens or a low-power microscope. It also comprises checking of thickness by using calipers, guages, templates and so on. Special calipers may have to be designed to measure internal thickness.

Although the method is very simple and convenient. But it requires great skill on the part of the inspector to locate the defects. Defects detectable by visual inspection are blowholes, rates tails, cold shuts, swells, burnt-in sand, surface porosity, or surface cracks.

Hot tears is an internal defect. But is often expends to the surface. And so it may be detected if observed carefully provided it is not too narrow to be visible to the eye.

Limitation of Visual Testing. Main drawback with this method is that the internal defects cannot be detected. Surface defects can only be observed.

Sound or Percussion Tests (Ring Tests or Vibration Test)

This also is a very old method although a number of variations and refinements have been made. Basically, it consists of suitably supporting the part of suspending it by chains etc. permitting it to swing freely and then tapping it with hammer. Weight of hammer blow is so adjusted that vibrations are set up in the casting producing a certain characteristic tone. This tone may or may not be changed in pitch or quality by the presence of discontinuities which tend to change the sound wavelength produced by the blows.

This method detects relatively large discontinuities in an otherwise homogeneous metal. It may be successful in simple shapes and uniform cross-sections. This test reflects the soundness of a piece of metal by the quality of the '*ring*' it produces. It is an easily conducted but rather crude test when the '*ring quality*' is determined by the human ear.

Recently inspection equipment has been developed to '*listen*' to the sounds electronically and compare the tone with that of a casting known to be sound.

Limitations of Sound Tests. It is difficult to judge the extent and harmful effect of the defect and locate the fault position.

Impact Tests

These may be destructive or non-destructive in nature depending on the quality of the casting.

A proper sized hammer is used to strike or fall on certain members of the casting, where defect is suspected. The casting containing harmful defects will break and so will be automatically rejected. Those having no defects will stand the test.

In another form, the casting is dropped from a specified height onto a steel base.

Limitations of Impact Test

(*i*) This method cannot be used in all cases owing to its very nature which may cause damage to the casting.

(*ii*) It cannot be very reliable and sometimes even the defect free castings may break.

Pressure Tests

These are employed to locate the leaks and test the overall strength of the parts *viz.*, valves, fittings, boilers etc., required to carry fluids in service under pressure.

Fluid used in testing may be water, air or steam. Water is generally preferred because it is incompressible and less danger is involved even if the casting shatters due to pressure. Pressure for testing varies from one and a half times to two times the working pressure.

Pressure is generally applied by means of small hand pump for safety reasons. A leak if not located immediately, may be detected on the pressure gauge.

Steam test has an advantage because steam can pass through smaller holes or openings through which water may not pass readily. Heat of steam may cause minute cracks due to expansion. For safety, castings are first tested hydraulically and then under steam, the pressure used being higher in case of water.

For testing pneumatically, the casting is immersed in a tank carrying water and air pressure is applied. Air bubbles are formed if there is a leak.

Magnetic and Fluorescent Powder Inspection

1. **Magnetic particle inspection** is used of iron or steel and their alloys possessing magnetic properties. In this method, the casting is first magnetised. Iron fillings are then sprinkled over the path of magnetic field. Filling align themselves in the direction of the lines of force. This distribution is proportional to the strength of the magnetic field.

If a casting is free from defects, particles will be distributed uniformly all over the surface. If a defect exists, the iron fillings jumble round the defect. The reason is that a discontinuity in the casting causes the lines of forces to by-pass the discontinuity and concentrate around the extremities of the defect. The depth at which the defect occurs can also be judged by studying the concentration of the particles. Considerable experience is, however, necessary to judge the defects correctly.

The casting is magnetised by passing an electric current (A.C. or D.C.) through it. A.C. is used when high surface sensitivity is desired and DC. is preferred where defects are to be located beneath the surface.

Other methods used for magnetising the castings are—

(*i*) By placing the casting between two magnetic poles, and

(*ii*) By placing the casting in a coil carrying D.C. by wrapping a flexible cable round the casting.

Iron powder may be applied either—

(*i*) dry by a hand shaker or bulb blower, or

(*ii*) wet by spraying or pouring over the surface.

When wet, the powder is carried in suspension form in a liquid like kerosene or carbon tetrachloride.

2. **Fluorescent powder inspection** can be used on all materials, but detects only surface defects. Castings on non-magnetic materials may be immersed in a warm suspension of fluorescent powder in penetrating oil. The suspension penetrates even minute cracks and pore. Excess suspension is washed away in warm water, and the casting is dusted with a drying powder. This draws some of the suspension from the cracks to the surface, where it fluoresces and is readily visible under ultraviolet light.

3. **Dye-penetrant inspection** is a variation of fluorescent powder inspection wherein a coloured dye is suspended in penetrating oil ; rather than fluorescent powder. The use of ultraviolet light is thus obviated, but defective areas are somewhat less readily seen.

Advantages of Magnetic and Fluorescent Powder Inspection

(*i*) These methods of inspection detect fine surface cracks and flows more readily than radiographic examination.

(*ii*) They are also considerably cheaper than radiography.

Radiographic or X-ray Examination

Radiography can be utilized for inspecting casting of any metal. Materially, the techniques are not different from medical investigations.

Radiant energy from a X-ray tube, radium sulphate capsule (radium or gamma-ray radiography), or radioactive cobalt is passed through the casting, or section of the casting, and recorded on a film held against the opposite surface. Defects in the form of voids or cracks are recorded as blackened areas on the film, since the radiant energy moves more easily through the less dense regions.

Interpreting radiographic films of castings correctly requires considerable skill and experience. Following defects are readily disclosed by radiographic inspection : Sand spots, cracks, internal

and external hot tears, unfused chills and chaplets, shrinkage, sub-surface gas or pin-hole porosity and discontinuity or collection of discontinuities exceeding about 2 to 3% of the casting thickness.

X-ray radiography, as compared with radium radiography enjoys :

(*i*) shorter exposure times ; usually minutes rather than hours as required with gamma-rays.

(*ii*) better definition,

(*iii*) clearer images.

It is relatively very high in first cost and maintenance having limited manoeuvrability. It requires the casting to be brought to the machine.

Radium radiography, is particularly applicable when castings are extremely large and inspection has to be done at the site. In addition, many castings can be radiographed simultaneously by placing them in a circle around the capsule and exposing overnight.

Radioactive cobalt has characteristics similar to radium. Radium pills can be rented for unlimited times at low cost.

Electromagnetic waves having low wavelengths varying between 10^{-6} and 10^{-10} cm called X-ray are used as a means of insepection. X-ray have properties similar to those of light waves, but have much shorter wavelengths lying outside the range of humans sensitivity. X-rays can be defected by a sensitive photographic film. Due to their shorter wavelengths, these waves can penetrate materials that are normally opaque to light. Shorter wavelength is required to penetrate the denser materials.

X-rays are produced by an X-ray tube. Tube carried two copper elements, the cathode and anode which are sealed. Cathode carries an electrically heated filament which generates electrons. Electrons are driven across towards the positively charged anode, when they strike the tungsten target fixed to the anode. Striking electrons cause their kinetic energy to be partly converted into heat which is conducted away through the cooling fins provided on the anode and remaining energy converted into electromagnetic waves called '*X-rays*'.

X-rays pass out of the tube through a window in the form of a beam. Their intensity is controlled by controlling the current which passes through the filament. Wavelength of the ray is

inversely proportional to the voltage applied between the two poles. Thus, for shorter wavelength, higher voltage has to be applied.

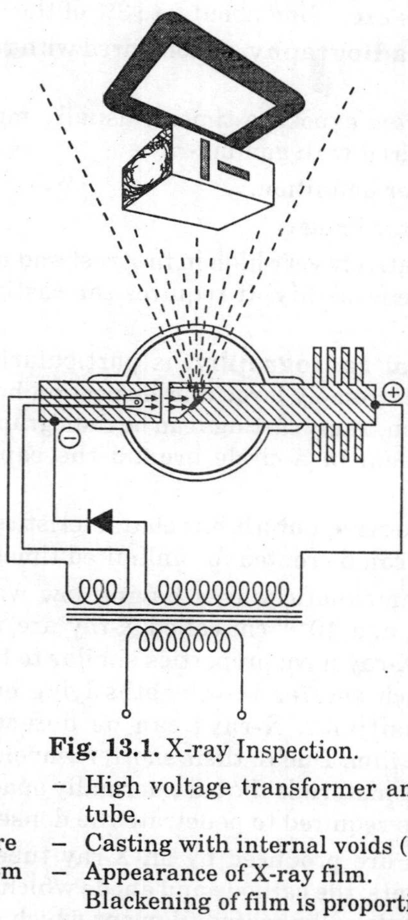

Fig. 13.1. X-ray Inspection.

Top – High voltage transformer and X-ray tube.
Centre – Casting with internal voids (black).
Bottom – Appearance of X-ray film.
Blackening of film is proportional to thickness of the internal defect.

The casting under inspection is kept against the X-ray. If there is cavity of a hole, the rays meet less obstruction and so penetrate more freely than at the place where metal is more solid and dense. The rays penetrating and emerging out of the casting are absorbed by a photographic plate. Thus, the part of the photographic plate opposite the defect receives more rays and is exposed more than the rest of the plate. This produces a contrasting image on the negative.

For getting more accurate results, special films with an emulsion coating are used. Sometimes, in place of a photographic

plate, fluoroscopic screens (made of materials which fluorsence when exposed to X-rays in a dark room) are used. For protecting the viewer from continuous exposure to the rays, the image of the screen is observed in a mirror. The mirror is so placed that the observer is out of the path of X-rays. Voltages for X-ray machines depend on the metal density and thickness. 150,000 volts machine may be used for steel sections upto 25 mm thick.

Gamma rays (like X-rays) emitted during decomposition of radium are used for inspecting casting. Their wavelengths range between $10^{-7.5}$ and $10^{-10.5}$ cm. They can penetrate metals more easily since they are shorter than X-rays. The method needs expensive protective equipment and is not so common due to high cost of radium.

Electrical Conductivity Method

Current is passed through the casting and the same is read on an ammeter. The casting having imperfections offers resistance to the flow of current and the same is shown by a drop in the reading.

Limitations of the Electrical Conductivity Method

(*i*) The method is difficult to apply practically due to variation in sectional thickness, size and metallurgical structure.

(*ii*) The method cannot be used directly unless a suitable standard is developed for a given lot of castings.

Penetrants Method

It consists of applying a thin penetrating oil to the surface of the casting. It is allowed to stand for some time so that the oil passes into the cracks by means of capillary action. Oil is then thoroughly wiped and cleaned from the surface. If the casting has any surface cracks, the oil remains in these cracks and tends to seep out.

For detecting the defects, the casting is painted with white wash coat or powdered with talc. It is then viewed under ultraviolet light. The oil is fluorescent in nature, is easily detected under this light. Thus, the defects are clearly revealed. For estimating with a fair degree of accuracy the form and size of the crack the amount of penetrant coming to the surface has to be closely observed.

Applications of Penetrants Method

(*i*) It is used to detect small surface cracks in castings which cannot be observed with a naked eye.

(*ii*) This method can also reveal those surface defects which are not revealed by radiographic inspection. It is, therefore, often used to supplement the radiographic test.

Limitations of Penetrants Method

Although this method shows up the finest surface defects in a magnified form, interior defects where the penetrant cannot reach, cannot be detected.

Supersonic or Ultrasonic Testing of Castings

It is comparatively very recent development. This method holds very encouraging prospects in near future owing to the high degree of accuracy with which the results are revealed.

Working Principle

It is based on the principle of reflection of high frequency sound waves. If the surface under test contains some defects, the high frequency sound wave when emitted through the section of the casting, is reflected from the surface of the defect and returns in a shorter period of time. If the section is homogeneous and free from defect, the wave is reflected back after travelling through the whole of the section. In this case, it takes longer lime to return to its source.

To detect the length of time, an oscillograph is used. The path of the travel of the sound waves is plotted on the oscillograph screen where it can also be measured.

Advantages of Supersonic Testing

Over other methods is that—

(*i*) the defect, even if in the interior, is detected and located accurately,

(*ii*) the dimensions of the defects can also be quickly measured without damaging or destroying the casting.

Applications of Supersonic Testing

Ultrasonic reflectoscope is used for finding sub-surface defects, *e.g.*, cracks and shrinkage cavities in large castings.

A flat surface is prepared on the casting against which a quartz crystal is pressed. A thin film of oil insures good contrast. Ultrasonic vibrations are sent through the crystal, and their reflections from any free surface are picked up and recorded on an oscilloscope. Position of the defects within the casting can be found accurately by a calibrated scaling system on oscilloscope.

Dimensional Control

Initial castings from a new pattern are usually carefully measured in a layout room to ensure whether the casting conforms to blue print specifications. Gauges are specially constructed to permit rapid check of particular casting dimensions during a production run.

Smooth Surface Finish

It is always a desirable characteristic. It is described by a number which is an average of the heights of the peaks and depths of the voltages on a casting surface. The number may be 'simple arithmetical average' or a 'root mean square average'. The two types of average are practically very nearly the same within 10 or 15%.

Casting surface finishes vary from about 2250 micromillimeter for smooth moulded plaster castings to over 7500 micro mm for heavy casting made in coarse sand. The degree of surface roughness on as cast surfaces is determined by visual comparison or by use of a direct-reading surface roughness indicator known as 'Profilometer'.

In profilometer, a stylus is drawn carefully over the surface. An electronic pitch-up translates the simple from the stylus into an average surface roughness reading.

Other Tests

These fall more in the category of acceptability standards, but which are considered inspection tests, are listed below :

(*i*) **Chemical analysis** for determining whether composition is within allowable limits.

(*ii*) **Metallographic test** as a check on grain size, non-metallic impurities, sub-microscopic pinholes type and distribution of phases present in the casting structure, and response to heat treatment.

(*iii*) **Mechanical test** includes the following :

(*a*) **Tensile test** for determining ultimate tensile strength, yield strength, elongation and reduction of area.

(*b*) **Bend, Notch bend, Impact and Transverse tests** for determining ductility and shock resistance.

(*c*) **Fracture** of the rough casting to check apparent soundness.

(*d*) **Pressure testing** of as-cast or mechanical unit to pressures in excess of service requirements.

(*iv*) **Hardness test.** Hardness is determined by measuring resistance of metal of deformation by penetration with a steel ball, or indentor. Hardness reflects ductility and tensile strength of round metal. Rockwell, Brinall and Seleroscope Hardness testers are most useful for checking castings.

QUALITY CONTROL IN FOUNDRIES

General Consideration of Quality Control

The raw materials, the finished product, the equipment and methods of each plant should be subjected to some effective form of quality control. In the larger and more progressive foundries, a quality control department is maintained which is just as essential as the engineering, sales, or production department. The application of statistical quality control methods is gaining favour rapidly and is effectively reducing the numbers of men needed for this important work.

Important Features of Quality Control

Management must know

(*i*) What needs to be controlled.

(*ii*) How to control it.

(*iii*) Limits of quality required by each phase of the manufacturing concern.

(*iv*) Specifications imposed by the consumer.

The foundry should realize that high quality is just as important to its welfare in terms of future orders as it is to the consumer in terms of machining costs and delivery dates of machines for which good castings are critical component parts.

In addition to effective organization and component personnel to handle a quality control programme, a set of control charts including statistical analysis of sampling frequency and methods must be determined. The methods vary with material and conditions of its use. All incoming raw materials should be considered as possible control items.

Melting stock and *scrap* should be checked and sorted according to a routine specification, as should *fluxex*, *coke*, *sands*, *clay* and *binders*. Sometimes a chemical check is adequate, but often a physical or performance test should be made.

In a steel foundry, *bentonite clay* used for bonding sand is one of the most critical materials as its quality varies widely from truckload. Since all the properties of a moulding sand depend primarily on the quality of the binder the latter should be accepted after proper performance test. '*Liquid limit*' test is an approved standard of acceptance by the steel foundry industry for bentonites.

Quality control test for incoming new sands include chemical analysis of SiO_2 content and a cumulative curve showing grain size and distribution of clay content for natural sands. The properties of mulled sand should be checked statistically for green and dry strength, green and dry permeability, and moisture content. These tests serve mainly to insure that the muller operator is carrying out his predetermined routine of adding proper ingredients and adhering to the proper mulling cycle.

Other tests to control mulled sand quality are flowability, hot strength and deformation, etc., but these are primarily useful for research and development work and need only be used as an occasional statistical routine test.

Cores should be tested for compressive or shear strength, permeability and colour as routine control checks. Oil or resin should be given an incoming service test. Core ovens should be carefully controlled by thermocouples properly placed to be sure baking is uniform throughout the oven.

Flasks that are weak or worn, warped, of wrong size or shape, and blessed with loose pins also responsible for scrapped castings. Flask quality must always be controlled, preferably by routine checks made at reasonably frequent intervals.

Molten metal can be checked for quality by rapid chemical analysis at proper intervals and by certain quick tests at the furnace.

Fracture test can be used to check the carbon content of steel and to determine the presence or absence of gases in bronze. A more accurate and rapid test for carbon in steel is the magnetic or hardness characteristics of a small, quenched specimen.

Slag tests are useful, particularly for steel making in open-hearth and electric furnaces. The colour of the slag coke and the

flow length in a special mould measure the slag properties, which in turn reflect melt quality.

Fluidity tests, in which metal from the furnace is poured or soaked by controlled vacuum into a flow channel of a suitable size, are very useful. Since temperature (superheat) is the most significant single variable influencing the ability of molten metal to fill a mould, the fluidity test is also an accurate indicator of temperature. The fluidity test is less needed, except as a research tool, for lower melting point metals.

Vacuum degasser is a very important and simple quality control tool for molten aluminium. Hydrogen gas impairs the strength and utility of aluminium alloy castings seriously. It is, therefore, very important to determine its presence in the melt. A small sample of the melt is dipped into a ceramic crucible and placed quickly under a vacuum pump. As the metal solidifies under reduced pressure, any gas present in the melt forms exaggerated cavities in the freezing, sample which can be assessed in severity by cutting the sample and observing the cross-section.

Quality control records should be kept and used for developing specifications for performance and raw materials acceptance. Foundrymen perform most dependably under a system of checks and records. Also, good records permit quick solutions to problems.

Daily clinics have proved valuable in which bad castings are placed on a table and causes of these discussed with the workmen. The value of the quality control programme should also be recognised and implemented by occasional management conferences.

There is increasing emphasis on quality control in all manufacturing processes. It is, therefore, desirable to seek the counsel of experts before setting up an extensive programme for better understanding of quality control and the use of statistical sampling.

QUESTIONS

1. Explain the merits and demerits of radiographic inspections.
2. Explain the following :
   (*a*) Magnetic particle method
   (*b*) Ultrasonic testing
   (*c*) Penetrate testing.
3. Explain in short the X-ray and gamma-ray techniques of Non-destuctive method of testing.
4. What are the gamma-ray sources for non-destructive testing? Compare gamma-ray radiography with X-ray radiography.
5. Write short not on :
   (*a*) Limitations of destructive methods of inspection.
   (*b*) Advantages of super sonic testing.
   (*c*) Explain in short the various quality control tests for the incoming materials in the foundry.

14

Heat Treatment of Castings

Introduction

Heat treatment of castings involves the improvement of properties by bringing about certain permanent structural changes. Latest demands for good quality castings have made heat treatment an indispensable step between casting process and finished product for engineering use.

Engineering properties of an element or an alloy depends solely on its structure, *viz.* (*i*) atomic structure, (*ii*) crystal structure, (*iii*) micro-structure, and (*iv*) macro-structure.

(*i*) Atomic structure refers to the distribution of electrons, protons, neutrons, and other particles in the atom. Different elements have different atomic structures and hence different properties and behaviour.

(*ii*) Crystal structure refers to arrangement of atoms in the material. Engineering metals and alloys have simple crystal structures *viz.*, face-centered cubic (f.c.c.), hexagonal close packed (h.c.p.) and body-centred cubic (b.c.c.). Mechanical yielding or deformation of materials occurs mainly by movement of line imperfections, called dislocations, along definite slip systems (the combination of crystallographic planes and directions).

(*iii*) Microstructure is made up of micro-constituents (phases) present in the material. The kind or phases present in the material are governed by the type of interaction among atoms of its constituent elements. Micro-structure is generally observed through the microscope by magnifying the specimen surface 100 times or more. Engineering properties of a material depend on its micro-structure *i.e.*,

(*a*) Number of phases and size and shape of grains present in each phase.

(*b*) Intrinsic properties of phases.

(*c*) Relative amount of each phase.

(*d*) Distribution of phases.

(*iv*) Macro-structure of a material (observed with the naked eye or smaller magnification of about 5 times) refers to the presence of inhomogeneity, seggregation, dendritic growth, inclusions, etc. Material remains weak and has poor plastic properties unless these defects are eliminated.

Atomic and crystal structures of materials are governed by the laws of nature and hence can not be altered without imposing external constraints of temperature, pressure, electric field, magnetic field, etc. *e.g.*, α iron (b.c.c.) can not be made as ductile and malleable as gold (f.c.c.) because plasticity of each is fixed by nature itself. However, fundamentals may be exploited by heating α-iron to over 910°C where it transforms to γ-iron, f.c.c. structure with better plastic properties is obtained. This is the reason steel castings are always forged, rolled and extruded within austenitic temperature range. Similarly, the strength of a material, otherwise fixed by nature, may be improved by inhibiting dislocation movement with the help of coherent precipitates. This fundamental is utilized in practice through (*i*) age-hardening of non-ferrous alloys, and (*ii*) secondary hardening of tool steels.

Microstructure and macrostructure of material are not rigidly fixed by laws of nature and hence may be controlled in practice. These structure of the casting are controlled by heat treatment. During heat treatment, the casting undergoes phase transformation, which involves changes of phase from one form to another. By comprehensive understanding of theory of nucleation and growth, control of phases, their distribution, etc. are achieved.

Phase transformation is caused by two basic mechanisms :

(*i*) Nucleation of the new phase at preferred sites *viz.*, impurities, grain boundaries and along certain crystallographic planes of its parent phase ; and

(*ii*) Growth of the new phase at the cost of the parent phase.

Various heat treatment processes in commercial use today fall under two categories :

(*i*) Anneal-quench-temper treatment for castings of plain carbon steels, alloy steels, and cast-irons, and

(*ii*) Solutionize quench-age treatment for non-ferrous alloys.

Both these treatments can produce a material many times stronger than the '*as-cast*' alloy, and a material with substantially increased hardness, improved ductility and impact strength.

Other heat treatments are used for various special purposes :

(*i*) *Stress relieving* for removing internal stresses which otherwise might later causes warpage of failure.

(*ii*) *Annealing, Normalizing and Spheroidizing* for producing special combinations of properties in steel castings.

(*iii*) *Malleabilizing* for transforming cementite of white iron to graphite '*nodules of malleable iron*' with consequently increased ductility.

Heat Treatment of Plain Carbon and Alloy Steel Castings

It is basically concerned with control of entectoid decomposition, *i.e.*, transformation of austenite to pearlite by the reaction

$$\gamma\text{-Fe } (0.8\% \text{ C}) \xrightleftharpoons{723°\text{C}} \alpha\text{-Fe } (0.02\% \text{ C}) + Fe_3C \ (6.67\% \text{ C})$$

Rate of decomposition is governed by the rate at which the carbon atoms diffuse through austenite, because ferrite and cementite do not form in the micro-structure until local concentrations of carbon are about 0.02% and 6.67% respectively. If time allowed for redistribution of carbon atoms is not sufficient, entectoid transformation may not be complete. Data for transformation kinetics, etc., are represented in a condensed and handy form as T-T-T. diagrams.

Transformation Products in Steel. In slow cooling, sufficient time is allowed for redistribution of carbon atoms (to about 0.02% in ferrite and 6.66% in cementite), which causes their nucleation and growth in alternate layers and results information of coarse pearlite. Nucleation rate increases with greater super cooling. Hence, a somewhat faster cooling yields fine crystals of ferrite and cementite, *i.e.*, fine pearlite.

Transformation to pearlite, when suppressed by very rapid cooling, austenite is transformed into '*bainite*', on holding in the range of 220–400°C. Due to an extremely high nucleation rate, cementite and α-ferrile grow as extraordinarily fine needles instead of lamellae. Hence, baimite has a needle-like structure with a dispersion of sub-microscopic carbides in a highly strained ferrite matrix.

On rapid quenching to temperature lower than 220°C (a still higher cooling rate) austenite is transformed into a highly distorted needle-like phase called '*martensitic*', which is extremely hard and brittle and has carbon atoms trapped as a supersaturated solid solution.

Heat treatment process of steel castings may be grouped into two categories :

(*i*) Process based on heading in the austenite range and subsequent cooling *viz.*,

(*a*) Normalising,
(*b*) Full Annealing,
(*c*) Isothermal annealing,
(*d*) Homogenisation,
(*e*) Hardening,
(*f*) Tempering,
(*g*) Martempering and Austempering.

(*ii*) Processes based on heating in the ferrite range and subsequent cooling *viz.*,

(*a*) Soft Annealing,
(*b*) Strive relieving,
(*c*) Antiflaking treatment.

Stress Relieving

While shaking the castings from the mould, high internal stresses are locked in the structure. These stresses arise from :

(*i*) Uneven cooling rates of various sections of the casting.

(*ii*) Resistance of the mould to normal solid construction of the casting.

These stresses can be large enough to result in severe warpage of actual failure of the part during subsequent finishing operations or in service.

Castings are often given a *thermal stress relieving treatment* for removing objectionable stresses :

(*i*) *In steel castings,* stress relieving is conducted by heating to about 590°C and furnace cooling. This treatment does not alter the metallurgical structure of the casting. If only permits the locked stresses to '*creep*' out.

(*ii*) *In other metals,* stress relieving is generally conducted at somewhat lower temperatures ; grey C.I. is heated between 430° and 590° C, and most non-ferrous metals to 200–260°C.

Time required at the above tempratures is generally between 1 and 5 hours.

(*iii*) Castings, which are too large to be completely heat treated, can be given local stress relief treatment. Areas, which are known to be subject to internal stresses, are simply heated with the aid of a gas torch or other device.

The main disadvantage of this method is that severe stresses may be caused at other portions of the casting, in the region between the heated and unheated zones.

Stress relieving may also be accomplished wholly or partly *by mechanical means*. But such methods are not common. *viz*.

(*i*) Casting surfaces are sometimes shot peened for eliminating surface tensile stressess and introducing surface compressive stresses (to improve fatigue life).

(*ii*) Residual casting stresses are, re-distributed by stressing beyond the yield point, *e.g.*, overspeeding turbine wheels, using autofrettage for prestressing large gun barrels.

Excessive speed or internal pressure in autofrettage process induces some plastic flow in the metal, reducing internal stresses and adding desirable stresses to counteract service loads.

(*iii*) In large complicated castings, stresses can be reduced by inducing vibration in them mechanically at low or room temperatures.

Heat Treatment of Non-Ferrous Alloys

All cast alloys are subject to microsegregation. Solution (homogenization) treatments are often used for eliminating or minimizing concentraton differences.

These treatments (*i*) improve casting ductility, particularly in ingots which require subsequent working ;

(*ii*) dissolve certain desirable constituents in the structure lattice for making the alloy amenable for subsequent hardening treatment.

Most of the aluminium and magnesium castings for structural or load-bearing uses produced today are sold in the heat-treated condition, and most of these heat treatments involve a solutionizing step.

Non-ferrous alloy castings are generally subjected to two types of heat treatment for improving their engineering properties :

(*i*) Homogenisation

(*ii*) Solutionise quench-age treatment.

(*i*) **Homogenisation.** During solidification of a liquid alloy, coring or dendritic segregation associated with inhomogeneity in composition occurs due to thermal and constitutional supercooling. This is common isomorighous alloys like Cu-Ni, Au-Ag, etc., resulting in low toughness and poor plastic properties. Cored cast structure is therefore not desirable and is to be eliminated by suitable heat treatment.

The process involves heating the cast alloys at elevated temperatures for several hours. Homogenisation (or equalisation) of composition occurs spontaneously through the action of diffusion.

(*i*) **Solutionise quench-age treatment.** This treatment is invariably given to almost all non-ferrous alloy castings in which the solute component has solubility with decreasing temperature, *e.g.*, the alloy of Al-Cu, Al-Ag, Al-Mg, Al-Si, Al-Zn, Al-Mg-Cu, Al-Mg-Zn, Cu-Be, etc. Strength and hardness of heat-treated alloys are much higher than those of as-cast alloys.

Heat treatment process (also called "*Age-hardening*") involves heating the alloy casting to a temperature where it forms a homogeneous single phase, followed by quenching to retain the solute component in unstable supersaturated state and subsequent aging in the range 100°–200°C. During aging, the solute atoms are rejected and form a cluster as a coherent or semi-coherent precipitate. The strained fields around a coherent or semi-coherent precipitate inhibit the movement of dislocations with increase in strength and hardness.

Precautions. (*i*) Treatments are often conducted at temperatures not far below the melting point of the alloys ; taking great care to assure that even slightly excessive temperatures are not encountered in any position of the heat-treating furnace.

(*ii*) Care should also be taken to assure that the temperatures are not much below those specified. Solution treatment temperatures be held within ± 10°F.

(*iii*) Furnace control equipment used for solutionizing treatments shoud be checked for accuracy at frequent intervals.

To determine uniformity of temperature throughout, thermal surveys of the furnace should be made.

Age Hardening

Solution treatment improves the ductility of cast non-ferrous alloys, but effect yield and ultimate tensile strengths only slightly. Age-hardening is frequently employed for improving these properties. A solution-treated alloy *e.g.*, aluminium–4.5% copper alloy in a supersaturated solid solution after it is quenched to room temperature. Some aluminium alloys age sufficiently rapidly at room temperature that treatment of elevated temperature is not necessary.

4.5 per cent copper-aluminium alloy requires an aging treatment at 150 to 200°C for 3 to 10 hours. Magnesium alloys are generally aged at about these same temperatures. Temperature control in the aging cycle is equally important as in the solutionzing treatment.

Time-Temperature Transformation for Steel

Castings. When carbon steel castings are heated above a definite temperature, the metal structure becomes a single-phase solid solution, just as done by non-ferrous alloys. In the case of steel, the solid solution is called '*Austenite*'.

Temperatures necessary to form an austenitic structure depend on the chemical analysis of the steel part. For plain carbon steel, the temperature is predicted from the iron-carbon phase diagram. As a carbon steel casting is cooled below the temperature where austenite is stable, products of transformation begin to appear in the microstructure. These products as the mechanical properties of the casting strongly depend on the rate of cooling.

Considering eutectoid (0.8% carbon) steel, if a small casting of this composition is furnace cooled after heating to austenite temperature range, the structure transforms to coarse pearlite. If rate of cooling is somewhat more rapid *e.g.*, in air cooling, the pearlite formed is finer resulting in higher strengths.

Still faster cooling results in an even finer structure with still higher strengths. Finally, a cooling rate may be so rapid that no pearlite may be found in the microstructure. The structure so formed called '*Martensite*' is hard and strong, but extremely brittle. Martensite is useful mainly in that subsequent tempering

operations alter it to a structure having excellent combinations of ductility and strength.

Annealing and Normalizing

Annealing (Full Annealing). This heat treatment is for steel castings. It homogenizes the structure and refines the grain with good ductility and lower tensile and yield strengths. It is often used to improve machinability.

Procedure. Annealing is performed by heating to the austenite region and holding long enough for homogenization of the austenite grains. Casting is then furnace-cooled to allow formation of relatively coarse pearlite.

Homogenizing temperature is usually 85 to 110°C above the critical temperature. Castings are held at this temperature for one hour per 25 mm of heaviest section.

Normalizing. It is a widely used heat treatment for steel castings, where homogenization is followed by air cooling. It improves tensile, yield and impact properties compared with annealed material.

In carbon and low-alloy steel, the microstructure after normalizing is composed of pearlite with some ferrite.

In more highly alloyed steels, some bainite or martensite may be present. In this case, normalizing is followed by a tempering treatment.

Normalized structure is quite sensitive to variations in rate of cooling. Mechanical properties vary with varying section. Cooling should be as uniform as possible throughout. Stacking castings too closely together or leaving them on a hot truck hearth during cooling should be avoided.

Quenching Steel Castings

Heat-treatment cycle which (when feasible) produces the optimum mechanical properties in steel casting is the '*Quench and Temper Treatment*'. It involves quenching from austenite temperatures at such a rate that the only transformation product formed is '*Martensite*'. A subsequent tempering operation carried out primarily improves ductility.

For forming a completely martensitic structure, the quenching must be sufficiently rapid so that cooling rates in all portions of the casting are greater than the '*critical rate*' *e.g.*, all

portions of 0. 8% carbon steel casting mould have to cool to below 740°C in less than 5 seconds for complete transformation to martensite. In most cases, either an oil or a water bath is used for quenching. Water cools more rapidly of the two.

For the centre of a heavy steel casting, such a high cooling rate is not possible irrespective of quenching media. To obtain martensite more easily, a number of alloying elements like nickel, chromium and molybdenum are added to steel. These elements permit martensite to be formed at much lower cooling rates. In other words, they increase the hardenability of the steel. Steels alloying element mainly to improve hardenability are termed *'Low-alloy Steels'*.

Of all steel heat-treating operations, quenching is probably the most delicate operation :

Heavy casting with uniform section may be quenched in water with little difficulty. However, sectional variation may result in uneven cool and consequent internal stresses causing cracking or distortion of the casting. To circumvent the problem :

(*i*) A great deal of ingenuity is often required.

(*ii*) If possible, oil or an air blast should be used as a quenching medium.

(*iii*) Steel parts may be quenched in jigs to minimize distortion.

(*iv*) Thin sections should be removed from the quench tank before thick ones or the entire casting should be removed and quickly tempered before it reaches room temperature.

Tempering

This treatment always follows quenching, and may follow normalizing. It is carried out from slightly above room temperature upto about 70°C. Tempering time varies upto above one hour for each 25 mm of heaviest section.

Tempering imparts some ductility and impact strength to the alloy. It is done by precipitating carbides so that after tempering the structure of a previously martensite casting becomes ferrite with precipitated carbides. The size of the carbides increases with increasing temperature.

Fine structure obtained at low tempering temperatures is termed. *'Troostite'* at high temperatures. *'Sorbite'*, and still higher, *'Spheriodite'*. The mechanical properties of the steel castings markedly depend on tempering temperatures. In steels containing

more than 0.7% manganese or appreciable amounts of nickel and chromium, tempering in the range of 425 to 600°C followed by slow cooling induces a form of temper brittleness.

Heat Treatment of Grey Cast Iron

Grey iron castings for most purposes do not require heat treatment. It is usually possible to produce a casting with requisite strength and hardness in the as-cast condition by adjusting all composition. Except for parts to be machined to close tolerances and for parts of widely varying section size, stress-relieving treatments are sometimes required.

For grey iron, stress-relief treatments are usually conducted at 430 to 600°C. Sometimes, machinability of grey iron castings is improved by an annealing treatment *viz*.

(*i*) Low-temperature anneal.

(*ii*) Medium anneal.

(*iii*) High-temperature anneal.

Low-temperature annealing converts any pearlite present to a graphite. It is performed by heating the casting to just below critical (700 to 760°C) and furnace cooling or air cooling.

Medium temperature annealing is carried out at higher temperatures (790 to 900°C). It is used when sufficient pearlite solution is not obtained at lower temperature.

Higher temperature annealing is similar treatment at 900 to 950°C. It is used if massive carbides are present in the cast structure which must be dissolved.

By heating grey C.I. to just above the critical temperature region (for pure iron-carbon 723°C, for commercial grey C.I. 730 to 820°C), the flake graphite is left undissolved but the matrix becomes an austenite, iron of about 0.8% carbon. The matrix is thus 0.8% carbon steel, which can be hardened in the same manner as steel.

By heat-treating, the mechanical properties of most grey irons are not greatly improved because the flake graphite particles act as stress raisers, casting failure or relatively low loads. However, quenching and tempering treatments improve hardness and wear resistance and for this purpose, they are sometimes used.

Quite often, surface-hardening treatment is used. In this surface is hardened by heating and rapidly cooling and subsequently tempering. Centre of the casting is unheated retaining its as cast structure. For rapid surface heating, gas torch for flame hardening is used.

Heat Treatment of Malleable Cast Iron

It is an iron of strength and toughness exceeding that of grey iron. The improved properties are due to its graphite being nodular in shape as compared to the flakes in grey iron.

For production of malleable iron, the casting, of an iron of such analysis, which freezes while (*i.e.,* having no free graphite) is used. To obtain the desired structure and properties, the casting is then heat-treated. For procuring a totally ferritic matrix, the most common malleabilizing treatment is a two stage anneal—

(*i*) **In the first stage,** the casting is heated 900 to 950°C. The massive carbides dissolve at this temperature and *'temper carbon'* nodules precipitate. Casting is held at this temperature until the structure consists of austenite and temper carbon. It is then cooled rapidly to about 760°C.

(*ii*) **In the second stage,** the casting is slowly cooled through the critical region (for ordinary malleable C.I. 700 to 760°C), thus dissolving any pearlite that may precipitate and reprecipitating it on the already existing graphite nodules. Depending on section thickness and composition, a complete annealing cycle requires from 18 to 72 hours.

Pearlite malleable castings have been growing in popularity with today's increasing need for higher strength castings. Malleable iron contains either pearlite or other iron carbide temper products in the matrix. For ferrite malleable iron, mechanical properties are :

5500 kg/cm^2 ultimate tensile strength, 3000 kg/cm^2 yield strength, 20% elongation ; these for pearlite malleable iron are 7000 kg/cm^2 ultimate tensile strength, 600 kg/cm^2 yield strength 2% elongation.

Malleable iron castings are tough and easily machinabe, and are produced by heat treatment of white cast-iron in an oxidizing or neutral atmosphere, so that part or all the carbide of iron is transformed into temper carbon.

In the Whiteheart Process, the carbon in the carbide of iron (cementite) is mainly removed by an oxidizing (decarburizing) are packing, the residual carbide is partly converted to temper carbon modules, but there is always some pearlite in the structure with its proportion of iron carbide.

Table 14.1: Comparison between Whiteheart and Blackheart Malleable Cast-iron

1. Composition :

	Whiteheart		*Blackheart*	
	As-cast	*Annealed*	*As-cast*	*Annealed*
Total carbon	3.50	1.20	2.80	2.60
Graphite carbon	Nil	0.70	Nil	2.60
Combined carbon	3.50	0.50	2.80	Nil
Silicon	0.60	0.60	0.90	0.90
Sulphur	0.20	0.20	0.08	0.08
Phosphorus	0.06	0.06	0.06	0.05
Manganese	0.02	0.02	0.35	0.35

Whiteheart	*Blackheart*
High carbon charge (over 3%) can be melted in a cupola. A large proportion of carbon is removed from metal by oxidation in annealing, and a small amount of graphitization occurs in thick sections.	Lower carbon charge must be melted in open-heart rotary or air furnaces requires a higher melting temperature than White-heart. There is an insignificant loss of carbon on annealing. A lower total carbon iron (2.4%) gives higher strength and ductility than if carbon is raised to over 3% to permit cupola melting.
Silicon content is low for thin castings, and somewhat higher for thicker castings to promote modular graphitization in thick sections, which cannot be adequately decarburized.	Silicon content must be low to produce white iron but sufficiently high to promote graphitization throughout the section in annealing.
Sulphur content need not be low because it assists in production of white cast-iron.	Sulphur must be low to avoid excessive brittleness in the as-cast condition.
Phosphorus must be low in comparison with grey-iron practice and, therefore, hematite pig iron and steel are the usual furnace charge.	Phosphorus must be low large proportions of steel scrap and refined iron are used in the furnace charges.
Manganese must be low in order to leave sulphur free to exert its influence in stabilizing iron carbide to prevent the formation of graphite during solidification.	Manganese content need not be so low as for Whiteheart the carbide in this lower carbon is more stable than in Whiteheart.

In the Blackheart process, the iron carbide is wholly or partly converted into temper carbon and ferrite in a neutral packing without decarburization. In both processes, it is essential that there should be no graphite particles in the as-cast structure of the white iron.

2. *Microstructure*: As-cast. Must be free from graphite for both processess ; any graphite flakes would grow, and produce a very weak and brittle structure similar to that of burned firebars.

Whiteheart	*Blackheart*
Annealed. A white band of ferrite next to the skin, pearlite and ferrite midway with increasing pearlite towards the centre together with a few black patches of graphite (temper carbon), particularly in this section.	No pearlite is present in normal blackheart in annealed condition, *i.e.*, no combined carbon present. Structure consists of white crystals of ferrite with scattered black nodules of graphite (temper carbon).

Pearlite malleable is blackheart which has a modified annealing to leave some pearlite in the structure, it is stronger but less ductile than normal blackheart.

3. *Fracture after Annealing :*

Whiteheart	*Blackheart*
White and crystalline with a dull grey edge at the skin of the casting.	Dull black appearance with a thin grey edge. A bright crystalline fracture indicates unsuitable properties.

4. *Machanical Properties :*

Whiteheart (Tensile test)			*Blackheart (tensile test)*		
Maximum stress (tonnes/cm²)	*Elongation percentage*	*Cold bend test*	*Maximum stress (tonnes/cm²)*	*Elongation percentage*	*Cold bend test*
4	6	70°	3.8	12	120°
Due to presence of pearlite (0.85% carbon steel) in the centre of the section, whiteheart breaks with a hard, crystalline fracture.			Blackheart is more ductile then whiteheart. Both have surfaces easily machined at high speeds.		

5. *Section Limits :*

Whiteheart	*Blackheart*
Upto about 50 kg and 25 mm maximum thickness, decarburization is only effective to about 12.5 mm.	Heavier and thicker casting are made in blackheart because temper carbon charge occurs throughout the section, *i.e.,* it is not a surface reaction, but an internal breakdown of the iron carbide.

6. *Mechanism of Annealing Treatment :*

Whiteheart	*Blackheart*
Carefully packed in finely divided hematite iron or, 25 to 12.5%, and spent ore, 75 to 87.5%, in annealing boxes having lids diluted with sand and clay. Slowly heated to 975°C, soaked for 3 to 6 days, according to thickness and composition.	Carefully packed, to minimize distortion, in inter blast furnace slag, mill scale or sand, slowly heated to 900°C, soaked for 2 to 3 days, cooled very slowly, the complete graphitization until temperature is below 650°C when it is safe to cool them quickly in air.
Cooled fairly quickly in one day to below eutectoid temperature (say 650°C) and then more quickly by drawing boxes into air.	However carefully the boxes are packed, some castings distort in annealing, but can be cold straightened without difficulty.
When temperature is raised above 723 + 30°C, the pearlite changes to austenite, and at higher temperatures the carbide or iron is absorbed by the austenite (solid solution of gamma iron) and an oxidizing gas from iron one dissociates the iron carbide in the surface layers. Carbon issues from iron as a gas ; it passes through iron-ore packing and burns away on the outside of the box. As carbon is extracted from surface layers, further carbon migrates from centre to outer layers of	When pearlite charges to austenite on heating above eutectoid horizontal, and cementite is dissolving in gamma iron, relatively higher silicon content iron allows some of carbon to separate as free graphite. As temperature is raised and maintained, more cementite is taken into solution in austenite, from which further carbon separates and builds up the graphite already formed. Reactions continue, but as arustenite holes some carbide of iron in solution,

casting, and decarburization continues until total carbon content is considerably reduced.	castings must be cooled very slowly to afford time for balance of carbon to be precipitated. Solubility of carbide decreases with falling temperature, and so as to obtain maximum ductility, all carbide of iron must have been changed to graphite and ferrite before temperature crosses the eutectoid horizontal at about 723°C.

Heat Treatment of Ductile Cast Iron

Most of the ductile iron castings are used in the *'as cast'* condition. By properly controlling composition and cooling ratio, castings with all-ferritic matrix (ferritic ductile iron) or with all pearlitic structure (pearlitic ductile iron) can be produced in the as-cast condition. Heat treatments used to develop the strctures are :

(*i*) If carbides are present in the as-cast structure, *'ferritic ductile iron'* can be produced by annealing at 700 to 760°C.

(*ii*) *'A pearlite matrix'* can be produced by normalizing.

(*iii*) *'Martensitic ductile iron'* (iron with tempered martensite matrix) is obtained by quenching and tempering.

Table 14.2: Typical Properties of As-cast and Heat-treated Ductille Iron

S. No.	*Structure*	*Thermal treatment*	*Typical Mechanical Properties*			
			Tensile treatment kg/cm²	*Yield strength kg/cm²*	*Elonga-tion%*	*BHN*
1.	Graphite + Ferrite	As-cast (for annealed)	5000	3500	20	180
2.	Graphite + Pearlite	Normalized and tempered (for as-cast)	8000	6000	6	279
3.	Graphite+ Tempered martensite	Quenched and tempered	10,000	8000	5	310

Table 14.3: Heat Treatment Problems, their Causes and Remedies

S.No.	Problem	Causes	Remedies
1.	Cracking	(*i*) Internal stresses resulting from thermal and structural stresses.	(*i*) Cool slowly in martensitic range applying interrupted quenching, oil quenching, martempering, etc.
		(*ii*) Failure in tempering just after quenching.	(*ii*) Temper before temperature reaches about 100°C.
		(*iii*) Improper quenching media.	(*iii*) Useless severe quenching media.
		(*iv*) Improper preheating.	(*iv*) Proper stress relieving is advised. Small holes in massive castings be plugged. Fixtures be used if necessary.
		(*v*) Higher hardening temperature causing grain coarsening of austenite.	(*v*) Check austenising temperature and normalise before hardening.
		(*vi*) Poor design	(*vi*) Avoid sharp corners, projections, abrupt changes in section.
2.	Distortion	(*i*) Transformation of retained austenite.	(*i*) Apply sub-zero quenching or multiple tempering.
		(*ii*) Overheating or under heating.	(*ii*) Check austenising temperature and control.
		(*iii*) Improper tempering.	(*iii*) Apply stabilising elements or sub-zero quenching.
		(*iv*) Severe quenching parctice.	(*iv*) Use less severe quenching media.

(Cont....)

S.No.	Problem	Causes	Remedies
		(v) Insufficient stress relieving.	(v) Apply stress-relieving before hardening.
		(vi) Unpredicted thermal stresses.	(vi) Use quench fixtures to balance the mass.
3.	Warpage	(i) Insufficient stress relieving.	(i) Apply stress-relieving before heat treatment.
		(ii) Stress reduced before non-uniform quenching (or heating)	(ii) Hold the casting in proper position employing spray or agitated quenching.
		(iii) Improper support during heating.	(iii) Support with bricks, used coke, cast iron, etc.
		(iv) Unbalanced design.	(iv) Use proper quenching, jigs, fixtures, and straighten the casting after treatment.
4.	Failure to fully harden	(i) Severe decarborisation.	(i) Furnace with controlled atmosphere or salt bath for heating be used.
		(ii) Non-uniform heating due to insufficient holding time of too low hardening temperature	(ii) Check austenising temperature.
		(iii) Tempering temperature and time too high.	(iii) Specified temperature and time to be used.
		(iv) Quenching not quite severe.	(iv) Use more drastic quench.

S.No.	*Problem*	*Causes*	*Remedies*
5.	Excessive or insufficient hardness after tempering	(*i*) Tempering temperature too high. (*ii*) Low tempering temperature or insufficient holding time.	(*i*) Anneal, reharden and temper at correct temperature. (*ii*) Second tempering with proper temperature and holding time be opted.
6.	Oxidation and decarborisation	Higher heating temperature and oxidising atmosphere in the furnace.	Use controlled atmosphere furnace or heat in boxes with carborising agent or cast iron chips of heat in salt bath.
7.	Soft sports	(*i*) Contaminated quenching liquid. (*ii*) Quenching bath too hot. (*iii*) Improper agitation. (*iv*) Decarborisation and excessive scale formation.	(*i*) Clean, filter, or change the liquid periodically. (*ii*) Check the martensitic transformation temperature. (*iii*) Use spray quenching or a liquid bath with proper agitating device. (*iv*) Use furnace with controlled atmosphere or heat in salt bath.
8.	Burning	Heating for longer periods at high temperature in oxidising atmosphere causes : (*i*) First stage of burning (grain boundaries enriched in carbon). (*ii*) Second stage of burning non-oxidised coolies and flowholes). (*iii*) Third stage of burning (iron oxide inclusions).	 (*i*) Use homogenising followed by double annealing. (*ii*) Forge and then anneal. (*iii*) No remedy.

QUESTIONS

1. Explain the difference between the heat treatment process of annealing and normalising for steel castings.
2. Give the heat treatment procedure for the following :
   (*a*) Aluminium alloy castings
   (*b*) Steel castings
   (*c*) Magnesium alloy castings.
3. Describe the process of producing malleable-iron castings.
4. Give in short the engineering properties on which the quality of structure of a casting depends.
5. Explain how the stress can be relieved from the casting.
6. Describe the heat treatment of non-ferrous alloys.
7. Write short notes on :
   (*a*) Annealing
   (*b*) Normalising
   (*c*) Quenching.
8. Write in short, heat treatment of
   (*a*) Grey cast Iron
   (*b*) Malleable cast Iron
   (*c*) Ductile cast Iron.

15

Modernization of Foundries

Introduction to Modernization

To an average person, a foundry conveys an idea of

(*i*) a dark, dirty and smoke-filled place carrying heaps of sand, coal, ashes, and metal at different places :

(*ii*) the persons working in a foundry sweating and breathing noxious fumes during the casting processes.

In many of the foundries in this country, such a picture exists upto the present day. Thus, there is a great need for modernization in this particular branch of industry.

Modernization, if adopted, finally leads to

(*i*) Increase in production.

(*ii*) Improvement in quality of the product.

(*iii*) Lowering down the cost of product.

(*iv*) Improving the working conditions in the shop so as to enable the workers to lead a safer, healthier and happier life.

To achieve the above aims, modernization can be carried out at a number of places in the foundry. Broad classifications of the fields in which modernization is possible are :

(*i*) Modernization in production methods and equipments for improving the production both qualitatively and quantitatively and lowering the cost of the product. This field of modernization is generally referred to as *'Mechanization of Foundry'*.

(*ii*) Modernization for improving the working conditions, which also help indirectly to increase production and lower the product cost.

Types of Foundries

Foundries are classified according to the nature of work undertaken by them and their organisational framework as under :

1. Captive foundries
2. Jobbing foundries
3. Production foundries
4. Semi-production foundries.

1. **Captive Foundries.** Such a foundry is an integral part of some manufacturing organisation. All the castings made in a captive foundry are consumed in the products manufactured by that organisation.

2. **Jobbing Foundries.** They generally produce small number of castings of a given type for different customers. Sometimes, they have facilities for mass production.

3. **Production Foundries.** They are highly mechanized and can produce castings economically on mass scale.

4. **Semi-production Foundries.** They are combination of jobbing foundry and a production foundry in respect of their nature of work. These accept both job work as well as production on mass-scale.

Also, foundries are classified as under :

1. Ferrous Foundries :

(*i*) Steel foundry (for plain carbon steel, low and high-alloy steels).

(*ii*) Grey cast iron foundry.

(*iii*) Malleable cast iron foundry.

2. Non-ferrous foundries :

(*i*) Aluminium and magnesium alloys foundry or light metal.

(*ii*) Copper, brass and bronze foundry.

(*iii*) Lead, tin and zinc-base foundry.

Plant Layout for Foundries

It is defined as a floor plan for determining and arranging the machinery and equipment of a plant, whether established or contemplated, in one best location, to permit the quickest flow of materials at the lowest cost and with least handling in processing the product right from receipt of raw materials to shipping of finished castings.

A plant with lower production costs and overheads is better able to maintain its relative production activity. For cutting down

production costs, all non-productive plant activities are eliminated or reduced to a minimum. A good layout provides for full utilization of available equipment for production, material handling devices, manpower effecting maximum saving in processing.

Advantages of a Good Layout in Foundries

(*i*) Effective Use of Available Area: Plant layout if well-planned offers an opportunity to place equipment and services in such a way that results in the most effective co-ordination. Locating equipment and services in such a manner that they can perform multiple functions, developing up-to-date work areas, and operator job assignment for full utilization of labour, tends to improve utilization of plant area.

(*ii*) Improved Utilization of Labour: Proper plant layout allows designing individual operations, the process, the flow and material handling in such a way that each workman is able to apply his activities to the best overall plant effort. Balancing labour to production needs to machine requirements eliminates situations where operator's time is not utilized to the maximum.

Laying out equipment for facilitating maintenance reduces the requirement of maintenance personnel. Improved handling leads to further incorporation of mechanical means minimizing requirements of both direct and indirect labour.

(*iii*) Improvements in Manufacturing Process: They may be both in method of processing and control of the process, which may result from :

(*a*) Reduction or elimination of delays by improved arrangement or better work balance between operators or machines.

(*b*) Smoother material flow in the process by analysing materials handling problems, incorporating new methods and equipment and incorporating techniques of automation or automatic handling thereby reducing interruptions in the flow.

(*c*) Improved control through methods for identifying, counting, and inspecting goods in process.

(*iv*) Improved Efficiency in Plant Service: It is obtained by considering problems of maintenance, service equipment and building during layout planning, improvement in utility distribution systems give maximum flexibility and facilitates future re-arrangement and expansion.

(*v*) Improvement in Materials Handling: It is improved by better location of equipment, reducing handling distances, and closely co-ordinating the entire handling activity. Application of

standardized materials handling units reduces the use of the variety of handling equipment, permitting greater flexibility without sacrificing efficiency and reducing investment.

(vi) **Minimum Equipment Investment:** Planned machine balance and location with minimum handling load distances, and planned machine loading reduce investment on idle or partially loaded units. This applies to service and maintenance equipment, materials handling equipment, office equipment and production machines.

(vii) **Improvement in Quality Control:** Good layout incorporates quality considerations so as to ensure maximum quality control and minimum cost. Analysis of production process necessary for proper plant layout requires determination of quality control factors and inspection locations.

(viii) **Improvement in Employee Moral:** Layout which provides for employee convenience and comforts inevitably boosts moral of employees, *viz.*, correct lighting, proper cooling and ventilation, noise and vibration control, sufficient and convenient rest rooms and lunch facilities lead to efficient job performance and reduced idle time.

Planning a Foundry Layout

To realise the maximum potential of a layout for a new foundry, a systematic procedure must be followed as under :

1. **Analysing the Product to be Produced** *viz.*,

(i) Annual tonnage.

(ii) Type of castings to be produced ; their range of sizes, weights, and composition.

(iii) Maximum piece weight.

2. **Determining the Process for Manufacturing the Product.** Operation sheets are prepared or developed for each product. For the purpose of layout, only the sequence of operations is required initially.

Castings are classified as light, medium, and heavy or according to the quantity required. Workplaces for moulding, core making, melting, inspection, etc., are logically located. Before deciding the details of layout, the various processes to be broadly considered first to suit the casting requirements are green sand, skin dried, dry sand, machine moulding, shell moulding, CO_2 process, etc.

3. **Preparing Layout Planning Charts.** These charts are very important as they serve as media for first tabulating and then combining various factors, *viz* ;

(*i*) Flow process showing all operations, moves, storages and inspection in sequence.

(*ii*) Standard times for each operation obtained from time study or pre-determined time standards.

(*iii*) Machine selection.

(*iv*) Machine balance.

(*v*) Manpower required.

(*vi*) Material handling load, method, and equipment required.

A full review and analysis is required at each step for completing the layout planning chart. After this, layout of manufacturing area involves primarily a conversion of layout planning chart data to the physical plant statistics.

4. **Determining Work Stations.** Requirements for machine, operator, materials, and service areas are determined by using man-machine and/or operation charts and scaled work station sketches/models.

5. **Analysing Storage Area Requirement.** Before actual layout both size and location of storage area is studied with relation to production activities. Three types of storage are generally included in the survey, *viz.* ;

(*i*) Storage of raw materials,

(*ii*) In-process storage, and

(*iii*) Finished goods storage.

6. **Determining Minimum Aisle Widths.** Clearance around various machines, equipments and between departments is determined before beginning layout. Aisle width, depend mainly upon materials handling methods and equipments, work station clearances, requirement and pedestrian traffic are carefully decided to avoid future production problems.

7. **Determining Office Requirements.** This will depend upon the scope of operational activities. Exact space requirements are worked out and provided in the layout.

8. **Considering Personnel Facilities and Services.** It includes allowing for such items as first aid, lunch and refreshment rooms, lockers, rest rooms, parking, etc.

9. **Surveying Plant Services.** This includes utilities *viz.*, compressor room, pump house, waste disposal equipment, maintenance, cooling, dust extraction and ventilation.

10. **Provision for Future Expansion.** It includes sufficient provisions for addition of new product lines or for increase in demand of existing product.

11. **Preparation of Layout Plan.** In this plan, locations of all plant and equipment, work stations, facilities, storage spaces, aisles, etc., are indicated clearly.

Foundry Mechanization

'*Mechanization*' is defined as utilization of machinery for performing the work previously done by hand. Machinery may be used for :

(*i*) Preparing sands.
(*ii*) Preparing moulds and cores.
(*iii*) Transporting and powering the molten metal.
(*iv*) Transporting the sands, moulds etc.

According to the quantity and type of production, the extent to which the mechanization can be adopted, varies considerably. In view of the economy and practical reasons, the scope of mechanization is limited. It is not recommended for small production work and for production of large sized castings. Mass-production foundries making large quantities of relatively few types of castings may be mechanized to a much larger extent or completely.

Figure 15.1 gives suggested layout for a mechanized foundry making only repetition work. Completely mechanized foundries are employed for making automobile parts, electric motors, portable tools, sewing machines, electric fans etc., where a repetitive work of mass production of small-sized parts is undertaken.

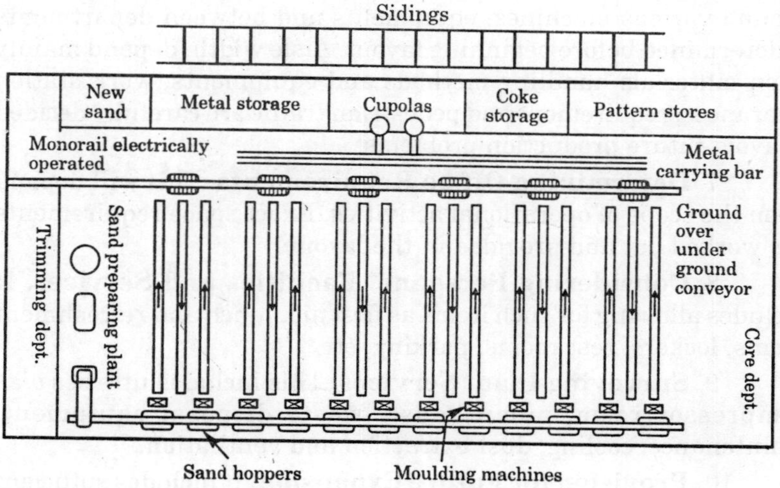

Fig. 15.1. Layout of Mechanized foundry for small repetition work.

Merits and Demerits of Foundry Mechanization

Advantages of properly planned and programmed mechanization are :

(*i*) Increased production from a given floor space.

(*ii*) Higher degree of accuracy, closer tolerance and better surface finish.

(*iii*) Many laborious manual operations *viz*., mixing and preparing sands, preparing moulds, handling of various materials etc., are eliminated. Hence, enormous saving of labour with consequent financial savings and faster work.

(*iv*) Due to increased production and better working conditions increase in the wages of the workers and rise in their standard of living.

Limitations or disadvantages of mechanization are :

(*i*) It is not adoptable for small jobbing foundries particularly those having little or no repetitive work.

(*ii*) The use of machines and consequent saving in labour gives rise to unemployment or retrenchment of workers.

(*iii*) Substitution of machines in place of men causes a gradual disappearance of the art of hand moulding.

Elements of Mechanization

(*i*) Mechanized sand preparation units.

(*ii*) Dust and fumes control equipment.

(*iii*) Moulding and core making equipment.

(*iv*) Melting, pouring and shaking out units.

(*v*) Material handling equipments and conveyor systems.

Sand Preparation Units

The sand mixture then prepared by mechanical equipment contains thoroughly distributed moisture. It is free from lumps and is delivered in a '*silky*' condition. Equipments used in the sand preparation works are :

(*i*) Magnetic Separator, (*ii*) Gyratory Riddle,

(*iii*) Rotary Sand Kicers, (*iv*) Sand Muller.

(*v*) Screenerator or Sand Aerator,

(*vi*) Sand Disintegrator,

(*vii*) Sand Reclamation Units.

Magnetic Separator. The moulding sand, which comes from the shake-out station, is made free from all iron particles and foreign matters before reusing it. Magnetic separator separates the iron pieces, wire nails iron shots etc., from the sand.

Magnetic separator consists of a magnetised pulley over which rolls a flat rubber or canvas belt. The pulley may be either or permanent magnet type or of electromagnet type carrying D.C. magnetising coils.

Working. As the beft rolls over the pulley, the sand and non- magnetic particles fall freely off the belt vertically downwards. On the other hand, the ferrous objects tend to cling to the belt due to magnetising effect and drop off only when the belt has left the pulley.

Gyratory Riddle. After the iron pieces are separated the sand is usually passed through a screen or riddle for removing the pieces of dry sand core, hard lumps or sand and other refuse.

Mechanical or gyratory riddle (Fig. 15.2) can screen the sand at much higher speed as compared to hand riddles. For a production foundry, they are a must.

Working. These riddles are operated by compressed air or electric motors. The pneumatic riddles which are operated by compressed air, consist of an air cylinder, a reciprocating piston and a screen fitted to the end of the piston. The reciprocating action of the piston moving through a very short stroke length causes screening action of the riddle.

Fig. 15.2. Gyratory Riddle.

In the case of riddles which are operated by electric motors, the action is due to gyratory motion. The screen is supported from a frame to which is also attached an electric motor. An unbalanced wheel is attached to motor shaft. As the shaft rotates, it causes the wheel to move out of balance. This gives, a wobbling motion to the screen.

In production foundries, the riddles having revolving or deck type screen are used. These can handle larger quantities of sand in a shorter time.

Rotary Sand Kicker

A definite improvement over hand mixing is use of a rotary sand kicker which straddles long heaps of sand, previously moistened with water, and mixes the mass with vigorously rotating blades as the machine moves along the row.

Sand Muller (Fig. 15.3)

'*Mulling*' is the process of kneading and working sand for the purpose of distributing the ingredients into a homogeneous mixture. The function of muller in a foundry is to condition the moulding sand for making it fit for reuse.

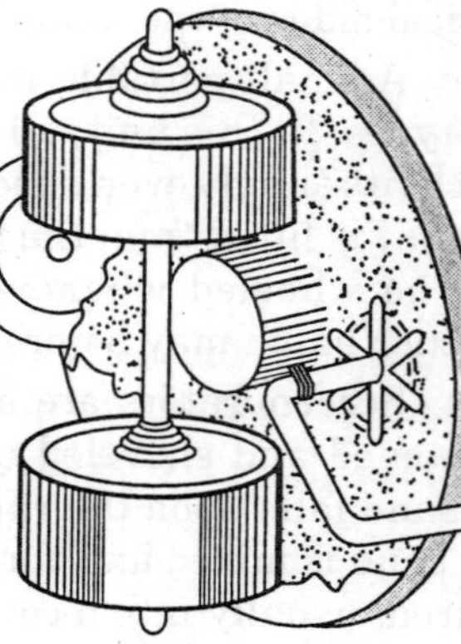

Fig. 15.3. Sand Muller (Rotating pan type).

The muller generally consists of a cylindrical pan in which two heavy rollers roll in a circular bath about a vertical rotating shaft. Two ploughs are also carried with the rollers. They scrap the sand from the solids and bottom of the pan and bring in the front of the rollers.

The rollers are set slightly off the true radius so that they move out of centre and produce a smearing action on the sand. They are mounted on rocker arms so as to enable them to move up and down according to the quantity of sand in the pan. However, in order to prevent crushing of the sand grains, they are kept raised by about 6 mm from the base of the pan in the lowest position.

Generally, the muller is equipped with cooling arrangement for cooling the sand and adding moisture if necessary. If required, binders etc., are also added to the moulding sand before mulling. After mulling the sand is discharged through a door in the case of the pan. Figure 15.3 shows a small sized muller equipped with cooling mixer having a holding capacity of 15,000 litres.

Modern sand mixers, or '*mullers*', operate on one or two general principles in which tempering and mixing are accomplished :

(*i*) With thick rimmed, heavy, metal wheel rotating relatively slowly over moistened mixtures, of sand and clay.

(*ii*) With lighter, thinner, rubber-covered wheels spinning rapidly over and through the mass.

In the former type, the wheels are always rotated with their axes horizontal and the full weight of the wheels on the sand. The wheels may move with the pan held stationary, or the wheels may be mounted rigidly with the pan rotating. In either case, the wheels are not power-driven but are rotated by friction against the sand. Power keep the sand stripped and in position under the wheels.

In the latter type (high speed unit), the wheels rotate with their axes vertical and the sand is stirred vigorously against the vertical sides of the mixer shell.

A small portable unit is a compromise between the above two types. In this unit, all working parts are mounted into a cover which fits snugly over specially shaped wheel barrow. After mixing the unit is lifted from the wheel barrow by crane. The mixed sand may be wheeled whenever it is required in the foundry shop. Another batch may be prepared in a second wheel barrow.

Screenerators are often used as mixers. After use, sand is moistened and shoveled upon a vibrating screen, through which the sand falls upon the rapidly spinning, wheel or belt (Fig. 15.4). The sand is mixed and thrown from the belt or wheel into a pile as desired, usually into a corner of the shop or against a three-sided backboard.

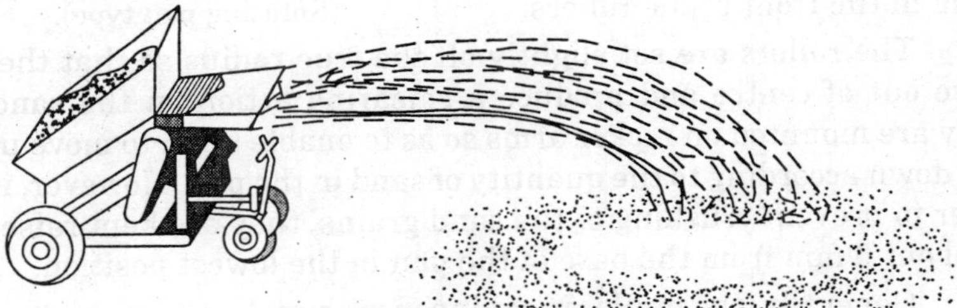

Fig. 15.4. Screenerator.

Aerator

After conditioning the sand in the muller, it is sent to an aerator in which the sand grains are separated and each grain is made to flow freely and smoothly in the direction of ramming.

The capacity of the moulding sand to flow freely around the pattern and get packed is termed as *'flowability'*. Aerating improves the flowability of sand.

Mechanical aerating is accomplished by whirling the sand at a high speed by an impeller or rotating paddles towards the

inner walls of the casing. Rotating paddles consists of a set of rods, each having a number of combing figures arranged radially.

The aerator may either be

(*i*) In the form of a separate unit, in which the mulled sand is charged through a hopper from a bucket, or

(*ii*) It may be attached directly to the outlet of the muller. In this case, the mulled sand passes through the aerator and is discharged through a door in the bottom of the aerator casing.

In heavy duty type sand aerator known as '*Sand Disintegrator*' the sand is fed to a charging hopper from where it falls into the pin baskets. The sand is seized by the pin baskets rotating in opposite direction and is loosened, aerated and cooled. The sand so prepared ensures the manufacture of perfect moulds with smooth surfaces.

Considerations while Preparing Sands in Mechanised Foundries

(*i*) Whatever type of mixer is used, care must be taken to remove large, hard lumps of sand and metal pieces. For this purpose, equipment is sometimes simple like vibrating screens, or eleborated like magnetic separators, crushers etc.

(*ii*) Core sands can be mixed in any of the above units or in spug mills or bakery-type mixers. Core sands and moulding sands are usually mixed in separate units to avoid contamination.

(*iii*) Fundamental purposes of mixing are considerably different between moulding and core sands, *viz*.,

(*a*) In moulding sand, the energy of mulling is required to plasticize the clay and hasten the absorption of water by clay.

(*b*) In core sands, it is only necessary to coat the sand grain as uniformly as possible with oil and water, or with resin.

(*iv*) A typical mulling cycle comprises addition of a weighed amount of sand of the mixer together with predetermined amounts of clay and other dry ingredients. They are mixed dry for about 2 minutes in the slow-speed mixer. After this water is added and mulling continued for about 5 minutes. For high-speed muller times are correspondingly shorter.

Reclamation of Sands

It is the process of restoring used foundry sand to as nearly its original condition as possible.

Methods of reclamation of sand, are classified as :

(*i*) Dry reclamation,

(*ii*) Wet reclamation,

(*iii*) Thermal reclamation,

(*iv*) Combined Wet (or Dry) reclamation plus Thermal reclamation.

Applications. (*i*) Sand reclamation is desirable only when the cost of operation does not greatly exceed the cost of new sand *i.e.,* it must not exceed the cost of sand plus freight charges.

(*ii*) It is indicated only when sand is used in relatively large quantities and is principally applicable to synthetic-type sands.

(*iii*) It is particularly applicable to steel foundries where much new sand must be used for facing each new mould.

Limitation. In natural sands, complete reclamation, in which all clay and residue is washed from the grain, will be expensive in terms of wasted clay which may be as high as 12 to 18% compared to 3 to 4% bentonite in synthetic sand.

Advantages of Reclaiming Sand

(*i*) Properly reclaimed sand is equivalent in performance to new sand in all respects.

(*ii*) Problem of finding places to dump huge quantities of used sand is solved. Expensive loading and hauling of used sand eliminated.

(*iii*) Expensive and troublesome storage of new sand in quantities is eliminated. Thus, huge inventories are not required.

(*iv*) Extremely high freight costs of new sand are saved.

(*v*) By reclaiming all sand, there is tendency to skimp on the use of new sand facing to the determinent of casting quality.

(*vi*) Storage of reclaimed sand is automatic. Thus, the troublesome task of unloading cars of sand is obviated.

(*vii*) Sand (by reclamation) is available at constant moisture content and of consistent quality particularly grain size and grain size distribution.

For imparting properties like green and strength, collapsibility, permeability and flowability and for modifying mould-metal interface reactions or for adjusting grain-size distribution, materials like fire clay, bentonite, lignins cereal binders, linseed and proprietory oils, starches, resins, iron oxide, wood floor, etc., are added. These materials form a coating around each sand grain. This coating varies in thickness.

(*i*) with the amount of these materials added, and

(*ii*) with the number of times the sand is used without reclaiming.

Dry Reclamation of Sand

It removes fines like silica flower, spent and free clay, finely fractured sand grains, and iron oxide particles.

Iron and steel particles are usually removed by magnetic separators. Lumps are crushed and screened. In simple dry reclamation, the aim is achieved by screens and air separation. By using pneumatic scrubber, tenacious coatings on the sand grains are partly removed.

In one type of dry reclamation system, iron and steel particles are first removed by magnetic separation and used sand is fed to a scalping screen. Lumps left on the screen are either discarded or crushed and rescreened. The sand passing through the screen enters the pneumatic sand scrubber unit, where the grains are repeatedly picked up and rubbed against each other to scrub off the coatings. Sand grains now travel to an outlet while fines and dust are separated from the air.

Limitations. It does not restore the sand to its initial quality since some clay and organic and carbonaceous materials may cling to individual sand grains.

Wet reclamation of Sand

In its purpose, it is similar to dry reclamation. *i.e.,*

(*i*) to remove fines and foreign materials, and

(*ii*) to clean the individual sand grains to tenacious coatings.

In a well-designed wet reclamation units, complete removal of clay is obtained. In one type of such unit, used sand is first passed through a magnetic separators and screens, as in dry reclamation. It is, then, mixed with water to form a slurry, passed to a primary classifier for removing fines and to a wet storage tank.

The sand-water slurry next enters one or more sand scrubbers which rub the sand grains against one another for removing the adherent clay. Sand scrubber is simply a tank with a large propeller immersed in it. The propeller rotates at high velocity in the sand-wear slurry, creating the '*, ubbing*' action.

The slurry now moves to a secondary classifier for—

(*i*) removing fines created in the cleaning operation,

(*ii*) obtaining the desired sand grain-size distribution.

In the end, water is removed from the sand by a filter and drying unit.

Limitations. Wet reclamation does not, however, restore sand to its original quality. Some carbonaceous and organic residues remain on the individual sand grains.

Thermal Reclamation of Sand

It comprises of heating used sand to 650–800°C in furnaces which are usually of multi-hearth type. Carbonaceous and organic material are removed effectively by this treatment, *i.e.*, burning. Oil-bounded sands having no clay bond can be fully reclaimed. To assure proper grain-size control of the used sand, thermal reclamation sould be combined with screens and classifiers.

Applications

(*i*) This system has been used with success in several non-ferrous shops, which perform predominantly oil-core moulding.

(*ii*) It is also effective for reclaiming shell mould sand.

Limitations. There is little effect on the clay loading of sand grains. The furnace heat may make these coating bond still more firmly to the clay. It is, therefore, not adequate for most shops because it does not remove clay.

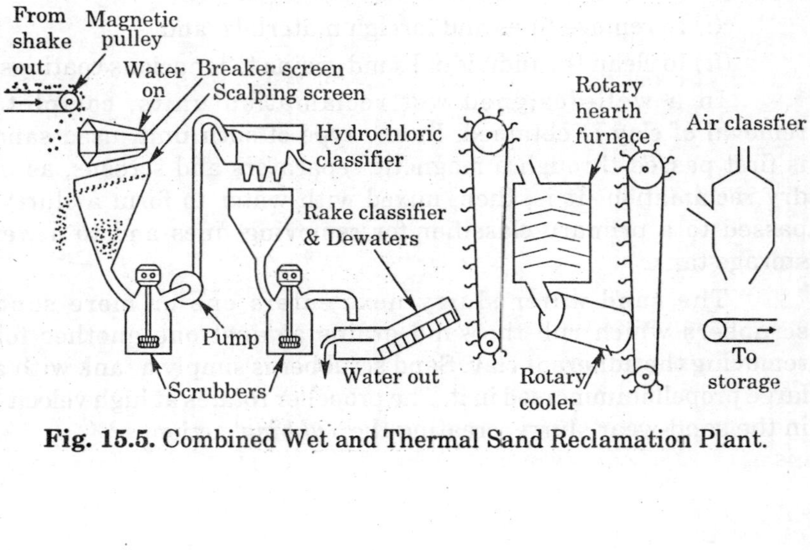

Fig. 15.5. Combined Wet and Thermal Sand Reclamation Plant.

Combined Wet and Thermal Sand Reclamation

In this system, the benefits of both thermal reclamation and wet reclamation are realized, and reclaiming foundry sands to their original quality is possible.

Characteristics

(*i*) Fines, adherent clay, organic and carbonaceous material are all removed.

(*ii*) Except for a slight iron strain and slight pitting and etching of the individual grains, the sand is restored to its original grain size, shape, and distribution, and the castings made from such reclaimed sand are fully as good as those made in new sand.

Figure 15.5 illustrates a combine wet-thermal system for complete sand restoration. Components of the wet system are similar to those described earlier.

The used sand, after passing the wet portion of the system is classified and dewatered. It then enters a rotary multi-hearth furnace for thermal treatment at 650 to 850°C. Finally, the sand is cooled, reclassified and stored.

Equipment for Fume and Dust Extraction

When a fully mechanised scheme is designed, the question of fume and dust extraction must be borne in mind so that this plant may be suitably located in the general layout. This problem must be considered at the following main points :

(*i*) At the pouring point.

(*ii*) The knock out and knock out belt.

(*iii*) Screens.

(*iv*) Bucket elevators.

(*v*) Chipping or fettling benches.

(*vi*) Grinders.

At the pouring point, various methods of extraction are in use. Where a continuous power mould conveyor is used, it is usual to provide a continuous extract hood on the far side of the mould conveyor opposite the ladle.

To ensure that all fumes are drawn into the extraction duct, the velocity of the air being extracted through the grills is calculated. Under these conditions, fresh air is injected into the foundry at this point. The duct is situated over the extraction duct and directed

down towards the bottom. Thus, an air curtain is provided within which fumes are trapped avoiding the draughts produced by the constants air extraction from the building.

At the knock-out, a similar system may be provided for access to the grid top after placing the ducting and hoods in position, is possible. If this is not possible, an extraction may be arranged immediately below the grid. The latter system has disadvantages that (*a*) a great deal of sand may be extracted and (*b*) the extraction headers may be blanked from the fumes by the knocked-out sand.

The dust carried a way from these extraction point is collected and disposed off in a number of ways, the most simple being the cyclone.

The cyclone is of cylindrical shape. The dust laden and contaminated air enters at the bottom where it is given a whirling motion due to which the heavier particles of dust separate at the bottom. Air is then allowed to rise in a spiral fashion through plates while water flows downwards. Thus, a resistance in the passage of air is created. Air is completely cleaned and washed by this process. Clean air is led out into the atmosphere and the contamination collect at the bottom from where they are removed periodically.

Necessity of Dust and Fume Control. Dust and sand particles are charged in the air during (*i*) mixing and sand preparation, (*ii*) moulding work, (*iii*) fettling and shake-out operation.

Fumes are produced during melting and pouring operations. Some molten metals like lead and its alloys produce very poisonous fumes. These fumes as well as dust particles should be collected and the air should be maintained clean in the foundry shop for healthy working conditions.

Equipment for Moulding and Core Making

The basic requirement of a mechanised foundry is suitable machines for moulding and core making. These machines are designed for performing most of the work previously done by hand. They help in

(*i*) Making moulds faster.

(*ii*) Producing castings to a greater degree of accuracy and uniformity.

(*iii*) Making use of semi-skilled workmen.

(*iv*) Lowering the production cost.

Different types of Moulding Machines are discussed below. The operations performed by these machines include—

(*i*) Ramming the moulds either by jolting, squeezing, slinging or a combination of the first two.

(*ii*) Rolling over the mould, rapping the pattern, drawing the pattern from the mould and placing the mould on a roller conveyor for sending to drying section or to assembling section.

Depending on the design of the moulding machine, it performs one or more of the above operations.

Machine Moulding

Production of uniform castings by hand moulding from loose patterns requires considerable moulding skill :

(*i*) to make the joint,

(*ii*) to draw the pattern correctly without enlarging the mould cavity, and

(*iii*) to cut the ingates and risers.

When large quantities of castings are required, moulding machines are employed, the patterns mounted on plates with runners and risers attached. For snap flask work on squeeze machines the pattern plate may be double-sided, *i.e.,* carry the drag portion of the pattern one side and the cope portion on the other side.

Moulding processes may be classified according to whether the mould is prepared by hand tools or with the aid of some moulding machine as

(*i*) Hand Moulding.

(*ii*) Machine Moulding.

Hand moulding is generally found to be economical when the castings are required in a small number.

When similar castings are required in large quantities, hand moulding being more time taking and laborious, becomes expensive. Moreover, for making a good mould by hand, considerable skill is needed. Machine moulding is generally employed at such places.

There are many types and makes of machines, all of which have their particular application. There is no universal machine which will efficiently make every type of mould. The use of machine in the foundry has made it possible for the industry to compete on a sound basis with other trades, like steel and brass stamping, bakelite and similar plastic moulding.

Moulding machine is a machine for producing moulds by applied mechanics. Objects are (*a*) to eliminate manual fatigue and

(*b*) to remove the necessity for skill in producing a good mould. With the simpler types of machines, these objects are only partially attained. For obtaining efficient outputs, a certain amount of energy and skill is necessary. The production of a mould entails two main operations to perform :

(*a*) Ramming the sand to a correct density.

(*b*) Removing the pattern from the mould.

Advantages of Moulding Machines

There are factors other than quick production which are advantageously gained by the use of moulding machines :

(*i*) *Uniform density of mould hardness,* resulting in a correct standardization of casting finish.

(*ii*) *All runners, ingates and risers can be moulded.* The correct size of gating is very important, and obviously, difficult to reproduce manually with accuracy on individual moulds. For machine moulding practice, the correct size and type of gate is established and mounted on the pattern plate resulting in a correct reproduction with each mould.

(*iii*) *Correct shape and size of the finished casting.* Very often with hand moulding work, castings gain in size and weight owing to excessive rapping by the moulder for drawing the pattern clearly from the mould. With a machine-operated pattern draw, this enlargement of the mould size is eliminated.

(*iv*) *Long life of the pattern equipment.* Loose patterns made of mahogany, or pine, rapidly deteriorate owing to the fact that they have to be rapped and spiked for drawing them from the mould. Such damage is eliminated by machine-moulding.

(*v*) *Less skilled worker can do the job,* whereas in hand moulding, greater skill is required.

(*vi*) Machining allowance may be reduced.

(*vii*) Due to steadier lift of the pattern from a machine ; less taper is required for machine made moulds, and great accuracy secured in core fitting.

Classiffication of Moulding Machines

The moulding machines may be broadly classified into two categories :

1. Hand operated Moulding Machines.
2. Power operated Moulding Machines.

Hand Operated Moulding Machines or Hand Moulding Machines. In these machines, one or more of the operations like ramming, pattern drawing, moulding, mould rolling over, etc. are performed by the machines which is manually operated either by a hand lever or pedal control. These machines do not make use of any external power. The operation of drawing the pattern is performed mechanically and more accurately than is possible by hand, but the actual ramming is a manual operation.

According to the type of operation performed, the hand moulding machine may be of :

(*a*) Pattern-draw type, or

(*b*) Pattern draw and Squeeze type.

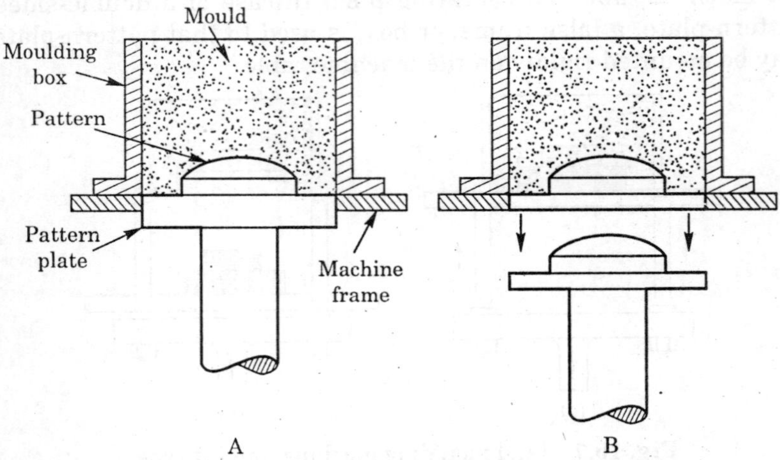

Fig. 15.6. Principle of working of plain stripper type pattern-draw head operated moulding machine.

A–Position during ramming.

B–Pattern withdrawn.

Pattern draw hand operated moulding machines make use of suitable arrangement for withdrawing the pattern from the mould after ramming the sand. Pattern draw arrangement may be one of the following types :

(*i*) **Plain stripper type pattern draw machine** consists of a stationary frame or table which supports the flask, a moveable pattern plate on the top of which the halved pattern is screwed, and an arrangement for moving the pattern-plate consisting of a rack and pinion or an arm and a lever.

For ramming, the pattern plate is kept in raised position, the flask located over the machine frame, and the sand is filled in and rammed by hand ramming.

For withdrawing the pattern, the pattern-plate is lowered by pressing the foot-pedal or lowering the hand lever, the flask remaining supported on the machine frame.

The flask, which carries the sand mould, is then removed from the frame and sent to the casting section.

(*ii*) **Pin-lift or push-off type pattern-draw or straight-draw machine.** In this arrangement, pattern-plate along with the pattern remains stationary while the moulding box complete with the sand mould is raised, being supported on four pins passing through the pattern-plate.

A single sided pattern plate is employed, and this is fixed to the machine table with locating pins. In case of a double-sided pattern-plate, a false frame, or box, is used to that pattern-plate may be mounted rigidly on the machine table.

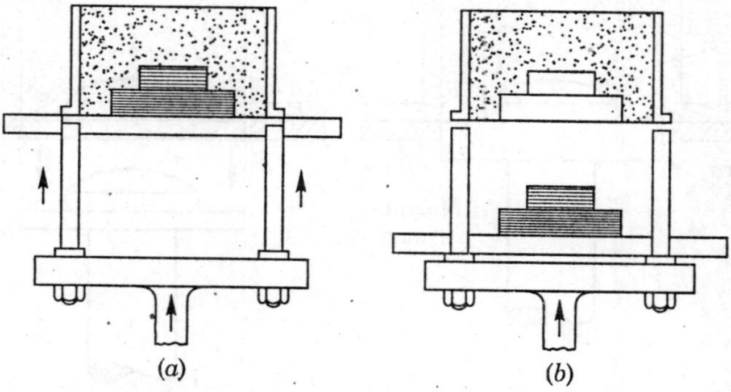

Fig. 15.7. Hand moulding machine. pin lift type.
A–Ramming position.
B–Ejector pins have moved upwards to push or lift the mould away from the pattern.

After fixing the pattern-plate securely to the table, the moulding box is placed on the locating pins and filled with sand, rammed up and strickled off as usual. Runners, risers, venting etc. is then made. Machine is now ready for performing its part of operation. The lever which lifts the box off the pattern, is moved slowly and at the same time, the operator raps the table or pattern-plate with a mallet. Rapping is continued until the mould is drawn clear of the pattern, when the lever is operated more quickly until the maximum movement is obtained.

The mould will remain in the topmost position without holding the lever. Thus, the operator can remove the mould off the machine on to the floor, or conveyor. Then the operating lever is

returned to its original position and machine is ready for dealing with the next mould.

(*iii*) **Roll-over type pattern draw machine.** In this arrangement, the moulding box is clamped to the pattern-plate having pattern half attached to it. The pattern-plate, which carries the pattern, can swivel on two trunnions fixed on two sides. After filling the sand and ramming by hand, the whole assembly of the pattern plate, pattern and moulding box is rolled over and brought into horizontal position.

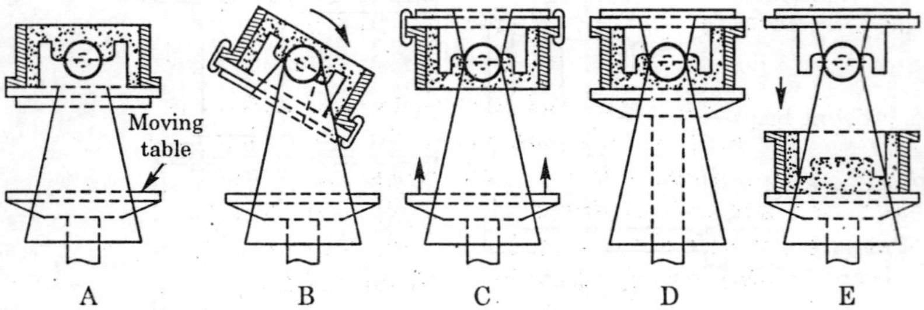

Fig. 15.8. Hand moulding rollover machine.
Mould lowered away from the pattern.
A–Hand ramming position.
B–Mould clamped and being rolled over.
C–Mould rolled on over hand plate locked.
D–Moving table raised to receive mould.
E–Moving table and mould lowered away from pattern.

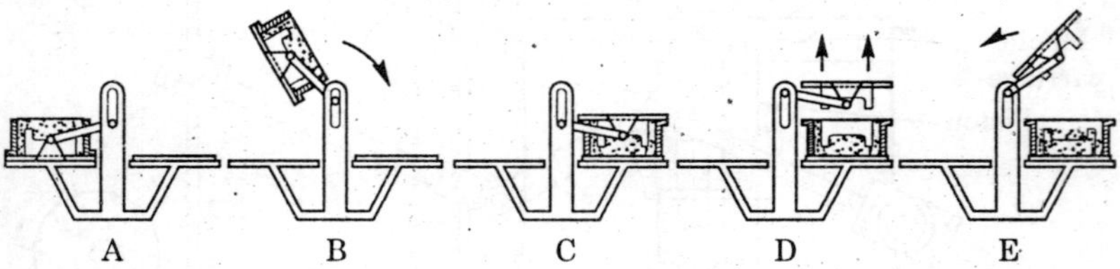

Fig. 15.9. Hand-moulding rollover machine.
Pattern drawn upwards from the mould.
A–Ramming position.
B–Rolling over.
C–Mould resting on equalized table.
D–Pattern drawn upwards from mould.
E–Pattern rolled back to ramming position.

The table underneath the mould is then raised till it comes in contact with the box. Now, the clamps are released and the table along with the mould lowered, leaving the pattern and the pattern

plate in the inverted position (Fig. 15.9). The up and down motion of the table is obtained by means of toggle lever action.

In some hand-operated moulding machines, there is also a provision for ramming the sand mechanically by means of squeezeaction. One of such machines in which pattern withdrawal is combined with the ramming operation, is shown in Fig. 15.10.

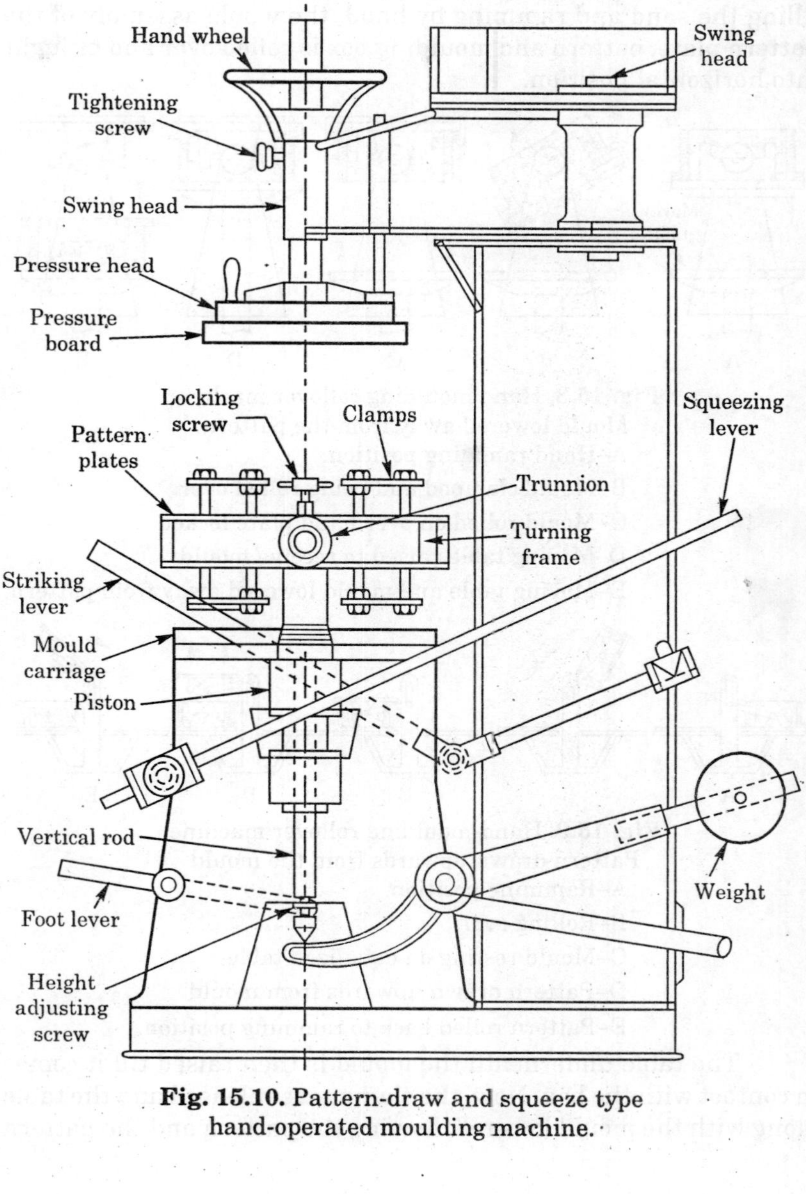

Fig. 15.10. Pattern-draw and squeeze type hand-operated moulding machine.

This machine consists of a C.I. column to which following are supported :

(*i*) Squeezing mechanism.

(*ii*) Pattern drawing mechanism.

(*iii*) Turnover type frame for mounting boxes.

(*iv*) Swing type pressure head.

The squeeze piston operates in a cylinder by a combination of toggle lever and track and pinion mechanism. The squeeze-action is obtained by pressing a hand lever. The pattern is drawn by foot pedal which actuates two vertical pins supporting the turning frame. The turnover unit holds two snap type moulding boxes, one on either side by means of quick acting clamps.

The unit can be located positively after turning in horizontal position. A pattern-plate is screwed on each side of the frame and to each of the pattern-plate, one halved pattern is attached.

For ramming the sand, the squeeze-plate is fixed to the swinging type pressure head. To suit the depth of squeeze, the pressure head can be adjusted in height. It can also be swung clear of the moulding box by rotating it through 90°.

Power Operated Moulding Machines

Power-squeeze and ramming machines, operated compressed air, hydraulic power, electromagnets, or a high-speed impeller, reduce the labour of ramming. On certain patterns some hand tucking of the sand and hand ramming into difficult position may be necessary, and operations such as stricking off the excess sand must be carried out by hand. These machines generally make use of pneumatic or hydraulic action for performing various operations during the moulding process *e.g.*,

(*i*) Raising or lowering the table for pattern withdrawal.

(*ii*) Ramming the sand by squeeze, jolt or combined squeeze and jolt action.

(*iii*) Rolling over the moulding boxes, etc.

The manual labour and fatigue is very considerably reduced and the production rate of moulds is greatly increased due to the use of external power. These machines are also named after their principal functions like hand moulding machines, *e.g.*, pneumatic jolt roll-over pattern-draw machine in which the sand is rammed by jolting action with the help of compressed air, the mould inverted and the pattern drawn out mechanically.

Moulding machines working on a present automatic cycle are also available. Various operations required for preparing the

mould are performed automatically one after another in proper sequence and the moulds, which are ready for assembling, are passed on from machine to a conveyor for transporting to the mould assembling and pouring section.

In these machines, the arrangement for pattern drawing is basically similar to that used in hand moulding machines. Three principal methods for ramming the sand are employed :

1. By squeezing.
2. By jolting.
3. By slinging.

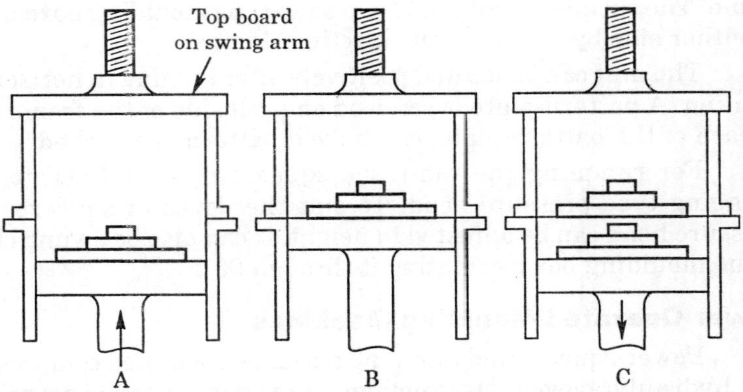

Fig. 15.11. Power-squeeze machine. Using down-sand frame.

A–Before squeezing the pattern is below the mould joint. Distance 'A' is adjusted until the squeeze action produces a level mould joint.

B–After the surplus sand has been squeezed upwards into the mould.

C–Pattern drawn from the mould on the return stroke.

1. Ramming by squeezing. In this method, the flask is filled level with the moulding sand and the sand is squeezed by a pressure board using hydraulic or pneumatic pressure till the desired density is attained by the mould. In some cases, electromagnets are used for obtaining the squeeze action.

Limitations of the Squeeze Method

(*a*) By squeezing, the sand is packed more densely at the top where the squeeze board presses against the sand and the density decreases uniformly with depth. The density is found to be at the parting plane. The hardness of the mould is thus affected by the variation of density, *i.e.,* it varies with the depth.

(*b*) Squeeze method is, therefore, limited to moulds not more than 150 mm is depth.

(*c*) Where the moulds contain green sand cores, this method is not satisfactory because the sand cannot flow into the core cavities of the pattern and may remain loose near the cavities.

2. **Ramming by Jolting.** In this method, the flask is filled with the moulding sand and the table supporting the flask is then raised mechanically and dropped in succession. The sand gets rammed due to sudden change in inertia at the end of each fall. The action of raising the table and dropping it is called '*Jolting*'. By varying the height of the stroke, the amount of sand heaped on top of the mould and the number of strokes, the density and hardness of sand can be controlled. This method is in more general use than squeeze method.

Limitations of Jolting Method

The drawback with this method is that the sand is rammed hardest at the parting plane and around the pattern and remains less dense in the top layers. Hand ramming of the mould at the back after completing the jolting action is, therefore, necessary.

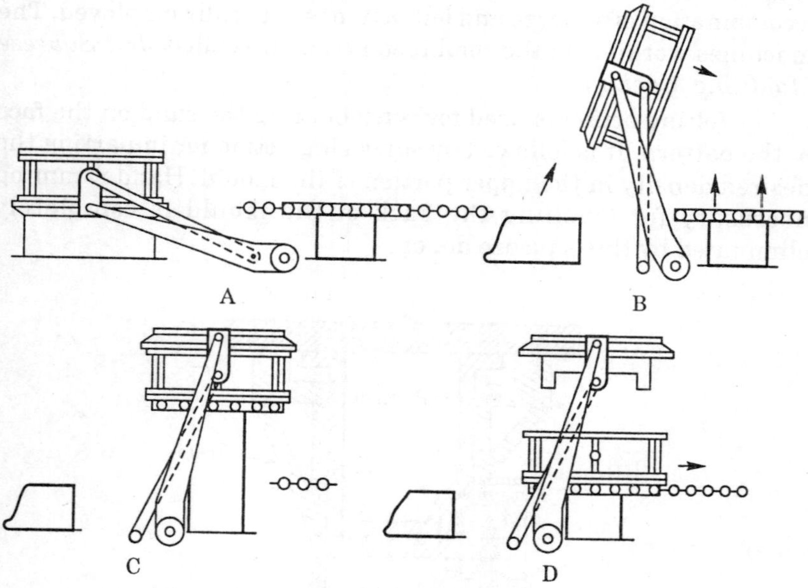

Fig. 15.12. Jolt-ram, Pattern-draw machine with roll-over attachment.

A–Mould rammed and plate clamped ready for rolling over.
B–Mould being rolled over.
C–Equalizer table raised to receive mould.
D–Mould lowered away from pattern. Pattern and machine plate rolled back to the jolting position.

Working Principle of Jolting Machine

The table, which supports the moulding (Fig. 15.3) box, is mounted on a cylinder called '*Jolt cylinder*'. The cylinder is raised and dropped in succession by the entry and exit of compressed air underneath its base.

When the cylinder is in dropped position, it presses against a value causing it to open and allowing the air to enter the space underneath the cylinder base. High pressure air causes the cylinder to rise till it uncovers an exhaust port when the air rushes out and pressure falls down.

As the cylinder drops down, it again presses against the valve and opens the air entry. The jolt cylinder along with the table are thus raised and lowered in quick succession to produce the desired jolting action.

3. **Ramming by Jolting and Squeezing.** For overcoming the drawbacks of both squeeze and jolt principle of ramming and to obtain uniform density and hardness in all portions of the mould, a combination of squeeze and jolt action is generally employed. The machines working on the combined action are called '*Jolt-Squeeze Moulding Machines*'.

Jolting action is used for consolidating the sand on the face of the pattern. It is followed by squeezing action for imparting the desired density in the upper portion of the mould. Hand ramming necessary for levelling the back of the mould is completely eliminated by this squeeze action.

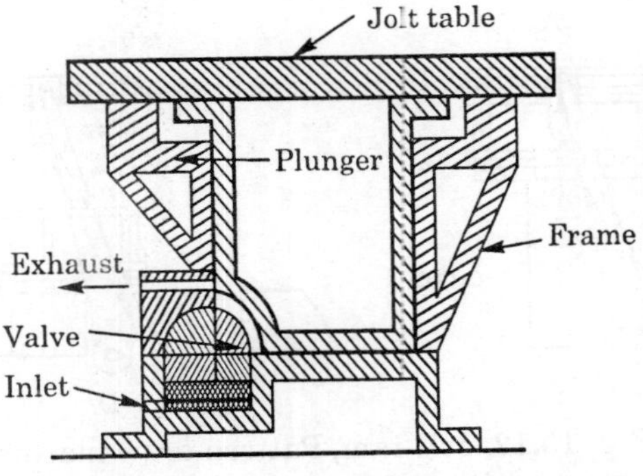

Fig. 15.13. Principle of working of Plain jolting moulding machine (Working on compressed air).

Figure 15.14 illustrates the operation of Jolt-squeeze-roll-over moulding machine :

A– The pattern, mounted on two sides of a match-board is placed between the empty cope and draw flask, with the drag side up. The drag half of the flask is filled with sand, and assembly jolted.

B– After striking off, a squeezer plate is placed over the drag and the assembly inverted.

C– The cope half is then filled with sand and both halves are squeezed simultaneously.

D, E– Finally, the cope is removed automatically, the pattern drawn from the drag by hand, and any necessary finishing of core settling is done before reclosing.

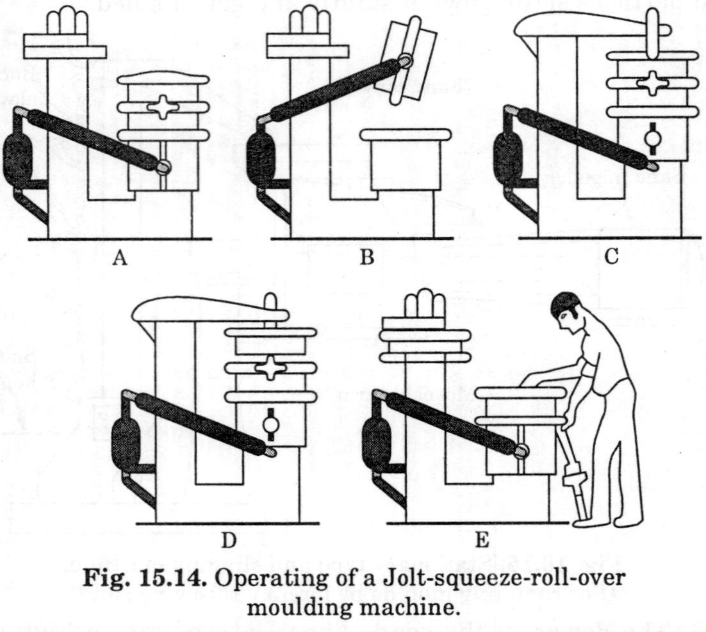

Fig. 15.14. Operating of a Jolt-squeeze-roll-over moulding machine.

Jolt-squeeze moulding machine is so constructed that both jolt and squeezing actions are obtained one after the other. The table is attached to a cylinder piston called the '*jolt piston*'. This piston is raised and dropped in the jolt cylinder by the action of compressed air. The jolt cylinder is an integral part of the squeeze piston and the latter can move up and down due to air pressure in the squeeze cylinder. Upper surface of squeeze piston remains in contact with the bottom of the table.

During jolting action, the squeeze piston lies solidly on the base of its cylinder, and lift of the jolt piston causes the table to rise.

During squeezing action, the jolt piston and cylinder side along with the squeezing piston, thus, raising the table through the desired height. This method combines the advantages of (1) and (2) and produces a mode uniform hardness throughout the mould.

4. **Ramming by Slinging.** Figure 15.15 shows the main parts of a stationary sand slinger. In slinging operation, the consolidation and ramming of sand is achieved by means of impact with the pattern.

Basically, the sand slingers consists of an arrangement for throwing a stream of sand at a high velocity downwards through a slinging head on to the pattern. Owing to the rapid ejection, the sand particles settle down instantly and get rammed.

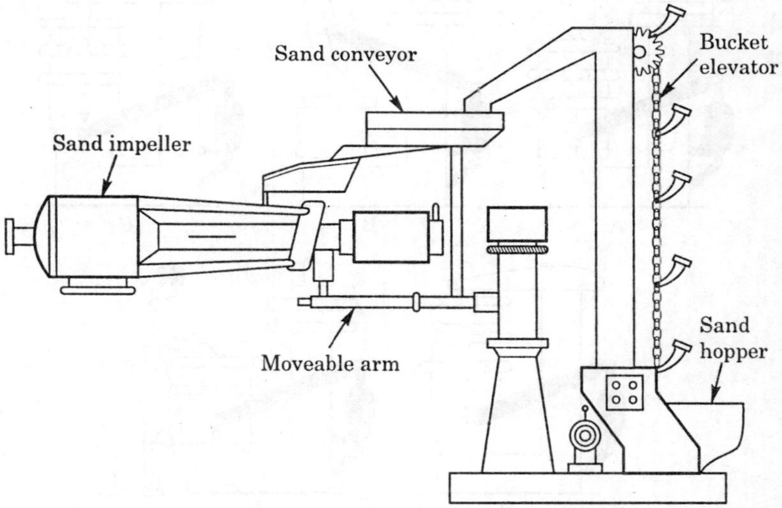

Fig. 15.15. Stationary type and slinging machine.
(For ramming moulds by forcibly throwing sand)

The design of the sand slinger incorporates a high speed rotary impeller, pipes, a band conveyor, bucket elevator and an ejecting head attached to a swivelling arm. For attaining uniform density of sand all over the mould, the ejecting head can be moved over all the parts of the mould box.

Moulding sand is thrown in small handfulls by means of a high-speed rotary impeller plate or cup. Very high rates of ramming are achieved upto 0.35 cubic metre per minute, and it is customary to provide each sand slinger with its own sand preparation plant or to provide an ample supply of sand by conveyor belt from a central sand plant.

The head of the sand slinger must be kept moving to obtain a satisfactory and uniform mould hardness ; sand collecting in a pile leaves soft places in the mould. More sand slingers are used in iron than in steel foundries.

There are three classes of sand slingers :

(*i*) A stationary type with sand-conveyor system,

(*ii*) A tractor type, which cuts its way through and reconditions the sand heaps as it goes along, and

(*iii*) A portable type, which can be slung by crane to any part of the foundry.

Mobile type large sized sand slinger suitable for a steel foundry is equipped with hydraulically controlled lifting unit, interchangeable sand pin and electrically driven transporting bogie. Its capacity may be about 20 cubic metres per hour and arm length of about 6 metres.

Mechanical Production of Cores

Operations required to produce a core are :

(*i*) Place sand in core box and ram firmly and evenly,

(*ii*) Finish off core flush with top open edge of box,

(*iii*) Place core plate in position on top of core,

(*iv*) Turnover core box and plate,

(*v*) Vibrate,

(*vi*) Withdraw core box, leaving core silting on core plate,

(*vii*) Pass core to stove.

First operation in the making of core, *i.e.,* the ramming of the core sand can be accomplished by four methods :

(*i*) Hand-ramming of the sand into the core box,

(*ii*) Blowing of sand into core box,

(*iii*) Jolting of the sand in the core box,

(*iv*) Vibrating and compression by squeezing sand into core box.

Like moulding machines, a number of types of machines have also been developed for rapid production of cores. Suitability of a particular type depends on the following factors :

(*i*) Number of cores required.

(*ii*) Size of cores.

(*iii*) Intricacy and design of cores.

Core making machines commonly used are :

1. Core blowing machine.
2. Core drawing machine.
3. Continuous core making machine.
4. Roll-over core-box draw machine.
5. Jolt roll-over or ; Jolt pin-lift core-box draw machine.
6. Sand slinger for cores.

1. Core Blowing Machine. In a production foundry, coreblowing machine is an indispensable equipment for core making. Core sand is forced into the core box from a sand reservoir with a stream of high velocity air at a pressure of about 55 to 70 gm per sq. mm. The core box has a number of vent holes suitably located so that on intoducing the sand, the air may be ejected through these holes. The sand is packed instantly in the core-box due to high velocity air.

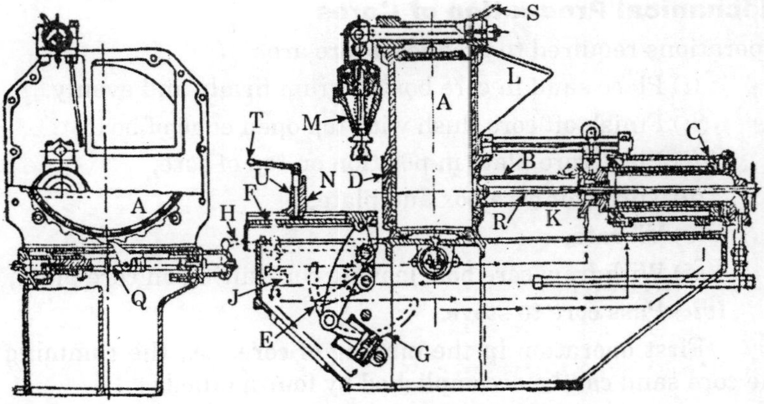

Fig. 15.16. Core-blowing machine.

A–Container drum	B–Cartridge
C–Main cylinder	D–Blowing plate
E–Cam lever	F–Table
G–Table cylinder	H–Operating valve lever
K–Shooting valve	L–Hopper
M–Upper clamping piston	N–Table clamp
Q–Drum turning piston	S–Lever
T–Bolt	U–Safety stop.

Core blowing machine shown in Fig. 15.16 is suitable for core boxes of maximum dimensions as follows :

Height 350 mm, length 500 mm, width 250 mm. Capacity of sand drum 200 kg, and that of sand cartridge 1200 gm. Consumption 1 cubic metre of free air per minute.

Working. For operation, the core-box is placed on the table *F* with the sand entrance of the box in line with the nozzle of the blowing plate *D*, the table being adjustable for different heights of core box by means of the cam lever *E*. Upper clamping piston *M* is positioned by the handwheel so that the ball clamp is about 20 mm from the top of the box. This clamp should be over the middle of the box, and can be moved longitudinally by loosing the lever *S*, and sliding the bearing rod to the required position.

The table clamp *N* should be brought up to the back of the core box, leaving about 20 mm clearance for the clamp operation. The clamp is then screwed down tightly to the table by means of the bolt *T*, the safety stop being inserted in the dowel holes immediately behind this clamp. The handle of the operating valve *H* is then turned through 90° from the '*off*' position, actuating both the upper clamping cylinder *M* and the table cylinder *G*, the cartridge *B* moving forward, and being filled with sand from the container seal moving the rubber ring in the blowing plate.

The handle *H* is then momentarily depressed to open the shooting valve *K*, allowing the air in the main cylinder *C* to eject the sand from the cartridge through the blowing plate into the core-box. The valve lever *H* is turned to the '*off*' position, so as to release the core clamps and return the cartridge, the drum-turning piston *Q* being at the same time actuated automatically, so as to allow the sand to fall, and fill the cavity left by the extrusion of the cartridge.

When the capacity of the box exceeds that of the cartridge, additional '*shots*' can be given by returning the valve handle only 45° back from the '*on*' position, then, after the drum has rotated, returning the handle to the '*on*' position and repeating the blowing operation. By returning the valve handle only half-way back, the cartridge is returned without releasing the clamp. The container drum *A* can be refilled through the hopper *L* without stopping production, and should always be kept as full as possible while blowing.

Useful Hints and Suggestions for Overcoming Snags and Difficulties in the Technique of Core Blowing

(*i*) Core boxes should be checked periodically to see that joints are in good condition and that, if possible, the end at which the box is blown is at exact right angles to the bottom of the box.

(*ii*) Always have plenty of sand in the machine, otherwise air will quickly become worm.

(*iii*) Owing to even ramming and greater permeability of the core, venting is not always necessary.

(*iv*) A blown core in its green state is softer than a hand rammed one, but after baking the core will be at least twice as strong.

(*v*) A worn hole appearing in a core is often due to the core box not being a good fit at the joint, or the box not square on the machine, and thus sand leaking from the box.

(*vi*) Soft sport appearing on a core are usually due to,

(*a*) Air being traped in the box. This is overcome by drilling a hole at the affected place and inserting a vent specially made for this purpose.

(*b*) Sand by passing at the place where the core is soft. To overcome this, direction of the shot may be altered so that sand is blown direct against the affected spot. Any sharp corners may be slightly chamfered.

(*vii*) Blowing nozzle of the machine should be as small in diameter as the smallest diameter of the core box, when this diameter is in direct line of shot. If this is not done, the box may tend to be blocked before the core is fully blown.

(*viii*) Use a small diameter nozzle for blowing a long core and as big a nozzle as possible on block cores.

(*ix*) Wires should be dispensed with. But, this depends entirely upon each particular core in regard to casting conditions, etc. However if wires are necessary, they can be either placed in the core after blowing or by fixing small pegs in the box to hold the wire in position while blowing. These pegs if possible, should be filled in the box print.

Core drawing Machines

These machines facilitate in drawing off the core boxes from the cores, particularly for core boxes with deep draws. The core-box with core sand duly rammed in, is placed on a core-plate which is supported on the machine bed. From one side, the core-box is placed in contact with another vertical plate. This vertical plate is vibrated so as to produce a rapping action on the core-box.

After rapping the core-box is raised leaving the core on the core-plate. Sand is rammed by hand either with a hand hammer or

a pneumatic rammer. Portable type penumatic rammer is particularly useful for core making and moulding work as it is a very handy, convenient and simple tool.

Continuous Core making Machines

These machines are used for preparing cylindrical cores of uniform section in various sizes. Cylindrical cores, being most commonly used are prepared in long lengths on these machines and are kept in stock. Such cores are, therefore, called *'Stock Cores'*.

When a core of a certain diameter and length is required, the same is taken out of the stock, cut to desired length and used after having tapered down the ends.

For preparing the stock cores, the core sand is filled in a hopper of the machine. From the hopper, it comes into a cylinder. It is then forced from the cylinder through a die of the desired size by a horizontal rotating screw.

Roll-over Core-box Draw Machines

These machines are just like the *'roll-over pattern-draw hand moulding machines'* except that these are of smaller size and are used for withdrawing the core-box from the core.

Jolt roll-over or Jolt pin lift core-box Draw Machine

This machine again is similar to the corresponding machines described under *'moulding machines'*.

In general, these machines are similar in size and often the various operations *viz.*, jolting rolling over, drawing etc, are performed by hand.

Sand Slinger for Cores

Sometimes, a sand slinger similar to the one used for moulding work, is used for medium and large sized cores. Usually, it is of the stationary type. It differs from the core blowing machine in that the sand is forced into the core-box by means of an impeller. On the other hand, in the core blowing machine, the sand is forced directly by the air pressure and no moving part like impeller etc., is used in the machine.

Recirculating Drying Stove

All modern ovens employ forced-drought air circulation for giving at least 20–30 air changes per hour, this is essential for the

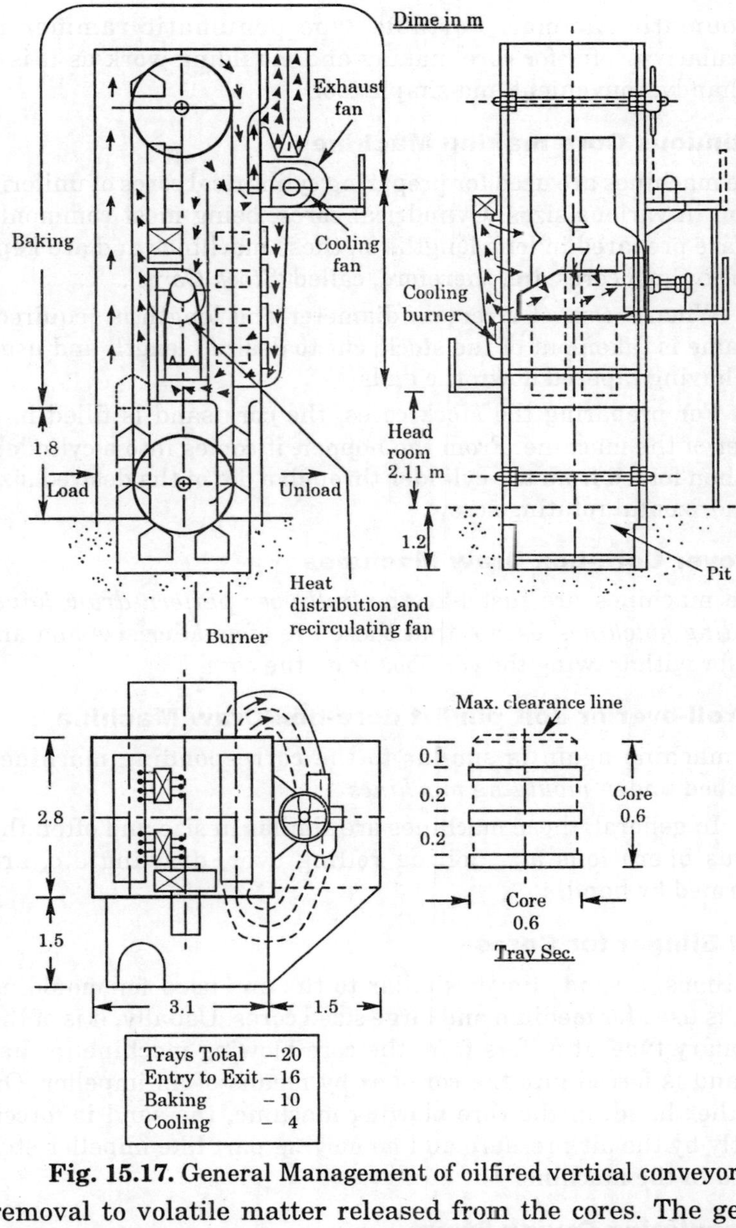

Fig. 15.17. General Management of oilfired vertical conveyor.

removal to volatile matter released from the cores. The general arrangement of an oven of vertical conveyor type is shown in Fig. 15.17.

High velocity air circulation enables to maintain a constant temperature throughout the whole of the drying or baking zone, and answers a rapid transfer of heat to the work, and thus a minimum baking time.

When the amount of work is sufficient, it is obviously most economical to segregate, in separate ovens, the cores required short, medium and long baking cycles. Partial cooling of cores after baking is achieved by extending the conveyor beyond the heated baking zone, through a chamber cooled by natural draught, before unloading.

For complete cooling, additional forced draught cooling air is essential, and it is sometimes preferable to allow a length of cooling conveyor equivalent to that employed in the baking zone.

Types of core stoves. The type of stove to be used in any particular foundry depends on the class of core and the quantity of core made. Various type designed for this purpose are :

1. Drawer-type stoves.
2. Batch-type stoves.
3. Continuous-type stoves.

1. **Drawer-type stoves.** A core shop engaged on medium quantities of small core installs a coke or gas-fired drawer-type of stove. This stove consists of a heated chamber into which are fixed a series of shelves, or trays. It is so designed that one drawer, or tray, can be withdrawn, cores loaded or unloaded, and the drawer replaced without undue loss of heat.

The heating of the drawer of fixed tray type core stove can be from a coke fired unit from which hot air is circulated evenly, and a constant temperature maintained. This type is made with gas burners as an alternative method of heating.

For larger quantities of cores of possible greater varieties in size, a fixed-shelf type of core may be used.

2. **Batch type stoves.** For drying the large quantities of varying shapes and sizes of cores, a series of batch-type core ovens should be installed. Batch type core oven is a permanent brick-built oven so designed that a rack of cores to be dried may be placed into the oven, the doors closed and then, after a predetermined time, the rack can be withdrawn and replaced by another rack of core so brought on a bogie.

Batch-type stove is usually heated by a coke fire box, with suitable fan and damper arrangements to enable each of the stoves in the series to be maintained at any required temperature. The

flues are usually built into the base. Each stove has a hot-air inlet at the back of heating chamber and two exhaust outlets to a suitable chimney at the front of the chamber floor. Doors of these stoves are of a balance-weight type, which lift vertically. They are, however, securely held in their working position by cam-type retaining clamps.

3. **Continuous-type stoves.** For foundry engaged on mass production of cores of uniform size and type, a continuous type of drying stove should be installed. It consists of a vertical steel chamber ; into this two steel chains are fixed by means of steel shafts and sprockets at the top and base of the stove. A series of steel carriers are slung between these chains.

The operation is such that at the base of the stove, the carrier is loaded with cores. The rack, of carrier, is then slowly lifted into the heating zone, and is allowed to pass through this heat for a period of time which can be regulated. This time varies from one to three hours. The carrier then travels round the stove and returns to its original position. Cores can then be unloaded and further cores placed on to the carrier for drying.

The heating of a stove is by a fire box from which hot air is blown into the heating oven above the loading position of the stove vertical type stove assures a continuity of core-shop operations and provides maximum core drying in a minimum of floor space.

In certain core shops mechanization has been such that core drying is done through continuous stoves which are built horizontally and through which a pendulum conveyor passes. Cores, after being made, are placed on a series of pendulums. These pendulums pass through a horizontal chamber heated to a specified temperature. Conveyor speed in conjunction with length of core stove is such that cores are allowed the correct baking time.

For large cores, logic-type stoves are essential. These stoves consist of heating chamber, governed to temperatures of 260 to 265°C, giving suitable quantities of circulating air. Large cores are loaded on different types of logics made to suit the particular stove conditions.

Core shop Mechanisation. Mechanical aid can be used in the core shop for the following operation :

(*i*) Unloading of sand from transport vehicles into storage hoppers.

(*ii*) Drying of moist silica sand and conveyance of dried sand to storage hoppers above the mixers.

(*iii*) Sand mixers.

(*iv*) Delivery of mixed core sand to core makers.

(*v*) Delivery of finished cores from core maker to drying stoves.

(*vi*) Handling of cores from drying stoves to finishing and inspection section.

(*vii*) Return of core plates to core makers.

Sand for mixing of oil sand must be dried before use, and, therefore, any mechanisation in the core shop must cover sand drying equipment. Various types of Sand Drivers are :

(*i*) Rotary kiln or revolving-drum type drier.

(*ii*) Vertical cone-shaped drier.

(*iii*) Horizontal stationary-type drier.

Dry sand storage hoppers should be placed above the oil sand mixers, and be so arranged that measured batches of sand can be fed into the oil-sand mixers. Handling of mixed oil-sand is achieved by one of the following methods :

(*i*) Rubber belt conveyor

(*ii*) Bucket type conveyor

(*iii*) Batch trucks and logics.

Plant layout in core shop governs the method which is employed to deliver the mixed sand to the core makers.

Mechanical Handling of Cores

1. **Before stoving.** Mechanical handling can be applied after the cores are made and have to be transported to the core stoves, as follows :

(*i*) Using batch-type stoves and a portable core rack, placed along side core maker's bench. Core maker places the cores on the rack. When full, rack is conveyed by a special bogie to the core stove, and an empty rack placed alongside the core maker.

(*ii*) Transporting cores by roller tracks (conveyors).

Drawback is that green sand cores collide and distort from coremaker's benches to core stoves due to bumping.

(*iii*) The ideal method transporting green cores to the core stove is by means of a steel band conveyor.

(*iv*) Pendulum, or suspended-tray type conveyors may be used for conveying the cores from coremaker's benches to the point at which they are lifted off into the stoves.

In some cases, pendulum conveyor may pass through a horizontal type drying stove.

2. **After stoving.** As cores are taken from the stove, they are placed on a conveyor, preferably of the pendulum type, which, if correctly arranged, allows the necessary cooling time before they arrive at the inspection and dressing department.

Turntables

For large scale production of castings, use of turn tables provides a highly mechanised system. A turn-table consists of a circular revolving platform on which a number of moulding machines are mounted. Pattern-draw type moulding machines are used and sand ramming is carried out by a stationary sand slinger.

As the turntable revolves at a slow speed, several operations for preparing the mould are performed. In this case, each worker has to perform only one operation. So, he quickly becomes familiar with the same ; thus helping in production of castings at a very rapid rate. Using turntable saves floor space considerably.

Melting, Pouring and Snake-out Units

In the proceeding pages, various equipments used for melting have already been discussed. The type of melting equipment needed depends on the factors *viz.*,

(*i*) Metal to be melted.

(*ii*) Quantity of metal required.

(*iii*) Quantity and purity of metal desired.

(*iv*) Availability of fuel.

Recent Cupola Development—Type of Cupolas

In recent years, there have been several developments in cupola practice. They have come into use primarily because of increased labour and material costs :

1. **Water-cooled Cupolas.** In this type, the melting zone is water-jacketed or the steel shell in this zone is water-sprayed. Water cooling saves both refractors and maintenance costs. Water cooled copper tuyeres are also often used. On large cupolas, say over 90 cm inside diameter, savings are worthwhile.

Water-cooled is justified where more than eight hour's operation is required. In special cases, upto one week's operation or more has been obtained without dropping the bottom.

2. **Hot Blast Cupolas.** The addition of hot blast has been increasing steadily for economy in coke and to permit of a higher proportion of steel scrap being used in cupola charges. Hot blast enables.

(*i*) poorer quality cokes to be used,

(*ii*) reduces the loss of silicon in the cupola,

(*iii*) increases carbon pick-up.

Three different systems of preheating are :

(*i*) **Air Preheater System.** A specially designed air preheater heated by oil, gas or other fuel is used. It is normally a tubular type heat exchanger in which fuel is burnt in a combustion chamber and the products pass over either the outside or inside of the tubes, the air blast passing over the other surface.

(*ii*) **Combustible content of waste gases from cupola and their sensible heat utilized to heat the blast.** About 95% of the top gases are drawn through a combustion chamber and burnt with air. The products of combustion pass through a metal recuperator to heat the blast.

(*iii*) **Gases drawn off the cupola through a off-take just above the melting zone and their sensible heat used for preheating the blast by a recuperator.** Hot blast system described (*ii*) is most used :

Top gases from a cupola normally emerge at 350°C to 500°C. They usually contain 12 to 16% carbon monoxide. Their sensible heat and calorific value together amount to about 1600 B.Th. U. per cubic metre. These gases are drawn off below the charging level by means of gas off takes. The charging opening is narrowed drawn forming a construction, so forcing the gas through the recuperative system.

The hot gases usually pass through a dust catcher which may be in the form of a cyclone. Then, they pass through a combustion chamber located just ahead of the recuperator without much loss in temperature.

Types of Recuperator. Two types of recuperator in use are :

(*i*) Radiation type. (*ii*) Covection type.

(*i*) **Radiation Type Recuperator.** It consists of a heat-resisting steel cylinder of 60 to 100 cm diameter through which the hot gases pass and radiate on to the cylinder walls. Air is passed in contraflow around the outside of this cylinder. The air passage is

formed by putting a cylinder of slightly large diameter outside the inner, or '*radiation receiving*' cylinder. Space between the two cylinders called '*annulus*' is small enough to ensure fairly high air velocity. This air is given a spiral or vertical flow by means of guides.

All hot gas ducting is lined with insulating bricks and hot-blast main insulated on the outside. A chimney is normally mounted on the type of the radiation recuperator for increasing the draught. For controlling this draught (regulating the proportion of gas passing through the recuperative system) a stack damper is installed. About 75% of the cupola top gases pass through the recuperative system and the balance passes out through the cupola charging opening and then to the stack, keeping a pressure at the charging level and preventing air being drawn into the system.

(*ii*) **Convection Type Recuperator.** It usually consists of a tubular heat-exchanger in which the products of combustion of the top gases either pass through the tubes, or over the outside of the tubes, the air passing over the other surface. In a convection recuperator, the resistance is much higher than in a radiation recuperator. Generally, an exhaust fan is provided for sucking the gas through the combination chamber and recuperator.

Most of the heavy dust is removed in the dust catcher. Recuperator element also accumulate dust. To avoid impairing the efficiency of heat transfer, means for cleaning out the dust at intervals, are provided.

Large cupolas have no open mouth for charging, but a closed top with a bell and hopper system is provided. In this case, all the gas is passed through the recuperative system.

Advantage of Hot-blast Cupola

(*i*) Reduced coke consumption.

(*ii*) Ability to use low-grade high ash cokes.

(*iii*) Ability to melt and carburize a higher proportion than normal of steel scrap for manufacture of C.I.

(*iv*) Reduce silicon loss.

(*v*) Ability to produce higher casting temperatures.

All these advantages cannot be obtained at the same time *e.g.*, if lowest coke consumption is required, then the steel scrap proportion should be curtailed.

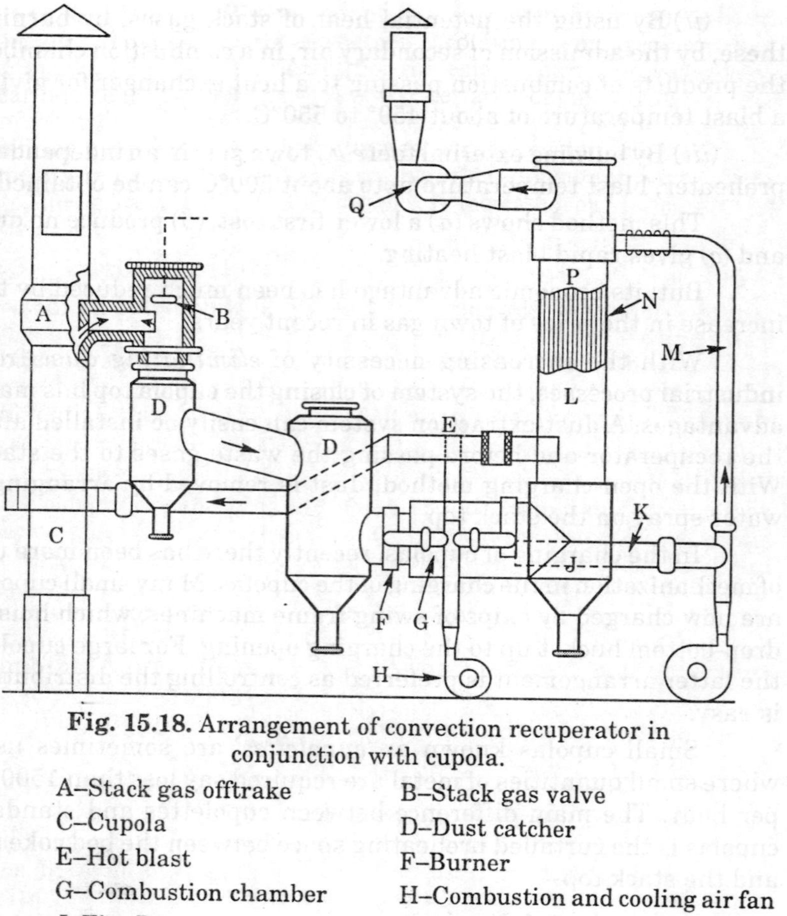

Fig. 15.18. Arrangement of convection recuperator in conjunction with cupola.

A–Stack gas offtrake	B–Stack gas valve
C–Cupola	D–Dust catcher
E–Hot blast	F–Burner
G–Combustion chamber	H–Combustion and cooling air fan
J–Fire Box	K–By pass
L–Combustion gas	M–Cold blast
N–Air flow	P–Convection recuperator
Q–Waste gas fan.	

Blast preheating can be effected :

(*i*) By using sensible heat of stack gases, by circulating air for combustion through tubes or chambers around the cupola shell for producing blast temperatures upto about 300°C. For obtaining a much higher temperature, some of the gases are bled off through a off-take situated just above the melting zone.

The gases pass around the outside of the tubes in the recuperator. After two reversals of direction through three banks of tubes, the blast enters the wind belt at a temperature of 450° to 550°C.

(*ii*) By using the potential heat of stack gases, by burning these, by the admission of secondary air, in a combustion chamber, the products of combustion passing to a heat exchanger for giving a blast temperature of about 450° to 550°C.

(*iii*) By burning external fuel *e.g.*, town gas, in an independent preheater, blast temperature upto about 500°C can be obtained.

This method shows (*a*) a lower first cost, (*b*) produce no dust and (*c*) gives rapid blast heating.

But, its economic advantage has been much reduced by the increase in the price of town gas in recent years.

With the increasing necessity of *eliminating dust* from industrial processes, the system of closing the cupola top has many advantages. A dust-extraction system can easily be installed after the recuperator and before passing the waste gases to the stack. With the open-charging method, dust is removed by arranging a water spray on the stack top.

In the charging of cupolas, recently there has been more use of mechanization in the charging of the cupolas. Many small cupolas are now charged by skips of swing frame machines, which hoist a drop-bottom bucket up to the charging opening. For large cupolas, the latter arrangement is preferred as controlling the distribution is easy.

Small cupolas known as '*cupolettes*' are sometimes used where small quantities of metal are required say less than 1500 kg per hour. The main difference between cupolettes and standard cupolas is the curtailed preheating space between the bed coke top and the stack top.

Cupolas using Auxiliary Tuyeres

This type of cupola has apparently since been abandoned ; and today is merely a matter of historic interest. In this cupola, there were in addition to the main tuyeres, auxiliary tuyeres disposed spirally up the stack.

In this design, incomplete combustion in the lower part of the cupola was deliberately aimed at, with intent to avoid oxidation. The arrangement of the auxiliary tuyeres was considered to promote fractional combustion of the carbon monoxide higher up the stack, so as impart extra heat to the descending charges, for promoting a higher tap temperature and a greater fuel economy.

It was claimed that success or failure of regenerative tuyeres was entirely a question of position and arrangement.

Balanced Blast Cupola

Principle of Operation is that of controlling the air supply at the main tuyeres by means of individual screw valves on each tuyere. These valves are fitted to the wind belt and control the air supply to the bottom row of tuyeres. Two rows of small auxiliary upper tuyeres are provided above the main air valves and also draw their air supply from the wind belt.

This auxiliary tuyeres are not regulated like the main air valves, but the amount of air admitted at each can be adjusted during the initial melts ; after which they require no further adjustment. Air supply is divided between the main and auxiliary tuyeres by setting the main air valves. Closing these results in less air passing through the main tuyeres and more through the auxiliary tuyeres, and *vice versa*. Thus, air can be adjusted between the main and auxiliary tuyeres to suit different working conditions ; and hence the term *'Balanced-blast'*. For producing iron of the required temperature with the most economical coke consumption, there is an optimum setting of the main air valves.

Advantages. (*i*) Reduced coke consumption.

(*ii*) Lower sulphur pick-up.

(*iii*) Ability to melt successfully charges with large proportions of steel scrap.

(*iv*) Higher initial tap temperature and maintenance of a high temperature at the spout throughout the melt.

Cupolas using Oxygen Enriched Blast

Much information has been published on the use of oxygen enriched blast in cupola melting in recent year. Air contain 80% by volume of nitrogen, which is of no use in the combustion of coke and also exerts a cooling effect in melting. The addition of 1% of oxygen to the blast is thus equivalent to an increase of 5% in the volume of air delivered to the cupola.

The advantages claimed for using oxygen are generally similar to those obtained in hot blast melting, comprising :

(*i*) A saving in coke.

(*ii*) Ability to use coke of poorer quality.

(*iii*) A reduction in initial melting time.

(*iv*) An increase in melting rate and top temperature.

(*v*) An increassed carbon pick-up.

(*vi*) A reduction in the loss of silicon and manganese, and in overall melting loss.

(*vii*) A reduced sulphur pick-up.

(*viii*) Slag is more fluid and there is less tendency towards bridging.

Limitations : (*i*) Lining wear is increased, chiefly due to the increase in temperature.

(*ii*) Use of oxygen is economically less favourable in steel making, because of the smaller oxygen consumption too small for cheap generation and two large for using oxygen cylinders.

Applications : (*i*) Continuous use of oxygen enriched blast appears not to be economical in its present stage of development. But, it can usefully be employed as a '*booster*' for the first tap of the day's operation.

(*ii*) When the cupola is operating irregularly and the metal tapped is below normal temperature, the introduction of oxygen into the blast will rapidly restore the cupola to normal operation. For this purpose, a battery of cylinders, with regulating valves, should be employed.

(*iii*) In a jobbing foundry producing thin walled grey iron castings, it has been found very useful to inject cylinder oxygen into the blast pipe upto 4% enrichment for a period of 3 to 5 minutes whenever it is necessary to increase tap temperature.

The intermittent injunction help to prevent bridging, but does not remove it once it has started. Oxygen enrichment is more effective with a positive displacement blower than with a fan.

(*iv*) Oxygen is sometimes injected into the molten metal help in the receiver, for the purpose of superheating. Use of 5.6 cubic metres of oxygen per tonne of iron is said to raise the bath temperature by 80°–100°C.

8–10 cubic metres per tonne bring the metal temperature to 1500°–1520°C, when carbon begins to burn vigorously. With iron initially at a temperature of 1380°C, the carbon can be reduced by 0.2 to 0.3% by injecting 7–10 cubic metres per tonne.

Oxygen pressure should not be less than 5/6 atmospheres, the size of oxygen nozzles varying from 2-3 mm for a melting rate of 3 tonnes per hour, to 4 to 5 mm for one of 8 tonnes per hour.

Mechanical Devices to Minimize Manual Labour

In a mechanized foundry, suitable means should be employed for minimising the manual labour and substitute it with mechanical

devices as far as possible. The extent to which such means may be employed depend on factors *e.g.*,

(*i*) Type and condition of equipment.

(*ii*) Economical feasibility of installing such means.

(*iii*) Floor space available.

These mechanical devices vary from equipment to equipment. In general, they are used for the following operations :

(*i*) Handling the charge *e.g.,* pig iron, coke, flux, etc. and bringing it near the furnace for charging ; using a crane, lift truck, turnover truck, belt conveyor or bucket conveyor system.

(*ii*) Sending the charge upto the charging door as in a cupola and discharging it into the furnace. Generally, a skip-hoist type conveyor is used for sending the charge up. This arrangement consists of a charging bucket mounted on wheels and is guided by a vertical or inclined track. The bucket is raised or lowered along the track by a reversible electric motor through a cable.

When the bucket reaches the charging door, it operates an electrical limit switch which braces the motor instantly and after some time lag, reverses it. The bucket is lowered in a pit for convenient loading.

For large size cupolas, conveyance of crane type is used, *i.e.,* the bucket is raised by a crane from the loading station and carried into the charging door horizontally.

Two types of Discharge Bucket for Charging

(*i*) *With Skip-hoist Arrangement.* Top discharging bucket is used which is automatically inverted as it enters the charging door of the cupola.

(*ii*) *With Crane-type Arrangement.* Bucket is bottom-discharge type. In this case, the bucket has a hinged bottom door which swings open for discharging.

The arrangement with either top or bottom discharge bucket is commonly employed for open-hearth furnace, air furnace and electric furnaces.

Molten metal is taken into ladles and carried to the pouring floor by means of a crane. The metal may be poured.

(*i*) Keeping the ladle stationary in the crane and moving the moulds one after the other on a roller conveyor, or

(*ii*) Keeping the moulds in a line and moving the ladle every time a mould is filled with the metal.

When castings have cooled down sufficiently, the moulds are carried by a crane or conveyor to a '*shake-out station*'. Here, the moulds are vibrated or shaken in such a way that the castings along with the sand come out of the moulding boxes.

Shaking operation is performed on a grating having a sand conveyor underneath. Sand separated from the castings passes through the gate and is carried to sand reclamation plant. Castings and emptied moulding boxes remain on the grating. Castings are then sent to the fettling and inspection shop and moulding boxes are returned to the moulding section.

Shake-out Machines are of many types :

(*i*) *For small sized moulds,* a stationary grating installed at a small incline may be used. When moulds are jarred and dropped on the grating, the grate allowing the sand to pass through the grating and the casting, moulding box, bottom board etc., remain on the top.

(*ii*) *For small and medium sized castings,* vibrating type shakeout is commonly used. It consists of a perforated plate or a grille of heavy section fastened to a vibrating frame. After placing the mould on the grille, the frame is vibrated by means of an electric motor. The sand in the mould gets loose and drops through the grille.

Vibrating frame is connected to the fixed machine frame through compression springs. Thus, transmission of vibrations into the foundations are largely eliminated.

(*iii*) *For heavy moulds,* shakeouts used are of bumper type. Mould is placed resting on two heavy hinged type beams. The free ends of the beams rest on motor driven cams. When the cams rotate, the beams are raised and dropped through a small height, thus giving a jarring action to the mould.

In all cases, the shakeout machine should be fitted with a hood and a powerful dust suction device for preventing fine sand and dust particles getting charged into the air all round.

Material Handling Equipment and Conveyor Systems

For rapid and economic production of castings on a large scale, material handling equipment is a great asset to a foundry shop. Foundry is a place where the largest quantities of materials have to be handled. Materials to be handled in a foundry are in many different forms and each of these requires a different type of

equipment. The main items handled on large scale in a foundry are :

(*i*) Sands	(*v*) Core sands
(*ii*) Moulds	(*vi*) Cores
(*iii*) Molten metal	(*vii*) Furnace materials *e.g.*,
(*iv*) Castings	(*a*) metal to be melted
	(*a*) coke
	(*a*) limestone
	(*a*) return-scrap from fettling section.

Handling of Sands

Moulding sands are to be conveyed from one place to other for various purposes. Equipment used for carrying sands mechanically are screening.

Purposes of Using Conveyors in Production Foundries

(*i*) For conveying used sand from shake-out station to riddle for screening.

(*ii*) For conveying sand from screen to magnetic separator.

(*iii*) For conveying sand from magnetic separator to reconditioning plant, *e.g.*, muller and aerator.

(*iv*) For conveying reconditioned sand to distributing section.

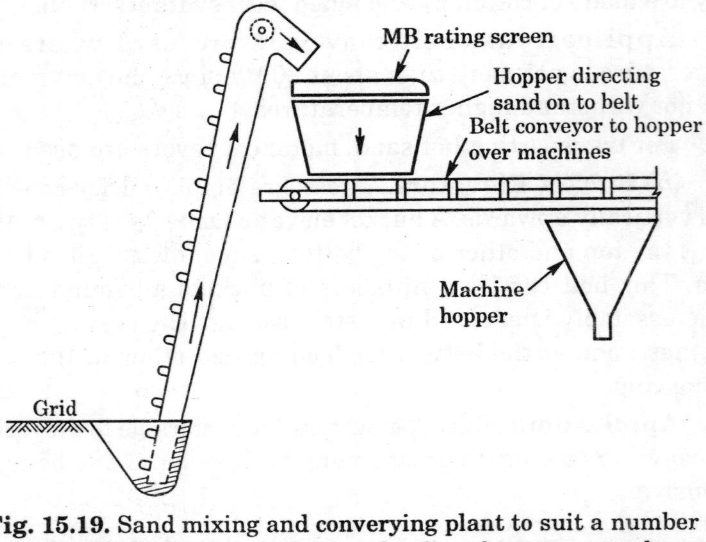

Fig. 15.19. Sand mixing and converying plant to suit a number of machines. (Elaborate layout for supply of sand to numerous hoppers).

(*v*) For conveying sand to moulding machines, sand slingers etc.

(*vi*) For conveying new sand from stores to mixing or conditioning plant.

Types of Sand Conveyors commonly used :

(*i*) **Belt Conveyor.** These are commonly used for conveying sand from one place to another for horizontal and inclined travel. They consist of an endless belt, two pulleys '*head and tail pulleys*', rollers or idlers for carrying the loaded belt and returning the empty belt, belt tightening mechanism and belt cleaners.

The hand pulley drives the belt. It is connected to electric motor through a reduction gear. It should be of fairly large diameter for providing full traction. For preventing sand from spilling and keeping it in the centre, the carrying idlers or rollers are in the three pieces. Each set consists of three rollers ; one horizontal in the centre and two slightly inclined on the sides. To avoid too much sagging of the belt under load, the idlers should not be spaced very far away.

When using the sand conveyor for an inclined travel, the angle of incline should not be more than 25°C for tempered sand and 15°C for silica sand so as to prevent rolling back of the sand.

Conveyor belts are available in various sizes and strengths. They are made of cotton plies bonded with synthetic rubber.

Applications. Belt conveyors are used where sand temperature is not more than about 300°F since the belt material does not withstand higher temperatures.

For transporting hot sand, metal conveyors are used.

(*ii*) **Bucket Elevators**. These are employed for conveying sand vertically upwards. A bucket elevator consists of two pulleys ; one at the top and other at the bottom. An endless belt rolls over them. This belt carries a numbers of buckets all round and the whole assembly is encased in a steel casing. The casting has two openings ; one at the bottom for feeding and other at the top for discharging.

Applications. Bucket elevators are preferable to the inclined belt conveyors owing to great saving in floor space and being less expensive.

(*iii*) **Apron Conveyors.** These make use of over-lapping steel plates, hinged at the ends in such a way that when assembled, they serve as a belt.

Advantage. They can be used for conveying materials which are too hot to be carried by a belt.

Drawbacks. 1. As compared to belt conveyors, apron conveyors cannot be used at high speeds.

2. There are chances of sand spillage and leakage through the plates.

3. Maintenance cost and initial cost are higher.

(*iv*) **Flight Conveyors.** It is used for distributing the sand to the work stations from an overhead trough. It consists of two endless chains which move on sprockets fixed at both ends and carry steel plates called '*flights*' at certain intervals.

As the chain moves, it causes the flights to move in the trough and force the sand to enter the openings in the hoppers.

(*v*) **Reciprocating and Oscillating Conveyors.** Sometimes, sand conveyors are made of the reciprocating and oscillating type. A crank pin and connecting rod produce reciprocating action.

This conveyor is made of steel plates which are fastened together and held by two beams. An electric motor produces the oscillating action.

Applications. 1. This type of conveyor is used for short travels where excavation depth for continuous type conveyor is not available.

2. Oscillating conveyor is sometimes used for conveying hot sand and hot castings.

(*vi*) **Mono-rail Conveyors.** These are frequently used for carrying sand, casting, molten metal, furnace charge, etc. Sand is filled in container or buckets which are of drop bottom type. These containers are carried from one place to other on an overhead monorail. The conveyor is either manually operated.

(*vii*) **Crane.** An overhead travelling crane may be more convenient for carrying the sand for small foundries engaged in jobbing work. Sand is filled in a bottom discharge bucket, which is transferred by means of the crane.

Main Sand Storage Hoppers. These may be square or circular with a tapered bottom feeding on to a rotating table discharge. Or, they may be rectangular in shape, again with a tapering bottom. The hopper floor consists of a belt conveyor by which the sand is discharged.

In the former case, a cone is either fitted to the top of the rotary table or suspended in the hopper itself a few metres above the rotary table.

Handling Moulds

Moulds require to be conveyed from the mould production section to the place where they are poured. Also moulds may require to be conveyed past a pouring station where the molten metal is poured into them while they are in motion. After pouring and cooling, the moulds are conveyed to shake-out operation, the emptied flasks, moulding boards, etc., are returned to the mould production area.

In a mechanized foundry, all these transportation operations are carried out by a suitable conveyor system. Mould conveyors commonly used are of the following types :

(*i*) **Roller Conveyor.** It consists of two beams fixed on trestles of suitable height and support laterally arranged rollers on the top. Roller conveyor may be either of gravity or power-driven type :

Gravity roller conveyor is that in which no power is used for driving the rollers and moving the moulds. Roller ends are fitted in sealed bearings and the operator pushes the moulds causing them to move on the rollers. The beams are fixed at a slight slope so that the moulds move by gravity.

In *power driven roller conveyor,* some of the rollers at fixed intervals along the conveyor length, are driven by power from an electric motor. To enable co-ordination of mould movement with mould production, the drive is generally provided from variable speed motor.

Applications. Power-driven roller conveyor is only adopted in a mass production foundry owing to high cost whereas gravity roller conveyor is used for both jobbing as well as production.

(*i*) **Car type of Pallet Conveyor.** For carrying moulds in large scale foundries, pallet or car type conveyor is the most efficient means. This conveyor consists of pallets made of steel plates or cast iron. These plates are mounted on wheels which can roll along

a narrow gauge track. Moulds are placed on the pallets and are pushed manually. However, in continuous drives, pallets are joined with a clamp and driven from one end by power.

Application. Completely mechanised work is possible by means of the pallet conveyors. They are of continuous type and carrying moulds from the mould production area to the powering station and from there to the shake-out place after giving adequate cooling time.

The moulds in a continuous process of preparation on a battery of moulding machines duly assembled are placed by the operator on the pallet conveyor which takes them to pouring station.

(*iii*) **Overhead Conveyor.** In small foundries, an overhead conveyor of mono-rail type is sometimes used for carrying the moulds. The completed mould is placed on the conveyor platform and the latter is moved by an overhead mono-rail to the pouring floor. The same carrier then moves to shake-out station after solidification of the casting.

Handling Molten Metal

Two systems are commonly followed for pouring the molted metal into the moulds :

(*i*) **Where a continuous conveyor is not used,** the moulds after completion are conveyed to storage area on a roller conveyor. Molted metal is brought in ladles to this area with the help of travelling crane or hoist and is poured into the moulds.

(*ii*) **Central pouring System.** It consists of conveying the moulds to a central pouring station on the pallet type continuous conveyor. Molten metal is brought in ladles from the furnace on a mono-rail type overhead conveyor and is poured into moulds while latter are in motion.

Mono-rail conveyor can be synchronized with the motion of the mould conveyor so that the ladle travels along with the mould while the pouring is going on. After pouring the metal, the ladle is moved to the next mould manually. Mono-rail overhead carrier may be power driven or manually operated.

Handling Castings. After removing the castings from the moulds at the shake out station, they are conveyed to the cleaning and fettling section on a suitable conveyor. For conveying the castings, suitable types of conveyors are :

(*i*) **Plate-band or Apron plate Conveyor.** It consists of the plates together and mounted on a continuous chain moving on

power driven sprockets. This conveyor is used in many foundries for carrying the castings to the fettling or inspection section. It can be used for both horizontal and inclined travels. Also, it can be used both for short as well as long distances.

(ii) **Rollers Conveyors.** These can be used for carrying castings in the same manner as moulds. Gravity type roller conveyor is particularly cheap to instal and also suitable for small foundries.

(iii) **Oscillating Conveyors.** It is sparingly used for conveying castings. However, it is employed more frequently for sands than for castings.

(iv) **Overhead Chain Conveyors.** These are very frequently employed for conveying the castings from the shake-out station to the shop blasting room for cleaning.

An overhead conveyor carries castings in hooks suspended from the chain. The conveyor alongwith the castings enters the shot blasting chamber from one side and leaves it through the exit on the rear side.

(v) **Slat Conveyor.** This is a double-chain conveyor. It carries the surface consisting of a series of steel or timber slats which do not overlap. It is, therefore, unsuitable for conveying sand. It is used for handling, castings and empty moulding flasks.

QUESTIONS

1. Give in short the classification of modern foundry's.
2. What do you mean by plant layout of foundries? Give the advantages of good foundry layout.
3. What do you mean by foundry mechanisation? Give its merits and demerits.
4. Describe the following with simple sketch :
   (a) Gyratory riddle
   (b) Sad muller
   (c) Aerator.
5. What do you mean by Reclamation of sand? Give its advantages.
6. What are different methods of reclamation of sand? Explain each in short.
7. Explain the working of Fume and Dust extraction equipment.
8. Describe with simple sketch construction and working of pattern draw and squeeze type hand operated moulding machine.

9. Write short note on :
   (*a*) Power operated moulding machine
   (*b*) Core blowing machine
   (*c*) Drawer type stove.
   (*d*) Batch-type stove.
10. Differentiate between water cooled cupola and hot blast cupola. (*ii*) Give the advantages of Hot blast cupola.
11. Explain balance blast cupola. Give its advantages.
12. What are the types of sand conveyors? Explain reciprocating and oscillating conveyors.
13. Explain in brief :
   (*a*) Apron plate conveyor
   (*b*) Overhead chain conveyor
   (*c*) Slat conveyor
   (*d*) Oscillating conveyor.